I0148150

THE CAIAPHAS LETTERS

(Second Book of the Kahana Chronicles)

BY ALLEN E. GOLDENTHAL

Copyright© 2003 By Allen Goldnthal
First published in New Zealand in 2003
By Charon Publishing Ltd.,
Palmerston North, Manawatu 5453
www.publishontheweb.com
1st Edition
ISBN 0-9582098-1-2

Val D'Or Publishing
2nd Edition 2016
ISBN 978-0-9942559-3-8

DESCENDANTS OF ALCIMUS

Letter From the Author

To my family members both near and far, the heritage you share has spanned the centuries and everyday you'll learn more about yourselves by studying the lives of our ancestors. Cherish the dreams and hopes that we have carried from generation to generation, for if not through ourselves, then at least through our descendants we pray that these may be fulfilled. We are a family from which many have risen to answer the call but only a few have succeeded in achieving the mandate that has been thrust upon us. It is a heavy burden but one which cannot and must not be avoided. Since the first time that we heard the summons in the marshlands of Goshen we knew that there was only one option and that was to obey. Our destiny was formulated a long time ago and in time of great need we are called upon to change the world. Two thousand years ago there were those of us called upon to do exactly that. The world was changed but not in the manner in which it was intended. Certainly not in the manner that those involved hoped would happen. Over the next twenty centuries we suffered for this grievous error in judgment but perhaps now we can succeed where those others left off and set the record straight. The story you are about to read has derived much of its information from two ancient manuscripts authored by members of my family, the *Toldoth Yeshua* and the *Hazak Amanah*. They provide a historical context to events and individuals that lived during that turbulent time when a new voice came out of the wilderness, crossing the Jordan River and changed the world.

Prologue

"EEEEEAAAAHHHHHHH!!!!"
My wife's scream ricocheted like a bullet from the kitchen, penetrating the stillness of what had been shaping up to be a very lazy Sunday afternoon on my part. I had my feet up, a bottle of Speight's pale ale in hand, and the All Blacks were just about to come on to the field. So much for relaxation. Even the best laid plans are doomed to failure. Her scream was much louder than the accompanying sound of a pot or some other such item falling to the floor and reverberating excitedly against the burnished Mexican tiles that we had just recently installed. God, I hope those tiles were as good as the salesperson claimed them to be. Now this could be costly, those tiles weren't cheap.

I ran to the kitchen immediately, finding my wife trembling uncontrollably as she stared wide-eyed and motioned frantically out the window as if she had seen a ghost.

"So what's happening", I asked calmly, placing my hands on her shoulders in an attempt to help her relax. She shook off my hands, a clear sign that I wasn't helping the situation.

"Look. Look there." She pointed towards the hollyhocks. "He's over there. See him?"

"Who?"

"I don't know who," she screamed at me. "If I knew who, I wouldn't be this upset. He's some kind of pervert. He's been watching me and he's wearing a dirty trench coat!"

I scanned the gardens only to catch a glimpse of the stalking stranger. I saw him clearly. Hair, unkempt, dowdy, stained beige trench coat and looking like he had just stepped off an air plane. The fact was that I knew that is exactly what he had done.

"See! Do you see him? There's some creep staring at me from our back yard! So what are you going to do about it? Go out there and chase him away! Call the police! Do something instead of being useless!"

"What are you talking about?"

"There, look there!"

"Yea, I see him…that's John."

"John who?"

"Pearce. Didn't I tell you he was flying in today?"

"No! You didn't! You never said a word. I can't believe you didn't say anything. How could you? Couldn't you have the decency of letting me know something that's this important? He scared me half-to-dearth. I hope you're satisfied! And look at me! Look at this house! It's a mess! I didn't have a chance to clean up anything. How could you?"

"I'm sorry, I forgot."

"You always forget. It's never ever different. You're always doing something stupid like this!"

"I'm…"

"I don't want to hear your 'I'm sorry'. You're always saying you're sorry. It doesn't mean anything anymore. You can't keep saying it and expect me to say, that's fine. I've had it up to here." She made a cutting motion across her neck which made me think long and hard about something else which I won't mention.

"Well I am. I can't say it any other way. "

"I've had it. I'm so-o-o mad at you. I'm going upstairs. You talk to John or whatever. Don't speak to me. Don't even try to come upstairs. I have to cool down. I can't believe you did this to me."

"I really am sorry."

"Urrrrgh." She clenched her teeth and stormed from the kitchen. Her every foot step pounding against the matai floors of the hallway and all the way up the winding rimu staircase. The last sound I heard from her was the slamming of the bedroom door. Unfortunately, it's all very déjà vu. I really must make an effort to become more considerate. I know I was wrong but how do you stop yourself from repeating the mistakes you've made from the first day you managed to climb out of your crib. The point of fact was, that I was sorry. Whoever thought there could be a limit to saying sorry?

I briefly considered following her up the stairs but then thought more rationally about it. Discretion before valour! Probably best to let her cool down. My wife's a blonde but I'd swear you can actually see her hair transform into flaming red tresses when she gets mad. I wouldn't stand a chance. Better take care of my visitor instead. Give her some time. She'll calm down. I'll make it up to her later.

I opened the back door and poked my head outside. Watching him examine a fejoia hanging off the tree, I thought I'd better get him inside before the neighbours start ringing the police about some strange little man in my yard. Pearce had an instinctive knack of making himself irritating. It was over a year since he had walked into my life; let me rephrase that. Over a year since he intruded uninvited into my life.

"John, get the hell in here! What do you think you're doing walking all around the property?"

"It's beautiful, Doc. We don't get many houses that look like this back in Canada. You know that. So, I was just having a good look around it. It's a grand old home. And get a load of this. What are they?"

"Yes I know, yes it is, and that's a fejoia. You can eat it. Now get in here before you cause a disturbance. You've already scared my wife half-to-death."

"Geez, Doc. I'm sorry. I was just waving to her. I didn't think she'd get upset."

"Don't even mention you're sorry. I've been through that discussion already. It's definitely one word we can all do without right now."

"Well, let me talk to the little woman. I'll set things straight." John flashes me a smile as if he believes that's going to work some magic on my wife.

"John, trust me, you don't want to speak to her right now. Why can't you just walk to the front door like everyone else?"

"Like I said, I have an appreciation for these old homes; couldn't stop myself from looking around. It's just so amazing. You have a really nice house here. So how old is it? Turn of the century?"

"It was built in 1903 to be exact. And yes, we do appreciate it, and enjoy it tremendously. So come on in. Have a quick look around, satisfy your curiosity, and then we'll get down to business."

"Thanks Doc for your gracious how do you do. It's really good to see you again too!"

"I don't know if I'm glad to see you or not, John. I'll let you know when my wife speaks to me again."

"Well, Doc, you should be glad in other ways. We sure had a

good run with Blood Royale. Every Saturday paper we featured it in, sold mega-copies and then it went to hardback print. So, it's not as if we did a wrong by you."

As I walk John through the main floor, I take a moment to think how I'm going to respond. "I'm not complaining financially, John. You have to understand, there's more involved than the almighty dollar. The notoriety and the subsequent scrutiny were devastating to myself and my family. Even my own relatives have shied away from us. They don't know if I'm crazy or merely deluded. You see, not everyone in my family, is as in tune with our ancestors, as I am. Sure, they know about some of the legends in the family, but that's all they know. Some quaint stories passed down without any hard basis in fact. Then you have me, telling tales that are steeped in hard factual evidence and they can't comprehend where it's all coming from."

John followed me attentively through my home as I showed him each room, with their kauri walls and eleven foot high ceilings, until we came to the ornate spindles of the majestic Victorian fireplace in the salon or living room.

"Wow, Doc, what a room!" he gasps.

"The decision to buy this house was based on this room. My wife took one look from outside that window and said this was it. Have a seat; we'll make ourselves comfortable in here."

Pearce leaned himself back into the engulfing overstuffed pillows of one of the floral couches.

"To continue where we left off…but surely they must have had some clues from the family legends you spoke of?"

"Perhaps they always had some instinct of something special but now that the limelight has been focused upon anyone with the same surname, they're crumbling under the heat. Easier to say Allen is deranged than to admit that we have a very interesting but bizarre history. Some prefer to have the past buried."

"Does it matter?"

"For God-sakes, Pearce, I'm living in New Zealand now! How much further can you get away from the hoopla?" I shot upright from my seat on the couch facing opposite Pearce's and my eyes knifed directly into his heart.

Pearce recognized he may have crossed over the threshold with his flippant remark. "I thought you were here because of your job?"

"I don't have to search for employment in the last outpost before Antarctica. There's plenty of opportunity in North America. One runs away to New Zealand!" I shook my head in disbelief. The rage began to drain from my expression.

"Seems like a nice place to me, Doc."

"It's an absolutely beautiful place John," I corrected him. "Don't get me wrong. None of us have any regrets being here. I don't know of any other country in the world like it, and coming from Canada, that says a lot. Majestic scenery, relaxed life, great people, but it is about as remote as you can get. And that's the biggest plus I have going for me. It's not like there's going to be a line-up of people knocking at my door to interrogate me."

"Except for me."

"Right. Except for you. And I must admit, I'm surprised that you got on to a plane as quickly as this. I didn't expect to see you for another six months or so. So what's up?"

"Well, that's the good news, Doc. Ever since we published your book, it's like the head office has become mission control. Everyone's trying to find you. Thousands have phoned claiming to be a relative of yours and therefore entitled to a piece of the action. Even more have threatened to sue, saying that you stole their story line. But most interesting of all have been the ghouls."

"The ghouls?" That was a strange terminology, I thought.

"Yes, the guys in government issue suits. That's what we call them at the office. You know, the Men in Black. The NSA guys."

"And just who are these ghouls? Pardon my naiveté but I'm away from the loop so to speak."

Pearce leaned forward as if he was going to reveal the identity of who shot Kennedy. "They're the guys that when you try to pin them down as to where they're getting their directives, they respond 'No Such Agency.' They're invisible. Like we say, they're ghouls."

"So let me see if I have this straight. The good news is that I'm popular, or at least my book is. The bad news is that I'm probably as good as dead because of some secret agency that is trying to track me down!"

Pearce just nodded in silent agreement.

"That's just wonderful," I thanked him sarcastically though I think the nuance escaped him.

THE KAHANA CHRONICLES

CHRONICLES

(BOOK TWO)

A Family History

CHAPTER ONE

"Oh, wonderful! Now I'm being pursued by a mysterious government agency. Did you even bother to find out what they wanted?" This was beginning to sound like a nightmare to me but I knew that Pearce had the capacity to exaggerate, so I pressed him for more detail.

"They want to know where you got your information. Apparently the book touched on some issues that were not publicly known. They tried to get our file on you but I keep that well-hidden. Privileged information of the press and all that. So, they ended up empty handed. I'll don't think they'll be back to bother us."

I tapped my right index finger against my forehead in an obvious display for Pearce's benefit to think harder. "Now, why would you suppose they would be interested in some insignificant piece of historical literature? Have you asked yourself that question?"

"Perhaps, you pissed off a bunch of people. Not like the Pope is going to be your best friend after your exposé on his predecessors being a bunch of mass murderers and conspirators."

"No, that's not it. The truth on the Papacy has been known for quite a while. No big secret there. The Popes all know they have the biggest track records as sinners than anyone on the planet. To them it would be just one more book that they recommend their loyal adherents and good Catholics don't read. After all, sixteen centuries of paedophile priests haven't caused their congregations to disappear, so why would this?"

"So, what do you think it might be, Doc?"

"Can't you see, John? It's GLEEM."

"Why would you think that?"

"Because it's a project that always was more than just theory. Certainly, it was theoretical when explaining my personal circumstances but as I revealed to you, there's enough circumstantial evidence to support it without holding me up as a test case. Imagine the unlimited potential of identifying the proteins and enzymes that constitute a memory. Imagine the ability to produce these in a lab and then inject them into a subject when you need an acquired ability or information. How much would it be worth to you to see what thoughts flashed through the mind of a Pulitzer Prize winner? Or taking a more nefarious approach, consider what this would mean to the fine art of interrogation. The military would have a field day. Capture the descendant of a high ranking officer or official and download all his significant memories by basically tapping into all that has been genetically placed into storage."

"Gee, Doc, you're making it sound like something from Stephen King." Pearce saluted me with a mock shudder.

"Except it's real," I cautioned. "GLEEM has taken on a life of its own. Other researchers are already claiming that they can provide the research to prove it."

"So, why would they want you?"

I pointed my finger at him, giving it a little wag as I did so. "Think about it, Pearce. Think carefully."

"Nah…they couldn't. They wouldn't. Would they?"

"If you were working on a project, wouldn't you want to make certain that you had the best lab rat money could buy? Why work with unknowns when you can prejudice your testing by starting with a fully loaded, accessorised, turn-key model!"

"But you wouldn't let them."

"Of course not! Not of my own free will. How many Canadian military men do you think willingly offered themselves to the CIA testing of LSD in the sixties? Do you think they all volunteered? Raised their hands and said, 'Go ahead, mess with my brain?' Why would you even think that they'd give me an option? They were all deceived. That's how these black box ops operate, isn't it?"

"I just can't believe it…it's too fantastic to be true." Pearce held up his hands and then spread them in a gesture of denial.

"You're the one that told me these 'ghouls' came to your office. I didn't make that up. And if you really believe it's because they couldn't get a library card, so they came to get a copy of my book directly from you, then you're fooling yourself. They meant business; serious business."

"So, what do we do?"

"What can you do? That is the million-dollar question. You protect yourself the best way that you can. I keep the light shining on me so that if I suddenly disappear from the world stage, then people start asking questions."

"You have a plan?" Pearce leaned forward in his chair as if to avoid detection by hidden microphones. He's probably even more paranoid than I am.

"Of course I have a plan. The same one I had when I let you know where you could find me. I didn't provide that information so that you would fly twelve thousand kilometres just to say hello. I figured we have work to do. The only difference now being that I just won't release another book to be published in serial by your paper. No we get involved in very serious work. We start putting down on paper everything that's in my head. My entire family history; every individual, every event, every detail until there's nothing left to reveal."

"And how does that protect you from some guy trying to get a sample of brain tissue?"

I winked all-knowingly at Pearce. "That revolves around another theory I have. I don't believe GLEEM remains in a constant structure. Once activated, I believe it becomes simply another construct within the brain, not any different from any other cerebral material or activity."

Pearce's facial features adopted a mask of complete and utter confusion. "Come again?"

It was time to think of an appropriate metaphor. "Think of it like a ZIP file on your computer hard drive. As a zip file, it stands out as being different. Identifiable, unique, but inaccessible in its current state. Then you run your zip programme. Think of that in terms of the trigger enzyme. Once activated, it unfolds the file and turns it into whatever file your computer normally processes. It becomes no different from any other execute file, word processing file, spread sheet file, etcetera. Unrecognisable, totally stable and unremarkable."

"So, there would be nothing to find but how would they know that?"

"Because, if they do have such a project under way, which I suspect they do, then whomever is the team leader would think very similar to myself. They would know it, just as I know it. And they'd also know that once I've exhausted every titbit of information stored in my neural network, then there would be nothing there to test for. Instead of being successful, I would render their programme a colossal waste of money. I have to eliminate the raw storage mechanism, so that there's nothing for them to retrieve."

"Well, where should we begin?"

"You know, Pearce, you asked me that very same question once before. But then I told you we couldn't start at the beginning because there wasn't that much time left in your life span. I'm going to have to re-examine that comment. I think the beginning is very much where I have to take you. Did you come prepared?"

"You should know me by now, Doc." Pearce reaches into his pockets and withdrew a collection of writing utensils, a pad, and his indispensable tape recorder. "So, what's this one about?"

"I think I should start by giving you a little more detail on my genealogy, John. You've already got a conception about the significant role played by my family, the Kahana but, I think it's time to answer the big question, why this family?"

John interrupted my train of thought with his over-exuberance. "I thought that was pretty obvious from *Blood Royale*. You made it clear that the Kahana were descendants of good ol' King David. Oh, and by the way, my wife wanted me to tell you that she loved your story. She said it confirmed everything she figured about you."

"I'm glad Mrs. Pearce liked it. Now if you let me continue...." I didn't wait for his consent. "True, there was Davidic blood but that certainly wasn't the Kahana's origins. Just so happened that the Kahana married the daughters of the Royal House of Israel on a constant basis and therefore the two families became quite inseparable. The two became as one. The rod and the sceptre were intertwined. You've heard of that expression before, rod and sceptre, right?"

Pearce stared upward at the ceiling, trying to recall his old Sunday school lessons.

"Vaguely," he responded.

"Well, let me refresh them for you. As you recall from your initial investigation, I am also known as Avrum Aryeh-Zuk."

"Right!" Pearce exclaimed. "I remember that."

"Anyway, it's an interesting Hebrew name since it's not used too routinely. In fact, it's almost never used. Translated, it's Abraham, the righteous lion. It's the righteous lion part that we'll concentrate on because that's the unusual part. Lots of my predecessors were known as Aryeh-Lieb, the lion hearted but only two bore the same name as mine."

"How far back we talking, Doc," Pearce interrupted.

"That's a good question, John. If I wanted to, I could take you easily back one hundred generations. Three thousand two hundred and eighty years to be precise."

"You're kidding!"

"Do I look like I'm kidding?"

"Wow, that's amazing. I just can't believe it." Pearce still shook his head in obvious disbelief.

I understood just how difficult it was for him to accept a concept of infinite lineage. Even I'm awed by my own origins when I sit down and think about them. But then again, it's those origins that have gotten me into this hot water.

"Well, believe me, it's true. How do you think I have all these family histories? It takes a lot of intermarriage between the same families to achieve GLEEM. It just doesn't happen. It's almost as if it's predicated. As if there's an unseen hand intentionally manipulating the entire process."

"How's that?"

"One thing I've noticed over my years of research is that none of the significant families developed in isolation. In fact, the world was quite a small place even without the internet. Distinguished families of one country, intermingled freely with those of another, and so on, and so, on. The Caesars married into families that ruled Syria, Mesopotamia, Judaea, and Africa. Those in turn, would take brides from India, the Indo-Sino peninsula, and the steppes of Asia. And this would be repeated on a continual basis. Not only did they know of each other's presence, they were in constant communication. So our first mistake is to think of historical events in isolation from the rest of the world. It wasn't true. They were all co-developing within a global concept. The Global Village already existed, even way back then. So I can show you intermarriages between families separated by thousands of miles that you never dreamed possible."

"Sort of like Natronai marrying into the Carolingian family."

"Exactly, John. There's a member of a Jewish royal family marrying the daughter of the Frankish king. Suddenly, all the perceived isolations imagined by our present day concepts of history are blown away. How does a Jew marry a Catholic? That's not supposed to happen in the eighth century, is it? We don't give it a second thought in today's society, but back then we perceive it to have been a forbidden event. Yet, all our documentation suggests it occurred with regular frequency between prominent families of the times. Jews have essentially been a monogamous society for thirty centuries, yet all our kings, advisors and leaders were permitted to marry as many woman as they wished. There were always these exceptions provided to the families of prominence. Here, help me out with this."

I launched myself from the couch and walked over to the television cabinet. In between it and the wall, I started to pull out an extremely large roll of laminated paper.

"What's this?" Pearce asks as he assisted me in removing the scroll from its storage space.

I cautioned him to wait a second. "Just help me unroll it and you'll see for yourself." Taking the one end, Pearce started to unroll the document across the living room floor.

"Hey, how big is this thing?", he questioned as it continued to spread, running out of floor space and stopping up against the leg of another couch.

"It's six feet wide and almost twenty-five feet long. Each name is written in five point and if I recall correctly, there's about forty-three thousand two hundred names on this scroll."

"Is this what I think it is," he sputtered, his jaw dropping to the ground as he got down on his knees to get a closer look.

"My family tree. Over two decades of work and not finished by a long shot."

"But how?"

"Like I said, prominent families married other prominent families. That was the way of the world back then and the same holds true now. Nothing has changed. So when the Royal family in Britain talks of its roots back to the king of Judaea, they're not fabricating. The legends are supported. The only difference being is that on my tree I can demonstrate the where and the how."

Pearce crawled all over the scroll, looking at names, scribbling down bits of information here and there. "I can't believe it! You have what looks like every king and queen in the world on this chart. Wow, look here! The Flavians."

"You know about the Flavian Dynasty?"

"What can I say, Doc, I like military history. I also like historical epics. Saw Masada three times. But I don't understand, how can the general of the Roman eastern legions be tearing into the Jews and here it shows he had a Jewish ancestry?"

"Easy enough. The Flavians were of the Senatorial order of Rome. Not quite Equestrian in that they originated from poor beginnings, but Vespasian's great grandfather began a solid merchant empire that was highly successful under Vespasian's brother, Flavius Sabinus. This one here, Titus Flavius Sabinus, did his government stint in the Middle East. No better way for a merchant class family to move up the ranks than marry into royalty. The Herodian-Asmonean ruling family of Judaea was very close to Rome and one of their daughters, to be specific, Mariamne granddaughter of John Hyrcanus, marries Vespasian's relation. And not only that, if you look here, it happens again. See, where Titus Vespasianus is in a relationship with Berenice, daughter of Agrippa King of Judaea. If it wasn't for the Roman Senate threatening to remove any support from the Flavians, Berenice could have very well become empress of Rome."

"But how is it, no one recorded this information regarding Vespasian's Jewish ties before?"

"That's where you're wrong. It was recorded and that's how I got my information. GLEEM is only responsible for just so much information and knowledge that I have about my family. The rest comes from research. And the art of research is knowing where to look."

"Hey, wait a minute, some of these names over here are mythological guys. You can't be serious about including these!"

I laughed at his observation, but just for the moment. Not enough to make him uncomfortable. "What's a myth, John? If anything, it's nothing more than a cultural difference."

"I don't get it."

"Then think about it. Without attacking your beliefs, you believe that God had relations with a woman, and through her had a son. I believe that in a time of great evil and slaughter, a man rose in Judaea unlike any other man, who could look past the veil of hate and chaos and could visualise a world of love, peace and harmony. That he had a unique ability to inspire those around him to see the world in much the same way that he did. But ultimately, he was executed by the same society which he tried to mould into a better place. I see a great man, you see a demi-god. As far as I'm concerned, you're adhering to a myth but with some basis in fact. Is that not what *the Caiaphas Letters,* which I released years ago trying to say? Our starting points determine our beliefs and where we disagree is that fine line between myth and reality."

"I'm still disagreeing with you, Doc. Come on now, Hercules, surely you can't believe a television show character has a place on this tree? You're stretching my belief a little too far there."

"Let me tell you a story about a man that never cut his hair, had the strength of probably ten men, and pulled down an entire building on his head, killing himself and his enemies. Nice myth."

"Wait now. Samson and Hercules are two entirely different issues here."

"Are they, John? Think about it. Two men of great strength, both accomplishing superhuman trials and labours, and both of them have God or a god as a protector. Where's the difference? It's all a matter of reference points. We're grounded in the Judeo-Christian heritage, so Samson is okay, but a Samson like character living in the Greek world isn't. How can we justify one and condemn the other?"

"So you're saying he was real."

"As real as you and I. Because of his tremendous feats, the stories got exaggerated and his birth gets attributed to Zeus, but when you strip away all the added tales, you find him to be a real person, living a real life and accomplishing great things. Like everyone else on the chart, he has a normal lineage. Strangely enough, he's contemporary with Samson. During that 11th and 12th century BC, these strong men were quite acceptable in everyday life. They rose to prominence easily and everyone made a great deal about them. After all, Samson was a judge for quite a long time. Yet when you read the stories about him, you realize he was one of the least likely men to have been considered judge material. Nevertheless, he was."

"So where are you, Doc?"

"Look here." I draw his attention to the bottom of the chart. "That's me. There's my immediate family."

"Once again, wow Doc! I can't believe you have all this information. Hey, is this right, over here? When you trace back yours and your wife's family they join up way back here too. That seems a little odd to me. This can't be for real. All the people in the world and you want me to believe that your two families link up twice in a thousand years?"

God he's thick! "Is any of what I'm telling you sinking in, John?" I felt my blood pressure rising. I've come to like Pearce in a peculiar way but sometimes it's like talking to the wall or worse.

He was fully aware that I've grown irritated. "Sorry Doc."

"Don't be sorry! Just open up your mind a little. Where do you think our feelings of attraction stem from? Why are you drawn to a certain hair colour, a look, a particular sounding voice? You spot these characteristics and you're immediately attracted to the individual. In another case, you can't even stand to be next to a person. You haven't exchanged a word, you barely look at each other but nonetheless, their being there just makes your skin crawl. You don't even have a clue why you feel that way. All you know is that you've got to get away."

"GLEEM?"

"Yes, GLEEM. The people we want to be with are determined long before we're even born. And we seek them out based upon the genetic input that drives our limbic centres. Then again, your ancestors may have encountered a woman that made their lives absolutely miserable. So much so, that it became imprinted within their genetic code. Now all it takes is to just see, smell, hear a person that triggers that encoded memory and you can't wait to put as much distance between you and them as possible. But don't get me wrong. I'm not trying to say that all our choices are predetermined. No, we're still free to make our own mistakes, even if those choices are being influenced by our past."

I saw the light beginning to dawn in Pearce's eyes. Dim glow mind you. "In many ways I'm not very different from Natronai Kahana. Look here!" I point to Natronai's name on the chart. "You see, what I told you about the Kahana in Gaul being an offshoot of my family is basically correct. What I didn't tell you is how close an offshoot. Here's his first wife, Ruth. The one he left behind, and his son, Achunai, whom he never saw again. Follow this line down and it eventually comes to me."

"So, you're a descendant of his first marriage."

"Yes, from both his brother-in-law, Mar Papa and his firstborn son, Achunai, because their lines both intermarry a few generations later. That's a pretty hefty double imprint, especially from a son who still shared a full genetic complement from his father, still followed the life of Natronai from a distance, and learned as much about his father's life as he could. Because no matter how long apart, nor how distant, a son will always love his father even to the point of hatred. But it's a hatred based purely on love and longing, which becomes soured by resentment and anger. How much better to intensify the memories regarding his father to the point that they are so ingrained that they become GLEEM."

"And your meeting up with your wife?"

"Simply this unseen hand I referred to earlier. The surviving member Bernard, as you might recall from the closing chapter of *Blood Royale*, eventually made it back into the family by marrying a later descendant of Achunai. Now you have Natronai's genetic matrix entering by two different portals. The intensity of his feelings for Alda, his love for the Carolingians, whatever triggered his responses of affection, admiration, etc., are now being passed down. My wife is a Carolingian through a series of accidents. Most significant accident being Antoine the Great Bastard, son of Philip the Bold. Antoine was probably Philip's favourite but being the son of the maid didn't score him too many points in taking over the family kingdom. So instead, his father gave him all of Freisland, which the French occupied and controlled at that time. He needed a princess to rule with him, so understandably, he took her from the ruling families of the area which were all Scandinavian.

The descendants of Harke had control over the people, so he took to wife, Margaret Harkesdottir also known as Margaret of Haakon. They had a son, Henicke, or Henri in French, Harkeama; the last name translated from the Freisian as Harke's son. In this case, it would not have been unusual to adopt the mother's surname since Henicke Great Bastard's son didn't have a nice ring to it. Antoine had no family surname to carry on, but Margaret did. Henicke called that part of the country from which he ruled, Harkemastadt and the furthest region of his state was called Harkema Opiende and for centuries, the family held sway over the country. By the way, the names are still used in Freisland to this day. The town of Harkema still exists. But as events changed in the Netherlands, the family of Harkema faded away, recorded in history but becoming nothing more than a footnote in the overall scheme of things. Although one genealogist in a letter to me still referred to them as a bunch of bastards. So I guess some things never really change.

So all those centuries later, a descendant of Natronai encounters a descendant of Charlemagne and immediately they are attracted to each other. That's Genetically Linked Enzyme Enhanced Memory in action. Pure and simple."

"That's great," Pearce commented with a surge of enthusiasm. "Almost like these lost souls you see in the movies that float around for generations until they can inhabit someone's body so that they can come together again."

"Sort of. I guess." Perhaps Pearce still doesn't get it!

"Getting down to business, where do we go from here?" Pearce switched gears without a sweat. He was now convinced and wanted to push on. I guess in retrospect, at the end of the day, it's going to be the books that sell, not some chart that covers three hundred square feet.

"*Caiaphas Letters,*" I responded very matter-of-factly.

"You've already done that," Pearce protests.

"But not the way it should have been done. Not without all the little secrets I intentionally didn't bother to reveal as I was concerned how the public would react. Now we don't have any of those inhibitions any longer."

"Why now?"

"Well, now it doesn't matter, does it? I have to clear my data bank, so to speak, in order to keep your 'ghouls' away from me. What the readership chooses to do with the information I'm about to reveal is their business. I now have my own personal agenda."

"It's going to be different, right?"

"Very different. Let's go to the kitchen, prepare ourselves a coffee and then we'll get down to business."

"Did you want to see how the Mrs. is doing, Doc?" Pearce suggests to me.

"Hasn't been enough time for her to cool down. Like I said, she's a Carolingian. I'm better off avoiding her for the time being. So how do you want that coffee?"

"Double, double."

"Okay, I'll start telling the story while we wait for the water to boil. Try not to interrupt me this time!"

JERUSALEM: 70 AD

Oh, mighty God, guide my hands and my thoughts. Hear the request of thy humble servant, son of Abraham, son of Isaac, son of Jacob, son of Aaron and son of Zadok. Protect those that are closest to me from harm and evil. Watch over them in these troubled times. Let me walk in your footsteps, Oh Lord. Guide me on the path of righteousness. Keep me from the evil that surrounds me. Help me to achieve the tasks that you have laid out before me. Let me vanquish my enemies and in so doing, spread you Holy Name throughout the world. My heart and soul are yours to command Oh Lord. Do not forsake me. Amen.

Throughout the centuries of mankind's existence, throughout every eon of human achievement and suffering, there has been only one eternal truth. Once in an infinity, God speaks to one of his creations, delivering His word to be passed on through the generations. The word of God doesn't always find approval in the mouths of men, so that which was originally unalterable and sacred becomes adulterated. One truth in essence spawns many lies.

The words of God would be lost forever if it weren't for His promise never to forsake the chosen guardians of His teachings; one family, unending, the repository and keeper of the one and only truth. This which I am about to tell is one such story, kept sacred and untouched in the generations extending to myself. A story that will forever change the history of mankind either for better or for worse. There are so many truths to tell, and so many which now circulate amongst the people but which conflict and others which are too fanciful to extend any belief. Some feel safe in their assertions because they say that the original story no longer exists in written form. That with the destruction of the Temple, it has now become smoke and ashes and therefore no document exists any longer which records the exact details of those event many years ago.

As is often the case, those that fear the truth have deluded themselves into believing that the burning of a book could remove it forever from the realm of mankind. I say nay, nothing could be further from the truth. The book of which they speak was nothing more than the product of my wife's grandfather's mind. It sprung to life the moment he read its words aloud to his son, whom in turn read it to me.

For we are the family of the Kahana, and the truth has been entrusted to us to keep safe and protect against the ravages of mankind. From the days of Aaron, my ancestor, we have all pledged to keep the Word, and we have not faltered nor failed in our duties for over twelve centuries. Why would they presume that we would do so now?

All who listen to my story now, be prepared to know the truth. For I am Jeshua ben Gamaliel, High Priest of the Temple of Jerusalem, of the House of Phiabi, and it is time now to give life to the stories entrusted to me for an eternity as I fear my enemies will soon end my life. To my son Joseph, I charge you now to commit this story to memory so that you too will preserve it through all of time. We must guard closely what transpired those fateful years, as those events will certainly alter the course of history now that the Temple is stained with the blood of Zealots.

I whom I suspect will be one of the last of the priests to serve in our glorious Temple; I whom was last to speak with the Lord, Our God within the Holy of Holies. None of what has come to pass should be seen as the end of days, merely the beginning. For the Lord has clearly sent us a message and now it has become important that we listen and learn, bringing the Truth as a blinding light to the world before others have an opportunity to distort what was clear to all of us at the time.

I will pass on the words of my father-in-law's father, the grandfather of my good and loving wife, Martha. For who knew better than he what really occurred during those years now long past. Who knew better than Joseph Caiaphas? Let his words speak for themselves.

None saw with the clarity of Caiaphas. None knew what would transpire as he had foretold. He surely knew that in time they would prove to be the destruction of our civilisation as we know it. We stand on the verge of losing everything and it all began with events from forty years ago. Now it is time for all to recognize that his words were not meant for our generation only, but for the world to come. Ours will be a long and terrible winter of oppression. Praise be to my father-in-law's father, Caiaphas, his last few years taken from us by the hands of our oppressors, but we must see that his words will last forever and shall never be forgotten.

CHAPTER TWO

"What was that all about?" Pearce stood perplexed, cup of coffee in his hand, with tape recorder whirling away in the background.

"I guess before I move on in the story, I should tell you a lot more about my background."

"I thought we had gone through all that last time?" Pearce fired back his comment. "But now you're throwing in guys from way back and talking like this is a séance with them using your body as a medium. Who's this Joshua guy and what's he got to do with anything?"

"Jeshua, not Joshua," I corrected him. "And I mean the real family history. The nitty-gritty. You've just heard the tip of the ice berg when we last got together. When it comes right down to it, you don't know a hell of a lot about me."

"Well, enlighten me, Doc. You can never give the readers enough background. But don't go throwin' in too many names. They don't really like that part. Too confusing." Pearce was giving me a lecture on people.

And there's living proof sitting across from me, I thought. "My world is that of being Kahana. Three thousand, two hundred and eighty years of descendency. In fact, I am the ninety-eighth generation of the Kahana. Can you comprehend that, John?"

Pearce nodded his head in patronizing confirmation. "If you say so, Doc."

"Well, good. It's one thing to say you're the ninety-eighth generation and another thing to prove it. And I can prove it my sceptical friend. What I'm about to tell you will probably shake you down to your boots. This is what was missing from the initial publication of *Caiaphas Letters*. That unknown quantity that most readers couldn't put a finger on but may have suspected."

"Like my wife," Pearce interjected, beginning to catch my drift.

"Exactly like you wife. What did she say? Ah yes….he's holding back. Well, she was right. I was holding back a considerable amount of information, which would have gone a long way in explaining some of the events in that book. Now we can rewrite it the way it should have been done in the first place."

"Doc, do you really think that the public wants a revised edition of *Caiaphas Letters*? Didn't exactly set the charts on fire, you know."

"They will want this one! This will make the first release look like a classic comic book. No one wanted to read those either. Plus, I'll be able to provide a considerable amount of detail that will keep me in the forefront of the public and out of the hands of any agency that may be trying to sequester me away. Right now, that's my primary focus, self-protection through total revelation. Don't you agree, Pearce?"

"Hey, it's your call. I'm just the recorder, remember? My editor will be more than happy to take whatever you're willing to offer."
Pearce adjusted himself in the seat, trying to look relaxed but I knew he wasn't too certain about my idea. After all, his job was to sell his company's magazines and papers and I'm pushing what on the surface looked like old news. He was gambling that I'd live up to my word and this version was going to be very different. It was a safe gamble but he didn't know that. He didn't really know me!

"You see John, I am the son of Joseph, the son of Chaim, the son of Simon Wolf, the son of David, the son of Jacob the Professor. This is the Jacob that had the liaison with the Empress Elisabeth of Austria. He became the first Goldenthal. The name was presented to him during his early stay in Germany and eventually adopted by all of his close relatives. They recognized that it was important to adopt the European system of surnames if they were going to become an influential family in Europe. Others, a little more distant in the family chose to stick with Kahana, converting it from a title into a surname. How influential we were is still open to debate."

"And what about this little tryst, he had with the Empress?" Pearce's eyes light up as he thinks about a romance angle to the story. "Don't you think that would be a better story to tell at this time?"

"No but without going into too much detail here, I'll give you this very brief outline. Jacob gets to know the Emperor Franz Josef pretty well. Franz Josef marries Elisabeth, a young girl of sixteen from Bavaria. He now has to educate her to the ways of his world because Vienna and Bavaria were light years apart. Jacob being a doctor of philosophy, fluent in several languages, knowledgeable in Aristotle and other Greek philosophers, a poet and authority on Dante's Inferno, and totally at ease in both the Western and Middle Eastern civilisations, appears to be the right man for the job. So he takes over Elisabeth's personal education, and she sees far more of him than she does any other man, even her husband. And most of these tutoring liaisons take place in her own quarters. Now, as history has shown, there is some evidence that Franz is pretty low on the fertility scale, some say to the extent that he was either sterile or more likely homosexual and therefore not really interested in his wife 'Sisi' even though she was a ravishing beauty. He soon has a daughter, dark with close set eyes, very Mediterranean looking. Not at all like anyone ever born to his family before. By two, this child, Sophie, is gone, dying during a trip to Italy. A lot of suspicious co-incidences you might say, especially concerning a mother-in-law that detests Elisabeth and never bonded with her new grandchild for reasons unknown but chose to accompany them on this trip to Italy along with her personal physician. The rest as we say, becomes history. Similar features are shared by a son born a little later and his life becomes cloaked in mystery, especially when it becomes involved with an event known as 'Mayerling'. Sure, one can say it's all speculation but there's enough information available to support what I will eventually write. "

"Such as?" Pearce inquires.

"Like I said Pearce, that's a book in itself that's still to be written. I'll save it for another time. I mean, even the reasons why Jacob is in Vienna at all, has to do with a warrant for his arrest back in Brody, Galicia. There's no short story where he's involved. But back to the mainstream. So Jacob is the son of Joseph Kahana, who just happens to be the Rabbi in Brody, just like his father before him, Abraham. Now Abraham is the son of Zeev Wolfe, who's the son of Shalom Shakna Kahana. This is where the names start to get interesting because they start becoming metaphors. So Shalom Shakna, which translates at 'the Peace of the Spiritual Cloud," is the son of Aryeh Lieb Kahana, whose name sounds a bit like mine but means 'the Lion Hearted' as I mentioned before. I guess you could say that they expected some kind of revolution or revelation when he was born but it didn't happen. That's the trouble when you give your children monikers that imply great deeds. They often have to live up to expectations that never materialise. But getting back to the story, Aryeh is the son of Yusef Kahana. Now Yusef lived in the late sixteenth century and early seventeenth. According to some, he was a very prominent Rabbi himself. Prominent enough to marry Reisel Heller, the daughter of the Yom Tov Lipman of Heller, a rabbinic sage of the time and his wife, Rechel Ashkenazi.

This last bit of information was provided by a colleague doing research on the Kahanas as well. You see, John, all aspects of the family are so significant that the research is being conducted from the various segments. David, who was researching from the other end, was looking at the Kahana and stumbles on to the Goldenthals through the material he's looking at. I stumble on to his research coincidentally about the same time from my perspective. My research provided no indication of Yusef, or Yaakov Yusef as he's called in my colleague's notes, being either scholar or rabbi but instead, the eighteenth generation from the Mar Rav Hilai, which makes him very prominent amongst Jewish society. He'd almost be considered a prince. The anticipation of his bringing forth an enlightenment or radical revolution of the people and age would have been considerable."

"Did it happen?"

"No…not really. More disillusionment. Things didn't improve for the majority of people. The Maharal, also known as Rabbi Judah Lowe, in Prague was the most prominent figure of the time and he was using a Golem to bring about change."

"A golem…?" Pearce had a quizzical look on his face with the mention of the Golem.

"So you've heard of that before," I questioned.

"Yep, Doc…an artificial human. A bogeyman. Now you want me to print fairy tales as well? I know that this golem character was possibly Mary Shelly's basis for her Frankenstein monster."

"Hey, the Maharal wasn't in my family. But I will let you in on a secret. Yusef's father, Yaakov Kahana, had to take on the Maharal and this Golem. No proof, just a legend but pretty interesting which I'll also write someday."

"So, you really want me to believe in a Golem?"

"No and yes. You're just going to have to wait until I get to telling you that particular story. Even legends in my family have a foundation in historical fact. It does help explain why Yusef was somewhat of a disappointment. Even his father played a more significant role in the overall scheme of things. Anyway, back to the main story before I digress any further. Now, Yusef was the son of Yaakov, the son of Natun, the son of Avrum Aryeh, son of Yakub, the son of ...."

"Just a minute, Doc. If the number of generations between people is so significant, where do you fit in?"

"What do you mean, Pearce?"

"Like this Yusef is eighteen generations down from this big shot guy, wait a second, let me check my notes…, this Mar Rav Hilai and because of that great things were expected. Now you told me that you got your name because of certain expectations. So I figure you have to be some special number from the measuring stick too."

"How very perceptive of you." I congratulated him. "Well, you're right. Certain numbers play very major roles in Judaism. Eighteen because it also spells 'chai', the word for life and in reverse it is the short form for the tetragrammon or initials of God. But also of importance was twelve. Twelve tribes, twelve showbreads, etcetera. I am the twelfth generation from Aryeh-Lieb Kahana and therefore considered a patriarchal father. I will play a prominent role more so for the raising of one of my children, grandchildren or great-grandchildren to a level of vital importance. Remember, my grandchildren will be the hundredth generation from Aaron. What could that possibly entail? Right now, it's anyone's guess but history says they will be significant!

Even though my full Hebraic name is Avrum Aryeh-Zuk, I doubt very much if my father even had a clue why he was naming me this way. Nine months afterwards I would never see him again, so providing a family heritage was probably one of the least important things on his mind. Then again, fathers disappearing totally into oblivion also happened to have traditional aspects in the family as well, so perhaps he didn't even know that he was following a pre-set pattern. A lot of what we do is predetermined and very little we do can change it. Anyway, my mother struggled to grasp the words that made up my name properly, which only gave my brother a free license and a wonderful opportunity to ridicule me since he would always refer to me as 'Broom Air Sick'. When I'd protest to my mother, she'd comment on the effort my brother was making to say the name correctly. I didn't think that it was that difficult! But later, even the Rabbis at the Hebrew school had difficulty with it, recording my name on all their documentation instead as "Abraham Isaac" which to them was deemed the more correct, version of my name. But if we're ever going to finish this story sometime this decade then let me get back to it and stop interrupting me!"

CAESAREA, JUDAEA: 37 AD

For your eyes only, my son!

I am writing this letter to you Elioneai, at the same time that I'm preparing my belongings for the long voyage. I don't want you to fret for me, my son. As I look out the window from my chamber, I do not know if I'll ever see this view again. It is with a sadness that I depart, but if God is willing, my bones shall be buried in the tomb of my ancestors. I do not now when, or how this will come to pass. I only know that it will. I can be grateful only that your mother, Annah, is not alive to see me this way. She would never accept my being so sad and solemn. I have to express my real thoughts in this letter to you, which I will arrange to have delivered once my ship has left the port of Caesarea. Please watch over your brother for me until I return, either on the strength of my own to legs or in a box. He tends to be hot and tempestuous and now is not the time for him to vent his anger.

It is important to me that you understand the reasons for these recent events. It is not as though they come unexpected to me. So much has transpired over the last few years that I can barely recognize what was a normal way of life and what has been thrust upon us.

It came to pass that I was no longer to wear the priestly ephod, having done so for nineteen years. And they chose my brother-in-law, Jonathan, son of Anan to stand in the sanctuary in my stead, but he did not know how to please our Roman overlords. That was a talent that I had finely honed over two decades. To say one thing to the Romans, yet do another and still have them think that all was done according to their wishes, which is an art all to itself. Jonathan could never be that man. He could barely control his temper, let alone mask his sentiments towards a man like Pilate.

So they cast him out of office and put his brother Theophilus into the holy vestments of Aaron. Now all who knew him would say that Theophilus was not suited to be high priest by anyone's accord. Yet, here we are a year later and still he serves in that office. Your mother once said that Theophilus was always the most temperate of her siblings, kind and helpful to a fault. He has proven himself to be a very good puppet. At least he will no longer have to contend with Pilate as the master of his strings.

Life at my age was intended to slow down and let me reap the rewards of my children and grandchildren. Yet, with every passing moment, my world appears if anything, to be more hectic and overpowering. The notice from the Roman Senate that arrived today was a summons that cannot be overlooked. I really don't know if my sailing to Rome is good news or bad news. For once, my outwardly powers of perception appear to have failed me. The future has become nothing but a dark landscape upon which I cannot even find the remotest sign to guide myself.

If I am being summoned for what I believe will be accusations regarding my role in the Samaritan uprising, then it could mean that I will not be returning to this land of my own accord. At least there may be some redemption in my final days. I'll be able to see that Pilate is summarily charged for his cruelty once and for all. How ironic that we may both be meeting our ends but from two diametrically opposed positions. Me, because they have come to suspect my involvement in the events and insurrections over the past few years, and the Procurator because of his cruelty in putting down such insurrections of which I speak. Who says that there is no irony in this life?

Is there no one that can understand what has happened in this land of ours? The world has changed, and most of our people don't even realize it. It is as if all that we understand to be true and correct has been stood on its head and we must open our eyes and see for the first time. Even I did not appreciate the extent of how much our lives have been changed. Whether it be for the worse or the better, it makes no difference because none of it can remain the same in the face of such pressures. Even our Samaritan cousins recognize it, and they are the last to see anything, thick-headed and dim-witted as they are.

Pilate was justified in loathing them. Their rededication of their Temple on Mount Gerzim would have been a prelude to disaster. And this Simon Magus is no fool. Trust me in this matter. He is not a light that shines a clear path to follow. Keep our people from him. He has abilities, that I will concede, but just what may be the source of his powers I do not know. They are unlike any that the Lord has bestowed on any man in the past. If he truly had the ability to divine where the Samaritan's sacred vessels are hidden, then there would have been no stopping the Samaritans as they would have rampaged through the streets in celebration of their restoration. I would not want to have been a Roman standing in front of that unruly throng at that moment. Had I been Pilate, I would have similarly interceded before the event as well. At least by doing so he was able to prevent immeasurable Roman casualties and all it cost him was the death of several thousand Samaritans. Knowing Pilate, he would have considered that a cheap price.

It has always been his problem though, that Pilate doesn't commit these atrocities because he has to; he does so because he enjoys it. He derives great pleasure in death. He is a black force that has only spread darkness upon this land. That is what has earned him his summons to appear before the Senate. But once I've had the opportunity to make my defence before that august body, they'll have a much better picture of the man they sent to Judaea a decade ago to rule in their name.

Was I involved in Pilate's campaign of murder? Is that not one of the accusations that will be laid against me? Not to my knowledge. I have more pressing problems to deal with than a Samaritan magician and his crazed followers. It has not been that long since the settling of our very own problems in Jerusalem. Now, in that matter I will admit I was very involved. And in that matter I failed miserably to achieve my goal for it was my intention to bring about the necessary changes that would restore our predominance within our own land. I was certain that the prophecies had been fulfilled and it mattered not to me that I had jeopardised our entire existence by tying our entire religious and judicial structure to the robes of one man. Unfortunately I failed him as much as he had failed me.

Pilate tried so hard to have me condemned for my involvement in that matter but he could prove nothing. I was cautious enough to ensure that all my machinations behind the scenes were concealed but from a trusting few. Now to have myself brought to Rome to appear before the Roman courts on charges that most likely Pilate has trumped up regarding the Samaritan issue seems almost ludicrous. But nonetheless, I go because it is my just punishment for my failure to save a good man from his premature death; a death that I cannot wash my hands easily of.

My great plan had come to naught. Our people are still oppressed, and Rome still hangs like a turbulent thick cloud over our Holy of Holies. A priesthood that is nothing more than an object of derision that a procurator plucks like a lyre, appointing and dispensing with us as he feels the urge or if someone should pay the price to have him do so. All because I failed in my mission. I failed God in the task he had assigned to me. If that be my shame then I will go to my end knowing that it has been ordained for all things are known to the Lord and this is but a part of his plan for all of us.

I only ask my son that you remember all that I have said to you, as the time will come when we must try again to deliver our people from this evil that tries to decimate us. We have passed through the darkness in the past and each time we have found our way into the light. If I should not be here to lead, then it is your task, and those of your descendants to do so. We have all eternity to succeed. Keep well and safeguard your family for me. I will miss seeing my grandchildren. May the Lord keep them safe until my return.

Blessed be the Lord, our God!

CHAPTER THREE

"So you're going to tie all this in at some point, right Doc? Because right now it's sounding a lot like your original story."

"I won't let you down, John. In fact, I was going to make the connection right now for your benefit. Now, I last told you about Aryeh-Lieb Kahana, my ancestor of twelve generations ago, but as you probably noticed, he was "the Lion-Hearted," not exactly the same name as mine, but nonetheless, a marker post in my genealogical data. It's saying, 'look here! We have someone of prominence in this line and you can forget about looking at the divergent lines; very typical of any aristocratic lineage. One particular family rises to prominence to the exclusion of all others. It's a way to prevent dilution within the families. King David had to do it with the families of the priesthood. There were just too many of them. So he chose a single descendant of Aaron, brother of Moses, and said, 'From now on, your family holds the high priesthood. All others are excluded.' It probably wasn't considered too fair at the time to the others, but it worked. Otherwise the process of selecting a new high priest would have proven to be horrendous."

I waited for John's pen to go back to the paper before I continued my train of thought. "So, if Aryeh-Lieb of twelve generations ago was a marker, then who was the marker before him? Let's start again at the Aryeh-Lieb Kahana. He was the son of Yusef Kahana, the son of Yaakov, the son of Natun, the son of Avrum Aryeh, the son of Yakub, the son of Natai, the son of Avrum, the son of Yusef, the son of Jacob, the son of Achunai, who was in turn the son of Aryeh Zuk Kahana. And now twelve generations from the last marker we have this Aryeh-Zuk Kahana. That's if you include both as part of the set of twelve. I hope you recognize that he bears the same name as mine. He was a marker but more significantly he suffered very much like me!"

I released my body from the surrounding comfort of the wingback chair and walked over to my bookshelves. These weren't as ornate as the library cases of my old home where John last spoke to me. No old carved doors and stained-glass cupboards. No, richly oiled wood with its perfumed fragrance of bouquets of flowers. Just plain old shelves, but still holding my greatest treasures, my books. I pulled a small little leather bound book from the shelf. It measured no more than five by three inches.

"Here, take a look at this." I gently placed it into his outstretched hands.

"Looks old," Pearce commented.

"It is old. Almost four hundred years old. Printed in Amsterdam in the seventeenth century but containing the collected thoughts of Aryeh-Zuk Kahana from three hundred years earlier."

Opening the cover, Pearce looked inside, turned a few pages and then placed the book on the glass covered display table. "It's in another language."

"It's in Hebrew. A medieval Hebrew to be exact. Like Latin, Hebrew was still used by the scholars of eastern studies and by the Jewish religious leaders. Not exactly a lingua Franca but still quite accessible."

"So what does it say?"

"The book is entitled Hazak Armanah. Which translates as the 'Testimony of Strength.' or 'Unyielding Faith.' Problem with ancient languages is that one word could have multiple meanings and I can only guess at which one they were using. Either title conveys the author's sentiments quite strongly. Within its pages, you quickly realize that my ancestor suffered from the visions of his illustrious ancestors in the way that only GLEEM can produce. Difference is, unlike myself, who can rationalise the condition through present day genetics and scientific discovery, poor Aryeh-Zuk must have considered himself a man possessed. His discourses on alternative history race back and forth, portraying the play of time's events from a spectator viewpoint. And he saw a lot. Those that recorded his words probably considered him divinely inspired. Mainstream Judaism would have branded him a heretic. The Christian world would have viewed him as dangerous. And the political forces of the time saw him as a threatening cloud on the horizon, which left unattended, would release a torrential flood across their lands."

Pearce sat forward on the couch, eager for the climax. "And

the point is…?"

"And so, they did to him in the fourteenth century what they did to all other potential threats; they gave him to the inquisition. The greatest mechanisation of organised torture mankind had ever produced. And poor old Aryeh-Zuk probably didn't want the visions in the first place. He already was a tortured man when they finally broke his bones."

"But why? What could be in the book that they were so afraid of?"

"As always as history has proven, it was the greatest threat of all. It contained the truth! Of course, even Aryeh-Zuk's truth would have been biased and corrupted by all the ancestral visions he suffered. But nonetheless, it was seen as an alternative truth and therefore a considerable threat to established beliefs.

"How did he die, Doc?"

"Morbid curiosity, Pearce?" I considered his question somewhat offensive. Aryeh-Zuk's death or means by which he died mattered little to whether his words should be given credence or not.

Pearce shook his head back and forth innocently. "Readership. When we write the editorial to accompany the story, it's facts like these which sell. You may not realize it but people are intrigued with death. The greater the shock value, the more likely they'll read the storyline."

"I guess they do, at that. There was probably quite the audience watching my ancestors intestines ripped from his body while he was still alive. Why should it be any different now? Imagine having a butcher's hook inserted into your belly and through a series of pulleys, it's withdrawn along with most of your insides. That passed for entertainment!"

"And did they get the confession they wanted?"

"They got what they wanted. He died screaming. And his wail like a banshee is still burning in my memories!"

"How's that possible, Doc?"

"I would suspect his son must have witnessed the entire episode. Obviously it had been significant enough to impact and be stored in his memory."

"How horrible." Pearce's eyes were staring blankly at the wall behind me. I could tell that he was playing out the scene of Aryeh-Zuk's death in his own mind.

"Yes, how horrible for all of us!"

ROME: 37 AD

Dearest Elioneiai,

I am writing this letter to you from Rome, my son. I know that my departure from Jerusalem was quite hasty and that it most likely took everyone by surprise. My apologies for the discomfort that I have brought upon you all. I had very little choice in this matter. I am relieved that there are so many of my former colleagues and friends that reside in this city that my stay here has been most comfortable. Though I am considered to be under house arrest, there are no restraints on my movements. I have had the opportunity to visit the Jewish districts of the city. I believe many of the Senators that will hear my case are predisposed to our religion and teachings.

My host, Lysimachus Alexander, has been very generous putting his household and servants at my disposal. For the most part, it is not unlike being at home in Jerusalem. There is nothing lacking, except being able to see my family. That I miss most of all.

There is no date set for my hearing in the Senate. Rome, as great as it is, seems to be at a standstill. The word on the street is that the Emperor Tiberius is on his death bed. As insensitive as this may sound, I have no prayers to offer on his behalf. The Emperor has not exactly been a benefactor of our people. After all, it was he that chose the series of procurators that have ruled over us with their corruption. We cannot overlook that it was his guiding hand that shaped our world.

Lysimachus believes that should the Emperor die, there will be good fortune to follow. Do you recall, Agrippa, Herod's grandson, Elioneiai? I know that he has been absent from among us for a long time but he should not be forgotten. All these years he has been in Rome under the auspices of the Emperor. Like myself, until recently he has been under house arrest, free to come and go as he chooses but now he is in prison awaiting sentencing by the Emperor for failure to pay debts. It would appear that our royal heir has burrowed a lot of money than he should have from some very influential people in this city. His non-payment of these loans could very well earn him a lifetime in prison. But as Lysimachus believes, Agrippa will be released upon Tiberius's death. It is only the Emperor's distaste for our prince that put him in prison in the first place. Many owe debts within this city without incarceration.

I believe my host is correct with his assumption. Should Tiberius succumb to his illness, then it is most likely his nephew Gaius Caligula will become emperor in his stead. Caligula is Agrippa's oldest and dearest friend. They are like brothers, having been raised together. I would expect Agrippa to be released immediately if this should prove to be the course of events. This would be very good news for us.

Although Agrippa is not a religious man, I'm assuming that he'd want to rule over us to the best of his ability. That would mean the restoration of all of the old institutions. Caligula will likely give Agrippa the freedom to do so. I have always said that it is better to be governed by one of our own. Even the worst of our own people is preferable to the best foreigner.

And of course, we are all expecting for Agrippa to present my appeal to the new Emperor and obtain my release. Even if Caligula merely refers my case to be handled by a court administered by Agrippa, it would mean that I'd be coming home. So as you can see, Lysimachus's news of Tiberius's pending demise is being met with renewed optimism.

I don't think Tiberius could ever understand us. Unlike his step-father, Augustus, he never made an effort to do so. We were merely a problem that he inherited and his primary focus became Romanising us. Had he paid any attention to history, he would have seen that that was the worst advice he could have been offered. We have been a thorn in the side of every occupying force since the time of the Babylonians, and not of them ever succeeded in breaking us. If I have the opportunity to appear before the courts in his presence, I will try to give him the details of this lesson, so that he may understand that for all the problems we may have been to him over the past twenty years, he was the chief author of his own torment. And should he pass away prior to an opportunity to do so, then I will make an effort to educate his successor in the proper means to administer Judaea, Galilee, Idumaea and Peraea. Only when they realize that we will bend, but we will not be broken will they be able to understand our indominatable will.

I will keep you informed of the events of my scheduled hearing as they transpire in this accursed city. I do not know how soon it will transpire or whether I will merely be informed about my release that is presuming that it will happen, but I pray that it will be soon. Successors to the throne in this city seem to have a way of expediting events, and I pray that this happens as soon as possible.

Until my next letter, keep well and be strong.

CHAPTER FOUR

"And back to this expected tie-in, Doc?"

"It's coming. You'll put it all together soon enough. I'm pretty certain of that."

Pearce adjusted himself but the look of discomfort was obvious on his face. Thus far, I haven't really provided anything different from the previous version of the *Caiaphas Letters* but that's what was so much fun about our meeting today. I had the upper hand. He had to go back to his publisher with something different and the tension and pressure he under was beginning to mount. I knew what I was going to say as we progressed the story line but he didn't have a clue. The smirk on my face must have been terribly annoying to him. But it was my dime and he was just going to have to wait.

"Now Aryeh-Zuk was the son of Nathan Kahana, who was the son of Avrum Kahana, who was the son of Jacob, the son of Nathan, and he was the son of the Yom Tov Kahana. Yom Tov was one of the great scholars of his time. That was the recognition given to him but as you've probably been counting, that was neither twelve nor eighteen generations from the last "Lion" of the line. So let's take it back even further. And the Yom Tov was the son of Jacob, the son of Natronai, the son of Mar Rab Hilai, whom I mentioned earlier. And he in turn was the son of Hananiah, the son of Haninai Kahana, the son of Huna, the son of Chunai, the son of Mar Papa. Now Mar Papa was the brother-in-law to Makhir Natronai, who was also called Theodoric."

"You pointed that out on the chart already," Pearce commented, a slight tone of irritation in his voice.

"Yes, but now we're counting generations and the numbers become important.

"But you said you weren't directly related to that particular Kahana family."

"No. I said I wasn't directly connected to his family in

France. But as I pointed out earlier, I am a descendant of the wife that he left behind. The one called Ruth Bas Kahana. She was the mother of Achunai. So I'm still a descendant of Natronai but through the family he left behind in Baghdad. Now do you understand? I also told you that the last Bernard made it back East and re-entered the genetic chain at some point, passing along his memories of events that transpired, but he was not a direct line to me, having come back through the females of the family."

"So they are interconnected," Pearce sighed understandingly.

"Now you've got it. Now you understand the workings of GLEEM. It requires the repeated injections of the same DNA into the genetic line over and over again. That's why it's unique and relatively rare. Artificially, your government ghouls can probably now remove the protein structures from a particular candidate, replicate them through Polymerase Chain Reaction techniques, then inject the copies into the test guinea pig, but for it to happen naturally it took a lot of interbreeding."

"So why aren't you strumming a banjo," Pearce joked, his feeble attempt at humour not going over too well. I ignored it and he picked up quickly not to make any further hillbilly jokes.

"By the way Doc, we had a lot of amateur historians writing in to our office saying that you were mistaken in your claim that Alda was a sister and not Charlemagne's aunt."

"My, you're getting a little capricious, John. Why not just sit back and relax while I tell this story?"

"Don't mean to challenge you, Doc, but it might be a mistake."

"Not on my part! Alda was the oldest of the siblings. She helped raise her brothers. Whether she was a daughter of Bertruda is questionable. It would have been very unusual for Pepin not to have had more than one wife or concubine. Older half-siblings were often referred to as aunts or uncles. It's Charlemagne's references to Alda that lead people to call her Pepin's sister. Furthermore her age was far closer to Charlemagne's than to their father's. And since we know that Charles Martel died in 741, how can we explain a daughter born in 738 AD to a man almost eighty years old and to Swanhilde, who would have been an old woman by that time as well. Pepin would have been twenty-four years older than his sister. Not very likely."

"Okay. I understand now. You made your point."

"Good, now we can get on with this story."

"So who's being testy now?" Pearce laughed thinking that he almost got himself one up on me.

"Touché! Tu ne trouve pas le vrais quand tu serche dans merde!"

"What was that?" Pearce inquires.

"Just a French expression saying, 'Yes, let's get on with it.' So, let's look at the chart again. Here's where it starts getting interesting."

"Sounded like a lot more than just get on with it," Pearce objected.

"Forget about it and look at this." We get down on the floor and start crawling all over the tree scroll. Following Mar Papa backwards, he's the son of Achunai-Amaniah, the son of Natronai Kahana, the son of Nehemiah, the son of Mar Rav Achunai, who was married to Addah. Take a look at her father. Do you recognize that name? You should! That's the one and only Bustenai, the exilarch during the transition from Persian rule to Arab rule in the Middle East. He went toe to toe in *Blood Royale* with Othmar if you recall."

Pearce nodded in recognition. "I see that you're from the not so likeable female side again, Doc. Wasn't it he that talked about his wife being a shrew when compared to his other wife, the Persian Princess?"

"Ah, I see you did learn something from my previous book. But that's what I've been talking about. Bustenai's family line is through the Davidic monarchy. But most often they took wives from my line being the Kahanate and vice versa. But if you follow through his second wife, Izdudurdad, you'll see, that the Persian line is blended back into the Kahanate until it's indistinguishable. That was the problem when the Viceroy Rosbihan was saying there were too many kings in Baghdad. Natronai, it turned out was the one that had to go."

Pearce started tapping at one of the names on the tree.

"What is it?" I inquired.

"This daughter of Yhosdegerd, I know that name from somewhere before."

"You should, Sheherezad was quite famous."

"Now, how do I know it?" Pearce scratched his head in an

attempt to jog his memory.

"You grew up with it, like almost every other child. Aladdin, Ali Baba, forty thieves, genies, and so on."

"Nah, I still don't get it. Can't place the name."

"She was the teller of the Arabian Nights stories. You know, a thousand and one Arabian nights. Bustenai was her protector, Othmar took her as concubine because of it, but she was still the great granddaughter of his arch enemy, Khusroe. That meant she always had to be in fear for her life. And she wasn't exactly enamoured to Othmar, who happened to be an old man by then. But it even got worse when Al-Husain, the son of Ali, became Caliph and took her as a wife. Coming from the desert, he wasn't exactly as sophisticated as the courtesans she had been accustomed to, and he certainly wasn't as tolerant as Othmar. So she told him stories at night. Primarily because it endeared herself to him, thereby reducing the threat of execution, but also because in order to listen to her tales, he wouldn't be trying to force himself on her. By making her heroes all named Ali, he couldn't help but listen. Stroke a male ego and you have a willing audience."

"So that's her! She was a real person. I didn't know that."

"Not too many people do. She's become almost as mythical as the stories she told. But she was as real as you or I. And as real as the characters and events of the Caiaphas Letters are. So while you look at the chart some more, I'll give you a little insight of what's happening in Caiaphas's world."

ROME: 37 AD

My blessing upon you, Elioneiai,

You should know that while those from Judaea and Samaria suffer and struggle, there is a particular segment of our people that don't share our concerns. In fact their complete disregard for our situation has become quite the topic of discussion amongst the Jewish community, here, in Rome. Far greater than any discussion that we might engage in back in Judaea. I find that quite odd.

Of course it is the Essenes of whom I'm talking, those communities living in the desert hills by the sea, seemingly too distant to grow weary under Rome's heavy hand. For almost two hundred years now they have lived in isolation, rarely venturing from their villages, concealing their strange customs and ways of their brotherhood from us.

It is surprising therefore that there is one of them preaching in the streets of Rome and in the name of the Baptist. He talks endlessly about their devotion to purity, their ritual of immersion on a daily basis, and how this is not to clean their bodies but to purify their souls. In his simple dress of clean, white tunic, and his strict adherence to dietary laws that are far more rigid than even those of our fundamental beliefs, as inconceivable as it may sound, he is gaining adherents amongst the Jewish population of this city. Can you believe that? And now I have come to understand that he is even gaining a following from amongst the gentile population of Rome itself. I must confess, that I do not understand the Roman mind. How is it that they can oppress us and condemn us, and yet a segment is so willing to follow our customs? This worries me, because it is obvious to me, that it would not be difficult to gain a fellowship of worshippers that would follow any charlatan claiming to preach the true scripture.

Right now, these follower of this Essene named Eli, are proclaiming that they are the true believers in the Torah because they are living by the precepts laid down by the Essene's long dead, Righteous Teacher. Most of them don't even know who this Righteous Teacher was, other than a former High Priest of Jerusalem, whom was deposed and exiled, and then killed. But the fact that I am currently in Rome has fuelled their religious hysteria, since it was our ancestor Joacim that was put into the position of High Priest in his stead. Antiochus King of Syria deposed Onias, not us. Let them go vent their anger against the Syrians in this city, not at me! It was probably for the bet that Onias was removed from the position, because by then it had become the heredity position of a single family and that was never what had been intended by Moses, or even by David.

But worst of all is the belief being spread amongst these new adherents that the Righteous Teacher is not dead. That he was merely removed from this world and that he is due to return at some time, leading an army of the Holy Hosts against the Sons of Darkness. The coming Armageddon is all detailed in the book Eli

44

reads from, entitled *The War between the Sons of Light and the Sons of Darkness.* Surely you would expect the people to see through this ruse but that is not the case. It is bad enough that the Pharisees have confounded our faith with their beliefs in the immortality of the soul, but now the Essenes have gone even further with their version of a resurrection including the restoration of the physical body. Not all my assurances that the prophet Ezekiel was writing purely metaphorically and symbolically can sway their belief in these obscene fantasies.

These beliefs endanger our very own structure of the afterlife that was provided to us by Moses and Aaron. For they let us know that all things come from God, and in the end, all things return to God, and that is that. When we die, our spirit returns to the Holy Presence, the Shekinah, and we become one with the Eternal Spirit. God's purpose was to have us fulfil his instructions while we walked in the world of the living, not some contrived fantasy of a world after we have been long departed. Such nonsense smacks of the pantheon of gods that the Romans and Greeks have tried to force us to follow since the dawn of time. It's idolatry and self-worship of the most vile kind for it masks itself in a cloak of Judaism that is not acceptable.

Everything that Eli is expounding is profane to my ears. He talks of the Essene's adherence to a celibate life, since fornication is looked upon with contempt because it violates the spiritual cleansing of their souls. No wonder they need a resurrection of the body in the end of days. Without procreation, they are doomed to extinction. God has clearly demanded that we go forth and multiply, and here's this sect proclaiming otherwise. It is ludicrous!

This prophetic mission of theirs must be discouraged. Should I not be able to return from Rome for some unforeseen reason, I am hoping, my son, that you will undertake this responsibility with all haste. I never recognized how dangerous the Baptist truly was, until now. When he first began his preaching, I once travelled to the Jordan, at the northern border of Samaria to hear him speak. He had great personal magnetism, dressed in the traditional garb of an ancient prophet, forsaking fine linen for the furs and skins of animals. This John the Baptist was a fine orator, sincere and resolute in all that he preached, and the light of divine purpose clearly shone in his eyes. I grant him that in admiration even all these years after his death. He practiced his ritual immersion on all whom declared that they accepted his teachings. He changed the lives of all whom he came in contact with, just as he opened my eyes to a world that I had not viewed prior. I bet you are surprised that I admit to that.

He was the hope for the poor and oppressed. "Salvation is at hand," he would proclaim, and the people were buoyed by his conviction. Like this Eli, he preached the imminent return of the Righteous Teacher but not in the offensive manner that this second rate sermoniser is doing in Rome. John was very reluctant to reveal any details, saying only that the one of whom he spoke would bear the mark of the Almighty, and the Baptist was not even worthy to carry his sandals.

But as in the case of so many prophets of the past, John placed his faith in the Lord, forgetting that on earth it is the kings and rulers that make the laws. Herod Antipas was a weak vassal of Rome, harmless in most respects, but John's verbal attacks would send him into a furious rage. Especially since the Baptist accused him and Herodias of adultery because of her being the wife previously of his brother; a pretty serious accusation, considering that the punishment for Herodias by our religious laws would be stoning to death. The Baptist didn't overlook the crime against nature either since both Antipas and Herodias were half siblings, which is condemned in the eyes of God. Antipas had no other choice but to rid himself of the potential threat John represented and the rest as we say is history.

So, after this long dissertation, I can only recommend that you be on guard. The proof that mankind wants to be led astray is in this man, this Eli. Do not try to reason with a system of beliefs that defies logic. It is the dreamer's mentality, and as a result, man cannot separate reality from fiction. The stronger the desire, the more easily followed is the illusion. The more convinced someone is to live within their madness, the easier it is for others to believe in the lies. What is most amazing is that once there are more people believing in these falsehoods then it is the actual truth that becomes the lie. What is truth, Elioneiai? It's whatever one is led to believe.

I have become cynical, I know it. But being here in Rome does that to one's mind. It is a city filled with cynicism.

Be well.

CHAPTER FIVE

"I disagree with you there, Doc!" Pearce protested as I sat back in my chair and took a long awaited sip of coffee.

"Disagree with whom, Pearce?"

"Well, with...I mean...you know what I mean. With what Caiaphas said."

"I think I have to show you something. Perhaps it will help you understand once and for all what is going on here. Back to the chart!

We have some choices to make now. I can take you back to the same point, either through Bustenai's ancestry, or we can look at that of his daughter Addah's husband's line. It all depends whether I take you through the royal line from David or the priestly line from Aaron. If you saw how many times these two families intermarried then it's almost incestuous."

"Guess I can expect some banjo strumming after all, eh Doc?" Pearce's repeated attempt at a little Appalachian humour was beginning to wear very thin.

"Anyway," I continued, "following the line back from Addah's husband, Mar Rav Achunai, who was the son of another Natronai Kahana, this one the son of Nehemiah, the son of Haninai Kahana, the son of Achunai Kahana, and his father before him was also named Natronai Kahana, and before him Nehemiah Kahana, and before him was Rav Kahana, son of Nathan Kahana, and he was the son of Kahana. Now that was the first Kahana by the way and I'd say he must have been very important because the name stuck as a surname or title for a very long time afterwards. And this Kahana was the son of Ananiah, the son of Judah Mar. And Judah Mar was the son of Sharaf, and that leads us to a very interesting chapter in history. Sharaf was the grandson of Mar Sharafa. These names are highly significant. There are several translations but the message is loud and clear. A conflagration was expected. These two were expected to turn the world upside down. Armageddon was definitely expected. The time period was about 180 to 250 A.D. The family of Septimus Severus would have been ruling Rome at that time. They were Easterners with close ties to the Jews of Emesa. I would think the people thought deliverance was at hand."

"And…" Pearce inquired.

"And they were wrong. Another miscalculation in a long history of miscalculations. But once again, a story for another time, so back to the genealogy table.

Sharaf was the son of Judah HaCohen, who was the son of Mar Sharaf, who in turn was the son of Judah Cayafa, who was the son of Joseph ha Cohen, the son of Elioneus, the son of Joseph, and he in turn was the son of Jeshua ben Gamaliel. Remember him? You just heard from him talking about the situation of being the last High Priest of the Temple before Titus burnt it to the ground. Take a good look at the chart there. Because here's where my family does a switch from the male line to the female line. Jeshua was the high Priest in the temple around 69 AD. That means he was a member of the twenty-four sacred families. An ancestor of the Kahana line, who happened to serve as the Cohen Gadol. His father was Gamaliel but not the sage descended from Hillel with the same name. For your information, that was a completely different family. In fact, that other Gamaliel-Hillel family weren't even Levites but merely Pharisees that came to control the nation after the destruction of the Temple.

Now for Jeshua to have become the high priest, it meant that his father Gamaliel was either an Anian, Boethian, Kamithian, or Phiabian. There weren't any other choices at the time. Those were the only families serving in the chief position during that era. But strangely enough, his ranking in the families must have been fairly low because Gamaliel isn't provided with a lineage chart in any of the old documents I've researched. As Jeshua had said, Phiabian was his lineage, and because of it, he wasn't as esteemed as the other three lineages. What happened to the House of Phiabi, leading to its decline and being despised by the Pharisees is another story as well. What elevated his own status though, was Gamaliel's choice in a daughter-in-law for Jeshua. See, there's Martha, Jeshua's wife, and there's her father Elioneiai ha Cayef, and then of course her grandfather."

Pearce rolled backwards on his heels, landing on his bottom, an expression of shocked surprise ran across his face. "Holy shit, Doc. Is that who I think it is? Let me see that again!" Picking himself off the floor, Pearce scrutinised the chart more closely.

"It is him, isn't it?"

I nodded my head in confirmation. "In living Technicolor. Now do you comprehend the source of information in the Caiaphas Letters?"

"I don't know what to say, Doc. I don't know if having him as an ancestor is good or bad. It's almost like saying you're the son of Idi Amin. Not exactly a role model to live up to."

"Not a problem as you perceive it. You have to remember it's all a matter of perspective. A descendant of Caiaphas would have been held in high esteem at the time. So, in regards to your question it was definitely good. Because I see what I see, and know what I know, I have nothing but admiration for the man. He held on to his position for nineteen years. That was unheard of in those days. He knew how to walk the thin wire between two worlds. Very few could do it. Serve his people and his Roman occupiers at the same time."

"Yea," Pearce interrupts, "that's the whole problem. He served his Roman masters too well. And look what happened because of it!"

"You're missing the point, John." Obvious the revelation had struck an emotional chord or should I say discord. "He knew that at any moment, his traditional world could be obliterated. His beliefs, customs, everything were in my hands. Look! It really happened thirty-four years later. It wasn't as if he was being unrealistic. He had a mission. Preserve his people and his homeland and he did it. Perhaps if he had lived longer he could have avoided the catastrophe of the Roman-Jewish war, but he didn't and what happened, happened. I know exactly where he was coming from and I agree with his position. The needs of the many do outweigh those of the few. It's a simple equation."

"I can't agree with you, Doc. What he did was a crime, I don't care how you try to explain it. What he did to Jesus amounted to murder no matter how you slice it. He killed him!" Pearce was heated.

"That's the easy approach; the one that most will select. Look superficially and shoot from the hip. All I've ever asked from

Caiaphas Letters was that the reader viewed the situation from the other side. What I'm going to do this time though is give you all the reasons why my perspective has the clearest view. But before I do that, you have to understand Joseph Caiaphas's background. He just didn't appear from thin air. Like me, he was a product of his lineage. As the first Aryeh-Zuk, he bore a tremendous heritage."

"So you're saying, that he was the first of your line."

"No! Not exactly. He was the first to be called the 'Righteous Lion', as well as the 'Lion of Matthias.' The latter was the result of his family house or surname. And it's quite interesting when you think about it."

Pearce didn't have a clue what I was referring to. "How so?"

"Because being from the house of Kamithos, also called Matthias, in Hebrew they would have called him the Lion of Matthiah. Combined it would be pronounced Arimathea. In full, Joseph Arimathea. Does that ring any bells for you?"

"That doesn't make any sense, Doc. You're confusing two separate identities. It's obvious that they couldn't be the same person. I mean, just because someone has the same last name as a town doesn't mean they're one and the same. Look how many people have town names in our language. It's a common occurrence....isn't it?"

"Here's the first great revelation for you, John. There was no place called Arimathea."

"How can you say that?" Pearce twitched uncontrollably on the couch. I could see the carotids in his neck begin to pulsate as his heart went into overdrive. "I've seen lots of maps with it from the old days."

"No, what you've seen is a lot of maps trying to do reconstructions of what things looked like in the old days. And Arimathea shows up all over the map; thirty miles to the south, on the Dead, Sea, to the west, or anywhere else as anybody's guess. Because nowhere in the history of Judaea does anyone refer to a town of Arimathea."

"But that can't be true...."

"That's where lack of language skills can fool most, John. They'll tell you that Arimathea is the same meaning as Yir Mathea, which does translate as Matthias's City but as you are well aware now, Ari and Yir are two entirely different words. And if it wasn't quite a city they could have used Kiriot or Kirbet, but again, that's not Ari.   The best argument presented was that it was the name used for the town of Ephrathah.   If you say them quickly enough, I guess you could confuse the two. Only problem is that Ephrathah has always been Ephrathah, and if that was the case then he would have been Joseph of Ephrathah. Are you getting my drift?"

"But it could have been a city that sounded the same. One we don't know about now.   It could have just been a simple mistake."

"John, you have to think with the mind of someone in the first century AD, not as if you're merely looking back through history. You live in Toronto. When you die, you'll be recorded as living in Toronto. When your great grandchildren refer to you, it will be as their ancestor who lived in Toronto. No one is suddenly going to say Ottawa, because they feel like it. Because Toronto exists in their time, they will relate to it and you will always be John Pearce of Toronto. Do you understand? One, two, three generations later, he would always have been Joseph of Ephrathah, because it still existed.   They wouldn't have made up a non-existent name to replace one they could easily find on their maps. It's not logical. You're fishing for excuses and they don't hold water! Period! Consider yourself on a learning curve"

ROME: 37 AD

Dearest Elioneiai,

I believe a brief lesson in history is necessary for you to understand the framework in which events transpired. The last three decades have been tumultuous times, filled with insurrection, natural disasters, prophets of doom, and of course, messiahs.   So many messiahs. I grow tired of messiahs.

With the passing of Judas, the Galilean Zealot that terrorised the Roman forces throughout the provinces for a decade, the tax collection was strictly enforced, and all our people submitted to these foreign masters that had temporarily broken our spirit.   To disgrace us even further, they selected from amongst us those that would serve as their agents, gathering the head tax at the meeting houses, for it was well known that all of us would gather at the synagogues and community houses every Sabbath. They went as far as setting up their booths in the outer court of the Temple mount in Jerusalem, so that not only would we exchange our money to purchase the prayer offerings to be sacrificed, but a shekel would be taken on behalf of Caesar as well.

Now, during this time of the taxation there was an exceptional boy brought to the Temple for his consecration as a member of the congregation. Herod Archelaus had just been sent into exile by the Roman Legate of Syria, and Coponius, the new procurator had ordered a census and tax collection of the new provinces under his jurisdiction. It was during the time that Eleazar was High Priest in Jerusalem.

The obvious thought on most people's minds was not to register and thereby not pay tax at all! In those provinces still governed by Herodians, it would be their concern and therefore theirs to tax? But those living in the communities outside the land of Israel have failed to understand this and the Mediterranean sun has addled their brains. They have become more Gentile in thought than Hebrew, making some outlandish story of how everyone had to come to Jerusalem to pay the tax. Take every opportunity to correct them Elioneiai, otherwise their errors will be compounded one on top of the other until no one will recognize what truly did transpire. Is it any wonder that they tell of the star that guided them in those days? Not that this had anything to do with Yeshua's presence in Jerusalem when Coponius was procurator. This flaming star shone when Herod was king. For this was the Messiah Star that shines once every four hundred years, as it has done since the creation. The travels of this star have been recorded since ancient times. It was during that year that Herod went even madder than he had ever been before, his illness resulting from the disease which God had visited upon him, that ate at his bowels from the inside. When he saw the star, and his royal astronomers told him of its meaning, he flew in to a murderous rage.

The advent of the messiah meant the end of his reign, the termination of his dynasty once and forever. And he knew exactly from whence that threat would come. His own two sons from his wife Mariamne, granddaughter of Hyrcanus the Hasmonean. They would serve as the dagger that would pierce his cruel heart.

Alexander and Aristobulus would have to be eliminated if he was to elude his fate. So, like so many of his other enemies, Herod had his two favourite sons executed for the potential threat they represented. And amongst the people there arose a great clamour and mourning for Alexander and Aristobulus for they were well loved by all the population. And the mourners proclaimed that the firstborn sons of Israel had been taken from them and they cursed the king for what he had done.

Many children were born during the time that the star shone in the heavens. Whether one of these children was truly the messiah, I do know, for if they were, there is nothing to suggest that we have been delivered from oppression yet or soon to be. I can only pray that there is still a child born during this time that has grown to manhood but not made his presence known as yet. Whoever he may be, he would now be just over forty years of age when it is said that God will manifest his spirit upon his chosen when he has reached the age of wisdom and leadership.

The stories that have circulated have now become intertwined so extensively that the year of the Messiah Star is proclaimed amongst the followers of Yeshua to have heralded his coming and they make no mention of the two Hasmonean princes that lost their lives at this time. These stories are especially popular amongst the communities that have arisen outside of Jerusalem that spread the teachings of Yeshua. But then, it is not unusual for those that live beyond the borders of Judaea to have no use for facts or truths. Legends and tales are what they prefer, especially amongst the Galileans, for they are an uneducated lot.

And mark my words, Elioneiai, this will be a problem. Perhaps not so much for me since my days are still number in Rome, but most likely in your time because when I and all those that are contemporary with me have passed on, whom will be left to challenge and debate an opponent that twists the truth and creates his own history to support their beliefs? Truth is insubstantial, when all that you have to say can be buried beneath a landslide of myths and incongruities. This is why have chosen to spend my waning time on this earth to write down these thoughts and anecdotes on your behalf, so that you too will have the benefit of knowledge of these events.

Do not be disheartened as you face the swelling tide of deceit, my son. These are only the beginnings of the time of their distortions. Is not all this indicated by the prophets? Bear witness to me and I will tell you all that I know of. Just be reassured that the truth will prevail, no matter how long it may take, no matter how many generations may pass in between, it will conquer all that is placed in its path in order to make it falter.

Galilee, fair Galilee, is a land populated by people whom seemingly see a world painted in black and white when all about them is in colour. Yet, even so, they manage to sow the seeds of discord abundantly. Fishing and farming should have been their lot and messiahs should have been left to those that could understand them.

This kinsman, Yeshua ben Joseph, was but another product from a province that breeds messiahs like one breeds sheep. Ask his followers, and they know little of his background. In a single night that I spoke to him, I knew more of his history than those that now speak out as his chosen apostles. And his words to me I will pass on to you so that you will understand them and use them in your coming battle against the deceivers. And on this point I will be very clear, for those that will tell the lies of what never transpired will surface like the dew on the morning grass. In numbers so great, that they will be like the stars in the sky. For the stories that they will spread will be like a plague upon us, afflicting us sorely. Like a wind they will storm against us, and we will bend but we shall not break. Because the truth will always be our shield, protecting us from the evil that abounds.

My blessings upon you, Elioneiai.

CHAPTER SIX

"You have to realize that the Caiaphas Letters will always result in more questions being raised than answers ever being given. That was always my intention, John. You know that, I know you knew that, and the reader definitely knows they're in for a series of belief shattering revelations. That's what it's always been about. That's why I believe this new edition will still sell to those that already bought an earlier version. You'd be hypocritical if you say that you don't want to hear about it. It's what sells newspapers, and after all, that's what you do. So deny it all you want, but I know you better than you think."

Pearce just sat there, motionless, eyes wide opened, and not a single word made in reply.

"One thing you have to realize, is whatever you thought you knew...forget it! It's all wrong. Always has been. Tough to accept at first, but it's just the way it is. It applies to most of what we consider facts. Even the simplest facts are likely to be inaccurate. And the only way we can know for certain is by spending an awful lot of time digging up the truth.

So, either you're on board and we go ahead with my telling you what you don't want to hear, or we stop right now, and you can live the rest of your life with your head buried up your ass."

Suddenly finding his voice, Pearce objected to my accusation. "No Doc, that's just not true. I can accept that a lot of things we are led to believe aren't accurate but that doesn't' mean that they shouldn't be accepted. That's what faith is all about. And having faith is not always bad."

"Do you listen to yourself John? That's such a load of crap," I shook my head. "Blind faith is always bad. It's what sets men against other men. It becomes fanaticism and that can never be good. Faith led to a bunch of children following a deranged priest of to the crusades. And you know how that ended up."

"Things like that don't happen anymore. We have faith, but

we're also a lot smarter than back then."

"Are we John? That's where I'll disagree with you. I don't think we're any smarter. The bigger the lie, the more believable it is. Isn't that what Nazi Germany was all about? Telling the big lie!"

"Hey, that was sixty years ago," Pearce quickly interceded.

"Yes, so your point is...? What's sixty years? It's just a drop in the ocean of time. Might as well have been yesterday. We're not any wiser for it. You'll disagree with a lot of the things I'll have to say in this book. But that's okay. Over time you'll think about the points I'll raise, and then you'll start doing a little of your own investigation, and given time you'll find the truth out for yourself. That's all I'm asking from anyone."

Pearce relaxed a bit, slumping further into the couch. "So if I'm following you correctly, Doc., you're saying that Jesus of Nazareth was a relative of Caiaphas, but that's totally out of sync with everything we know about Jesus' family."

"And what do you think you know about his family?" I questioned Pearce. "Firstly, you have to remember, I'm not providing these details: the memories of my ancestors are. Secondly, Jesus never said he was descended from David. That information was presented in Luke and Matthew but neither was obviously in consultation with the other because they created two entirely different genealogies. In their attempts to give him Davidic ancestors they each picked a different son to spawn the tree from. So how's that for historical accuracy? What we do know from the New Testament is that his mother Mary was definitely from a priestly family as described when she visited her cousin Elizabeth, wife of the priest Zechariah."

"I don't know how you make that assumption" Pearce stared at me, searching for an explanation. "How do we know that?"

"Quite simple, John, you see, there's certain things you know when you happen to be descended from the Kohenim, like myself. And as a high priest I am very aware of the rules by which my ancestors lived by at that time. You couldn't marry a divorcee, or anyone considered unclean. You wouldn't marry anyone without a good pedigree. In fact, you only married someone from either the line of Aaron or from the royal family. So Zechariah was fairly limited in his options. Especially since members of the royal family were unlikely to openly identify themselves in Herodian Judaea.

Therefore, his wife was in all likelihood from the line of Aaron and since her parentage would be the same as Mary's then obviously she was the product of a priestly family. There shouldn't be any dispute there.

And that leads me to my next statement. That Mary in turn would have married either a descendant of the Aaronic or Davidic line, and since I've already commented on the difficulty the Gospel writers were having in establishing a Davidic heritage, then it only confirms Caiaphas's statement that Joseph was also of priestly descent through the same line descended from Joakim, as his own. What little information passed on through the gospels that support this conclusion is that the early names in the lineage attributed to Joseph by Matthew and Luke are all Levite names, such as Levi, Eli, Helkias and Matthias. Identical to the names found in the lineage of Caiaphas. I'll let you in on a secret John, if it looks like a duck and it quacks like a duck, then it's a duck!"

ROME: 37 AD

The Lord's blessing upon you and your family, Elioneiai.

It has been said by those in Rome preaching The Way, from Antioch, that I must repent for my sins, but they fail to realize that my sins are their passion. That was a fact I learned, only after committing the greatest error of my life. I let a man die, and in so doing, I created a god, which is now being idolised by a pagan world gone mad. Much in the same way that they have pointed their anger and resentment towards me, I fear that if left unchecked they will eventually swell in magnitude and direct their vile hatred towards all of our people, thereby threatening our survival.

Once again, I remind you my son, that it must be a mission that you and your descendants undertake, to correct these myths so that ultimately truth can prevail. This task will not be an easy one, but when has God's work ever been easy? Hear in Rome they have referred to our kinsman, Yeshua ben Joseph as the Nazarene, or as Jesus Christ they call him in the Greek tongue. Be wary of this name, for when he is no longer referred to by his Jewish heritage, then the true story of his courage and inner strength will be lost, and that which should fascinate us will no longer be recognizable.

In the second to last year of my ordination as High Priest of the Temple in Jerusalem, John the Baptist had been executed for the threat he represented to Herod Antipas. Poor Galilee, which had born the imprint of John most of all, was grief stricken and an entire populace mourned the passing of the Baptist. Many had heard him preach, while others had just heard the good tales about the man and the wisdom he espoused. Many became distraught by his sudden absence. One such person was Yeshua. To himself, John had represented a hope of universal brotherhood; a faith built on adherence, not birth right. I can only surmise that John's execution would have been unbearable to Yeshua.

How he must have longed for a new beginning; a chance to start over. Here he was, baptised by John in the Jordan River, only to have his dreams of spiritual fulfilment torn asunder. Forty-one years old, finally old enough to accept the spiritual calling and break away from his past as a tradesman and the opportunity was suddenly lost. His beloved father, Joseph, whom he adored, had died before Yeshua had ever attained manhood. With his death, it was necessary for him to become the provider for the household, which was not small. Though Joseph was an elderly man when he took Mary to be his wife, he still fathered a sizable family having other sons in James and Joazar. His brothers helped where they could, but the burden of the finances rested with Yeshua. Like his father, he had become a skilled and proficient carpenter; a builder of houses and fine furniture. A trade passed down through the priestly orders since the building of the first Temple for Solomon, for the guilds are all priestly vocations.

Hard labour had shaped him into a strapping young man. Taller than most, a half span's width less than four cubits, he stood. It was no wonder most looked in awe at him. But in spite of all these assets which drew the people to him, I must admit, I have never met someone so sad and alone. The loss of the Baptist only refreshed the painful memories of his father's death. I can only presume that the only men that he looked up to and admired were now taken away from him.

Suffering under this terrible hardship, he tore himself away from his family responsibilities and journeyed into the wilderness, searching for life's hidden meaning. Now this was the time of the spring fast, and for forty days he sought solace from the Creator. Whatever he may have encountered during that period, it changed his life forever. He became possessed by a mission and boundless determination.

Upon his return to civilisation, Yeshua was convinced that John the Baptist had passed his cloak of prophecy to him, much in the way that Elijah had passed his to Elisha. Yeshua returned to the Jordan Valley, preaching John's inspired message. He knew most of John's words, and he used his traditions and beliefs for the foundation of his own message. When Yeshua wanted to emphasize one of John's discourses in any particular instance, he would shroud his own answer in mystery, speaking in parables and riddles, forcing his listener's to dwell upon the lesson until it became ingrained into their conscience. It was a brilliant method by which to pass on life's lessons. Parables encourage discussion, force multiple explanations, and thus sow the seeds of learning. Inquisitive minds sought to interpret his discourses, teasing their intellect with messianic hopes.

Throngs of people gathered wherever he went, eager to hear his wisdom. At first, Yeshua confined his travels to northern Galilee. The area was populated by a hard-working, poorly educated class of Hebrews, with strong beliefs in legend and folklore. As I once mentioned to you, this is a land famous for its messiahs.

Similar to those that preceded him with messianic fervour, Yeshua selected a council of disciples to help him spread his message. The choice of disciples is very important. An unpopular choice could destroy the entire mission. There were to be twelve, the sacred, mystical number of our people, a clear sign of continuity with the past. Twelve tribes, twelve showbreads in the Temple, and twelve Minor Prophets that lived in the shadow of the three. Like any tradition, it nurtured the people's beliefs.

Yeshua selected his disciples, each different from the others, having the broadest appeal to the masses as possible. While visiting the shores of Lake Tiberius, Yeshua encountered the first of his inspired followers. Fishermen by trade, they would provide the necessary link to the common people. He chose wisely, for simple folk are unlikely to have complex ambitions. Capernaum has produced nothing of repute except for fish. But did it happen to move from its location when last I checked?

There was a man that confronted me here in Rome that

insisted he was there when Yeshua spoke in Capernaum, but was insistent that it was situated on Lake Hazor. He was obvious ignorant of the geography of Galilee, and I told him as much, doubting that he had ever been in the presence of Yeshua during the sermon.

Simon and Andrew were the first to answer Yeshua's calling. Andrew had been an ardent follower of the Baptist, and with the arrival of Yeshua it was easy to persuade himself and his brother to follow a new inspirational leader. They became steadfast, unswerving, unquestioning followers. Like most Galileans, they were skilled with the sword and were easy to rile, fighting without a moment's hesitation. They were guilty of drinking too much as well, and they were brash, easy to anger.

That is a nature very common to Galileans. Few have time for scholastic training. Most don't even know how to write or read. But they are strict adherents of anything that appeals to them as being sacred, willing to defend it to the death without compromise. An eye for an eye is the law, Elioneiai, but without compassion it is cold and cruel. Laws must each be valued on the individual merit, and of all God's creatures, it is only man that can temper his judgements through the mercy in his heart.

Yeshua knew immediately that his first two followers would never question his authority to lead them. In any sect, men like them become the pillars of its leadership. They are relentless in withstanding the onslaught of derision and contempt; bulwarks against the storms that rage against them. And Yeshua knew more men like these would only make him stronger. For that reason he found James and John, the sons of Zebedee. These two were called lightning and thunder, for they were storms unto themselves. Constantly challenging the other pair of brothers, Simon and Andrew, as to which pair was closest to their leader, vying for the privilege of sitting on his right hand sign and being recognized as his seconds in command.

But both sets of brothers were limited in their scope and Yeshua knew that in order to gain momentum, he needed a man of letters, someone who could record events and occurrences, as well as communicate with the more learned of his followers. As he soon learned, the educated don't go trailing after wandering prophets, and the learned no longer rely on deliverers to achieve their aims.

Unable to find such a valuable adherent, instead he approached a man named Levi, later to be called Matthias.

Levi could write and read. He was well-educated, as Yeshua had hoped, and he spoke several languages. But in spite of his assets, he was a tax collector. Despised by all, and friend to the occupying government of the land. It was not long until Yeshua's followers questioned why such a man would even be attached to them. Yeshua defended him vehemently as he knew that without Levi, he could never enter into Judaea. Levi gave him the ability to converse in Greek, Aramaic, Latin and Hebrew. Surrounded by his small retinue of five disciples, Yeshua travelled along the course of the Jordan, into the heart of Judaea.

I am tired now; I will talk more of this later.

CHAPTER SEVEN

Pearce one again had this lost expression on his face, as if he was waiting for me to fill in the blanks. Except that I had no way in knowing which blanks exactly he needed filled in. I suspected quite a few!

I broke the silence. "Are you having a problem with any of this, so far," I asked John.

"Just with establishing what Caiaphas may be lying about and what he's being honest about."

"Truth's a funny thing Pearce. When I first wrote Caiaphas Letters, there were those that read my book and assumed somehow I had found a cache of ancient letters from the first century AD. That is in spite of my making it very clear that all I have done is take these genetically passed down memories in my head and transcribed them into what I believed would be an easier format for people to comprehend. As first person letters, they do have much more of an impact. Yet, even after making this perfectly clear, you still have people insisting they are actual letters written by Caiaphas. So what is their truth? Definitely not the same as mine but probably just as strong.

Sometimes truth stares you right in the face and you still can't see if. It was always there in the Gospels. For example, the Jews didn't have the authority to put a man to death for a political crime. They could have put a man to death by stoning for a religious crime. They say it themselves right in the books. Yet they didn't do it! Don't you think that begs a few questions? So they took Jesus to Pilate, because he did have the authority to sentence a man to death for crimes against Rome and the Empire. And after that Jesus is nailed to the cross. So, who do you think gave the order for that to happen? Only one man it could have been, Pilate. He held the power to condemn or pardon. No one else. And yet if you ask anyone what's the truth about the crucifixion, they'll say the truth is, the Jews did it."

"I don't think it was that simple," Pearce stammered to reply.

"Why? Because years of Sunday school told you differently? And yet it was always there staring you in the face. It's one thing to read the Gospels, another to understanding them. Let's face it Pearce, we all believe whatever it is we want to believe. That is the definition of truth. That's what makes the world go around. The further from the truth, the better!"

"I don't agree with you. Not at all," Pearce resisted, his hands clenched as he held them in front of him as an unconscious threat.

"Once again, that's the choice you make. Because it is the likely truth, you choose not to believe what I've just said either."

"You're trying to confuse me Doc."

"I bet I am. You see, John, I just stated that we prefer to believe half-truths. You may disagree. Because that's something you don't want to admit to. If you agree that it happens, then you have to question all your beliefs and that's just too painful."

"That's too simplistic," Pearce argued, and I could detect the anger rising in his voice. "That's like saying we don't have minds of our own, and we just believe everything we get spoon-fed because we can't think for ourselves."

"Exactly! Now you got it!" I challenged back.

Pearce was stuck for words momentarily. "Well...like I said, it would mean we can't think for ourselves. I just can't buy that."

"Come on now, John. When did you ever have any independent train of thought that wasn't established by the institutions that rule over your life? Religious, political, educational and even familial. From the day your born you're fed fables and tales and most of us will never question them until the day we die."

Pearce half rose out of his chair. "So you're saying we're all brainwashed. A pack of mindless blithering imbeciles!" He was irate.

"Well, don't get excited, John, it's not as horrible as you make it sound." I knew I better calm him down quickly. He wasn't handling this well at all. I guess I had assumed incorrectly that a reporter would be more open minded than the rest. Still, there must be some fundamental beliefs that even the most open minded can't handle being challenged. I think I had found a few of Pearce's.

"It's like the old computer rule, 'garbage in, garbage out.' But I'm not saying every piece of information your fed is false or a half-truth, but what I am saying is that society establishes a level of harmony by ensuring that you tend to work with the same information as your neighbour. It's a levelling process that helps keep everyone on the same wavelength. You could imagine what it would be like if we didn't have that. But what our society feeds us may be completely different from another society, and that in turn has led to numerous conflicts resulting from what you referred to as brainwashing.

Let me provide you with an example. Now, most in my family realize that the Goldenthal family is pretty small and that we're all related to various degrees. If you come across someone bearing my last name, then it is a fact, he or she is a relative. I had mentioned my fourth great grandfather Jacob to you. Professor, tutor, linguist, and in some ways a Rasputin type advisor to the Emperor Franz Josef's family. It's recorded and for all intents and purpose would be deemed indisputable. Yet, even in my very small family of relatives, ask them about our distinguished ancestor and you'll get back stories like, 'he was the tailor to the Czar', or the one about, 'he and his brother were dentists to the Czar but couldn't cure his toothache, so they ran off to the West, leaving their families behind, never to be heard or seen from again.'

We're only talking about less than one hundred and fifty years ago, yet branches of the family have several stories that they already believe in each one straying farther from the truth. Another few generations and the stories won't even be close enough to find the resemblance any longer. There's even a historical book out there called *The Eagles Die* by Marek on the Hapsburg family, and it refers to my ancestor as a mad Hungarian, without ever naming him. Galician yes, Hungarian no!

So like I said, you'll tend to believe whatever society's beliefs and teachings are at the time, whether or not they're correct. That's the way it works. That's the way it's always been. Neither you nor I will ever change that. So why don't you sit back, relax, and listen to what else Caiaphas has to say? All I'm asking is that you listen."

ROME: 37 AD

Elioneiai, there is more I must tell you of this entire affair. I've heard this Barnabus speak of Pilate as if he were free of sin. How could anyone believe Pilate to be anything other than he was; evil incarnate. The mere fact that he is to stand trial before Caesar is a testimony to his character. Let me tell you about this noble Roman that Barnabus holds in such high regard!

It was nine years after I assumed the priesthood that a new procurator named Pontius Pilate was sent to Judaea. I never knew what favour the Emperor Tiberius owed this praetorian that forced him to appoint him as our governor, but I'm positive it was not due to any demonstration of political ability on Pilate's part.

He was an arrogant, lecherous man, bent on draining our country's wealth into his own personal coffers by the cruellest means. I'll always remember the day he arrived at the port of Caesarea. I journeyed to the port with a delegation from Jerusalem to greet him as was customary to do for all arriving dignitaries from Rome. As he stood on the ship's deck, I could see in his face the disdain he bore for the populace that gathered to herald his arrival. And immediately I knew then that he would be no different from the other procurators that had preceded him.

I've seen men like Pilate before. Unscrupulous by nature, caring little for the responsibility of administration, desiring only to make their fortune at the expense of the civilisations they plundered.

As he tried to disembark, the throng pressed forward and confined him to the edge of the pier. With little concern for welfare, he commanded his guard to use the flat of their swords to clear a path. The crowd panicked when the Roman soldiers drew their swords, as you could imagine. Whenever they have drawn their swords in the past it was to sow death and destruction amongst us. In the ensuing panic and attempt to flee, tens of people were trampled underfoot and subsequently died from their injuries. This is the Pilate we met on his very first day in our land. This is the man Barnabus tries to whitewash.

Further to enlighten you as to Pilate's character, unlike the previous procurators he refused to travel to Jerusalem and live in the capitol amongst us. Instead he chose to remain the Greek city of

Caesarea and had all government documents and records transferred there, as clear indication that he held Jerusalem inferior to Herod's port city built for Rome. He knew very well the insult he had done us.

Almost from the day we were introduced, Pilate and I failed to find anything in the other that we could admire. I represented a threat to his authority, and he was a threat to my society. We laid charges and counter-charges against each other in an effort to have the other removed from his position over the years we were acquainted.

Pilate made several attempts to have my priestly vestments locked behind the doors of the Antonia fortress, knowing that I wouldn't be able to preside over the religious ceremonies without the sacred attire. In retaliation, I presided over the Sanhedrin in which we dispatched several letters of condemnation to his superior's both in Syria and Rome. In those letters, we remarked on the intense cruelty with which he weighed out his brand of justice. Crucifixion had become so common a sight that the hills were often covered by forests of mutilated bodies.

His evil nature urged him to pursue even greater sadistic pleasures, and Pilate devised the torture of crucifixion in a head-down position to satisfy his depravity. Had it not been for the even-handed justice of the Syrian legates, especially Pomponius Flaccus, I don't know how we would have survived Pilate's tyranny. Every time Pilate exceeded his limits of power, the legate interceded on our behalf, dealing a severe blow to Pilate's political ambitions.

This period was also plagued with unprecedented civil unrest, precipitated by Pilate's legacy of terror. The sons of Judah of Gamala became popular leaders of the resistance more so because of Pilate than because of the martyrdom of their father. With every act of barbarism performed by the procurator, more and more of our people joined the resistance. He was too ignorant to realize that the more he crucified, the more martyrs he created in this land. Pilate was overheard once to joke that he'd soon have no Jews left to deal with at the rate he was crucifying us, but I suspect even he knew that through it all, his own life hung by the merest thread.

Our history of dealing with Rome extends back two centuries and they have known us to be steadfast allies as long as they have respected us. Pompey was well aware of that, as was Marc Antony.

And when Augustus defeated Antony, we made it clear to him that Antony had been our friend, but we would honour Caesar, as long as he did honour to us. And for half a century we have kept our half of this bargain and Rome has known peace and contentment in our land.

Pilate has done his utmost to wreak havoc upon this arrangement and it would not have gone unnoticed by the Senate. I can only assume that all the crimes he had committed have finally caught up with him, and the only defence he could muster, was to accuse me of being guilty of his sins. Now that thread has become a rope, and if possible, I will be the one to place it about his neck.

I pray that it may be so.

CHAPTER EIGHT

Intertwining his fingers, Pearce prepared to make a point. "I'll agree with you there," he commented, "Pilate was a pretty bad guy. Nobody said he wasn't. His entire washing his hands bit was just a clear demonstration of his hypocrisy." Probably without even realising it, Peace was wringing his hands as if they had just been washed. "But the fact remains; it was the Jewish court that brought him to Pilate in the first place. You can't overlook that."

"Ah, yes, the Jewish court," I reflected. Pearce had just brought up a subject that I would have eventually raised myself. "I won't go into too much detail, because it's better I let Caiaphas explain it himself, but there's one thing I will point out immediately and that is that Jesus never appeared before the Jewish court."

"What do you mean," Pearce flung himself forward, almost throwing himself off the couch.

"First of all, the Sanhedrin, as the court was called, consisted of seventy members. Same number that Moses had as his council of elders. Secondly, the Pharisees had gained a stranglehold on the Sanhedrin by this time, and they didn't really have a problem with Jesus, contrary what you may have thought when you read the Gospels. You see, the Pharisees were strong believers in resurrection, Armageddon, the whole messiah thing. Sure, they challenged Jesus but you have to remember, they're there, sitting and listening to him. A lot of them were his followers. Because in direct contrast to the Sadducees, they desperately wanted a messiah to show up. And thirdly, the Sanhedrin never met at night. It was a day job, just like any other job. At night you went home and you slept. And why meet at Caiaphas's house, if the Sanhedrin had an official meeting place that could properly hold all seventy of them. So there's a fourth reason why you have to interpret what was going on with a little more insight than has been shown over the last two millennia. I mean, come on now John, don't you ever wonder about the course of events as they're detailed in the Gospels. All of them sleeping in the Garden of Gethsemane, the high priests guards showing up to arrest them, a quick hearing at Caiaphas's home, Peter walking in as if he'd be welcome there, and then finally taking Jesus before Pilate the next day to get immediate sentencing at what would have been the most precarious time to do so, with over one million pilgrims having come to Jerusalem to celebrate the Passover. Don't you think it's just a little odd?"

"I never really thought about it. It all made sense to me before."

"And now?" I questioned whether he still held the same beliefs as he once did.

"I have to think about it," he responded. "There's an awful lot of information that you're throwing at me. How was I supposed to know the rules for the Jewish court? I admit, there was probably more I could have looked into but the bottom line hasn't changed at all. Caiaphas still sent him to Pilate, and because of it, Jesus still ended up being crucified. Court or no court, the end result was the same!"

"I won't argue with history," I gave Pearce his due. Jesus still ended up being killed, no matter how I explained the events, but it was important to make him understand the interplay of the personalities, as they alone brought an entirely new dimension to the entire story.

"But what if I told you that it was never Caiaphas's intention to send Jesus to Pilate. That his entire goal was to keep him under house arrest. That's why he used his own personal guard to arrest him, and why they were ordered not to use force, even though the disciples did draw their weapons in order to provoke a battle. If you recall, it went as far as cutting the ear of the captain of the guard, and yet there was no retaliation. Strange, don't you think?"

Pearce placed his left hand over his mouth. I don't know whether it was a sign that he was thinking about the little brain teaser I had just thrown in his direction or whether he was trying to hold himself back from saying something he'd regret.

"You don't have to say anything right now. I just want you to think about the course of events. And when some of Caiaphas's revelations are brought out on the subject, then give him the benefit of the doubt that perhaps there is an alternative perspective. Take everything with a grain of salt. Somewhere in the middle is the real story because you have to remember, Caiaphas is just telling it from his viewpoint. The Gospel writers told it from theirs and neither will be viewing it as a non-involved spectator. It's not about taking sides. But it is about looking at alternatives. Searching for a speck of truth in an entire sea of lies. By the time the *Caiaphas Letters* is finished in its telling you'll have a whole new outlook to deal with. Guaranteed!

ROME: 37 AD

So much has happened since my arrival in Rome. Every man has a story and every story concerns the machinations of some other man. They are a people obsessed with myths and legends. And the greater the myth, the more outlandish the tale, the more they choose to believe. Do not lose heart my son against the swelling tide of deceit. Remember Elioneiai, this is only the beginning of their distortions. Bear witness to me, for I will tell you all that I know. Remember, as the Cayef you are the protector of His truth. And truth shall always prevail, no matter how long it may take and no matter how insurmountable the odds against it may appear.

From the first time Yeshua spoke to me, I suspected that he must have lived close in contact with the Samaritan people, close enough that they had influenced his thinking and for which he always held them in contempt. Unlike ourselves, he made reference to Lord Almighty as the Geborah, the Power. As you know, this is the revered term of our half-breed neighbours. For Yeshua said to me, "the Son of Man is sitting on the right hand of Power." Now I would not condemn a man because he used Samaritan phrases, but I believe his affiliation with them influenced him in other ways, for how else could I explain his detachment to the Temple. Our Temple.

Our people pilgrimage to view its magnificence from all over the empire, just to pay homage, pray and sacrifice to God. Even Caesar pays tribute to the Temple coffers in order to have us sacrifice daily to Rome's well-being. So beautiful is its architecture that it is considered one of the wonders of the world. All nations speak of the White Mountain where the Jews pray. If every other Jew carries the image of the Temple close to his heart and nurtures it with affection in every waking thought, then how could Yeshua be so callous to call for its destruction and condemn its functionaries for being a den of thieves?   To go so far as to lead a foray into the Temple grounds and have his followers take possession of the outer court is beyond my comprehension.

How could he stand in judgement of the Temple and the Priestly order? From where could he have formulated his concept of the ideal temple? I can only think that the austerity of the Samaritan temple has preyed upon his conscience.   Let us not forget that following the destruction of their temple by the great king, John Hyrcanus, they have nothing left of beauty in their rebuilt sanctuary. Now their music is sorrowful and dirge-like, making ours look pompous in comparison. Though I admit to be viewing it as a non-involved spectator it never was about taking sides in an argument over who had the right to be called the servants of God.   There is nothing about their ceremonies that I would be envious of, but it may be that Yeshua felt that our ceremonies within the Temple of Jerusalem had become too ritualistic for his appreciation.

The early death of his father obviously did not help in his thinking, for his father's love for the Temple was not there to be passed down from generation to generation. What can a son from a priestly line do if he no longer feels the connection to the religious centre of his heritage? He adopts an attitude completely opposite from the expected in order to discharge his anger and frustration.

I expect no better from a Samaritan, but to have such disdain proclaimed from one of our own I find it unbearable. Alienated from his Levite roots, disgusted by the idolatry of his Samaritan neighbours, he acted as he only could; with malicious anger. How much he had been influenced by the Samaritans I needed to know, so when he appeared before me I asked, "Is it not true you're both a practitioner of Samaritan beliefs and deranged?"

He replied, "Whether I'm a believer from Samaria is insignificant, but I'm definitely not insane."

Does this response make one guilty of following Samaritan traditions, I cannot say for certain. But I do know that whatever he knew of them affected the way in which he viewed God's holy house in Jerusalem.

And when I asked him about his intentions to tear down the Temple stone by stone, he only responded that it was God who would punish this den of thieves. How it was to occur, he did not know and he would not venture to say. But Yeshua, did make this claim and went amongst the people professing the coming of a new kingdom that would deliver all people from the hands of oppression.

And just as Alexander and Aristobulus were a threat to the House of Herod, so to had Yeshua become a threat to the Empire of Tiberius. For anyone that would promote instability and insurrection was to be considered an enemy. How long did Yeshua think it would be until he drew the attention of Pilate?

And how long would it be before Pilate would accuse all of us of being in collusion to lead a revolt against our Roman occupiers? The more Yeshua spoke of the destruction of both the political and religious infrastructures that existed in Judaea, the closer we were all being drawn to the edge of the precipice with the constant presence of the Procurator pushing us at spear point from the rear. Time was of the essence if I was to avoid certain catastrophe of major proportions. I had to take action.

Of that which I had to do, I will speak of later. Tonight I am to meet with Agrippa. Oh, how blessed are we that we once again may have a Jewish King to rule over us! He has just been released from prison, though his incarceration was luxurious by anyone's standard but it was a foolhardy thing he did to hail Caligula as emperor, before Tiberius had breathed his last. Tiberius was not a man to be trifled with. Had Tiberius survived another day, I think he would have executed our new impending liege. Fortunately for him, Tiberius expired that night. Caligula has been proclaimed Emperor and Agrippa is his best friend. As friends, I can only believe he will be rewarded handsomely with a Kingdom by the new Emperor. Now I must see how this may all benefit my case.

Pray for me, my son.

CHAPTER NINE

"I need a break," I commented. "I think I'll make myself a sandwich. Are you interested?"

"Nothing for me Doc, I ate all that plane food on the way over and I think I better hold back for a while.

"That's okay. I think there was only enough left over corned beef for one sandwich anyway."

"Oh, thanks for offering then," Pearce responded sarcastically.

I was halfway to the kitchen before I retaliated. "Good to see you're back with me, John. I was afraid the story was becoming a bit of a sore spot for you and we wouldn't be able to continue."

"Just because you're trying to destroy every belief and concept I ever grew up with doesn't mean I'm going to resent you for it," John replied, a huge grin lighting up his face. "After all, what are friends for?"

"If I'm not allowed to wreak havoc on your world, then who is?"

We both had a good laugh at ourselves. I recognized we had let the situation become far more intense than we should have. It's a risk you take when you begin attacking religious dogma. I'm glad that Pearce had been able to come to grips with it on his own. It meant the rest of what Caiaphas had to say was going to be a lot easier on us both. I wasn't prepared to dilute what Caiaphas had to say.

I raided the refrigerator looking for the mustard, tomatoes and lettuce, neatly arranging them on the counter beside the sink before I began my search for the rye bread. If there's one disappointment of being in small town New Zealand, it's that you can't find a good rye bread when you want one. Pumpernickel is completely non-existent. A dark rye would be a miracle if I could find it. So I have to settle for this bread that is more like a day old garlic stick with poppy seeds spread over the top. It had to do, so I begin slicing it into a couple of pieces that I then spread a layer of hot mustard on. A couple of slices of corned beef a layer of tomato and a garnish of lettuce and it's all done. . I almost felt guilty of not having something that I could prepare for John while I ate, but obviously not that guilty.

Slapping the sandwich on to a plate, I headed back to my salon. "Feel like anything else," I yelled from the doorway. "Another coffee, beer…"

"No thanks, I'm fine, really."

"Okay then, I'll get back to the story as soon as I finish this." I relaxed back into my chair and took my first bite. "That is really good," I commented, licking my lips after I swallowed. "Funny thing, most people don't even recognize what the political crime was that Jesus committed while he was in Jerusalem. Most think it was something to do with proclaiming himself as King of the Jews. Being the messiah wasn't a crime, not unless you broke a few other laws because of it. Want to take a guess at which one he broke?"

"That's a tough one," Pearce scratched his head. "I never really thought about it. I just assumed that he got himself in trouble just by claiming to be who he was. Wouldn't that have been enough?"

"We're talking about a civilised world here, John. Roman law was the basis for the British law that rules over us. Jewish law, was some of the oldest in existence and had been refined over twelve hundred years by then. There had to be a crime, otherwise there'd be no charge. No charge and he couldn't be arrested. That's the way it worked then as it does now."

"I give up; what was it?"

Like most others, Pearce had never given it a second thought. And without knowing the crime, it's difficult to understand the punishment. Lots of people over that span of decades claimed messiahship, and none of the others were sentenced to death for it. In reality, the plague of messiahs was more like an infestation of mosquitoes. An itch that you have to scratch, but ultimately it goes away. Those that were put to death by Roman justice were leaders of armed insurrection, such as Judah of Galilee, or Simon bar Kochba. Sometimes even armed insurrection wasn't enough to earn the death penalty as in the case of John of Gischala.

"He turned over some tables," I answered quite calmly and

matter-of-factly.

"You're not serious," he inquired disbelievingly.

I nodded my head. "I'm very serious about it. All has to do with Tax Law and as you well know, you never go up against the taxman. That was probably single most threatening action he undertook. It wasn't mentioned in the Gospels just by chance, or because the author thought it was an interesting event that added colour and flair to the narrative."

"I don't remember anything that I would have considered very threatening about the story." Pearce thought long and hard about what he had learned in Sunday school. He shook his head repeatedly as if reaffirming that the story was no different no matter how many times he filtered it through his thought processes. "Just some tables where they changed the money. He didn't even take the money! Just knocked it on the ground."

"And did you ever think about what those money changers were doing there in the first place?" I asked.

"No, not really."

"Not really or never," I prodded.

"Well...never. It wasn't that important but you're going to tell me it was, aren't you?"

"Of course. I wouldn't bring it up unless I had some comment to make about it. I'll try to make it easy to follow. What do you think would be punishment if they caught you breaking into Fort Knox?"

Pearce looked at me as if I had suddenly lost it. "Fort Knox, Doc? What's that got to do with anything? You're pulling at straws with this one I'm afraid."

"Answer the question Pearce. What's the punishment?"

"You mean if they don't shoot you on sight when they catch you breaking in?"

"Yes, if they don't shoot you."

"Life in prison, I guess," Pearce took a stab in the dark.

"Pretty severe penalty for an attempted theft."

"Has to be," he lectured me. "It's the national reserve. The entire USA economy is dependent on the money in the reserve being secure and accounted for. Without backing up the currency, it's nothing more than paper."

"So you're saying, that because of the importance of the

reserve, then the penalty for attempting any criminal act against it would be more severe because of the resultant instability that could occur subsequent to the action."

"Yes, that's what I'm saying."

"Well, good because that's exactly what Jesus was doing at the time. The outer court of the Temple was very important to both the Romans and the Jews. The next court as you move inside the Temple was the court of women. No gentile was allowed into that court. So the outer court, also known as the Court of Gentiles was where all transactions between the Roman and Jewish world had to take place.

The Antonia Fortress connected to this court, giving the Romans complete policing authority of this outer court. Roman currency could not be taken inside the Temple because of the portrait of Caesar that was on the currency. Yet the people were expected to present their tithes to the Temple treasury and purchase animals for sin offerings within the Temple. So they needed to exchange their Roman currency for either a shekel coin that could be used in the Temple or for an animal that they would have sacrificed. Because the exchange rate was applicable to all trade between the Empire and its subject provinces, overcharging would have been a very serious crime. The destabilisation effect would have cascaded until it affected all the provinces and fair trade practices would be ancient history. Rome relied on imported grains and goods from its provinces and any inflationary spiral would have crippled the size of its imports.

Now turning a table in the Temple of Jerusalem, and the downfall of an Empire's economic stability may seem miles apart and almost impossible to demonstrate any connection but it's not as inconceivable as you might think. Accusing the money changers of illegal practices, scattering their scales and money across the court, would be the first trickle of an eventual waterfall. If the people all started to behave the same way, refusing to pay the exchange rate, then the moneylenders would have to react to the potential loss of income and start increasing the rate of denarii to the shekel. A doubling of the rate, and Rome's finances would easily be catapulted into a state of shock. Everything from the provinces would cost more and the Empire's treasury would be depleted. That's the crime! That's what he was punished for! Not for what he did but the risk of what he could have done and what could have been. A far greater threat than you can imagine. Maintaining economic stability was paramount to the operation of the Empire and no one was permitted to threaten that!"

ROME: 38 AD

During the daytime, Yeshua preached his message concerning the "Day of the Lord." By night, he and his companions rested in the homes of wealthy Judaeans whom were moved by his message. Some probably remembered him from the days of the Baptist, others probably took him in as part of the social adventurism that the idle rich seem to crave.

You might ask, "Which is more important, the man who speaks or the one who helps the people to understand?" In Yeshua's case, it was the latter, with Levi acting as interpreter, commentator, interpolator and revisionist. Levi was indispensable in the beginning. When people said, "No prophet has ever come from Galilee," it was Levi that talked of reciprocal kingdoms. Even though Yeshua may have known of such thing, it is not permitted for a prophet to sing his own praises. There is little tolerance for that amongst our people. Therefore Levi explained that in the past Judaean prophets preached in the Northern Kingdom. Now it would be northern prophets speaking in the Southern Kingdom. Yeshua's movement gained momentum, but still it could not draw upon the majority of the people. Only the dissatisfied fringe would lend credibility to a Galilean prophet with a tax collector for an advisor.

But let me get back to that which I spoke of before. Of those that came to hear Yeshua, one such family was the household of the Nasi. By tradition, such a family has been with us since the time of Nehemiah. Just as our brethren in Babylon of Parthia have a nasi, we too had a prince of the royal blood. Only through a son of David can we find God's mercy and grace to protect our land. The household of the Nasi consisted of three whom were young in age and very naïve. There was Miriam and Martha, and lastly Jochanan Eleazar whom was also called Lazarus.

Now Yeshua knew that it was necessary at that time to draw

upon new disciples that had Judaean roots. Of those he selected initially, only one was of any consequence. That was Simon the Zealot. Long associated with the son of Judas of Gamala, he brought a warrior's shadow to the clan. Simon was feared, admired, loathed, loved, but whether enemy or friend, he was respected. He could command hundreds, or even thousands. Despised by Rome, he was a folk hero to the Judaean farmers, attacking Roman patrols whenever they crossed along passes of the rocky mountain roads. Simon dealt ruthlessly with anyone he may have suspected of having Roman sympathies. Of course, to Simon, that meant anyone of the aristocracy, the priesthood, or with wealth. He detested them all.

A solid friend but a terrifying adversary, it was necessary for Yeshua to walk a fine line in order to keep Simon satisfied. That meant a shift in his preaching style with the inclusion of enough indicators and comments that an overthrow of the ruling powers was necessary.

The Zealots are a demanding lot. They care not for words but desire action. Because of this, Simon would sorely press Yeshua to launch an assault to bring the Kingdom of God to fruition. But Yeshua would reply that the Lord's time had not come yet, and only God knew the hour when it would happen. At that time they would fight in the name of God, but not a moment before. Talking like that was not going to keep Simon's war mongering heart pacified for long. And Yeshua was smart enough to realize that he needed a counterbalance to the Zealot in order to keep his tiny movement from tearing itself apart. For that reason, he never filled the twelfth position for the longest time. The last of the disciples would be the most important one of all. An individual that could give the movement the respect it craved, but without any blood on his hands. That man did eventually arise, and he proved to be the most tragic figure of them all.

In the meantime, Simon Zealotus would persevere, and eventually forced Yeshua into making a display of force. Now the events of this day are quite confused in their retelling, no help from Lazarus whom now resides in Epheseus of Asia Minor. The Nazarenes pass around letters that he writes under the name of John of Epheseus. Be not mistaken, Elioneiai, it is Lazarus that pens these documents, but he hides his face in shame from all of us, even the remaining disciples.

Here is the tale of events as it really took place at that time. Like Lazarus, I should know, because I was there in Jerusalem when they transpired. Unable to stay Simon's blood lust for long, and buoyed by throngs of admirers, especially the forces of the Zealots, he decided to march his disciples triumphantly from the desert of Judaea to the edge of the outer city of Jerusalem. This may have been his choice to try and pit his mission against the City of David, but I can tell you with most certainty that it was his undoing in the end. For it was during the twentieth year of the Reign of Tiberius and the Passover was quickly approaching. Jews from all over the empire and beyond came to the holy city for their traditional pilgrimage. Some had even heard of the gifted Nazorite and eagerly sought him out. Because of his vows, he was not difficult to find.

I don't wish to digress or belabour the point, Elioneiai, but this reminds me again of how even the simplest tale can get twisted and confused. It is well known that the Gentiles of this world are shamefully ignorant of our religion. They surely would not be familiar with the term Nazorite nor should we expect them to be. It would be miraculous if you could find one of them that was.

How do you explain to them that it is a personal vow between man and God, and that the individual that undertakes such a vow abstains from cutting his hair and drinking intoxicating beverages for a minimum of thirty days? The other-worlders have no personal god with whom they make such a vow and even if they tried to understand, they would only become more confused. Like Samson, they would think that a person's power had stemmed from his long mane of hair, and not from the inner strength that one receives when they walk with the Almighty. So for me to try and tell them that Yeshua had such a relationship with the Lord would be beyond their comprehension.

And his disciples followed suit, taking up the vow and adhering to its restrictions. Therefore, when I say that it was not hard for the visitors to find Yeshua in the city, it was merely because he stood out prominently from the mainstream of the population along with his followers.

Imagine the deadly combination, my son. The mass of people surging into the city while the Zealot constantly berating his companions and Yeshua for their lack of action. The Romans standing on high alert while making their presence known through force and harassing our people. There was no surprise that the situation ignited. Taking his troupe of adherents, Yeshua marched to the Temple grounds and ascended to the outer court. Within seconds he had turned over the exchange tables set against the inner wall. All the money that had been traded and that which was collected for the tax were scattered to the four corners of the Temple. It was already the middle of the day, so the amount we are talking about was not insignificant.

The disturbance did not go unnoticed by our overlords. They immediately sent a force from the adjacent Antonia fortress to suppress what they considered an attempted rebellion. With so many people filling the Temple grounds, it was impossible for the soldiers to reach Yeshua and his followers before they were able to disperse and disappear amongst the pilgrims. The money could not be recovered. Just like the man that had caused the problem, the currency was lost almost as soon as it hit the ground.

Since by law, all coinage of the realm produced by colonial and provincial mints was the property of Rome, then the exchange within the Temple served no differently than a banking house for the provincial government. An attack on a Roman institution was tantamount to treason. Whether Yeshua intended it or not, this episode was significant enough for Pilate to demand the immediate seizure and execution of all the rebels.

It really should be no surprise that Simon Zealotus was able to force the hand of Yeshua in this manner. After all, we must remember that the Zealotim are notorious for hit and run tactics against Roman sentries. An attack of this level would have been second nature to him. I still question if Yeshua was even aware of how he had played into Simon's hands. Where he may have been thinking the incident would be seen merely in a religious context, and that he was performing a cleansing of the house by removing the graven images that are struck upon each Roman coin, Simon would have known the true nature of the act. The Zealot had been trained well enough in Roman law to know exactly what the repercussions of the action was likely to have been.

I can only surmise that by forcing Yeshua into a situation where he would be hunted by the authorities, he thought he could get his leader to finally call for the liberation of his people. It was a foolish ploy, for even if Yeshua was to preach to overthrow of the

Romans, he had not the following in numbers to complete such a bold action. Yes, it was true that during the time of the Passover there were over a million Jews in the city as compared to the single legion of five thousand soldiers under Pilate's command, but that is where the Zealot and those of their ilk show their stupidity. Do they really believe that the slaughter of a legion would cause Rome to abandon their plans of domination? These are the people that have taken over the world through their military superiority. Whereas there is only now a single legion in Jerusalem, had such violence taken place as he had hoped, there would now be a host of legions within the Holy City. For every Roman that died, there would have been ten, no, more like a hundred to replace him. They would be like ants swarming over a drop of honey. They would come in such numbers to blot out the sun. That would be the world that we would now have to endure.

Do you see the dilemma now, my son that arose from such a simple event that occurred that day in the month of Nissan? Whereas, Lazarus may describe it almost in passing insignificance, I cannot remove the memory of that day from my mind.

Until the day I die, that day will live within me.

CHAPTER TEN

"I guess the hardest part of GLEEM is living with the memories. Can you understand that Pearce? Can you appreciate the fact that I have memories that aren't even my own? Memories that make me laugh, cry, fill me with terror, or even make me want to shout with joy. That is the world I live in. You're lucky. You just have to believe it, not live it!"

"But how do you know what's merely your own imagination or not?"

"How do I know? How do I know? How does a mother know the sound of her own child's cry in a room full of screaming children?

"But maybe they are only illusions. Like events you want to believe but never really happened." Pearce was trying hard to rationalise what he never would be able to comprehend fully.

The difficulty with trying to share your own experience with someone else reduces to the age old adage, 'You had to be there.' Certainly, I would be able to tell him of events, names, places, that no one else would be aware of, and with careful research, he'd be able to verify that I was correct, but that would prove to be a long drawn out process. I had done that with the first book, and our first meeting was the result of his investigating a story that indicated that I had access to information that no one else had.

That's all fine and wonderful, as long as the revelations aren't threatening in any manner. In that case, most people want to accept the concept and believe in GLEEM. But I could see it in Pearce's eyes. I had rocked his world far more than he could handle. Far more than he was willing to admit! The memories that were stemming from Caiaphas were undermining fundamental beliefs that he wished to preserve. For me to continue would only cause him to bleed more profusely. I guess I was beginning to question myself as to whether I had the right to do that. Now I was beginning to feel guilty.

"We don't have to pursue this any further, if you don't want to," I suggested, trying to gauge where he was actually at.

"What are you saying, Doc?"

"I guess I'm just getting the feeling that this is difficult for you. I don't know… perhaps our beliefs, even if based on half-truths are more important than knowing the whole truth."

"Hey Doc, you're not wimping out on me, are you?" Pearce had a broad smile on his face as he waited for my reply.

"I thought I may have disturbed you with the last disclosure." I tried to read his expressions but they were quite well hidden.

"Now how could information regarding an event like the turning over of the tables disturb me? I mean, I may have always believed that he was nailed to the cross for being the son of God, but even if it was for another reason, he was still killed. And what he did while he was alive, was the important part. That's what made him who he was. So why he was killed isn't that big an issue with me." Pearce held up his left hand, palm upward and shrugged his shoulders.

"I just thought that I had upset you. Something I saw in your face, like you were struggling with what I was saying." I tried to explain myself to Pearce.

"No, Doc. You're imagining things. I know what it must have been. For a while there, I was thinking about this whole GLEEM business, and I figured, if Caiaphas had seen Jesus, and you can recall certain memories of Caiaphas, then there might be this chance that you might also know what he looked like. That's right, isn't it?"

I laughed loudly. "You really are beginning to understand this entire GLEEM concept! There may be some hope for you yet!"

John laughed too. "Well, that's reassuring to know that I'm not a total cock-up. But seriously, what about my question?"

I felt my neck beginning to stiffen from all the time we had already spent sitting in the salon. Rolling my shoulders and stretching my neck in either direction, must have given John the impression that I was avoiding him. That was clearly not the case because I did have an answer ready for him. A very simple answer that I knew for certain he would have difficulty in accepting.

"Yes."

"Yes, what?" he blurted. "What's that mean?"

"That means, yes, I have seen him, and yes, I do know what he looked like."

Pearce was leaning forward so far at this moment that I thought for certain he was going to fall off the edge of his seat. "And…."

"And," I responded, "he didn't look anything like you or most others probably thought he looked like. I mean, look at the portrayals of him over the centuries. He looks practically frail and so pale that he had to be anaemic in the artist's mind and not to mention hair colour. Now how many blondes are you going to find in ancient Israel? Not many. And why always straight hair? He had waves and curls throughout a mass of very thick dark hair. His skin was a ruddy in colour, not this washed out flesh tone that the artists seemed to prefer. Caiaphas already touched on some of his physical attributes. He was certainly not a small man by any measure. When you're standing over six feet tall amongst a nation of people averaging just over five and a half feet, you're practically a giant. And with years of hard work as a carpenter and builder, you can imagine the size of arms he had. Not to mention hands, big, strong, walnut cracking hands.

Pearce just bobbed his head up and down as I spoke. I guess when it's explained in greater detail, none of what I was saying was going to be a major surprise. Of course he'd be Semitic in appearance, which automatically suggests to you the length of his face and features. Not to mention that hair colour, eye colour, even blood type would be consistent with the indigenous population. It was all just common sense. But over the years you come to realize that there's nothing common about common sense. Most people don't have it.

"But your children don't fit that description from what I see of the pictures over there and you're from a Semitic background too."

"You have a point," I agreed, "but my family is another story. I'll digress and provide a brief explanation. Everyone thinks of the Jewish community as closed and sticking to its own kind. And in a majority of the population that is very true. But historically, the affluent or aristocratic families were guilty of a high degree of intermarriage and assimilation as I mentioned earlier. If you recall from your Sunday class, when Ezra returned to Jerusalem following the exile in Babylon, he had to make rules banning intermarriage. In fact they were so stringent that he made husbands give up their wives and families if they weren't Hebrew. The target of these laws wouldn't have been the peasantry that married within their own villages, but would have been the more upscale, mobile personalities of the time. The reality of it all is that either most wives lied about their background or quickly adopted the religion. I doubt very many were separated by the new laws, otherwise I don't believe Ezra would have been high priest for very long.

You don't walk into a situation like that, make laws to upset the lives of the rich, powerful and influential, then expect to have a long life expectancy as high priest. And as you saw from my genealogy chart, the continued practice of intermarriage was rife in my family. So my having three out of four children blonde haired and blue eyed is not as surprising as you might think.

But coming from the small village background that he did, Jesus' ancestors would have been unlikely to have married significantly into any non-Jewish population. And for that reason, it's not surprising that he looked very much like I described to you."

"It's going to be hard to prove it," Pearce suggested. "You're going up against two millennia of dogma. And that means getting blasted from both ends. Not only the ones that insist he must have looked like the portraits in the icons, but the other fringe that will claim he never even existed, and therefore you must be fabricating the entire description. So it's not so much the case of myself believing, it's everyone else as well."

"That where time will be on my side, Pearce," I reassured him. "Just like the first time I came out with the book, enough historical evidence surfaced after publication that the issues I presented became both revealed and verified. That's why you had to use your detective instincts to hunt me down in the first place. My story revealed too many unknowns that turned out to be true. The same thing is happening now but you just don't realize it."

"Well short of pulling out of the ground his mummified body, I don't think you're ever going to be proven right about how he looked."

"What do you know about bone boxes, John, ossuaries?"

"Can't say I ever heard of them."

Pearce looked puzzled by my question. But he's known me

long enough to know that I only steer down paths that are going to lead somewhere. Even if it does take some time to do so.

"Don't worry, it's not something that's common knowledge. It wasn't around for long either. Back in the time of the Roman occupation, land for burial was becoming very scarce. Especially in Jerusalem. You could only double decker so many corpses before there wasn't any room left to do that either. That's how bad it was. So, from about 60BC to 70AD, the people of Jerusalem made use of bone boxes or ossuaries. They'd burry the deceased in a cave wrapped in the traditional linens and then after a year they'd collect the bones which were left, put them in a box, and then take the box back to their own home. This wasn't the practice for everyone. Having your own family burial cave in Jerusalem meant one of several things; you were either rich, an aristocrat, or from one of the twenty-four families of the High Priesthood.

And now after almost two thousand years, historical evidence for the existence of Jesus has come to light. Best yet, it's literally written in stone so it was intended to be a message for our time."

"What are you talking about Doc? No one has ever mentioned any of this. You'd think there would have been a big pow-wow or something if this is true," Pearce gave me his opinion.

Not that I wanted it. But with Pearce, you didn't have a choice. Right or wrong, he'd let you know what he thought about what you had to say. And this was one of those times.

"An inscription has been found on an ancient bone box," I informed him. "James, son of Joseph, brother of Jesus," I stated emphatically, "that's what was written on it. Do you get my point yet? This container provides the only New Testament confirmation of a central figure of Christianity. Do you realize that it is the first-ever archaeological discovery to corroborate Biblical references to Jesus? Don't you remember reading about any of this, Pearce?"

He sort of gave a half shake and nod combined. "Not really."

"Well it's only been revealed for a few years. And you should know about it. The bloody things on display at the Royal Ontario Museum in Toronto. Surely you must have seen something about it?"

"Vaguely," he now admitted. "I actually think I saw something about why it wasn't the real McCoy. Hard to recall exactly."

"There's been a lot about it. A lot of people without any credentials have been surfacing taking a shot at the authenticity of this ossuary, but I can assure you, it's the real thing. André Lemaire of the École Pratique des Hautes Études has studied the Aramaic inscribed on the box's side and confirmed that they show a cursive form of writing used only from about 10 to 70 A.D. Other tests have supported the ossuary's dating as being approximately 63 A.D. Guess when James likely died?" I challenged him.

"Sixty-three A.D.", he questioned back.

"Your right! Absolutely right. But to those that challenge the authenticity, there's something they have to realize. Although all three names were very common in Roman times, the statistical probability of all three appearing in that combination is extremely slim. Also, the mention of a brother on a bone box is highly unusual. The only explanation could be that it was-indicating that this particular Jesus must have been a very well-known figure. Want to take a guess of how many other ossuaries exist that mention a brother in their inscription/"

Pearce shook his head.

"There's only one other. That's how rare it was."

His interest was piqued now. I can see how important this could be from an archaeological standpoint but how does this confirm what you said about Jesus," Pearce pressed.

"Think Pearce! Remember what Caiaphas had said about Jesus being a distant relative. We've already discussed it in part. James was buried in Jerusalem. Lab tests performed by the Geological Survey of Israel confirm that the box's limestone came from the Jerusalem area. It meant he would have been placed in a tomb for the year prior to having his bones removed in the Jerusalem area. Like I mentioned previously, only the rich, the aristocratic and the priests had tombs in the area and they were the ones making use of ossuaries. It's already confirming parts of what I've told you today. Why would you doubt the rest will be confirmed shortly as well?"

"I'm still not following the connection," Pearce reasserted his failure to grasp the essentials I was providing. "So James was rich, or something, what's the big deal?"

I leaned forward and looked Pearce square in his beady eyes. He was taken back by my abrupt manner and tried to squeeze as far back as he could into his seat cushions to maintain a safe distance apart.

"You don't happen to be Catholic, are you John?"

"No, why do you ask?" he retorted, almost as if I had insulted him merely by making the inquiry.

"Oh, no particular reason. It would have helped me understand your reluctance to let any of this sink in."

"I'm still not following you, Doc," he replied. "Not that I'm denying it but how would my being Catholic explain anything?"

"It would explain everything," I advised him. "You see, if you were Catholic, you'd be wrestling right now with the Doctrine of Perpetual Virginity and therefore anything I had to say about James, his bone box, or his family would be shrugged off by you as non-pertinent and irrelevant."

"Is that so?" Pearce piped up defiantly. "I think that's a pretty broad brush you're painting eight hundred million people with."

"I don't think so," I replied calmly. "The Doctrine itself is the problem, not my brush as you called it. Mary's perpetual virginity means that Jesus couldn't have any brothers. So whatever details surface regarding Joseph's offspring is not a direct reflection on Jesus. In reality it looks like a protection mechanism specifically developed for times like these when this ossuary surfaces and behaves like an exposé. Only one other bone box ever uncovered mentions a brother. You know why, because it meant the brother was of great importance and therefore whoever's in the box gained his credibility because of his sibling. And since Hebrew had specific words for half-brothers, cousins, or whatever, there's no mistaking that the relationship carved in stone is that of a full brother. And as far as the deceased and whomever burred him was concerned, the Jesus mentioned was definitely the son of Joseph."

"Not to burst your bubble, Doc, but like you said, the names were pretty common for the time."

"Sure they were," I agreed, "but how many James son of Joseph were buried in Jerusalem at that time, having a famous or popular brother Jesus do you think there were. I can think of one."

"I'll concede that there's an amazing string of coincidences," Pearce offered, "But I still say that this isn't going to prove to anyone that what Caiaphas says about Jesus is true."

"Sure it does. Because like I said, essential details are being revealed which will be confirmed following the release of Caiaphas's statements. A bone box in Jerusalem, which meant a family tomb in Jerusalem, was a privilege shared by very few. Caiaphas has said that Jesus was from such a family. No one else has ever written that about him. And now the statement is being proven. And if one revelation is proven correct, and then another, and another, then the bottom line is that all of the revelations are true. Thirteen years ago they uncovered Caiaphas's ossuary. Now James. Let's see whose next."

I think that last comment sent a shudder down Pearce's spine. He opened his mouth to speak but then thought better of it. Part of him wanted to accept what I was saying, the other part was extremely worried that if I was right, a lot of beliefs were going to be shattered. He finally found his voice again.

"A lot of these findings are disproved later on. Who's to say this won't be the case for this bone box. Just look at the Shroud of Turin!"

"Oh yes, let's look at the shroud. But not now. There's a lot more that Caiaphas has to say before I go down that tract."

ROME: 38 AD

Elioneiai,

I must explain to you the presence of the Nasi in Jerusalem. For there must always be a Nasi if we are to survive as a people, even if there's no longer a titular office from which such a family rules. For God stipulated that the offspring of the royal family shall always grace our land. The rod and sceptre shall not depart from between Israel's feet, and if we are the rod of which God speaks, then so too will He preserve the sceptre throughout eternity. L'olum va'ed, as God had said, forever and ever.

But even though Cyrus the Persian let us resurrect our nation, he did so with the stipulation that we would not set over ourselves a king. Only as governors could the royal family have power, and at first, such a thing was acceptable. But who was Cyrus that he should tell God what could or could not be done. Such a thing could not last for long. When the Seleukids came to power they tried to officiate in the same manner, but the royal family would no longer be part of this mockery, so instead they ruled in quiet dignity, disassociated from any form of government, giving council when required but otherwise sitting passively, awaiting the time when once again they would sit upon the throne of our land.

Oh, certainly we have had other kings since then, from other tribes with no right to claim such a position. But see how easily Elioneiai they have been wiped from existence. They weren't of God's choosing. Hasmoneans, Herodians, a plague on their houses for being pretenders to the throne.

Now the young Nasi who calls himself Lazarus was different from the rest of his relations. He had the impatience of youth and the belligerence that spawns from affluence. So when Yeshua arrived in Jerusalem, Lazarus and his sisters Martha and Miriam sought an audience with the gifted teacher, hoping to receive a sign that their own rise to power had come. How do I know this? How did I know everything that transpired within the walls of Jerusalem at that time? My network of spies had even infiltrated into the ring of protectors that provided sanctuary to Yeshua and his followers.

This is what was reported back to me. As the family of the Nasi sat before Yeshua, Lazarus asked, "Is it not true that you are the Northern King that it is written must rule before me and be herald to the Davidic dynasty?"

"It is true, young prince," Yeshua relied assuredly. "From Ephraim, through the blood of Gideon, the Power has chosen me."

Now these words may sound abstract to you my son but they are as ancient as our own time honoured beliefs themselves. It was this very belief that let us tolerate the usurpers for the last two centuries. It is said that before a son of David shall reclaim the throne, his way will be prepared by a king from the Ephraimites. Ephraim was known to be the most powerful tribe and the true leaders of our people when we conquered the land of Canaan under the command of Joshua. For a long time they led us in battle and their judges reigned over us. From all the lands of Canaan, that tribe was given the choicest parcels and they waxed strong. When we looked for our first king, we searched amongst Ephraim and selected Gideon to be our ruler. Although he would not call himself king, he ruled over us and our land prospered. But like all those not chosen by God, his sons fought amongst themselves for the throne after Gideon died and the slaughter was great. Gideon had many sons, but only one survived to claim the throne and that was Abimelech. And this son did proclaim himself to be king over our people.

Now, it is well known, that along with kings comes the evil that all monarchies shed, and eventually the people rebelled against this overlord because of the taxes he levied against them in order to build himself a palace. The people killed this self-proclaimed king during their insurrection and swore they would not let another rule over them but instead the elders would rule.

But the memories of men are short lived and eventually Saul was anointed king, chosen from amongst the hill tribe of Benjamin, which lived in the south of Ephraim. A rift arose between the north and the south, and soon, David of Judah ruled in Hebron, simultaneously with Saul. Truthfully, even though it remained a single nation through the reigns of David and his son Solomon, it wasn't meant to be. The rift was to become a fracture that would never heal.

It has been said that there would never again be a descendent of David to rule over the united lands of Israel until a king from the north, a prince from Ephraim, came first to unify the provinces under his hand. That is what Lazarus was speaking of.

After his meeting with the Nasi, Yeshua was surnamed Gideon, of which you may have heard it spoken, and the fabric of his fate was woven. So entwined were the family of Lazarus and Yeshua that they would always be talked of together. Their destinies had become inseparable, their futures pledged, and Yeshua chose Miriam, the youngest sister, to be his consort. And to his consort he added the surname Migdalah, the tower, for like the eternal Tower of David, which stands in the city, she would be the everlasting continuity of the royal line. In the Roman world her name has been corrupted to Magdalene, but as you can see, it has nothing to do with the act of crying as the Latin suggests. After all, this was her name in Judaea, and here we speak Hebrew and Aramaic, perhaps one might claim even Greek. But Latin is a foreign tongue to us. Yeshua would not have used it to name his consort primarily because he did not speak their tongue.

The fire of redemption had been kindled, and many would be consumed in its flames. It was with trepidation that I stood and watched as the host of hundreds approached the city. I remember that day so very well. So vividly it stands out in my memory. Passover preparations were underway in the Temple. The sacrificial sheep were being carefully chosen as they must be free of all blemishes. In the Court of Gentiles which surrounds the Temple proper, the pilgrims purchased doves to present to the Levites for sacrifice. Some have said that the doves are merely a token donation to the Temple and not a true sacrifice, especially since there is not a dove for every purchaser. But this is not so. Whether their share is one half or one thousandth, the blessing of the Lord is for them alone, and the people all understand that. They give freely of their hearts. This is what God measures.

All that purchase these doves know that the Roman currency they carry is offensive to God because of the image it bears upon it. For the reason the exchangers sit in the outer court. The rate of exchange is set fairly, as it has always been since the time of occupation, based on the purchase price of a cattle beast. In this way, there can be no error, because the price of cattle in shekels is equivalent to the same price in silver denarii. For the poor that can't give, there is no shame for them. Their share is paid by the community, and a sacrifice is made on their behalf. No one has ever found fault with our system before. None complained, and none had ever protested, that is until that day.

When I heard the tumult arising from within the Court of the Gentiles, I ran quickly to stop the unrest. It was only a short distance from the Court of Priests, but in that time, Yeshua managed to overturn several tables and topple the cages of doves. Simon and his Zealots made certain that no one stopped him. The Levite guard ran forward, spears in hand, but I ordered them to hold their station.

"There shall be no blood spilled this day in the House of the Lord. Draw back you weapons. Tell your men Simon, to sheath their blades. If they keep them drawn, then I will order my men to remove them. But sheathed or not, no weapon shall cross into the Court of Women unless you are prepared to die."

"Sheath your dagger, Simon," I heard Yeshua say. "This is not the way it should be. I will use my words to do battle for me. I have come this day to cleanse this house, Caiaphas."

"By whose authority do you come, Rav?"

"Thus sayeth the Power that has sent me, My Temple should

be a house of Prayer, but you have made it a den of thieves!"

As I looked about the court I could see that the Pilgrims had filled the cloisters, eager to witness the challenge to my authority. Once more Yeshua had spoken of God as the Power. Ha Gibor, and the more I was convinced that he had been amongst the Samaritans for some time. For that reason I chose to speak to him as if he were an outsider, cut off from our nation and not worthy to stand on the Temple mount.

"Look around you Rav. Is this Mount Gerzim, where you speak? Where are your dirge-like songs that wail and bemoan that sad excuse for a temple? There are no bullocks here for the Power to ride. Here it is I that wears the ephod, for it serves me. I don't serve it as do the priests of Samaria, for they worship it as if it was a god to itself. You cannot condemn what you do not fully understand. You Galileans have been separated from us for too long. You look south and you see Samaria, and you make love to the Samaritan woman, and they infect your soul. This Temple, this Holy place that was built by your ancestors has become foreign to you. Open your eyes and see what is all about you. All that come here are entitled to the sacrifice if they desire, just as the sacrifice is the means by which the Lord blesses all. Even for those like you that live in the provinces, we make sacrifice for them. This is the custom, this is the law."

"I know the customs, Caiaphas. I know them very well. It is with your pride that I quarrel. Tell me Kahana, is a prutah the same for a rich man as it is for a poor one."

"A prutah is a prutah," I answered.

"Not so!" Yeshua refuted. "To a rich man a prutah is a useless coin to be thrown away as he pleases, but to a poor man a prutah purchases the sustenance to survive."

"And so it is," I replied, "a prutah is a prutah. The rich man casts it to the poor as alms, and each one appreciates its true value. That is a lesson that you should remember, Rav. Hurry and be gone now Yeshua, for this disturbance you've created has been seen by the Romans from the walls of the Antonia. Even now their sentries approach! Be gone quickly with you and your followers.

Before the centurion could make an arrest, Yeshua had disappeared into the throng of pilgrims in the outer court. A Roman tribune posted an edict for the arrest of Yeshua and his men. By turning the tables it was declared that he had led an insurrection against the Empire. The penalty for such a crime is death. The Romans do not believe in justice, merely retribution. I could only hope that Yeshua would return back to Galilee and leave behind these foolish notions that he possessed. Whether he realized it, which I sincerely doubt, he had violated the Roman Customs Office, under which the exchange tables are governed. Not even I possessed it in my power to protect him should Pilate insist on persecuting him for his crime. In Galilee, at least, he would be outside the procurator's reach.

But I knew that it was only a matter of time until he returned. He had said so, in as much as I could understand from his parting remarks as he fled from the centurion's men. "Your temple is doomed, Caiaphas. But by the third day that I return, I'll will raise it up and build it anew. I'm the cornerstone from which it shall be built."

We were destined therefore to meet again. He chose the tax year, two years from our initial meeting. If only I had known then what the future held for all that had come in contact with him. God forgive me, I did not know.

The stain is upon me; upon all of us. Upon this world! Forgive me my son.

CHAPTER ELEVEN

Sinking back into my chair, my eyelids were becoming very heavy. All this sitting and talking was extremely exhausting. Letting my mind drift off into little dark recesses of stored memories was beginning to make my temples hurt. Pearce may have thought this was all a simple process of hocus pocus but nothing could be further from the truth. If I was to try and describe it I would only say that it was as if a series of tracks were laid in all directions and sometimes the train would merely switch rails and move along without any hesitation and other times it would feel as it ran into a brick wall, unable to go any further. Multiply that by the hundreds of times it happened and you're on your way to a colossal migraine. And that's exactly what I was feeling now. One great big migraine!

"Not falling asleep on me Doc, are you?"

"We've been at it for a few hours. Perhaps we should take a break. No one would condemn us for doing so," I hinted.

"Only if you insist, Doc. I guess we have been going at it pretty hard."

"Yeah, I'm insisting on it," I remarked as I lightly rubbed the sides of my head with my fingertips praying for relief.

"So, let me tell you how I see it," Pearce started to fill in the gap of silence created once I stopped talking.

"Must we?"

Pearce stared quizzically. "So you really want to stop?"

"That's usually what taking a break means. I'm just going to lean back, shut my eyes and we'll continue this later." With that out of the way, I did exactly what I said. Pearce just sat dumbfounded as he watched me shut my eyes, lean back and forget that he was even in the room.

"And what am I supposed to do?" he demanded to know

"You're sitting amongst hundreds of books, some of which you'll never find in any library you'll ever go to in your lifetime, and you're asking me what you should do. Surely you can kill an hour in here without too much trouble. You were commenting earlier about the Shroud of Turin. Well there's got to be three or four books on the shelves specifically about that topic. Then we can talk about it later." I went silent once again, hoping that he'd take the hint and stop pestering me. No luck.

"I don't get it Doc. When we recorded *Blood Royale*, you went on for over a day non-stop. You never got tired then. What's the difference now? You getting old on me?"

"This time the memories are much more traumatic," I grumbled. "Harder to resurrect because someone in the past struggled so hard to keep them buried. But that's where taking a nap comes in handy. When I'm dreaming, I can usually absorb a lot more detail. Almost like watching a movie except I'm in it as the person whose dream I've inherited. Do you follow?"

"Well in that case, you'd better get some rest, Doc. I'll just keep myself busy until you wake up. I have a lot to look into with this Temple stuff. You and Caiaphas have spent a lot of time discussing this episode. Must be important because the Gospels sure didn't spend this much time on it."

I didn't bother to answer. I already felt myself slipping backwards through time, sensing sights and sounds that weren't from either my youth or my present. A parade of unknown faces raced by in a stream of vibrant colour. My salon had disappeared and suddenly I found myself in unaccustomed landscapes that stretched on as far as the eye can see. This was GLEEM at maximum intensity. Not just the retelling of an age old memory, but the actual reliving of events long since dead. This was what I could never explain to anyone that had never experience it. At our first meeting I tried to tell Pearce about those that had undergone life regression reading while lying on their psychiatrist's couch. They could rattle on about scrubbing a floor as if every bristle on the brush had a story to tell. The intensity of even the most mediocre event bursts with a luminosity that exceeds real life. Perhaps those that had experimented with mind altering drugs could understand what I could never relate with any clarity.

Soon I couldn't even hear the sound of Pearce rustling through the shelves of books, although my last thoughts were regarding his efforts to apparently make as much noise as possible in order to prevent my falling asleep. No such luck. I was being drawn towards a long chasm of rose pillared marble that appeared to be alive. Each swirl within the marble, spiralling and flowing like a river of liquid stone. And then I looked out from my grated window, the cacophony from a thousand muted voices parading through the cobbled streets of a red roofed city.

ROME: 38 AD

Today is a festival day, Elioneiai,

It makes me think of all the times I would take you and your brother through the upper city's streets to celebrate Tabernacles. Which reminds me, I have not heard from your brother Joshua in quite some time. What is he so busy with this time that he cannot find the time to write to his father? As I sit here at my writing desk, looking out this barred window of my apartment I am sometimes astonished by the beauty of this city. The red tile roofs contrasting against the whitewashed stucco of the walls is a thing of beauty. And it makes me wonder how this city of so much beauty and wealth can be so corrupt and evil. These are the mysteries of life, my son. The other great mystery is why your brother cannot find the time to write.

I had an audience with Agrippa, or should I say, he had one with me. It appears that he is awaiting approval from the Emperor to return to Jerusalem. His good friend Caligula has promised to make him King of Judaea. Normally I would not complain about this, but in passing conversation he questioned me as to whether I thought a Hasmonean should wear the priestly garments once again. What was I to say to a man that was key to my release from this house imprisonment? I avoided answering as deftly as I could but I know he saw through my reluctance to respond. It took us decades to erase the stigma of that family serving in the Temple and returning the function to the four families of the Kahana, representing the twenty-four appointed by David, himself, a thousand years ago. Was I to pretend that all would be fine, that I had no objection to whatever plan he might be hatching upon his return to the homeland. I could not support him and yet I knew that I could not express my objection lest he never secures the release I am awaiting. I do not consider myself that foolish. Instead I turned his attention to the general change in beliefs that is taking place in Israel.

I told him of Yeshua and how I considered all that he had said and done as being nothing more than an expression of this changing tide. To myself and my fellow Sadducees, it appeared that Yeshua had devoted so much of his efforts to mysticism and rebirth, that even his simplest comments had become enshrouded within an aura of Oriental esotericism. That would suit our Pharisee brethren well. They too, believe that every word has sacred, mystique significance. And similarly, they also look forward to the resurrection of all dead souls.

In my heart I know that this growing schism in beliefs will no doubt be our undoing. This is all the result of the Zoroastrianism that we inherited while we were exiled in Persia. And this younger generation, they have no respect for the old traditions.

I cannot believe in life after death, nor in this dualistic struggle of good versus evil. Those things are not of our faith. Beliefs such as these were not handed down to us and taught by Moses. Such teachings reduce our existence to insignificance; making everything we do merely a preliminary for death. It may appeal to the masses, because any excuse for a miserable life is preferred by them rather than having to work and strive to improve their lot. I cannot subscribe to this way of thinking. A man must work to study the Torah, he must work to provide for his family, and he must work to acquire the simplest of pleasures. By doing so, a man will be led by God to discover the true meaning of life.

It's an easy avoidance to claim that all of our miseries are caused by evil forces that we cannot fight against. God gave us free choice. We are victims only of our own insecurities and failures. There is no one else to blame. Only God and ourselves are in control of our destinies. That is the truth, but in many cases, it is the hardest truth to face.

There are only two things in this universe that are eternal— the Lord and the truth. It's not by accident that the word for truth in our language is what it is. Emet is made up of the first, middle and last letters of the alphabet. It symbolises that truth was the same at the dawn of time, the middle of time, and in the last days. It never changes. And therefore if it was true that in the beginning the Lord said that it was man's fate to live and die and nothing more, then certainly that is still true. Those who preach otherwise merely refuse to accept their own fate that they have created. They refuse to accept their own mediocrity.

But let me tell you more about that day that Yeshua and myself came face to face. He retreated hastily from Jerusalem, journeying eastward towards the Jordan. As he marched, people from all over the countryside went out to meet him. He would take them one by one into the river and anoint them in the baptism by water. The crowds began to grow and he ordained his disciples to begin baptizing in his behalf. No one, man, woman or child, coming to see them would be left unbaptized. Interestingly, did you know Elioneiai that Yeshua never performed the baptism himself. It was always his disciples doing so.

All this commotion, all this notoriety, it could not avoid falling upon Pilate's ears for long. As much as I resent Pilate for the man he is, one thing I cannot disparage is his ability to rule with an iron fist. He is like a fox, cunning and cruel, nothing escapes his watchful eye. Not now, not then. Yeshua was nothing more than sheep to the slaughter to a man like Pilate, and he would use his adversaries' own strengths to destroy them. Where Yeshua would preach love, he'd use that love to tear him asunder. When Yeshua would talk of strength, Pilate would render strength into weakness. While Yeshua appealed for the support of the meek, Pilate saw the misbegotten rabble as the weakest link, using their own fears and insecurity to turn on Yeshua and deliver him into the procurator's hands.

The only issue concerning Yeshua was for how long and how often Pilate would let him talk to the masses uninhibited. If he moved to quickly, he'd have no case to judge him with. Too slowly and Yeshua might just build his followers into an overwhelming force. He had to extend him just enough freedom to lure him back to the capitol where he could seize him without a violent confrontation. And in so doing, Yeshua continued to baptise by the river without hindrance. The more he felt free of Roman retaliation, the more his thoughts turned to his return to Jerusalem. Overconfidence was how Pilate snared his prey and Yeshua had become effused by such feelings, especially considering what happened next.

One day, before the arrival of the newly formed Roman division dispatched to Jerusalem, there cam an individual into the valley to be baptised. The missing piece of the puzzle that Yeshua had been so anxious to find. The apostle that would bring him full circle with his destiny. The conversation that these two had is quite well known to me. I had my spies amongst Yeshua's followers to keep me aware of his progress. And when they told me how one of our own kinsmen came to be baptised you can imagine my shock.

This was their conversation as related to me.

"Will you baptise me as well, Rabbi?"

Yeshua knew there was something strange about this man and his barbed question. "All men who wish to see the Lord most high must be washed from the sins of this world."

"If I am anointed, need I be baptised?" the stranger asked.

"Who has anointed you?"

"One whom is greater than you, Rabbi!"

"Then why seek me if you have no need? I have others to attend to that are not as pure as you claim to be. Be gone with you, for I have the Lord's work to do!"

"Who is greater Rabbi? Those baptised in the name of God, or those who are baptised by God, Himself."

"Only one of the High Priesthood could be so brazen and unashamed. But nonetheless, the hand of the Almighty has rested upon them, and even the most craven amongst them is greater than any of the multitude that I can procure."

"Then I am such a man, Rabbi, twice anointed just like you."

"What nonsense do you speak of?"

"Like you Rabbi, through the line of Zadok and by the Word."

"How do you know of my inheritance, priest?"

"Are we not all of one man's loins? How difficult can it be to see one's face in the mirror? You proclaim yourself to be the new Gideon but I know better."

"Was not Aaron loved more than Gideon?" Yeshua riddled. "Gideon was given seventy sons, but greatness only to one, whereas Aaron was given only a few sons, but each was greater than the previous one."

The stranger laughed heartily. "If I did not know better, Rabbi, I would think that you have insulted me in a very subtle manner."

"Perhaps so, priest. By what name do you go?"

"I am Judas, son of Joazar, son of Simon Boethus. I am the

Ischar, citer and scribe for the Holy Temple in Jerusalem. All the sacred writings of our people have passed through my hands, and the Lord in his mercy and wisdom has revealed their secrets to me."

"And why would He do such a thing priest?"

"For the time to come and that time is now and He has brought me unto you. You are a Messiah of Aaron that seeks a throne. I am a priest that needs a temple. The House of Bothias, though it be its right, is shunned from the high priesthood so that others less qualified may usurp that privilege. They treat us Boethians as if we were lepers, unclean and therefore unworthy to hold the office that is rightfully ours. In days past I heard you say that you would bring a new order to the Lord's house. If so, then I am the rightful priest to govern within its walls. In turn, I'll use my authority to legitimise your claim. The Lord has shown me the manner by which the time comes and what must be done to herald its approach. All of this is within my command, and I offer my services to you, Yeshua ben Joseph. The circle is now complete. Priest, King and Prophet intertwined."

Taking it upon himself to perform the baptism, Yeshua took Judas into the river and then lowered him backwards into the waters of the Jordan. "Consider this a pact between us. Arise Judas Iscariot. Arise my priest of letters."

So, Elioneiai, now you know the manner by which your kinsman Judas became linked to his Galilean messiah. That which had been nothing but the deluded preaching of a Galilean soothsayer has now taken on dangerous proportions. Whether it was Judas's folly that he desired that which his house had abused and squandered, or merely the fact that he coveted my authority, he would prove himself to be a most dangerous adversary. Some still remember that his was the last family to govern the Temple before the Romans began their procuratorship. Therefore the Boethians aren't tainted as being serfs for foreign masters. That alone would have given him the power to legitimise Yeshua's claim to be a restorer of the Temple's past glory.

There was no longer a vacant seat among Yeshua's disciples. He now had a man with superior knowledge and a noble upbringing to share his table. Do not underestimate the authority and reach that Judas had. He was the ischar, he had access to all the sacred writings and commentaries. Yeshua had advanced from Levi, who could merely record his teachings, to Judas that could now codify them, relate them to the prophetic texts and draw the connections to traditional teachings. Both the Torah and the oral traditions were at his fingertips and blessed with an excellent memory, he could recall any passage necessary to reinforce his arguments.

How fortunate for us that those same qualities that he possessed could also serve as vices. Judas had no tolerance for the others that made up Yeshua's inner circle. He frowned on any association with the unlettered, which happened to be the bulk of the disciples. You can understand his reasoning. How could such men even recognize the hand of God if they couldn't even read the words through which it would be revealed? The nature of Yeshua's mission was beyond their comprehension and Judas fought them fiercely over and over again as he tried to dispel their reliance on myth and legend.

But most notably, Yeshua loved Judas above all the rest. Only Judas had the knowledge that could lead to revelation. What Moses had been to God, so was Judas to Yeshua. Through Judas, his message would be delivered to the level of society where power resided, and through the powerful he would achieve his goals.

Yes, it was true that Simon the Zealot could command hundreds and even thousands but that was merely the control of bodies. Judas could master their spirit, their souls, and their minds. Only he could command blind unfaltering loyalty. This ability of Judas made his master blind to all of the other faults he possessed. And though trouble was brewing, Yeshua saw none of it.

As much as Judas held the other disciples in contempt, so did the others equally resent him. Simon Peter made no effort to conceal his hatred for the self-indulging priest. Like a kindling pot, the embers smouldered, awaiting the opportunity to burst into an inferno. And as those of Yeshua's followers relate to his downfall, they freely admit that it was this hatred that infested his disciples and ultimately consumed him in the end. When it was necessary to stand together, they could not do it and they let their master die as a result of their weakness.

As I so earnestly said, no man can ignore the fact that only he controls his own destiny. Yeshua failed to deal with his internal problems and in so doing sealed his own fate. That is the truth, my son!

CHAPTER TWELVE

I felt very refreshed following my short nap. That is until I heard the sound of Pearce's voice targeted from not more than a few feet above me. I opened my eyes and there he was, standing over me anxiously awaiting my return to full consciousness.

"Surely you have not been hovering over me all this time," I inquired.

"No, not at all," Pearce replied sheepishly. But his tone and mannerism suggested that he had been for quite some time. "So, what did you see?"

"Rome, white buildings, red tiled roofs."

"That's it? You can go to Rome now and see the same thing."

"True, but then I wouldn't have come across memories of Judas now, would I? And I suppose you're going to want me to tell you all about it."

Pearce was taken somewhat back by my attitude. For a moment, he was almost afraid that I was completely serious.

"Well of course, Doc. That's why I'm here. So that you can tell me everything and we republish this book of yours. If you were talking with Judas while off in never-never land then I want to know about it. I mean, this is about as close as it gets to having a time machine."

"Can't go backwards in time," I advised. "Forward maybe, but backwards, never."

"Pardon me, Doc, but what are you talking about now?"

"Time travel; you made a comment about time travel and I'm just expanding upon it. Thought you'd be interested in knowing that going back in time isn't feasible." I sat up in the chair, stretching my legs out while Pearce digested what I had to say.

Scratching his head he challenged my opinion. "I don't claim to be any physicist or anything, but I do recall being taught that Einstein had a theory that said it was possible. Faster than speed of light, backwards in time; something like that." Pearce waved his left forefinger annoyingly in my direction, emphasizing his point.

"Haven't you ever wondered why someone from the future has not come back then?

"That's easy because we haven't invented time travel yet. So no one has done the travelling thing yet."

"But John, this present is the future's past. They co-exist. We're actually history to someone in the future."

"I don't get it," he murmured.

"If time is like a book containing two hundred pages and we're on page eighty, then even though we don't know what happens in the next hundred and twenty pages, they still exist. Does that help at all?"

"Never was good at this physics stuff. But now I'm even more confused. If you're saying that everything exists at the same time, then why can't you go into the past? It sounds like a contradiction."

"No," I shook my head in rebuttal. "Not at all. Someone in the future, would have come back by now and we'd know all about it. Because we would simply be their past even though we can't think of ourselves as being anything more than the present. So you're probably thinking that it just hasn't happened yet. That's where I disagree. It can't happen. Even if you could successfully build a time machine, it can't happen!"

"You seem pretty certain about that Doc, but I still don't get it,"

"I'll give you a riddle, John. A man invents a time machine and goes into the past. He steps out of the machine and crushes an ant. He then goes back into the machine but it won't go forward in time. He can only continue to go backwards in time until such time that he depletes the power source. It's a time trap and he's the prey. So, tell me what happened." I know I must have had this smug smile on my face but I just couldn't help it. I know that there's no way that Pearce was going to solve this one.

Pearce rubbed his brow repeatedly with his left and his eyes flitted back and forth as he thought pensively. "He can only go backwards, you said. I guess the machine broke."

"The answer is the ant."

"What do you mean, the ant?" Pearce challenged me. "That's ridiculous!"

I laughed at his response. "Not at all. Let me explain. Had he not gone back in time, that ant would have lived. It just so happened that the ant was on the way back to his nest to tell all the other ants that it had located a termite nest. The ants would have mobilised for war and eliminated the termites within their territory. Instead, that termite colony remains undetected and goes on to develop into a fairly large colony over time. Some of the termites from that colony start invading a house in the neighbourhood, undermining the weight bearing structures. The house collapses and a young child in the house is accidentally killed. Had that child lived and grown to adulthood, he would have discovered the power source that fuelled time machines once they were invented. Since that future no longer existed, the time machine could not move forward because the path it had taken into the past no longer existed. One of the conundrums that results from splitting space and time."

"But that's only if he stepped on that particular ant," Pearce interjected, his index finger swiping through the air to make his point.

"Forget the ant. That was just one example. It could have been anything. What I was trying to say to you was that as soon as the time traveller leaves an imprint on the past, he's changed the future. Whatever the nature of the imprint, the chain of events will ultimately change the future."

"Oh...I get it. No matter what he does, the future's changed."

"Precisely! And that's why we can't have time travel backwards through time, only forwards. So I don't anticipate we'll be meeting anyone who claims to come from the future. And if we did, we'd just lock them away."

Pearce sat back in his seat and crossed his arms over his chest. "But that still doesn't stop you from going back in time with your memories. Or I mean Caiaphas's memories. So, are you going to tell me about Judas or not?"

"Couldn't have your story if I didn't, could you now? There's a lot to tell. Everything in its time and place. I just thought this little diversion would help explain a few things in our present."

ROME: 38 AD

"My son, my son, what have I done to deserve this? I should have been released by now, but instead they have reinforced the guards outside my apartment. Even those whom have normally visited me are no longer made welcome by the sentries. It is as if all of Rome has turned against me and I believe it is the result of my testimony before the Senate courts of yester morn. Should I be condemned for speaking the truth, then it is a sad time that has befallen us. A new Emperor, a new king, yet there is still no hope for us to be freed of this bondage.

I told them the truth, which they chose not to hear. For Pilate in his last years as procurator, became more corrupt and evil. Such is the character of those ignobles who purchase offices of government in distant lands that no patrician would care to rule. He swore he'd turn our country into a forest of crosses that would cover the horizons and that is exactly what he did as he delighted in his methods of devising torture. Yet, simultaneously, he was capable of showing great thoughtfulness towards Jerusalem. He completed the aqueduct that brought much needed water to our growing population. Do not misunderstand me, Elioneiai, as obviously those senators before whom I spoke must have done, for when I say thoughtfulness towards Jerusalem, I do not mean the people but the buildings and the structures. The things of stone. He cared more for these than he did for human life. Man was weak and frail, but his monuments would be eternal. He would build a Jerusalem that would stand as an eternal monument to his being. You may call his yearning madness, but I simply call it Roman.

To complete these tasks he sought, he required constant funding. Taxes could have been levied but that was a process too slow and too cumbersome for someone like Pilate. The Legate of Syria would not have agreed. Besides the populace was already poor. No, Pilate needed Yeshua to provide the pretext for the pursuit of his plans. And this is what I explained to the Senate had they been prepared to listen.

Unable to seize Yeshua in the Temple court because of the crowd, Pilate passed an edict that banished him from Jerusalem and the surrounding districts. All may have seemed tranquil while

Yeshua baptised his followers in the valley of the Jordan, but such was not the case back in Jerusalem. The people's obstinacy in refusing to surrender Yeshua was tantamount to treason. And for this the procurator demanded penance.

He sought his funds from the Temple treasury. I refused at first, citing that those funds were necessary for the day to day operation of the Temple. The responsibility had been handed to the twenty-four families since the time of David and reaffirmed by Octavian Augustus. He had no right to demand such a thing. But what did Pilate care of such things. Under threat of defilement and occupation of the Temple vicinity, especially during the Passover, I was left with no other choice but to comply. Sacred duty must always take precedent over sacred monies. To have the Temple defiled at that time would have desecrated the entire Passover celebration. But it was not enough to merely hand over the money; Pilate had to flaunt his victory, taunting us for being a weak and cowardly people. Such are words that do not go down well with us.

For as Jews, we are a warrior race. Born beneath the lash and scourge of the Egyptian sun, and forged in battle against every empire that has walked this earth. We have taken arms against the Canaanites and won. Driven the Moabites into extinction. Conquered the Edomites until they became one with us. Reduced the Philistines to nothing more than a series of coastal villages. One by one they fell, Assyrian, Babylonian, Persian, Medes, Greek, we fought, conquered and were conquered, each in its turn, but we have prevailed. That fire still burns within us and Pilate stoked it until it glowed red hot.

The people took up their swords and protested vehemently in the streets. Pilate was forced with his men to retreat to Herod's Palace but he seeded his assassins amongst the crowds at the same time. They moved swiftly and quietly through the streets, leaving a trail of death and destruction in their wake. Many fell that day, pilgrims from Galilee, Zealots from Simon's men, women and children. None were safe from his murderous assassins. Galilee mourned that day for its grievous losses and Judaea wept for its brave soldiers.

The senators did not care for me to call one of their own seditious and dishonourable. I think I may have inflamed their passions beyond reason. Rather than condemn Pilate, they may seek to raise him to the status of a protector of the Empire. Then he would walk free and I will spend the rest of my days in prison. Such irony! But let me speak of what other calamity resulted from that day; a day that changed the world as we know it.

The people called for the deliverer but he was unable to come to their aide. Yeshua was nowhere to be found and those in the city mocked him and accused him of hiding in the desert. So many had died as a result of that day he stood in the Temple. Even Simon Zealotus had lost much of his esteem. His power to lead men would wane severely from that day on. News of the people's condemnation for his failure to run to their aid reached Yeshua's ears and he responded saying that a prophet has no honour in his own country. Yet, at the same time he swore to make amends, deciding to return to Samaria and Galilee where he would attempt to restore and strengthen his power base. That was an undertaking he would have cause to regret. For everywhere that he went, he was subject to ridicule and anger.

It is often said that adversity hardens the steel in a man's character. Perhaps that was true for Yeshua. He must have known that the path he took would provide no escape. His only defence would be in his own death.

Travelling north, Yeshua entered into the heartland of Samaria. He must have certainly been aware that he could not remain there for long, because Samaria was under Pilate's hand as well. His presence was well received by the Samaritans. They heard of what he had done at our Temple in Jerusalem. They thought anyone that could desecrate our Temple must certainly be their Taheb, the one they seek as their messiah. And why not? Coming from Galilee, he spoke like them, even thought like them in many circumstances.

If he wanted them to become his faithful followers, he merely had to perform a single act. It was written in their ancient scrolls that the Taheb would reveal the hidden location of their holy vessels that had gone missing from their temple on Mount Gerzim during the days of Antiochus. They had no doubt that Yeshua could perform this miracle for them. They celebrated his arrival joyously, their priests labouring tirelessly to purify the grounds in anticipation of their dawning emancipation. The poor fools, they were blinded to reality.

There was no way that Pilate could remain idle while an insurrection was fomenting at his doorstep. As I told the Senators, as much as Pilate disliked us Jews, he despised the Samaritans even far more. He considered the Samaritans even more stubborn than us, which would be hard to believe. While the Samaritans prepared their celebration, a Roman garrison was dispatched to the city of Samaria. His instructions to his commander were simple. There was no concern for innocence or guilt; they were all guilty of living as far as Pilate was concerned. His men were ordered to rectify that. It was a senseless slaughter of men, women and children. All the leaders of the Taheb movement were publicly executed. Once again there was death and destruction in the wake of Yeshua's passing.

They wailed and lamented, filling the valley where Yeshua had set his camp. "How could this happen to us," they bemoaned.

"Who are you to question the ways of God?" Yeshua scolded them. "Since when does the Almighty answer to you? He has already shown his displeasure to your house. Why would you think He wishes to see his children split in two? Jerusalem is His holy city, and Solomon's Temple is his house. Can you not see that what has occurred is the result of your own folly? When the exiles returned from the Euphrates they refused to let you help restore the Temple, and in an act of spite you continued your worship in the ancient temple on Mount Gerzim. That was your choice, not God's. It is Jerusalem that we must cleanse of impurity. The Holy of Holies has been profaned by the stain of blood and we must take up the sword of heaven to rebuild it with blocks cut from devotion."

Unbelievably, he had stirred our Samaritan kin, and rather than stone him, they embraced him. That was an event that I had not thought anyone capable of. After so many centuries of hatred and revulsion for anything Judaean, he actually made them believe in the prospect of a united people. This probably concerned Pilate even more, and he issued orders for his garrison to make every effort to arrest Yeshua. When the Romans arrived in the valley, they came upon the Samaritans that had gone in search of their Taheb, but Yeshua was long gone, fleeing back into Galilee. By the end of the day, the valley was awash in blood.

The remnant of Samaritan leadership issued a resounding denouncement of Yeshua in an effort to appease Pilate and stop him from slaughtering any more of their kin, but also to put an end to any foolish thoughts of reconciliation between our two peoples. Such naivety could only result in pain and suffering. The proof lay strewn across the entire valley.

From his hiding place Yeshua issued this instruction to his disciples. "Do not go to the Samaritans any longer. By denying me, they denied their place in heaven. I brought a sword into their midst. I set sons against fathers, daughters against mothers. They'll have no peace unless those who live and follow my words prevail. Only then shall they share in the coming kingdom." That ban that he decreed still exists amongst his followers. Samaritans aren't allowed to join the sect. Let it suffice to say that Yeshua's detractors also played a hand in diminishing his Samaritan adherents by threatening to ostracise all who spoke of him from the community.

Yeshua returned to the Galilee where he felt most secure. Pilate couldn't pursue him there as it was beyond his jurisdiction. Herod Antipas ruled in Galilee and he decided to leave aspiring prophets alone, as long as they left him alone. Nonetheless, many doors were closed to Yeshua. New of what had occurred in Jerusalem and Samaria had reached their ears, and they grew afraid that the Angel of Death would follow him into Galilee. His teachings had become overshadowed with death's pallor, and many shunned him as if he was a leper. Often Yeshua was overheard to say, "A prophet knows no honour in his own land."

Those that knew him well were also shunned by the community. None suffered as much as his own family. His mother, brothers and sisters began to fall upon hard times. Their crafts and services were boycotted by the townsfolk. Mary sent word to her son begging him to abandon his prophetic mission and return home, permitting life to return to normal. Wherever Yeshua ventured, members of his family would appeal to him to honour his mother's request. Their efforts were in vain, for the more they embarrassed Yeshua , the further he became estranged from his family.

These were the events I related to the senators, and behind every statement I made was the inference of how all came to be only because of Pilate's intense cruelty. I doubt that they had anticipated that I would lay a set of accusations in their laps that would call for Pilate's incarceration. But that I did and now I am sequestered away in my apartment, a prisoner of my own condemnation.

Be well, my son. Pray for me.

CHAPTER THIRTEEN

"So where's Judas already," Pearce complained.

"Everyone in their time," I responded. "There's a lot taking place that you're not aware of. Judas has his role, but just not yet."

"Well, this is all very fine and dandy," he rallied, "but no one really gives a rat's ass about the Samaritans. They really don't come into the picture. They don't sell books!"

I shook my head. "Now that's where you're wrong, John. They're very much in the picture, just no one's bothered to take a close look. Just look what happened to Pilate. It was this incident with the Taheb slaughter that caused his dismissal and disgrace. What do people think? He just washed his hands and that was the end of the story. Not by any means. His misgovernment caught up with him and it was Caiaphas that was instrumental in seeing that it happened. How many people even bother to question as to what happened to the other players in the Gospels? If they did, they'd understand a lot more about what was going on behind the scenes. How can the history reconcile with the Gospels. Fact is, it doesn't." I made little quote moves with my fingers to emphasise my point. "Pilate and Caiaphas weren't buddy-buddy, in fact they despised each other. They were responsible for causing each other's demise. This doesn't fit well with the Gospel picture of things. That should set off a few alarms and get you thinking."

"Everything makes me think, Doc. Nothing is what it's supposed to be. How can history be so wrong?"

"Because it's so right. Everything took place because of the hatred between two men. Everyone else, and everything else was merely a tool to be used by Pilate and Caiaphas in their efforts to destroy each other. All that followed was the result of their perpetual battle."

Pearce laughed at my inference. "So that's all it was. A power play that ended up badly for all involved. Jesus was a bit player."

"Hard to accept, I recognize that. But for two millennia, all that we learned was focused on what Jesus said or what Jesus did. But it was those other two characters that gave it any credence. Judas, for all he was worth was just another pawn to Caiaphas. A piece on the chessboard that forced the checkmate."

I looked over to catch Pearce rubbing his chin which I always knew was his way of signalling that he was deep in thought. I just had to wait momentarily until he would spring into action. No way could he let this rest. I didn't have to wait too long.

"Okay," Pearce began his chain of thoughts, "it may not be obvious to the rest of us mere mortals how a belief in a son of God, a man possessed of great power, performing miracles that defy explanation, can be nothing more than the aftermath of the political struggle between two adversaries seeking personal gain. You're going to have to provide a lot more detail to satisfy the readers if you want them to buy your argument because I'm not convinced!"

"See, John, you haven't appreciated the Samaritans like I told you to. They really were far more than the rat's ass you accused them of being. There was one follower of Jesus, a Samaritan by birth that could perform greater miracles than his master. In fact he was so powerful that he almost single handily brought the end to Christianity. He's someone I don't think you knew about."

Pearce just sat without a trace of expression on his face. He wasn't prepared to argue what I just told him. But he knew that I was most likely correct. In the same way that all my stories we had discussed before passed careful scrutiny, this one would prove no different.

"But he had to be far more than human," Pearce made a desperate defence. "Why else would he have stood the test of time? Jesus said so himself. He said it, and he proved it, and that's why we believe."

"Did he?" I questioned. "Did he really say that he was the Son of God, John, or is that what others have said? That may be the problem. There's what he said, and then there's what the others said, and over time the two sources have tended to become confused. And interesting enough, it was Pilate and Caiaphas that seemed to be asking these exact same question two thousand years ago. Maybe we should have paid more attention to what they had to say?"

ROME: 39 AD

Elioneai, I had an interesting visitor today. A Jew from Tarsus that holds Roman citizenship. If that wasn't an interesting combination in itself, he's a tent maker turned bounty hunter. He wanted my blessing in pursing Yeshua's followers and bringing them in front the Beth Dins with charges of blasphemy. He's a worry. He claims to have letters of authorisation from Jerusalem. Wealthy, free to move throughout the Empire, and fanatical, this Saul may be a problem unless he is kept on a very short leash. He tried to argue with me that Yeshua claimed to be the son of God and therefore all of his followers are an anathema to everything we cherish and believe. No matter how much I insisted that such a claim was never made, this Saul refused to accept it. He was on a mission and nothing will deter him from it.

I'm one of the few people that spoke on a level man to man with Yeshua. I know he desired no divinity, in fact he constantly renounced it. Could he really be held accountable that the ignorant and displaced considered his refusals as evidence of his tremendous modesty? The misguided belief even split his disciples into bickering factions. After all, being Galileans, you wouldn't find too many men more ignorant in this world nor more displaced than that bunch.

The one they called Simon Peter turned to Yeshua and exclaimed, "You are the son of God. Act like it and it will be so. Our word will spread throughout the Gentile world. To them, worshipping men as gods is commonplace."

"Do not take my word to the Gentiles," Yeshua scolded him.

Such madness couldn't be tolerated by Judas either.

"Deny this falsehood unequivocally, or I'll leave. I'm a priest trained in the traditions and beliefs of Moses and Aaron. There is but one God and He does not have any sons", Judas challenged Yeshua to take control of the situation.

"I have not come to replace the laws of Moses," Yeshua insisted, "only to reaffirm them. How am I to be held responsible for the fanaticism that has arisen? It was never my intention to have them say these things. Do I not deny it frequently?"

"There is only one way," Judas instructed. "Remove the

blasphemers from our council. Those that wish to spread these lies have no place among us. They will only bring those in power down upon our heads if we let them continue with their lies."

Judas was right, of course but Yeshua could not afford to reject any of his Galilean apostles. Without their support he would lose his Galilean base. All that resulted was an intense hatred amongst the apostles. Simon may have hated Judas, but he feared him too.

"Was I not first?" Simon pleaded with Yeshua. "Wasn't he last?"

Yeshua apparently turned to Simon and in the calmest of demeanours replied, "Him who was first shall come last, and him who was last shall come first." The answer created a wound that bled profusely from Simon's heart.

"Let me sit at your right hand Rabbi," Simon begged. "Do not cast me aside like this."

"If my right eye offends me, then let me pluck it out. Do not force me Simon to take an action that I will regret. Do you not know whom I truly am? Is that not enough to deserve your loyalty? Right this wrong before you have no other choice. Now make ready to leave for we must go to the shores of the sea until all this foolishness is settled."

Simon prepared the small fishing boat to ferry them across the lake. The wind was favourable and it carried them to the village of Gerasenes, a town populated by both Jews and Gentiles, the latter whom made up the majority. But the attempt to flee did not go as planned. It is not a large lake, and it was easy to trace Yeshua's movements. So those that had dogged him as he marched through the valley continued to do so and arrived in the village in droves. Yeshua had no choice but to climb the small hill outside the town and speak to the people.

"You have heard much, yet you know so little," he scolded them. "With all you legends and interpretations through folk lore, you search for hidden meanings that continue to elude you. Don't make more of me than what I am. There are but two commandments to live by and you have forgotten them both. There is only one God and he will not condone any others, and secondly love your fellow man. You need no others!"

It was enough to squelch their insane notions for the time

being. To the Greek world, the offspring of their gods and humans is nothing unusual, but Yeshua made it clear that we are not part of their world and we never will be. So to hear this Saul of Tarsus try to say otherwise is a very serious situation. The mere fact that he pursues a lie will cause people to suspect it must be the truth or why else would he oppress them in this manner? His foolishness only lends credence to this absurd notion. He is a danger with his madman's mistaken quest and I fear he will adversely affect all that we try to achieve to eliminate the rift that is developing.

For the time being, Yeshua managed to restore common sense to all those that insisted that he pursue a course of deification. Almost in response to Simon's suggestion of taking his teachings to the Gentiles, Yeshua and a few of his disciples forced an entire herd of pigs over the cliffs that border the lake by Gerasenes. There would be no compromises. To follow Yeshua, one must adhere to the laws of Judaism. The dietary laws could not be forsaken. Those that would eat pig could not be redeemed. "A silk purse could not be made from a sow's ear,'" he preached. That eliminated most Gentiles unless they were willing to convert. But after you destroy the livelihood of several families, take the food from their mouths, and cripple their ability to hold on to their land because they no longer had the resources to pay the Romans the taxes, it is very unlikely that those people would have ever considered sacrificing any further to join his following.

The pig is symbol of all that is pagan and unclean with this world. By destroying that herd Yeshua had proved to Judas that he was not prepared to abandon to laws passed down to us by Moses. How could I object to such behaviour? I commended him for his action but condemned him for his continuance to speak in parables. To avoid once and for all being misunderstood, he covered his actions with riddles and now I have this Saul, whom I consider a most dangerous adversary because he will stop at nothing short of murder in meting out his vengeance. What can drive a man to hunt down his fellow man?

Before the Gentiles of Gerasenes chased Yeshua and his followers from their shores he performed one of his misquoted miracles. This again, Elioneiai is an example of how the outside world has no understanding of us Jews at all. His followers begged Yeshua to help them on their way by providing food to sustain them on their journeys home. What little supplies he and his disciples had were hardly going to feed anyone. He asked Philip how many loaves they carried between them and five were all he could muster. But Yeshua was not flustered in the least. It was the day before the Passover, so he instructed his disciples to go out into the village and ask those homes occupied by the Jews of the village to give whatever leavened products they might have to them rather than burn them in their ovens. For that is the day we must remove all leaven from our homes by noon but our Greek and Latin neighbours do not comprehend this.

The disciples returned triumphantly to the edge of the lake with twelve baskets full of bread and leaven, more than enough to feed the hungry followers. Since that event occurred, the story has become greatly exaggerated. They speak of the feeding of thousands, but they still retain some element of truth by mentioning the Passover was near. I think they fear to a degree of being accused of spreading lies. By retaining some truth, I believe they somehow feel justified in continuing to speak of this event as if it was some miracle.

Returning to Galilee, I believe Yeshua considered what he had done in Gerasenes would restore his popularity in his home province. Obviously, he could not be accused any longer of spreading heresy and blasphemy. But nothing that Yeshua had ever expected came to be. Clearly he was his own worst enemy but how he could have behaved any differently, I am at a loss for words myself. The events of Gerasenes grew as if they had a life of their own. It wasn't enough to tell tales of his creating food magically from thin air, they began to create a variety of explanations why he had his followers run the swine over the cliff edge. By the time he reached his family's village, reality had already fallen victim to hearsay and innuendo. Yeshua denied the allegations but as expected, there were always those that would deride him.

In Nazareth, Yeshua faced his greatest challenge. Awaiting his return were his brothers and his sister — James, Judah, Joseph, Simon and Salome. They were his harshest critics.

"Do you deny our kinship, brother?" they questioned him.

"Is it not you who turn your back on me brothers? Is it not you who fear to be judged on the basis of my actions? Truly, it is not I who has cast you off, but it is you whom have done this action to me. We are of the same flesh and blood, dear brothers and sister but we are certainly not kindred spirits. My soul pursues a different course from yours. The Lord has placed my feet upon this path."

"Do you truly claim to be our deliverer?" they taunted.

"How could I possibly deliver those that refuse to follow me? Let all men walk in my ways and they will be delivered. Cause me not to falter in my footsteps and all will find salvation," he instructed them.

"By whose hand?" Salome inquired.

"By the one, the only hand, the hand of our Lord! I'm only an instrument of His, a tool by which He applies His will. Those who seek His mercy shall find it through me."

"Then perform a miracle in His name and we will follow you gladly," they challenged him.

"Is this how to measure your belief, through shallow gestures? Is the Lord to be bargained with? Away with you for you are an embarrassment to the Lord."

"Prove you carry Elijah's mantle. We ask no more than has been asked of any other prophet."

"Shall we be guilty of condemning another of the Lord's prophets through this foolishness," Yeshua cautioned them.

"Elijah was put to the test. So was Elisha. Even Nathan had to undergo a series of tests. Why not you too, brother?"

"Bring on your test, if it is within reason then the Lord will guide me."

"There is a young boy in this village," Salome continued, "and on several occasions those that are disciples in your name have sat with this boy and tried to remove an unclean spirit that plagues him. We know that you are aware of this child's problem and that they have spoken of him to you. The child still succumbs to the falling disease. When they last passed through our town they said that only you had the power to release him from his torment. If you can do this thing then we will sing your praises and have no doubt that you are one of God's chosen."

"And what if I refuse this test? How can I perform miracles in a village full of disbelievers? What you ask is too much from any man."

"Not so," shouted Ben Meir. Ben Meir is the Rabban of that village and we have talked long of this event. At the time, Ben Meir thought he was acting in the best interest of all involved. "Elisha performed his miracles in a village of Shulamites, and Elijah achieved his miracles for a wayward King. And lest we not forget that Moses conducted his miracles to a world of disbelievers. So a village, my son, is neither too great nor too small. God's presence is in as small as a speck of dust and as great as the universe. There are no restraints on His will. Do as they ask, and I will vouchsafe for you. No harm will come to you whether you succeed or fail. If you're truly the hand of God, then there should be no fear of failure."

How could Yeshua refuse after the Rabban interceded? It was impossible. To turn away then would destroy his following that he had. Failures he knew could always be explained in a variety of ways. The boy was brought out of his house and led to Yeshua in the village square. Yeshua looked deeply into the boy's darting eyes. The child was obviously frightened.

"Keep your eyes on mine," Yeshua commanded. "How long have you been this way?"

"All my life," the boy could barely mouth the words, as the crowd pressed in closer and closer to overhear the exchange.

"Have you been faithful to the commandments of the Lord?" Yeshua asked.

"I have not sinned," the boy responded.

"If you have truly been faithful and believe in His mercy, then through your own strength we will cast the demon from you. Take my hands." Afraid the boy made no effort to reach out for Yeshua's hands. "Take my hands!" Yeshua shouted as he suddenly lunged forward to grab the boys own hands. "Grip strongly and pray for your release. Pray with all your heart and if it be clean, then God will make it so."

The crowd was engrossed by the melodic chanting that Yeshua began streaming continuously from his mouth. The sound was haunting and yet soothing, strange yet familiar. Suddenly the boy fell to the ground, gurgling and snorting while he fought for each panicked breath. His arms and legs flailed and thrashed uncontrollably.

"I order you demon, depart from this boy!" Yeshua screamed. The frothing from his lips became even more sever. "Depart I command you, in the name of the most high God!" Still nothing. Yeshua tried repeatedly, calling out to the Lord to release the boy from his torment. The convulsions continued for several minutes and then ended almost as abruptly as when it had started. The boy lay on the ground moaning in an overwhelming sweat.

His disciples broke into a chorus of hallelujahs and praise. They shouted to everyone that the demon had been cast out of the boy, but the townspeople only jeered at such foolishness. They had borne witness to these seizures too many times and knew that the boy was recovering from this one no differently than from the last. No one had been cured this day, and no one had been saved. They turned their backs on Yeshua and his followers, returning to their homes disappointed.

"Why couldn't you cleanse him Master?" those amongst his followers having the common sense to not listen to the false praises of the disciples asked Yeshua.

"Who are we to understand the ways of God?" Yeshua answered. "Though we see a mere boy and think him too young to be burdened by sin, the Almighty sees us with divine eyes. Our faith is truly tested when we continue to believe without the understanding of why there is suffering in this world. It is easy to believe when we are constantly handed signs to guide us but that is faith which is bought and therefore not worthy of our Lord."

"Liar," someone shouted from amongst the townspeople. "You have no special gifts! You are a fraud and a blasphemer. Death to the blasphemer!"

"Do not touch this man," Ben Meir warned the crowd. "I have given my word that no harm shall come to him, and so it shall be. To do otherwise would make me a liar, and then will you also condemn me to death?"

The anger in the crowd dissipated. No one would dare lay a hand on their Rabban. Ben Meir put his arm around Yeshua's shoulder and began escorting him away from the people. "Go away from here Yeshua before it is too late. Do not return to your birthplace, Yeshua ben Joseph, lest you be willing to forfeit your life. I cannot protect you. Though I know you mean well, there will always be those that will oppose you with violence."

And he was never welcome in his own home again, Elioneiai. This Yeshua freely admitted and even spoke of his teachings ultimately setting sons against mothers, and fathers against daughters. He recognized early on how divisive a force he could be. And even after his death, there are now those that want to viciously weed out his followers from the garden of our nation. Beware of them all, which is my advice to you! Do not fail to heed what I have told you!

CHAPTER FOURTEEN

"Epilepsy?" Pearce inquired.

"Most certainly," I answered. "Funny how many advanced medical practices were amongst the Jews, yet how little they understood the basics of disease. You look at the laws that Moses passed down concerning medical matters, dietary laws, cleanliness and hygienic practices, separation and isolation of those with disease, etcetera, and yet it was like they came out of the blue. We followed them almost fanatically, but never appreciated the modern medical basis upon which they were founded. I always wondered about that. Without knowledge of bacteria, viruses, infection, spread of contagions, etiologies, epidemiology, how did Moses know what he did? You're left with only two choices. Either he learned of it from some very advanced practitioners in Egypt and all of their ancient records have been lost to us, or else he did get it directly from God."

"Well, isn't it obvious that it came from God," Pearce blurted. "It's obvious! If it's beyond man's capability it can only be from God."

"Not that obvious, or else other civilisations would have caught on and adopted them. Remember, the development of Christianity meant rejecting almost all of these laws with no appreciation of what they actually achieved. When the plague swept through Europe and the Jewish communities were spared, it wasn't the laws that were attributed to this miracle but accusations of witchcraft. So something just doesn't add up. But don't get me wrong, I agree with you. Moses got these regulations from God. They were too out of step with anything any of the cultures had developed by that time. Either he had some window to the future, which I doubt, or the voice of God spoke to him and he followed blindly without ever understanding why."

"You surprise me Doc. I never expected you to admit that. Somehow I thought you'd have some other story about how this was all the result of a secret cult of surgeons, or something to that effect."

"Surprises me too. You already know that I'm a descendant of Moses' brother Aaron, which means I have a tremendous number of their memories within my cerebrum. And yet, any memories that would give some other explanation are notably absent."

Pearce wrote furiously as I spoke. His tape would capture my words, but what he would write in that little book of his were my expressions, my gestures, those things that the tape could never capture.

"Going back to the boy, the Gospel reports said that he was cured. In fact, I remember something about the pigs and the boy being connected. How's that?"

"Telescoped to be precise," I corrected him. "Two stories with entirely different origins being piggy backed, pardon the pun, upon each other until they are inseparable. All illnesses were believed to be the result of evil spirits. Those that understood the clinical signs of epilepsy were a little more honest in their assessment. But to uneducated Galileans, they'd stick to their original belief that when the boy finally relaxed he must have been cured. Their concern wasn't with what might happen later. They were dealing with the then and there."

"But other people knew that it was epilepsy, right?"

"Oh yes. People like Ben Meir, understood it completely but that doesn't seem to have been universal. In Roman society it was well known that epilepsy plagued the Julian family. It was commonly believed that the falling disease was a blessing of the Gods. That it imparted greatness to the afflicted individual. Good old Julius Caesar was proof of that. But Rome and Galilee were worlds apart, and to the common fishing and farming folk of a backward Jewish province, where God rewards those that are true believers and punishes those that are sinners, this boy was clearly possessed by demons. Jesus' failure to expel those demons was evidence of his being a false prophet, and no medical evidence to the contrary was going to sway that. So the only choice for the disciples was to continue to claim that they were expelled and what better way to do it than to cast those demons into a herd of swine and run them over a cliff. Tell the lie long enough and who's not going to believe it. Anyone that knew otherwise could easily be called a liar."

"So you're saying that the story as we have it written is a lie," Pearce challenged me with his usual finger pointing behaviour.

"I'm saying that his followers saw what they saw. In a world where exorcism was believed to standard practice then I don't believe they saw themselves writing a lie. And because there were at least three decades past from the time of the two events, to when they were written down, then telescoping is also a normal process. There was a very basic problem with Judaism of the first century BC and the first century AD, and that problem was that it forgot what God had said Himself. To Moses He said that he was the benevolent God, the wrathful God and the vengeful God. That meant that all things came from God. Good and evil flowed from Him. What this tells us is that what we perceive as evil is merely the opposite side of the coin of a God that has a purpose of action that we can't contemplate." I noticed John's facial expressions of furled brow and curled bottom lip and knew that he was giving this a fair deal of thought.

"But if one part is not correct, does that not make everything else incorrect?" Pearce's voice was troubled as he earnestly questioned his core of beliefs.

I was quick to reassure him; it was never my intent to undermine his faith. I guess in a way, blind faith bothers me because it leads to fanaticism and we all know what a malicious sword that can be, but faith in values and a moral system is essential for everyone. "You're missing the greatest miracle of all John. The hocus pocus is just that, smoking mirrors and magic tricks. Maybe for a ragamuffin bunch of Galileans it was essential, but not to the rest of the world. The miracle was that one man came into this world and changed it. Not just a little bit, or for a fleeting existence in time, but dramatically and for two thousand years now. And not like most others have done it, through conquest, enslavement, the pursuit of power. He did it benignly. That made Jesus unique amongst all the world shakers that have come and gone. That to me is a miracle. Don't you agree?"

"Well...I guess it is," Pearce's eyes lit up and his face relaxed so much so that the lines on his forehead receded. "I haven't really given that a lot of thought. But you're right, that is a miracle!"

I smiled contentedly as I nodded my head in agreement. He was beginning to realize what I had been saying all along. Now he was ready to hear the rest.

ROME: 39 AD

Elioneiai, I am beginning to feel so very tired. The physicians were in to see me today. They can't identify what ails me, but I believe it is all a result of my own despair. I despair that I will never see my homeland again. I despair that I won't see you or your brother again. I despair that I will not be laid to rest beside your mother as I have always hoped. The calling of one's self to their place of origin is extremely strong. I yearn to return home but every day that passes tears me further and further away that reality.

I can understand Yeshua's comments to me in those last few days. Rejected, abandoned, alienated, I believe he wanted to die, having very little reason to exist any longer. He made no effort to conceal this from any of us. You may wonder because of what I've just told you, why he would have continued in his mission. Or try to fathom why he would venture back to Judaea when he knew it would mean certain death. I think in retrospect, he knew all along what would be his destiny. As much as we were using him as a means to our own end, he was equally playing his advantage with us.

While in Galilee, his following was small in number but fanatical in their beliefs. As long as he remained in Galille, Yeshua knew that his roots could be nothing more than shallow, because as we all know, there is no credibility to anything Galilean. Judas could hardly be expected to be satisfied with such a small foothold to achieve his own aspirations, nor could Simon Zealotus feel of much use in a province even the Romans thought to inconsequential to patrol it with any regularity. The sons of Zebedee wanted a confrontation, but there was none to be had in Galilee. The infighting amongst the disciples was rekindled with a new intensity while they resided in our northern province. As I view it, Yeshua was left with no other option but to return to Judaea and attempt to reach the greater masses found to the south.

His stay in Galilee provided him with new insight and with Judas' careful attention to Biblical passages and haggadic traditions; Yeshua's impact was to describe it simply, staggering. The warrant for his arrest was enough to guarantee a large turnout wherever and whenever his spoke. Many may have initially come to jeer, but none that stayed and listened were unaffected by his words. The more they resisted, the greater his attention to explaining the prophecies. For this is the effect of the Essene teachings. They as a people, are far more with concerned with events of the distant future than with their current reality. This is not to say that the Essenes have a detached understanding of the prophecies for the opposite is especially true. They have built a culture based on living prophecy, and this ability to escape reality is what appeals to the people.

Let me explain more fully. The Righteous Teacher, of whom I talked about before, although concealed as to his true identity in their scriptures, is most likely the high priest, Onias, whom came long before us. He spoke in a most similar fashion to their teacher, and in fact identified himself with the suffering servant of Isaiah. His failings in life he interpreted as the anguish and torment that he must endure in order to fulfil the prophecies. The fact that he was incompetent in his position and that his failings to deal with the Greeks appropriately was ultimately destroying our privilege of self-rule. Following his replacement, the more he was chastised by the wicked priest, the more he would identify himself as the messianic hope of deliverance.

His defiance of the Hellenistic world ultimately led to his murder by his enemies, but because of his identification with the suffering servant, his followers believed that his death was merely the fulfilment of the scriptures. In their confused reasoning, his death was a guarantee of their success. Over the centuries, this perverted belief has gained numerous followers and the fanaticism of the Essenes has achieved an aura of both respect and admiration. The Righteous Teacher returns to lead the people into the final war at the end of time. Salvation arrives upon his return. And now a teacher returns to Judaea, defying the Romans that threaten them, and speaks in a manner reminiscent of the Essene's Righteous Teacher, what do you suppose the people would make of it?

Give Judas his due. He was clever enough to pattern Yeshua's presence after the Esseneic martyr. Yeshua was destined to become the suffering servant, the prophet preparing the way, uniting the people in spiritual liberation. But the Judas we all knew was not one prepared to share power with anyone else. Once Yeshua had outlived he purpose, Judas would find a way to wrest the power from him. Remember that the scriptures speak of the two messiahs to come in the final days. Judas could lay claim to being the messiah of Aaron, just as much as could Yeshua. But the prophecies also speak of the messiah of David.

This would present a more difficult situation, because it would entail a sharing of power with a prince of the royal blood. There were few that could fulfil this position. I knew it could not be Lazarus, because Judas despised the house of Lazarus. In his opinion, the royal offspring represented all the vulgarities of wealth without any of the moral trappings. The necessity for the messiah of David to die, would certainly have been agreeable to Judas, but this was not to take place until the war was already in its final days. Few could claim to have a mind as clever and cunning as your distant cousin Judas. He had a simple plan to rectify the problem.

The messiah ben Joseph provided an alternative to the messiah ben David. Since the family of Lazarus had already made it clear by anointing Yeshua that they considered him to be the returning king from the house of Ephraim, then it was already fixed in the minds of the populace that Yeshua was to represent the royal line. True, the messiah of the royal family would meet a tragic end after challenging the legions of the evil war lord, Armelius, but victory was assured, and the messiah ben Aaron would become the supreme figure.

Whether Yeshua was aware or not of the planned events that Judas had prepared for him, I do not know. It was hard to know exactly how close the relationship was between master and servant. But as I indicated, I believe Yeshua knew that he stood at the end of days in his life when he talked to me. It would suggest that he had accepted Judas's plan in its entirety.

Constant comparison to the ancient legends allowed the people to draw their own conclusions. It was a masterful plan, and the initial gains by the movement, minimal at first, soon blossomed with incredible speed.

But the plan went awry. The martyrdom required to succeed may have been acceptable at first when it seemed to be a long way off, but when it drew close actually transpiring, I think Yeshua underwent a change of heart. It was too late. Even I was unable to stop it from proceeding from my position of power. The threads of fate had already been woven and Judas soon learned that he was not equal to the task he had set in motion.

CHAPTER FIFTEEN

"Why is it that you insist on portraying Caiaphas as being a hapless victim? Even if he suffered at the hands of the Romans, it was minor in regards to what he had inflicted upon Jesus and his followers."

"Why do you insist on portraying Caiaphas as the villain?" I returned the volley. "If you examine the court structures of the time, you quickly realize the Beth Din was very limited in what it could and could not do. And Caiaphas was not a priest that would act independently of the Beth Din. Sure, he may have controlled it, but he always made certain that it was assembled even if it was only to rubber stamp one if his edicts."

"And how does that support your claim of innocence for the man?"

"Easily!" I retaliated. "None of the trial scene late that night could have taken place. True, Caiaphas had his own guards, which were sent out to bring him into custody but there couldn't possibly have been a trial conducted at night. The Sanhedrin or Beth Din couldn't convene without a majority present of the seventy members and the Gospel rendition only has a handful there." I lean back in my seat inviting Pearce to take the next shot.

"So that makes him even worse that you thought. He was breaking his own rules in order to see that Jesus got executed."

"Oh, come on now, John. Think about it. If he really did want him killed, as I mentioned before, he could have had him executed in the garden very easily. In fact they could have killed all of them at once, leaving no one to question their actions. A nice quiet execution, away from the eyes and ears of the public would have been far more suitable than a public execution through crucifixion. No, you have to believe he had him brought into custody for an entirely different reason. So let's just dump this Gospel mumbo-jumbo, as if the author was actually sitting in Caiaphas's house at the time and recording everything as the book would suggest. I can't believe how no one ever asks the question of how any of the writers were supposedly given first-hand information from what was a clandestine meeting conducted by those purported to be their enemies. Come now, do you seriously think it was possible?"

"Sometimes we don't know all the answers," Pearce argued in his defence. "Sometimes we have to accept things on faith. That's what religion is all about. I told you Doc, faith is what it's all about!"

"And I told you that's what blind faith is all about! The worst kind of faith there is. The kind of faith that keeps Christians, Jews, Moslems and whoever else wants to lay claim to being God's right hand at each other's throats. It's not good faith, nor can it ever offer salvation. Because in truth, it's what people have to be saved from. Truth doesn't always offer a smooth path. I do recall something being said by the first century leaders of the Christian church about that. Not to follow those that offer you the smooth path. What do you think they were warning you about? I think they were cautioning everyone against those that were telling the early followers not to ask any questions. A threat not to ask questions like 'how did they manage to get the transcript of Caiaphas's behind the door meetings'. Just accept it and base all your beliefs and hatreds on the virtually impossible. And the Arian Christians, and the Gnostics, and the Ebonites, they all had to disappear, because they asked too many questions and provided too many contradictory answers. Those wishing to make the path smooth had them all killed. Is that the type of faith you propose we all follow?"

Pearce went white. At first I thought it was white with anger but then I realized he was going white through shock. There was obviously something in his past that was triggering this kind of reaction. Funny, I've known Pearce for a couple of years now, and I guess I don't really know him at all. Of all the conversations we've had, his role was to be a listener. Other than a few comments about his wife, and what I've surmised from his mannerisms, I don't really know much of his past. And I've certainly never taken the time to ponder what my revelations might be doing to his sanity. "I'm sorry John. You know I'm not trying to turn your world upside down. I'm only trying to put it back on the tracks, one train car at a time. I hope you can appreciate that. Ultimately, you have to choose what you wish to believe, and no one else, not even I can do that for you."

"It's easy for you Doc," his voice cracked. "You have yourself to believe in. You've got views, imagined or real, and to you they're the 'be all to end all'. I don't have that luxury. All I have, all anyone has is what their parents gave them, good or bad, and if they lose that, then there's nothing left to believe in. Can't you see that, Doc?"

"Yes I can, John. I can see it very clearly. But you're wrong. My faith isn't in me, it's a faith in the men that have lived to shape and change this world. Once in a while one of them stands up and makes himself heard. Good men, great men! What goes wrong is due to what happens afterwards. The end result is just how distorted their messages become. But I'm not prepared to lose my faith because others have twisted the truth. I'll dig and sort through the past until I find that original message. I'm prepared to wrestle, and struggle, and both fight with and for my beliefs. That's the difference. Like Anan ben David said twelve hundred and thirty-three years ago, "Read the book, and if what you read seems good to you, then it is right." It's as if he's still saying it to me this very moment. So I do, understand what you're saying John, the only difference being, that if I haven't questioned any belief to the point of dissecting it a thousand different ways, then I've failed all those that came before me. Can't settle for anything less, not until it does seem good to me, so that I know that it's right. If I haven't given it the third degree, then I don't have the right to claim it as a personal belief."

"Then maybe I should feel sorry for you," Pearce commented sarcastically. "People like me can still be comforted in our beliefs even if we don't know the answers. We just have to try to do what God wants us to. And the trying is all that God expects from us. If we make mistakes, he forgives us. We die happy and you die while still analysing what's waiting for you on the other side."

"Never claimed that I was the lucky one. In fact, I think I've told you all along, Pearce, I'm the one that's cursed. My life's all about knowing not only if the shots were fired from the grassy knoll, but even more precisely, who fired them and what brand of chewing gum was in his mouth when he did so."

"Obviously Doc, you couldn't have had that great a childhood if you couldn't find the time to believe in the unbelievable."

"Childhood, whoever said I had one of those." We shared a communal laugh as we contemplated what my childhood must have been like. Pearce quickly grasped the picture. Being different sets you apart. And it doesn't take much to be viewed as different from other children. A weird laugh, hand me down clothes, a disfigurement, a stutter, you name it. And when other children cut you adrift, it can be a very lonely and cruel existence. So imagine how different children would view a boy talking about visions of other worlds, other lives as if they were part of his everyday existence. Pearce immediately got the picture. And it wasn't a pretty one. Children can be the cruellest of all.

"Guess, you haven't been so lucky after all, Doc. Would be hard to find other people that could appreciate what GLEEM was all about. Most probably would treat you like some pariah or something."

"Yeah, you've got it. You've got it so right!"

ROME: 39 AD

Take care my son. I have word that there are about to be some serious changes taking place in Jerusalem. Warn my brother-in-law of what might occur if Agrippa pursues his intentions of repeating the history of the Hasmonean kings of holding the priesthood as well. If this should be the case, it could be the end of the Temple as we know it. Never has anyone so unworthy held the office of High Priest. I would not be surprised if the King has broken every commandment handed down at Sinai. And worse, he has the support of the Emperor in doing so. This combination of Agrippa and Caligula will be the death of all of us.

And what is worse is that the King accuses us, the priesthood of being corrupt. That we have offended God and that he is only serving God's will of cleansing the Temple of defilement. This is reminiscent of Yeshua, the only difference being that Agrippa has the power and support to actually carry out his threats. I pray that I don't live to see this day when he places the mitre upon his head and the ephod around his chest. Perhaps my illness is in truth a deliverance sent to me by the Lord so that my eyes will never bear witness to such an atrocity.

I have endured much in my life, but never did I think that I'd have to suffer another Hasmonean forcing his way into the Holy of Holies. True, they can trace their blood lines back to Zadok but that can be said for many a priestly clan. Long ago it was recognized that that the twenty-four families would produce a legion of offspring and for that reason it was made contingent on only the oldest sibling of each line having claim to the position of Cohen Gadol. Four families are justified in sharing the office, and the Hasmoneans are not one of these. To usurp the position, as Agrippa intends, would set us back by centuries when families were at each other's throats. This cannot be allowed to happen again.

I did not allow it to happen when your cousin Judas spoke of bringing a Boethian back to power and I will not see it happen now. You must take our complaint to the Legate of Syria. Representatives from all the families must be there. Summon the Phiabians, the Ananians, those from See, and you my son will represent the family of Kamithos. Together we can prevent this travesty from occurring. As King of Judaea, Samaria and Galilee, there can be no objection to Agrippa laying claim but the Legate must understand there is no need to let him acquire more power than the Emperor ever intended.

The Temple must be spared from such a desecration. If we do not take action at this time, Agrippa will rally support to himself and like his ancestors, we will have to suffer God's wrath because of their indiscretions.

Strangely, that man from Tarsus was back today. It was if he knew of what laid upon my troubled mind because he told me not to worry, that the only crown that will rest upon the mitre will be the Tetragrammon. I never spoke a word of my concerns with the man, yet he knew. It was as if he was a messenger from the Lord and his words lifted my heart.

But I should know better, because this Saul of Tarsus is a spreader of lies and therefore he could never be the hand of God that he claims to be. He is a corrupter of truth, using the ignorance of his listeners like a weaver uses threads. He spoke to me of the esteemed Hillel being his teacher during his early years. He would have been so young that it is amusing to even consider him enrolled in Hillel's school. Unless he was there as simply a boy to run errands for the students. Whatever the case, he shows very little if any of Hillel's wisdom. And certainly none of his tolerance. More likely he would have been one of Shammai's students if he had been old enough to have been there at all. Shammai had a habit of striking everyone that crossed his path. He was the most miserable of God's creatures and to think that he was a teacher. What a cynical view of the world he would have taught his students.

On one hand you had Hillel preaching love and respect for all people regardless of their background and then you had Shammai preaching that a man must trust only in himself and especially to have no relations with anyone not of our faith. This Saul appears to have little respect for anyone else as well. And I strongly believe that he would hunt down Gentiles and any other non-believers, showing them no mercy. He could be one of those fanatics, not unlike the Sicarii, that consider the murders they commit to be the will of the Almighty. Hardly the type of person I want visiting me on a regular basis.

These are strange times, my son. A king has come to rule over us and yet I fear he is more Roman than Jew. A dead Jew is being proclaimed as the Messiah, yet he delivered no one while he was alive. The world is ruled by a family that makes sport of killing each other in order to sit upon the Emperor's throne. And here I sit in Rome, the High Priest of Jerusalem, stripped of my authority, my dignity, my life. What am I to make of all this? Perhaps the Essene are correct and that this is the beginning of the end time. If so, then at least we can embrace this madness with the realisation that a better world is soon upon us.

Pearce be with you my son.

CHAPTER SIXTEEN

"The concept of GLEEM is not new, John. At some time, every person on this earth has experienced a brief encounter with it. They just didn't know how to explain it. Like when you're in a conversation and something's said that sends a sudden shudder down your spine. The other party sees it, your change in expression, loss of concentration, the actual shiver, and when they question you, you usually say if felt like someone had stepped on your grave. Funny expression, don't you think?

"Haven't really thought about it," Pearce replied, all the time busy scribbling down in his notepad my anecdotes and sidebar off the cuff comments.

"Well, think about it. How could they step on your grave? You're not dead; haven't even been dead. Or have you? That's the question everyone should be asking themselves. Why pick a metaphor that suggests you've been dead at some time previous to the conversation?"

"GLEEM?"

"Oh definitely! The memories that were stimulated, or triggered by that conversation were from someone that's been worm food for some time. Consciously you aren't aware of it, but subconsciously, you most certainly are."

"Wow," Pearce dropped his jaw. "I never thought about it. But now that I'm giving it some thought, it really is an odd expression, isn't it. Why would anyone even say it? If it was purely for shock value, you could say something like, 'felt like I just got shot,' or 'my heart felt like it just got wrenched in someone's fist,' something like that, right? But we don't, do we?"

"We all do experience it. Just find difficulty expressing it. More developed in some, but that's all a matter of degrees. Tell you an interesting story. When I was in Vienna in 2001, I spent almost an entire week of living in the Twilight Zone. Never really thought about where my ancestor Jakob lived until I got there. I knew the address was 20 Postgasse Strasse, but that was just a name, nothing more. But once I was in Vienna, I knew it to be much more. In my mind I could see through the windows overlooking the Danube. The streets below, the trees lining the green iron rails that ran the length of the river and the sides of the bridge that was just thirty paces from the front door. But it was not until I actually went there could I confirm that the residence was on the river. From the central square, I could feel myself drawn to it. The emotions were hard to deal with. When my wife suggested that it was too late to go that day, I became angry and petulant. So I ignored her reluctance and pushed us onward.

And once I was on Postgasse, I just urged us along, because I knew we had to get to the river to find it. You can imagine my disappointment when I found that on an entire street filled with centuries old homes there's one missing on the street. Replaced by an ugly and out of place office building. Sure enough, Jakob's home was gone. And the lovely old green rails with their filigree are now replaced by cold unfeeling steel, but that as they say, is progress. C'est la vie, or should I say c'est la morte."

"Not to sound crass here Doc, but did you ever check to see if you might own an office building in downtown Vienna now, rather than a house?"

"Never got around to it. Guess I was too upset about not seeing a home standing there to have thought clearly. So much had disappeared in the way of records since World War II, that it will take some effort to sort it out. What little that remained of the family in Vienna was all shipped out to Theriesenstadt, never to return. There would have been several properties and most likely none of them had been sold properly or legally. One day I'll check it out, but it wasn't meant to be that day."

"Yeah, I guess it isn't something you think about at the time. But when you're ready to go back Doc, I'll make sure I book on the flight with you because there's a story line here that's bigger than the one you'd write about Jakob."

"It's a deal John. We'll go together," I assured him. "There were a few other unusual aspects I witnessed while in Vienna. My children were extremely comfortable there. Whether they were watching puppet shows in the central plaza, or walking through the back streets of the city, they were entirely at ease. No apprehension at all, which was noticeable in all the other cities they visited. It was like they were home too. Yet my wife, did not share the same sentiment and feelings. Vienna was a beautiful city, but it was too overwhelming for her. She couldn't get comfortable.

And I can say that, because when we were in Freisland, the northern part of the Netherlands, we visited her mother's home town and my wife's demeanour was completely different. She couldn't wait to walk down country roads, And even once or twice commented that she was certain she was on a path that she knew her mother had used when she was a little girl.

So yes, John, I do believe that we all experience GLEEM in our lives without even recognising it."

"Amen to that Doc. I can think of a few times I had that same feeling. I just didn't know it was GLEEM at the time. Makes a lot more sense to me now. Now the missus, she'd probably say, "I told you so," because she thinks she's an authority on you and you're writing. She's started to keep a little diary on events in the past that she thinks may be attributable to some of her ancestors. Even has gone as far as having her little hen party groups where all her friends get together to compare their GLEEM notes. You may not realize it Doc, but you've spawned a whole new industry."

"Whatever you do John, promise me you'll ensure that my life and theories don't end up as a board game. I think if that should ever happen it will be time for both you and I to hang up on any further collaborations. I can accept rigorous debate, contested theories, and the sort, but I wouldn't be able to bear seeing GLEEM ending up as a chance card in Monopoly."

"Naw, Doc. I don't think it would ever be a card in Monopoly. More like an entire game on its own," Pearce joked.

"Very funny, John. I'm laughing so hard my memory's fading. Perhaps there won't be any more stories for quite a long time to come."

"Don't be like that," Pearce commented, a wide eyed puppy-like look on his face. "It really is a very good reaction from the readership when you consider the effort they all go to performing their own personal research. You're like a guru, or something. It's like the Tolkien effect. This can only be a good thing even if it achieves a fraction of what Lord of the Rings did. You can see that, can't you? It's as if you've been granted immortality. In some way, you've had an impact and changed the world!"

"I can't believe you said that John."

"Why's that?"

"Why, because it was actually the most profound thing I've ever heard you say. From my perspective all I can visualise is the immortality of my ancestors. How they live on, generation after generation, and some have even achieved legendary status. But I've never thought that somehow I might join the elite few. And now that I think of it, naah, I don't see it happening. Perhaps the best I can hope for is a getting a movie or two out of the entire series."

"And recognition of GLEEM," Pearce added.

"That I believe is a matter of fact. A lot of research going into it. And this entire episode of men in black raiding your office suggests to me that it's already recognized by more people than you may be aware of. That type of notoriety I can live without."

"You know what they say," Pearce quipped, "Good or bad any publicity is good publicity."

I rubbed the side of my head. My right temple was beginning to throb. There was still a lot of history to cover. I was beginning to think that the burden was far more than any man should have to bear. I can honestly say that intentionally, I wouldn't wish GLEEM upon anyone else. At least not the full blown version as I experience it. It's hard enough for an individual to find their own identity without having the presence of several hundred others pervading their thought processes. Sanity is such a precarious gift, with us all straddling a very thin tightrope in order to preserve it. It doesn't take much to have us topple from the rope and fall crashing in a heap from which we might never recover. If GLEEM has that capability, then I can't see myself being lauded for heightening the public's awareness. I'd sooner leave the issue of immortality to my ancestors.

My thoughts were suddenly interrupted by the intrusion of Pearce's voice. "So, do you think your children will have it the same as you?"

"God, I hope not," I responded in horror. "It would be my desperate hope that they don't. At some point you're going to have to believe me that there is nothing to be envious of when it comes to this gift. There are a lot better ways to be special. Win a race, run for politics, work in Hollywood; these are far safer ways to be in the limelight."

"Still, to be able to have a window into the past has to have some value? You can't deny that, Doc."

"Is it going to change the world; probably not. Are you going to wake up tomorrow and live your life differently; probably not? Here's a better one. Would you consider yourself better off if you knew all the answers?"

"I'd think so," he replied.

"Don't think. It should be a yes or no."

"But it depends…"

"Depends on what?"

"On whether the answers are going to get me in trouble."

"Pearce, they always get you in trouble. The answers are providing nothing more than an alternative. Just because it may be true, doesn't mean that it's what we want to hear."

"Huh?"

"Now that sounded intelligent," I commented. "Try this one for size. If for example I said that aliens were a reality, how would that revelation be received? Some might throw a party to celebrate the news, others would hide in fear of the pending invasion, a paramilitary organisation may even arise to defend the Earth from invasion. People would die just from the hysteria they create within their minds from imagined or speculative developments."

"I guess I wouldn't want to know all the answers."

"I guess you're right."

ROME: 39 AD

If only I knew then, what I know now, Elioneiai. How could I foresee that Yeshua's supporters would not be there when he needed them most? All the planning, all the risks, and everything hinged upon the loyalty of his handpicked disciples. It is the one time that I find myself in agreement with Shammai. Trust no one, as everyone is capable of betrayal. Had I paid attention to that, perhaps our world would be a different place today. Alas, all I have is the memories of remorse of what should have been. And even then, they are memories of age, which may lead me to overlook some events, but I will not stray too far from the actuality.

As long as Yeshua adhered to the strategy that was laid out

for him by Judas, his following increased dramatically. But be aware of this, Pilate was ignorant of our customs but he was no fool. He understood all too well what was happening. And he came to the conclusion that the best way to defeat Yeshua was to be oblivious to him. The warrant for his arrest was not to be acted upon unless he openly defied Roman rule. In reality, it was a situation beautifully manipulated by Judas. He had carefully conceived a situation where any attempt by Pilate to detain or arrest him would only further encourage the symbolism of the suffering servant. Rejection and contempt only served to speed the momentum of the movement and this effectively tied the Procurator's hands. Even though his lack of intervention convinced the masses that Yeshua was under divine protection, Pilate could still not make a move against him for fear of a massive revolt.

Extended this freedom, Yeshua and his followers came once again to Jerusalem. It was the time of the festival of dedication, the Chanukah, and once again Yeshua stood before me in the Temple. I can only describe him as a man obsessed. I was in awe of him. He was an instrument of his beliefs. Add to that the words which were provided to him by Judas, and he was given the power to speak like the prophets of old.

"Whosoever refuses me, refuses God," Yeshua orated to the priests in the heart of the Temple.

"Blasphemer," they shouted in unison.

"A prophet shall find no peace amongst his own."

"Caiaphas," I remember one of the priests tugging on my sleeve, "remove him at once before he desecrates the Lord's house."

Personally, I was far more interested in hearing what Yeshua had to say. There was definitely something about him that intrigued me. I cannot tell you though what it was.

"Will you cast me from this sacred sanctuary?" Yeshua challenged me.

"Do you debate the holiness of this Temple, Yeshua," I asked him.

"Yes, I debate every single brick with which it was built!"

"Are you Samaritan that you would dare condemn the Temple of the Almighty God?"

Yeshua completely ignored my half-breed accusation. "Tell me Priest, which is holier, the flesh or the soul?"

"Not a difficult question," I answered him. "The soul is far holier because flesh was only made from the clay of the earth, but the soul was directly from the breath of the Almighty."

"Then by your own words, Priest, you condemn this structure. For it too is merely flesh, built to surround the soul of the people of Israel. It is the people that the Lord has sanctified, not this structure of bricks and mortar."

It was then that I realized what I admired most about him. Despite his rural background, his mind was sharp and alert, and definitely argumentative as if he was a student from the school of Shammai. Everything was black and white in that school, exactly as Yeshua was portraying the world. There could be no middle ground. So, I knew there was no point in denying Yeshua's accusations.

"How is it," I asked, "that you can speak for the Lord about what He finds holy and what He does not?"

"Because I am the servant of the Lord. The Lord and I speak as one."

With that comment, the priests became enraged. I think they would have stoned him then and there if it wasn't forbidden to draw blood nor display anger in God's house.

"You have come and said what you came to do. But know that you do not intimidate me. And I will not arrest you and try you on a religious charge no matter how much you blaspheme within these walls. Because I see what manner of ploy you are unveiling. Where is your mentor, your Judas, so that I may congratulate him on the excellence of the snare he has laid? Be gone for you are only like a gnat to me. I will not feed the fury of your followers by taking action against you." And with that, I had him escorted forcefully from the Temple by the guards. It should be obvious to all that had it been my intention to put him to death, I would have done so then for his utterances were enough to condemn him by our laws. What he had proclaimed was contrary to the Torah. In the Book of Leviticus, the Lord dictated his demand for us to build Him a Temple as a central gathering place for his children.

I certainly had the opportunity to mete justice against him and I did not take it. No one would have condemned me had I taken action at the time. But nonetheless, I refrained. Let that answer suffice to all those that claim that I wished to see him dead

May the Lord watch over you my son.

CHAPTER SEVENTEEN

The sun was beginning to set when I peered out through the window. Time loses its entire framework when I'm recounting memories. Hours pass like minutes, days easily slip by in the blink of an eye. But time is a most elusive prey. It can neither be tamed nor captured, sliding through your fingers like water. If we're lucky then we can make the most of it when we have it. Most often we're spectators not participators. When I relate the details of my histories to Pearce, I consider myself to be the greatest spectator of all.

"Penny for your thoughts," Pearce proposed, using a very old homily to try and resurrect the conversation.

"Just thinking about time. In the pure context, that is."

"And what exactly were you thinking about?"

"More or less, the same we talked about before. Time and space. The ability to move through each simultaneously."

"Didn't you say time travel was impossible, Doc?"

"Only if the direction was into the past. I did say that physically there were apparent safeguards that prevented movement into the past because they'd prevent the future from happening. But what I didn't say was that the future couldn't communicate with the past."

Pearce began writing furiously in his notepad.

"Subatomic particles could be the answer," I proposed. "Let's presume that Einsteinian Relativity is correct and anything moving faster than the speed of light moves backwards in time. If that's true, then particles such as tachyons which when released from an atom will move faster than the speed of light will by the laws of physic, travel into the past." I needed to get away from my burden of memories.

"Whatever you say," Pearce agreed, but it was obvious he didn't have a clue what I was talking about.
"You're supposed to say that tachyons don't exist. They're hypothetical. But let's say they do, and let's assume neutrinos are

tachyons. Therefore a controlled release of tachyons results in a controlled message into the past without physically disturbing the past, which resulted in an alternative future."

Hopping up and down, Pearce couldn't wait to fire his next question at me. "Sending a message into the past should also change the future in the same way because it would result in the person acting on the message doing something he would normally do."

"That's where I beg to differ. In this scenario all it does is create the pattern of events which had to happen in order for everything to have occurred in the first place. Step one you build a tachyon receiver and propose a code that can be translated when you receive the message. Step two, you wait. And you wait an awfully long time because you have no idea when you or someone else can finally build a controlled tachyon emitter. Then when you finally do receive an emission, in all likelihood it will not resemble your pre-planned code in any shape, form or manner. All you really have demonstrated is that the past can receive a message from the future. Proof of a theory but no benefit by which you could create an alternative future."

Restless and not knowing what to make of this new found information, Pearce tapped his pen against the paper repeatedly. It was a habit which I've seen him display over and over again. "So, is there anything gained from this exercise? Does this tie in with Caiaphas?"

"Proof of being able to transverse time is what's gained. As for a commercial value, that might be discovered later on. For now it would be nothing more than a science experiment. And who knows, it might even explain unexplained events from our past."

"Such as," he was quick to throw at me.

"I don't know, how about a huge meteor that wipes out thousands of acres and yet no evidence of the actual meteor is ever discovered. And this strike is so powerful that it lights up the sky for thousands of square miles, so that twelve midnight looks like twelve in the afternoon. Interesting phenomena early last century in 1908 and almost a century later we still don't have an explanation that satisfies all that occurred."

"So what are you suggesting Doc?"

"I'm throwing out a highly theoretical probability. Thirty-seven years later, two atomic weapons are detonated at relatively the same latitude. Fission of the bombs is going to release some subatomic particles moving faster than light speed. They have to go somewhere. Why not back in time? So that the energy they release has a physical effect back in 1908. But with a time shift, there's also going to be a spatial shift, so location of when they reach their destination is not exactly the same as where they were dropped in 1945. The earth rotates and perambulates, so you get a band of damage rather than pinpoint destruction. If this event should be proven to be a result of the theory, then who knows what else can be explained through the use of time travel."

"But it still really isn't time travel."

"Not if you think of time travel in an H. G. Wells frame of context. What he gave you was a vehicle by which his time travelling hero could move to and fro as he saw fit. As I postulated, the going back through time I don't think is possible for a traveller, but the going forward, that's an entirely different issue."

"So man will never travel into the past?"

"Physically, I don't believe it can happen."

"So you're saying if it's not physically then he may be able to? Other than your tachyon theory, what other way would there be?"

I stood up and went over to my bookcase. Searching through a pile of papers that sat in my in-out tray I found the little red A5 notebook that I kept for the purpose of jotting down my thoughts from time to time. I threw it into Pearce's lap.

"What this," his asked, his curiosity peaked as he flipped through the pages.

"That's a little something I started when my son asked me about time travel one day. I didn't have an answer for him at the time, so I decided I would think about it quite seriously, and whenever an aspect of my theory flashed into my head, I'd quickly write it down before it escaped me."

Still scanning the ruled pages, Pearce would pause now and then to digest a diagram or decipher some of the statements and formulae.

"This is yours?"

"No, whenever I go to sleep, little elves slip into the house and write these notes into my book. Of course they're mine. What kind of question is that?"

"I didn't mean it like that," he defended himself. "I meant it like in, neat stuff! I'm impressed. Like this diagram on how an expanding universe is actually closing in on itself simultaneously is fascinating. But the way you described this expanding, collapsing universe seems to suggest that if you travel to the other side of its spherical structure then you could go back in time. I might be looking at this wrong, but that's what it does look like."

"No, not wrong at all. If you were able to cross to the other side of the sphere, then you would be able to go to a point in time that very well could be in your past. But because of the fact that you're travelling on a tiny speck that's expanding outwards for most of its existence, you'll never make it to the other side. So it's not going to happen."

"So what about this page here describing movement through time using our thoughts?" Pearce pointed at a page around the middle of the notebook.

"I believe there are times when our thoughts can exceed the speed of light."

Cocking his head, Pearce signalled that he needed a further explanation of what this was all about.

"In order to believe you have to learn to disbelieve," I cautioned. "It took a long time to accept the theory of relativity. Now I'm suggesting we look at that theory, pick it apart, and say that in some ways it's right, but in others it just doesn't provide the answer. After all, to accept it blindly meant nothing was going to exceed the speed of light, since any object was going to shrink to infinity and become so heavy that it would weigh more than the universe itself. But you can't have a universal law that destroys the universe now, could you."

"Okay, so you can't exceed the speed of light, what's the problem with that?"

"I don't accept it. Light is proven to be both a particle and a wave. If you don't know how this was done, don't worry about, just accept it because its duality was proven quite a long time ago. As a wave, it doesn't adhere to the standard requirements for size and mass. So moving at the speed of light isn't a problem as it doesn't violate the theory. But as a particle, a packet, a photon it does. Shrinking to infinity that's fine. Just means we can't see it with our physical senses. A particle of light is too small to register in our own senses framework. But the theory says it should have gained incredibly in mass. This non measurable particle should weigh everything down in the universe. Light would be the heaviest object there is and this is not the case. And a black hole from which no light escapes couldn't exist because its gravitational pull wouldn't exceed that of a light emitting object which in a previous life, it was in the form of a star. So the black hole's mass has actually exceeded that of a light emitting mass. To do so meant its mass notched up beyond that of an object moving at the speed of light. Therefore inside the black hole its world is moving faster than the speed of light. I know this sounds like rambling to you but I will be making a point here that relates directly to our thoughts exceeding the speed of light."

"I hope so Doc, because you're losing me along the way. This relativity stuff is a little too extreme for me to comprehend. In fact I failed physics in high school."

Why doesn't that surprise me? Pearce must have been the ultimate science student...not! I doubt anyone else would have mistaken him for one either. But I was trying to make this very difficult subject as easy to follow as possible and I thought I was doing a pretty good job of it too.

"Okay, let me try this again. We can think of energy as electro-magnetic pulses. EM waves as we call it. Right?"

"Right," he responded.

"And you know what that means?"

"No."

"Then why did you say right, when I asked you?"

"Because I can understand electro-magnetic, but I just don't see what anything has to do with anything else." Pearce sat there shaking his head.

"Okay, back to scratch. If you understand EM then you should be able to follow this next bit. Go back to the E equals MC squared equation. We all know it but that doesn't mean we know what to do with it. But it's basically what Einstein gave us and we've been stuck with until proven otherwise. Let's rework the formula so that C squared equals energy divided by mass. Now the speed of light is a fixed value and therefore the square of it will also be fixed. So, as we move faster, we're going to need more energy both in producing it and releasing it. So E becomes bigger and bigger. You can think of it this way. If you're running to your home, you're going to burn up more energy than if you were just walking there. Which means you'll eat more when you get home to replace the increased loss of energy. This isn't rocket science by any stretch of the imagination. Just common sense. So more energy is being released which would make the numerator larger. If the denominator didn't increase proportionately, then the result of E divided by M would be greater than the square of the speed of light. And we can't have that, can we? So the rule says, if energy increases then mass has to increase to keep the value constant. And that's the reason you have a theory that says mass will increase infinitely as you approach the speed of light. But we know something is not right. Because small particles can approach the speed of light and they don't weigh a tonne. But they should be according to the theory. But if they're not a particle but a wave as they're moving, then they don't have the same constraints. They can go as fast as they want and mass doesn't become an issue. And if waves don't have these constraints then they can bend the rules which means they can go faster than the speed of light."

"I got you…I think."

"Well, hold on to that thought. Or try to hold on to it because that's what is at the centre of my theory. If waves can exceed light speed then they can also move through time. Now it has been demonstrated that at certain phases of sleep, the human mind can emit levels of electrical impulse energy that are greater in magnitude than what is required for normal thought. Alpha waves with sharp peaks. You've probably seen them on television documentaries. But a person sleeping is easy to measure. A person going through his everyday activities is a little harder to measure. Perhaps we do measure it but don't recognize it. Telekinesis, psychomotor activities such as ESP, Kirlian imaging, it doesn't really matter what aspect we see, it's all an emission of energy. And these abilities are probably within all of us. But what is essential to understand is that the brain can manifest these wavelength energies beyond the confines of our own bodies.

Now let's go back to talking about sleeping. Abnormalities such as alpha wave spikes are wave activity surges beyond normal acceptable parameters. They are indications of energy levels far beyond any use in the dream state. But it is this dream state that apparently eliminates any inhibitors that normally keep our electro activity at subdued levels."

Waving his pencil furiously in my direction, Pearce raised his objection, "Surely you're not suggesting that our dreams can take us back in time?"

"Why not? From my own experience, I probably have my most active dream state in the last hour of my sleep. And in that short time I can live an entire episode spanning several years of real life. The people involved, the events, may all be strange to me, but that's neither here nor there. What's important are the details. The myriad details of total inconsequence. The boring, mundane details of everyday life of total irrelevance. From the rising in the morning, the sitting in a class, the talking with friends, to sitting in the evenings in front of the television before I head off to bed. Every day, boring details of life, an ordinary existence, but totally complete. An entire episode of life, unabridged and fully recountable.

During my sixty minutes of slumber, I would have risen, been active all day, and gone to sleep over three hundred and sixty five times if I had dreamt about a single year. Once again, time is all a matter of reference and perspective. In this particular case, the compression was almost nine thousand to one. In other words, my brain was processing at a rate that is absolutely incredible. Neuroactivity that's out of this world. Obviously that velocity doesn't correspond to a spike measurement but it wasn't meant to.

Now I have to get you to think outside of your box, John." Pearce looked at me trying to guess what I was going to throw at him next.

"If we could in some way relate this measurement of time not only to progression but to distance as well, and think of our dream being a stream of energy packets called thoughts, then it is very likely that our thoughts had travelled very far. What distance can a thought travel, you ask? Can we correlate it to computer generated thoughts? Little bytes travelling across the world through the internet? Around the world in only a few seconds. If that should be the case, then a compression of nine thousand times would take it extremely close to the speed of light. So close in fact that it would project itself well into the future, all while our physical reality only aged a single hour. Reality and the dream world ceased to exist in the same time-spatial framework. Our dreams had become detached from our usual twenty-four hour clock. In fact our dreams had become travellers in time."

"Double wow, Doc. But not to be a devil's advocate or anything like that, once again what's all this got to do with Caiaphas?"

"Nothing and everything," I replied sedately.

"And you claim that I'm the one losing the plot line here," Pearce challenged my laissez faire response. "What am I supposed to write about this? That you decided that walking down memory lane was getting boring so you decided that rocket science was more entertaining!"

"Is that another attempt by you at humour, John?"

"Did you find it funny?"

"No."

"It wasn't meant to be. I've spent the five minutes listening to your dissertation, all the time expected it to tie up to the main reason I'm here, and it never did. So, what was the point if I can't use it in the story?"

"Like I said, it has nothing and everything to do with the story. Do you not think Caiaphas had some inkling of the future? A window onto a world that he was trying to prevent. One man usually doesn't make a world of difference if he lives or dies. Jesus did. With all the peculiarities in which his arrest was handled, don't you think Caiaphas had some idea of the future? Otherwise he would have ended up no different than John the Baptist. Just a head on a plate for the price of a dance. That should have been the scenario. Like they did with John, throw him in a prison, let the commotion die down, and then execute him when no one's paying any attention and that's the end of it. And that was done in Galilee where John had a strong following. Jesus was in Jerusalem where his support group was pretty thin."

A light turned on in Pearce's eyes and suddenly his entire face became illuminated. "So if I'm interpreting this right, you're suggesting that Caiaphas had some window into the future and because of it was holding off doing anything to Jesus."

"Why is it that we think automatically with GLEEM that an individual sees only into the past? If the genetic code gets hardwired to transport memories from one generation to another, why couldn't that same area of grey matter be tuned into a higher frequency?

Perhaps all those memories stimulate a higher brain activity while sleeping. We all know that the memories of a bad day can make us pretty restless at night. Who's to say having the bad memories of several hundred generations isn't enough to keep you restless every night of your life? Perhaps Caiaphas saw that the death of Jesus would result in the multiple attempts of genocide that have been perpetrated against the Jewish race since the fourth century A.D."

"But you have to have a basis which you've built upon to come to that conclusion," Pearce tried to lecture me on empirical process.

"Even better, I have his memories. So what he thought of the future, is just a memory from the past to me."

It took a few seconds for Pearce to wrap his mind around that conundrum. "So, if something scares the bejeebers out of him that he thinks is a vision of the future, then it imprints on his mind, and you inherit it as a one of his key memories."

"Exactly! Caiaphas doesn't fear Jesus alive, he fears what will happen when he's dead. So his entire effort is to keep a self-prophesising messiah with a death wish from actually dying."

"But that's certainly not the story that we've been handed down by the Church."

"That's where you wrong. That's exactly how they describe it. Jesus' ability to walk in and out of Jerusalem several times, Caiaphas manoeuvring at night in his own home to try and get Simone Peter to testify on his master's behalf, even his being taken into custody by the Temple guards before letting the Romans seize him is all designed to keep him alive. An extreme effort that placed the High Priest in a very precarious position and ultimately led to the charges brought against him by Pilate, which in turn brought Caiaphas to Rome to be tried.

"And all this because he saw into the future? Maybe he was just intuitive?"

"That's what being from the High Priests family was all about. Prophesy, visions, and extraordinary insight. Who's to say that intuition just isn't once facet of the entire process? But as far as I'm concerned, it goes hand in hand with GLEEM and hence my interest in manipulating time. So you see, I wasn't just rambling on as you may have thought, there was a purpose to it all."

"I didn't mean to imply that you were rambling," Pearce

apologised. "It's just I couldn't fathom how all this physics stuff was related to what our main subject was about."

"Well, let's remember you did ask, after all."

"I guess I did Doc. I'll have to be more careful next time."

"Now that was funny," I laughed. "It's not always easy to see the forest for the trees," I philosophised. "You know, even Einstein had a problem with quantum physics. He opened an entirely new world with his theories but because he placed limitations on his own universe, he couldn't deal with the fact that things may happen, simply because they can. Similarly, it's very hard for us to accept that there may have been a lot more than meets the eye about events of two thousand years ago. As I mentioned, it's all about perspective, and more so about time."

ROME: 39 AD

"Greetings Elioneiai, my son. Vile rumours are being spread of Yeshua's death by my hands, in the communities here in Rome. Such a lie spreads easily since no one from Judaea comes to Rome to speak openly of what really occurred during those dark days of Nissan. Even Yeshua's brother James has grown silent, and he I considered to be our best witness. Simon Cleophas has been the only one to speak of what really transpired but he does not hold any authority amongst this congregation here in Rome, even though he been appointed as spiritual leader back in Jerusalem. But what is truly ironic is that these rumours will actually be used in my defence against my accusers in Rome, for how could I be both collaborator as well as persecutor of Yeshua. For one to be true, then the other must be false, and currently the cries amongst those calling themselves Christians in this city are saying that I am a murderer. What a terrible situation to find myself in. To deny their cries would support those in the Roman Senate that wish to prosecute me. To agree with their defamatory remarks could win my freedom but bloody me with the mark of Cain, which would grieve me to death.

Whichever crime I'm tried for will ultimately bring the Gentile nations against us. The slander against me will be used to oppress all of our nation, for it will be an impossible task to pacify one faction without antagonising the other. That dilemma will be our haunting. For once I understand the words of Isaiah. We will be marked and scorned and rejected by all nations. And they will nail us to their trees, whip us with their scourges, and scatter us to the furthest lands. And this will be an inheritance that we will pass down through the generations until such time that the Lord sends us a deliverer to free us from the oppression that we suffer.

But you might ask, which was I truly, defender or persecutor. I think the true answer is neither. Of what these Christians claim that Yeshua had spoken I have little to agree with. I have no shared beliefs in their doctrines, but that does not mean that I stand against them. To me, they are no different than any of the other sects that we have spawned. They come and they go, mere spectres of Judaism's maturation. If some choose to consider Yeshua a prophet like Amos, Habbukuk and Zadekiah, then how is this any different than that sect in Alexandria that considers John the Baptist to be one too? Prophets come and prophets go. Is that not what we have always believed? Though Zechariah, when he was High Priest a long time ago said that the days of the prophets were over, I choose to disagree. If anything, they swell in numbers in times of trouble. Whether we listen or not is the deciding factor.

I do disagree with those that try to raise Yeshua higher than any of the original prophets. To these people, I challenge their attempts to judge Yeshua as greater than Elijah, creating stories of Yeshua that surpass each of Elijah's miracles. Prime example of their attempts concerns Lazarus, the story of his resurrection from a premature death and burial.

What had transpired then was the gravest error in all of the careful planning of Yeshua and his followers. And its outcome led to a further series of mistakes that in turn splintered the disciples and led to Yeshua's crucifixion. What I say now, Elioneiai, is from my position as witness and bearer of truth for these events. Of all that I have to tell you, this is by far the most important of events.

You must especially remember what I've told you previously about Lazarus and his sisters, Martha and Miriam. They were of the House of David that lived in Bethany. I told you of the two princedoms, that of Ephraim in the north and that of David in the south. And did I not tell you that the heir to the throne of David would not reign again until a king comes from Gideon of Galilee to rule first.

But now I will speak of things so mystical in nature that even amongst those few of us that have read of these things, only a few of us can understand. I was one that knew because as High Priest, the mysteries of the universe are as an open book. And Judas was one that knew, because as one of the Temple scribes he had access to such things. But to anyone else, they cannot make claim to know of such things, and whatever they thought they understood would be incomplete.

My son, what I speak of now is the mirror worlds, the realm of men and the Realm of God. Events which occur in heaven are mirrored in our own world. As the Lord suppresses evil within the seven heavens, so too, is it is our task to suppress evil in our world. There comes a time when Israel will battle against the evil of the other nations, taking arms against Gog and Magog. If Edom be Rome, then surely the time of coming is soon. In the other mirror world, the battle will be just as great, good against evil in its purest context. The messiah of the Lord against the evil Armilius. Both events shall coincide with the end of days, when Eden will be restored on earth.

The parallels run deeper than this. The messiah of the Lord is the messiah ben David, the greatest of David's descendants, but even so, the messiah ben Joseph must precede the Davidic messiah and therefore it is written that the greatest warlord to grace this earth will be a descendant from the house of Ephraim. This is the true essence of the mirror worlds, for each is a series of events complete unto themselves, yet inseparable from their counterparts in the other world.

There is only one notable difference. The messiah ben Joseph must die, then his body is to lay untouched for forty days at which time he'll be resurrected by the coming of the messiah ben David. Afterwards the two messiahs will conquer Armilius together, forever vanquishing evil from the universe.

These are what is written in the sacred books to which few have access but those that do rarely discuss because they are not easily comprehended by us mere mortals. Judas the scribe though, thought that he fully understood their meaning and he devised a cunning plan on how to use them.

It was following the Festival of Dedication when Yeshua and his adherents fled across the Jordan of which I have told you about previously. His consort, Miriam, feared for his life but to keep her safe she stayed at Lazarus's home, leaving Yeshua to suffer the anguish of his exile by himself. Though she was usually knowledgeable of Judas's intentions, but she had no knowledge of what he planned for Yeshua during the exile. Perhaps not even Yeshua knew at that time thatr Judas planned to turn his master into the suffering servant, and this meant that Yeshua was intended to undergo a terrible fate.

To the uninitiated they mistakenly believe there is but one world, but although I have knowledge of mirrored worlds, the same cannot be said for the House of Lazarus. Oh, they knew of the legends of the two kings and most certainly about the coming of the two messiahs, but I know for a fact that Lazarus thought they were one and the same. It must have been absolutely terrifying to Martha, Miriam and Lazarus, plagued by knowledge that they did not fully comprehend. How could they think any differently? As the family of the exilarch, they were the Davidic line, and that meant Yeshua would die, only to be revived forty days later by Lazarus.

Weak, timid Lazarus, the leader of the Lord's army was to be the key to Yeshua's revival. Not even Lazarus could believe that. And it was equally inconceivable to Miriam that Yeshua's entire fate depended on the strength of her brother. A man with no mystical power and certainly no divine guidance finding himself suddenly in a position to determine life or death over the man she loved.

Others may have argued that the forty days and nights that Yeshua spent in the desert, abandoned with no food or water by Judas, were equivalent to forty days in the grave, but those of us having greater knowledge of these hidden scriptures regarding the two messiahs aren't willing to accept anything less than the literal enactment of the prophecies. But poor Lazarus having partial insight into their content could not see any manner by which the death and resurrection could be avoided. As far as he was concerned, one of the Messiahs had to die.

What is truly amazing is that he and his sisters were able to concoct a plan, in spite of their fears for Yeshua, which would actually attempt to deter fate and correct God's intentions. It was Lazarus, himself, whom told me, "If Jacob was able to use cunning and lies to take the blessing from his older brother Esau, and God was still satisfied to bless Jacob, then surely he reasoned the fate of

the Messiah ben Joseph could be taken by his brother from David."
I rarely extend any credit in regards to intelligence to the family of
the Exilarch, but I must confess that I found Lazarus's argument
quite well founded from the perspective of historical precedent.
What he failed to recognize is that the scriptures and prophecies
cannot be bargained with and God has always been clear on that
point. But that would not deter him.

What they had planned went far beyond what could be
considered acceptable religious debate, but instead bordered on
heresy. Using a practice of controlling one's mind through burning a
specific incense and patterned breathing, a practice that
unfortunately returned with the exiles from Persia several hundred
years ago, and which was commonly practiced by those gifted men
known as Magi in Persia, they would place themselves into a trance
state bordering upon death. Even these Magi say that its practice did
not originate with them but with others that like themselves practice
magic in a world far to the east of the Indus River.

Of those that I have talked to that know of this practice, they
have explained to me that its implementation involves the
deprivation of all sights and sounds to the person involved. And by
doing so, the individual being worked upon begins to turn his mind
inward to the point that only the beating of the heart registers as a
sound, and even that can be slowed by the person's mind until it
barely beats at all.

Imagine it Elioneiai, their breathing becomes shallow and
infrequent and the body no longer moves but still, the individual is
not dead. Days pass, and some say even weeks, while in such a state
until there comes a trigger to revive them from this sleep of death.
As they transverse this death like state, the Magi say they are able to
commune with their gods, which makes such practice blasphemous
to us.

This is a vile, loathsome practice as much as it is a mystery,
for it mocks death and worst of all it mimics the Lord's power over
life. Men should not know of such things and only the trickster
Asmodeus could have given such knowledge to mankind. For is it
not this angel's mission to prove to God that mankind's creation was
His greatest error and held in contempt by the lesser hosts. Lazarus
and his sisters should have recognized the evil they were loosening
upon the world when they attempted such a thing.

They began their ill-fated plan while Yeshua was yet abandoned in the desert. Two plans in operation, each with the intended purpose of fulfilling the prophecies and each flawed from their inception. I still cannot conceive how Judas was able to persuade Yeshua to willingly enter the wastelands without any means to survive, and furthermore how he was able to convince the other disciples to let him go. Perhaps there was more to Judas's plan than we will ever know but whatever it may have been was intruded upon by the events within Lazarus's household.

The House of David began the ceremony in the flickering light of candles, while chanting a series of archaic versus over and over. And once Lazarus fell silent his sisters took up the chant as they lay their brother on a mattress of silkweed thread.

Deeper and deeper Lazarus's soul sunk into the depths of the underworld until for all intents and purposes his body appeared lifeless and only the merest of sparks ignited his consciousness. And in that state of unbeing, there spread the word throughout the village of Bethany that the Palestinian exilarch was dead! Sorrowful and bewildered relatives and friends flocked to the villa of Lazarus to mourn and grieve. But in their bereavement there came no physician to pronounce the official death as would be expected, and there was no Rav present to recite the Shemah. And it was Martha that did not permit either of these to take place prior to Lazarus being carried by tearful pallbearers to his tomb carved in the rock of the family garden.

His body was wrapped in linen from head to toe, but what all that were present found unusual was that his hands and feet were tied. All knew that this was not permissible by our customs and the fettering of the limbs is contrary to our laws. They protested to Martha, begging her to untie the bonds that would prevent the departure of the soul. "Release our brother from his earthly bonds," they shouted and demanded in unison.

But Martha would have no part of their protestations for to do so would risk that the state of false death would become in fact the real death of their brother. Once his body was laid within the tomb, she had the great stone rolled across the mouth of the cave, sealing Lazarus within to complete this deception of his death.

It was shortly after that representatives of the family came to my house to lodge their complaints. They requested that I send out my garrison to Bethany and seize the tomb so that they could properly prepare the body. They told me of all that transpired, the failure to pronounce the Shemah, the fact that no physician was procured to examine the body, and the customary application of spices and resins to the linen had not taken place. To have done any of this would have brought their deception into the open since they would have refused to let these be done

"Do not worry," I said to those that came to me, "your kinsman is not dead."

They looked upon me as if I was mad. But they knew not what I knew, of these sorcerous practices from the East. "I say so because of matters of which I am familiar," I instructed. And then I began to tell them of all that I knew. It was not long until some of them began to speak of the eerie singing they heard coming from the house of Lazarus the nights before. Others recalled the fragrant aroma of strange incense that filled the air. All these things when placed in their proper order made them realize the deception that had been played upon them. They realized that the fettering of the limbs was performed precisely for the reasons they objected to. The soul could not be allowed to leave the body because Lazarus was not truly dead. In anger they insisted that I make a stop to the charade immediately. But I could not, for I did not know what the trigger was that would release Lazarus from his slumber. Any interference at that time would likely cause the actual death of Lazarus and I could not bear to be responsible for his murder whether unintentional or not.

When those that had come to see me returned to Bethany, they confronted the sisters of Lazarus, insisting that they put an end to the charade immediately. You can imagine what happened following their outburst. Cousin against cousin, mass confusion, most didn't even know what they were arguing about, only that they had to choose one side or the other. There were still those that insisted that Lazarus was truly dead, but those that heard the reasoning and logic of the ones that had come to Jerusalem, saw the rational of their argument and knew it to be the truth. Still the sanctity of the shiva period of mourning became a battle ground.

Martha and Miriam sent an urgent message to Yeshua through their servants, not daring to go themselves because if they were seen to break the shiva then all would know that the death of

Lazarus had been nothing more than a charade. It was fortunate that they did so for it was then that Judas had to reveal that he had abandoned Yeshua in the desert where he was to survive without food or water. Upon hearing this news, the servants immediately rode into the desert and were fortunate to find Yeshua still where Judas had deserted him. As it had only been a matter of days and not the forty that were required, Yeshua had not suffered, other than the burning rays of the sun and the parching of his throat.

Relieved that he had been rescued, Yeshua knew immediately what his friends had done upon hearing the tale from the servants. And this is where I need you to pay particular close attention Elioneai, for it is important to know the words that Yeshua chose when he spoke of this situation, for he was very selective in his speech. He told the disciples that their friend Lazarus had become sick, cautioning them that he had been buried but was not dead, merely in a sleep of the righteous. But how do you explain such things to a mob of unruly and uneducated Galileans. They pressed him for a further explanation that they could fathom.

"Lazarus is dead," he swore at them in anger, frustrated by their failure to understand his original explanation. "For your sake I'm glad I wasn't with him, for you would obviously be swayed by those who have refused to mourn his passing. You'll see a man in his tomb, and you won't question if he is truly dead. When I arrive, he'll arise and you will see a man that lives again. That is all you have to know. Ask me nothing more!"

"Then let us go and witness this great miracle," they exclaimed.

"Know this," Yeshua instructed, "we will start out for Bethany but it will now be the fourth day since his burial before we arrive there. Along the way people will come and ask where we are going. You will tell them to join us for your master is going to raise a king from his grave. And we will say this to all that we meet and by the time we reach Bethany, we will be an army of hundreds, and this throng shall bear witness to what will transpire."

And just as he had planned, there were hundreds that accompanied him on his journey from the desert. All eager to bear witness to a miracle that defied explanation. A miracle as great as any that Elijah and Elisha had performed. In a small grotto outside Bethany, Martha met Yeshua and his party, defying the ban on immediate family members leaving the shiva house.

"Why have you taken such risks to leave your house," Yeshua asked when she arrived unexpectedly.

"Master, I am afraid that we have erred in our intentions. There is fighting within our house. The High Priest has turned many against our plan."

"What you did was wrong. I know why you did it, but it does not make it any less wrong. Why did you not speak to me first? Did you not have the sense to be fearful of what you did? What will happen if your brother does not awake? Then he will be truly dead, and everything would have been for nothing."

"Forgive me Master," she pleaded. "We only thought we were doing what was best. You must believe me."

"I do believe you but it was still wrong."

"You are the key to his release. It is your voice that will awaken him. He must feel your presence to break the trance."

"And what will all of this have achieved?"

"Then it will be said you are the true Messiah ben David and together with Lazarus you have fulfilled the prophecy of the two messiahs."

"Not so, Martha. Your plan doesn't make any sense. How is it that one like me from the north, not of the line of David can become that which I am not? You have brought the people against us. They will condemn this act, as much as there are those that already suspect it to be a ploy. The priesthood will demand that your brother stands trial for practicing such blasphemy. Do not forget that Saul was condemned for his contacting the dead Samuel through the necromancy of the witch of Endor. I will be surprised if we can emerge from this unscathed. For now we rely on Judas to find a way through the darkness. We listen only to him and seek his advice for guidance. Is that understood?"

Martha nodded obediently. She had been scolded, but even in his anger, Yeshua had not let anything step between them and his love for the house of Lazarus was as great as ever.

These words have been passed to me from those that I had as my ears amongst the followers of Yeshua. Similar words are spoken by one of the followers called Mark. I hear that he intends to write a book on his deceased Master. From what I have been told, he bears a true witness, but there are already others that have attempted to change his words. I fear that by the time a generation has passed, little of what Mark has to say will be recorded. Mark has said, that when Martha returned to Bethany following her meeting with Yeshua, she went immediately to Miriam, or Mary as he has subsequently named her, and she told her sister to go out of the house and greet Yeshua in the grotto. She was warned that there would be those of the mourners that would follow her and would scold her loudly because she broke the restrictions of the shiva. Of course, if Lazarus was ever to find the courage to tell his own story, then there would be no question as to what were the events that transpired. But then courage and Lazarus are two words that I would rarely use in the same sentence.

Martha told her to say the following words to Yeshua, loud enough that others would hear her. "Word has come that Lazarus shall live because Yeshua will raise his spirit. Had Yeshua been here in the first place, Lazarus would not have died." These were to be her words; she was not to add nor detract from them.

As instructed, Miriam ran from the house, and those attending her grief went out with her thinking that she was racing to the tomb hysterically. When they saw that she was heading to the outskirts of the town, they became alarmed. They ran after her, not realising that she had a predetermined destination.

When Miriam saw Yeshua in distance, she ran to him excitedly. She threw herself at his feet, bewailing her brother's death and screaming the words that Martha had given her.

"Take me to your brother," Yeshua demanded. "I'm here because the news your tragedy has come to me on angel's wings. Listen all of you whom have gathered here. I have heard from angel's lips while I wandered in the desert that Lazarus suffers the sleep of the living death. Do not be mistaken, he does not feign death, but there is a demon that lives in his body and suffocates his divine spirit from within. Woe to Lazarus, for he is now suffering an eternal torment. Take me to him Miriam, and I will free him from his bond of demonic death. He will rise and live again."

Those were obviously the words of Judas and each one had been selected carefully to fulfil a purpose. First, he wanted everyone to know that Yeshua had been wandering alone in the desert. Perhaps only for forty hours rather than the forty days but time would blur that difference. Secondly, the words were hose to beguile and confuse all those that had assembled. Talk of demonic possession would excuse Lazarus from feigning death because none could ever question the ways of demons. They knew that Yeshua had placed himself in danger of arrest by entering into territory under Pilate's governance, but despite the threat, he was willing to make the sacrifice to save a friend even though he made it clear that the resurrection would not be from the embrace of death itself but from that which mimicked death. Yeshua walked towards the town, crying as he did so, and everyone that saw him could only think of how much he loved Lazarus.

Martha waited for Miriam and Yeshua at the tomb. As soon as she saw them coming over the hill into the garden she ran toward him and threw herself at his feet, kissing them with her hair. Yeshua stood with his arms outstretched to all those in attendance, praising the Lord for bringing him to the tomb of his friend. He instructed the mourners to cease their wailing, claiming that today would be a day of life, not death.

"Spirit of Lazarus, awaken from your sleep!" Yeshua shouted through the cracks behind the great sealing stone. "Cast off the evil spirit that holds you as a prisoner. It is your friend, Yeshua that has come to rescue your soul. I have defeated death in my sojourn through the desert and the angels have sent me to do so on your behalf as well. By my command I release your burden. In the name of God, the Almighty and the Merciful, I order you to rise!"

At first there was only silence, a deafening, maddening silence. Then suddenly there were screams of terror emerging from the tomb. The crowd fell back paralysed with fear. Lazarus screamed over and over again.

"Quickly, roll back the stone!" Yeshua yelled at them.

Lazarus's relatives urged Martha to stop the proceedings immediately, fearing that they were witnessing the black arts of necromancy.

"Roll back the stone!" Yeshua ordered once again. "Those of such little faith, witness now the glory of God. Know that by what you are about to see, that the Almighty has sent me!"

As soon as the light entered the tomb when the stone was rolled back, the screaming from inside stopped.

"Come out," Yeshua shouted. "Come out, evil spirit that plagues my brother, Lazarus. No longer shall you be allowed to torment him."

There were only feeble whispers heard within the tomb.

"Did you tie his limbs?" Yeshua asked Martha.

She nodded to him.

"Praise be God. By doing so, you have prevented the demon from leaving the tomb and feeding upon all of us standing here. It has not been able to do so because of your foresight. But now that I am here, you no longer need to fear it. It won't be set lose in this world, for I do not will it. Untie Lazarus and set the unclean spirit free to travel the netherworld for all eternity."

Entering the tomb with their servants, Martha and Miriam untied Lazarus who now sobbed unrelentingly.

"Come to me, Lazarus, my brother," Yeshua urged. "We must pray together to the Almighty for the grace of deliverance that He has offered you today."

Staggering on legs that could barely hold his weight, Lazarus edged from the tomb and fell into Yeshua's open arms. While the shocked crowd stared amazement, Yeshua led his friend to a place where they would share the day and night in private. Yeshua bathed Lazarus's body, the final cleansing of the ordeal, and from a distance all that anyone could see was their two forms, dressed in white and talking together in private.

When word came to me of the details of what had transpired, I had to admit that Judas was a most worthy opponent. Although many like myself would realize that it was all a fraud, what Yeshua had said and done put him and Lazarus beyond our reach to punish them. What crime could I say had been committed? Belief in demons is now well entrenched in our religion, particularly amongst the uneducated. It is of little use to try and dissuade our people from these beliefs now. All they see now is that to release these evil spirits from their intended victims is considered a virtue and for Yeshua to have such a blessed power is far from blasphemous. Judas had proven himself to be a masterful strategist. But there was still a weak link because the house of Lazarus would always prove to be a thorn that would stick in one's sandal.

And so it was Elioneai, so it was.

CHAPTER EIGHTEEN

"Okay, I'll admit I'm not the sharpest tool in the shed, but you're asking me to accept an entirely different version of everything we've been led to believe." Pearce was absolutely frantic, the pen shaking and quivering in his hand as if it had a life of its own. His face had become flushed and the expression on his face was most disconcerting.

"No, I'm not asking you to do anything of the sort. I'm just relating memories from the past. It's your own mind that's doing the asking. And why? Because you have doubts. You probably always had doubts but you resisted the urge to search for answers. And now the difference is that where there were existing doubts I have supplied you with plausible explanations. Caiaphas has given you one. And that's disturbing. Because in your mind, his explanation is making a lot more sense than anything you've been spoon fed in Sunday school. So the question is not whether I expect you to believe or disbelieve but what are you going to do? It's not about me, it's about you."

"That's a crock, Doc. It can't be that simple and you know it!"

"Why's that Pearce, because it's too simple. That accepting events for what they really were would take away all the mystery, all the hocus-pocus. Is that what religion is all about? Is that why you think it was invented so that we could accept the supernatural, the things that go bump in the dark? Why not try to accept it as a morality lesson, a way to live our lives and make this world a better place. How about a guy that was just too good for the world he lived in. When things were bad, he saw good. Where there was hate, he found love. That's the miracle. Forget all this supernatural mumbo jumbo which only serves to detract from his real intent and purpose."

"If that's all there was, then it doesn't make sense," Pearce objected. "It wouldn't be a religion. Might as well just be some Eastern philosophy where we sit with our legs crossed and hum all the time."

"So what's wrong with that," I challenged. "Certainly would offer a lot more credibility than what I've seen so far from the so-called organised religions. I can aspire to live my life according to a great man. I'm doomed to failure if I try to live it on a scale of approval for a god."

"But that's okay." Pearce advised. "We're expected to fail. That's why we ask forgiveness. We can't possibly live up to the challenge that Jesus placed before us."

"Do you really accept what you just said? That we're doomed to failure and we accept that. That we don't have to challenge ourselves because all we have to ask for is forgiveness. Why would I even bother? If the goals aren't realistic from the onset, why in the world would I even try? At least if I know that there was a great man that trod this earth and set himself as an example of how we should behave, then I have a chance if I work hard enough that I can do the same."

Pearce laughed at my suggestion. "It doesn't make sense Doc. If all he was, was this really great man, then how can you explain everything that has been done in his name since then? Why hasn't there been a lot of others just as great in the last two thousand years?

On the contrary, it's the only thing that does make sense. Try and look at the entire history of the event as a whole. Can you even fathom how unique he was for his time? A world where life meant absolutely nothing, where a military power had subjugated the people of the living God. Can you even appreciate what this meant? Tyranny, oppression, slavery, murder, think of a word that describes the most despicable series of events that could afflict a people and that's the world that Jesus was born into. Picture your worst nightmare. Now you tell me that a man under those circumstances who can still find forgiveness in his heart for his enemies isn't a miracle in himself."

I could see from his eyes that Pearce was trying to deal with what was an extremely foreign concept to his upbringing. He kept making this opening and closing beseeching motion of his hands in my direction as if there was a point to be made but in reality Pearce was rendered speechless. "The deeper you try to look into the entire episode that framed Jesus' life, the more you see it for exactly what it was, and it's both disheartening and enlightening, sad and exhilarating. The ultimate paradox."

"Why can't there be more?" Pearce finally spoke.

"I'd like to think that there's a purpose to everything. What Jesus provided was a model that men can aspire to. A model within human capabilities and limitations. Isn't that what we find so marvellous about him? After all, if he really was superhuman, or a holy spirit, or even a god, what would his life have to do with any of us? We don't have godhood, or supernatural advantages, so how could we even think we could model ourselves in his image? But if he was a man, just a simple blood and bone human being, then suddenly there is a chance for all of us. Because whatever one man can do, another one can, and another, and another."

His chin sunk on to his chest, almost as if he had fallen asleep but I knew it was only a sign of his lowering of the barriers of his resistance further. Not that I viewed this as a conflict, but actually as something completely opposite, a welcoming. "So, did Lazarus ever write this in a book?"

"I thought I had mentioned earlier, or perhaps Caiaphas did, that Lazarus became a fairly significant writer. He moved immediately after the crucifixion to Ephesus. There, they called him John of Ephesus. And he did write a couple of books as you're aware that shed a lot more light on events at that time, as only Lazarus could have related them. Some might even say he was the most important writer of all, because he was caught up in this whole concept and idea of messianic hope, salvation and delivery. In spite of the disintegration of his plans, and the mishaps he and his sisters created in their efforts to herald the messiah, he still believed until his dying day that it was all coming to pass very soon."

"Never did."

"No, he died, Jesus never returned, but his book on Revelation is still viewed with the same single mindedness that it was back then. He thought he had written something so very simple. Even said so right at the beginning. But the world changed, not to mention the early Church chroniclers and editors also tampered to a considerable extent his writing, not only the events but the people involved as well, and what was intended to be easy became increasingly difficult to understand. And the more languages it was translated into, the harder it became to unlock the message he had buried within it."

"So John is Lazarus?"

"Is that so hard to comprehend?" I inquired. "John, Lazarus beloved disciple, the one who followed in the distance, he was called a lot of things throughout the Gospels. Most loved by Jesus, most hated by all the rest. He hid in Ephesus as much from the rest of his fellow disciples as from the Romans that were trying to hunt him down. I think he probably feared the apostles most of all!"

"And you certain of this?"

"As certain as Caiaphas was."

"And you have proof?"

"Pearce, if there's anything you're going to come away with after today is done, it's the truth. Trust me, Caiaphas is just getting warmed up. He's stored a lot of things up here," I pointed to my head with my right index finger and then bounced my finger against my forehead a couple of times, "an awful lot of things. Things which only he knew and which will make you think twice about everything you thought you knew."

"I still think that this entire episode may have been blown way out of proportion by Caiaphas," Pearce insisted in his usual off the cuff manner that tries to reduce everything to insignificance.

"You'd think so by the amount of press it received in the Gospels, wouldn't you? But that's why you should have been suspicious, with your reporter senses, right away. It had everything going for it. Intrigue, mystery, deception. Why so little attention? Here's Jesus having to risk everything by going back into hostile territory where Pilate is just waiting for the opportunity to arrest him, and not only that, he gives his biggest performance of his life, raising a friend from the dead before an audience of hundreds and nobody but John mentions it in his Gospel. That's not forgetfulness by the others, that's deliberate avoidance."

"But like you said Doc, it's the biggest single performance of his life, why would they intentionally avoid it. I just don't get it."

"Because it was a charade!" I blasted back at him. "Don't you see, they knew. The people knew, the priesthood knew, the Romans knew, everyone knew. I mean, Judas had instructed Jesus perfectly, and no one could touch him or Lazarus for what they had done, but the reality is that everyone knew the truth. You don't write into your Gospel an event that everyone's going to recognize as a lie or else it taints everything else you had to write and you end up with none of it being believed. Matthew, Luke, and with some coercion, Mark, didn't want to have even a breath of scandal associated with their Gospels. But Lazarus on the other hand, he was still seeking vindication. He still wanted approval of what he had done. He wasn't prepared to just sweep it under the carpet. He was held in disdain by the other leaders of the Church movement. This was his one chance at striking back and obtaining what he believed to be his rightful place in the hierarchy. By insisting on the truth of the entire episode he hoped his sincerity would demonstrate that he was the most beloved disciple. The thirteenth disciple of whom the others shunned but of which even Paul acknowledged as the one that Jesus loved best."

Pearce rested his chin in the palms of his hands which were now supported by his elbows planted firmly on the inside of his thighs as he sat facing me. "So by putting it in, he just pissed off everyone even more. Why bother?"

"Remember the part where one of the disciples ask Jesus after they saw him following the crucifixion. He asked, what do you want us to do about him, referring to the beloved disciple that followed them from a distance. And Jesus said, if I want him to live forever, what is it to you? In other words, hands off and Jesus was still making it clear that he'd bestow gifts of love on Lazarus to the total disregard of the others. My, how they would have hated Lazarus even more because of that statement by Jesus. And as for living forever, it is something that it appeared Lazarus might actually do, as he lived well beyond the age of most other men of the time. So when he released his gospel, most of his protagonists were dead and buried. They couldn't silence him. They couldn't ridicule, or lash out, or do any of the things they had done in the past to render him silent. He was in total control now and his writings showed it. It was as if he had become unleashed and his brand of Messianic Judaism was allowed to unveil itself. Remember he was an individual totally immersed into the messianic beliefs, the war of the Holy Host, the end of days, Armageddon and when you read what he wrote, you recognize how much his beliefs impacted the Christians that followed by creating for the them a parallel world of demonic hosts that challenged both heaven and our world relentlessly. He gave us the number of the beast and for the last two millennia it has terrorised every minute of our waking dreams."

ROME: 39 AD

Blessed be the name of God, Elioneiai. Only He has the wisdom to have foreseen all that would transpire. I have not been open to such understanding. The words of Gamaliel ben Hillel weigh now heavy upon my heart. "Leave these Christians alone, and they'll disappear like Theudas and Judas of Galilee before him."

How could a man of such learning have been so wrong? Never could he have comprehended what we were up against. This fanatic, Saul of Tarsus is a curse upon all our heads. He is like a rabid dog, hunting down his prey with sanctimonious obsession. In so doing he brings dishonour upon us and misery upon all that fall beneath the pounding of his fuller's club.

And then there is Simon Peter who says one thing and lets everything take place under his supposed authority. James claims that their church is not open to Gentiles, and yet here in Rome I've heard it said that Simon Peter has passed word through one Barnabus that they are welcome. Who knows what to believe, since Mark, who is Peter's closest companion writes that his master has said that the exiles must be kept separate from the Gentiles in all of the cities they inhabit. They are all a bunch of cackling women, with little value to their words.

Many of these problems I lay at Agrippa's feet. No sooner had he returned to Jerusalem to take upon his shoulders the mantle of kingship, he changed the order of the high priesthood to the family of Boethus: the same family that held the office back in the days of Herod. The same family that Judas was from. Unlike us, the Boethians do not have the tolerance for the Christians as we have. They blame Simon Peter for the death of their kinsman. It mattered not that Judas had turned his back on them and was harvesting his own plan that would have excluded them from any power. He was blood and they demanded retribution for the shedding of his life.

It was not hard to find proof that members of the sect had committed capital crimes. The murder of Judas was but one event. The murder of Ananias and his wife was another. They say that Ananias refused to give up all his possessions to the sect, for which an overzealous adherent exacted a heavy penalty. But to condemn so many for the crimes of a few, I cannot abide. The Boethians have begun a campaign of assassination of which I hear that Saul of Tarsus, of whom I spoke in the past is now their most relentless and cruel bounty hunter. I doubt Agrippa will tolerate that for long. But the damage has been done. Through his error of judgement he has created a rift between us and this sect that has birthed from our loins. But at least Agrippa thought better than to assume the mantle of High Priest for himself.

I have heard that there is an intensive search for James Zebedee for beginning a campaign of reciprocal violence in Jerusalem. It is amazing the things one can still hear even when kept a prisoner so many thousand miles away. This Zebedee is a violent man, even back in the days of Yeshua he was a wild one. But I fear his arrest will only start a spiral of violence that Agrippa will come to regret.

And still I think all this is because I failed to see what was about to transpire. I who have always prided myself of having a gift of seeing the obvious. A window into the future. I saw nothing. And it all stems from that foolish staging of death by Lazarus. Soon after Yeshua removed his friend from the tomb, he felt secure enough in his own popularity to return to Jerusalem. He was protected by the words that Judas had placed in his mouth of being accused of heresy. Spring meant there would be an influx at the same time into the city. More people to listen to the Galilean prophet. From all over the world would come an audience to listen to his pearls of wisdom.

It was within my authority to stop him. I could have put an end to this madness at any time. I could have prevented him from entering the Temple. I even could have placed him under house arrest but I feared his detainment would anger those whom sought after him. Why did I not do so? Why, Elioneiai? I will forever ask myself that question. And to this day I still cannot answer it.

And each day a new tale of Yeshua's treason against Rome reached my ears. Once it was said that the armies in Jerusalem would lay the city to waste. He urged his followers to be prepared for that day. Was that treason? One thing I could see clearly in the future was the legions of Rome doing that very thing. Rome is like a polished glass— it reflects what most want to see, not what lies beneath. Perhaps it is not untrue that I wished Yeshua to stir such feelings amongst the people that I dared not do myself. But if I was hearing of such things, then I can assure you, so was Pilate.

Yeshua continued the pressure, trying to force Rome's hand. Every parable, every story placed himself even more at odds with our occupiers. It was like a hot and humid wind. I could sense the conflict brewing like a storm in the distance. It was a tax year again, the sixth year in the cycle, and it was in this context that Yeshua decided to sink a dagger into the Roman belly. The tax is a despicable thing and evidence of our haplessness. Pilate had always been guilty of taking from the Temple coffers to provide funding for his many projects and personal needs. To compensate for his gross misuse of Temple monies, Pilate placed a surcharge on the offerings to raise additional funds.

Donations are given freely by our people, even when such a levy is placed upon us. In the past we have always been able to compensate for Pilate's greed through our gifts. Pilate was not immune to what he heard Yeshua speak. He was smart enough not to try to make an arrest with so many pilgrims in the city, but he also knew he required irrefutable proof of Yeshua's guilt. So the procurator made good use of his network of Jewish spies. They questioned Yeshua, trying to trick him into slandering the rule of Rome and thereby condemning himself. The inquiries were bothersome, but Yeshua answered deftly.

He failed to do so, though on that last day when a spy asked him why the tax should be paid to Rome.

"Whose face is upon this coin?" Yeshua inquired of his questioner.

"The Emperor," came the reply.

"And whose face is upon the coins of the Temple treasury?"

"None," the man said correctly. "It is forbidden that money intended for God should bear any image."

"Therefore the money intended for the Temple belongs to God," Yeshua informed his listeners.

"But if a man wishes to exchange these coins, is it not reasonable that a percentage of the coins in the Temple pay towards this service?" his questioner responded.

"What is Caesar's, give unto Caesar. But that which is intended for God is God's alone, and no man has a right to it!"

Yeshua was adamant.

Perhaps he said such a thing through anger, or even frustration, because the Yeshua I knew was not a careless man. He had openly accused Pilate of theft from God. Pilate already wanted him arrested for his upsetting of the tables the year before, but now he had put into words exactly what he thought of Rome's right to govern over us. As Roman procurator, Pilate had killed for saying much less.

I immediately sent word to Judas that I wished to see him that night, in the gardens of Matthias, my grandfather. I remember that meeting well. It was an unusually warm day, and the humidity seemed to carry over into that evening. I felt like a beggar in the market, trying to strike a bargain agreeable to everyone. Judas was clear in his wants. He wished to see Yeshua unite the people into a force that would defy Rome and achieve our independence. He went on to explain how Rome was weakest during the Passover, outnumbered three million to five thousand.

"If Yeshua persists in antagonising the Romans," I said, "he'll be arrested long before he achieves any of your intended goals."

"Don't worry Caiaphas," Judas replied in his gravelly voice, "Yeshua will do as I instruct. He'll avoid arrest. We've come too far to lose it all for a careless comment."

"I have word that Pilate wishes to take him into custody. How long do you thank you can avoid Pilate?"

"Long enough. Tonight we return to Bethany. Tomorrow Bethsaida, perhaps even the Upper City. Pilate doesn't have enough men to search beneath every rock."

"Forget what you think, what if Pilate manages to arrest him?"

"You know the answer to that as well as I," he smirked. "We can't allow that to happen. By permitting Yeshua to speak within the Temple, you have made yourself appear to be an accomplice. You think Pilate will stop with only one execution? We're all marked men!"

"You want me to defy Pilate? Are you mad? I'd be a fool to place my neck beneath his sword for the sake of this treachery you plan. This Yeshua is of your making, Judas! Guide him wisely, or don't attempt to guide him at all. There have been deliverers before this and I survived them all. Yeshua may create a more lasting impressions with his style, but like those who preceded him, he'll be swallowed like the rest."

"It's up to you to ensure that he isn't," Judas warned me. "A revolt is inevitable— you know that! If we are to succeed, then we must have a leader who can unite all the various factions that inhabit our land."

"And you believe that Yeshua is such a man?"

"As long as he's advised properly."

"And you will be that advisor?" I questioned promptly.

"No, we will be. He'll need your support as well. Are you ready to do what you know in your heart is required? Will you let God's people suffer immeasurably when you have had the tool placed in your hands to end such an abomination?"

"You ask too much!"

"You will hear from me when I have need," and with those words he spun on his heels and ran from the garden.

It was then that I realized how far I had become involved in this matter without even realising the depth I had sunk to. The fact that I had summoned Judas to my own house made me realize I was a willing participant in his scenario. It was not an unreasonable plot after all. I even toyed with the concept of a revolt controlled by the priesthood. By combining the people's passion for freedom, Yeshua's charisma, and the sanctification of the priesthood, we would have been a force to be reckoned with. Perhaps there is some validity to Pilate's accusation against me. When I hear myself talk like this, even I believe I may have been somewhat treasonous.

After Judas had left, I hastily summoned a meeting with the elder priests, including your grandfather. We had a raucous debate, with those for and against vilifying each other. If you ever want to see total anarchy my son, put a group of priests in a room and give them something contentious to debate. It is both an amusing and frightening sight.

"Stop!" I yelled. "We are faced with the greatest gamble of our lives, and you scream like children. The stakes are frighteningly high. There are only two options here to discuss. Either we crush Yeshua and his followers for fear of being linked to them, or we support his revolt in order to control it! Let me make it perfectly clear. Without our support, Yeshua will surely die and with him goes any opportunity for freedom in our lifetimes. The choice is to be made in this room. Now! We can either organize this rabble and fight for our freedom, or we can sacrifice one man so that a nation can remain in bondage. What shall we do, gentlemen? What shall we do?"

It is no great secret, my son. Even if this letter should be intercepted, the Senate investigation has already declared that my return to Jerusalem poses a potential threat to stability. But, at least I have the satisfaction in knowing that Pilate has also lost his case. He has been found guilty of excessive cruelty and oppression. I believe he is being posted to the furthest reaches of Dalmatia. May he rot in whatever hellhole they send him to. I'm afraid the next time you see me Elioneiai I will be wearing a burial shroud. But know this, I have no regrets regarding my involvement in the events of the time.

Did I ever tell you that I had a vision of the coming battle? I saw it all. The burning of Jerusalem, the crushing of our armies, the enslavement of our woman and children. But it was a time beyond my years. And I thought to myself, if this is to be our future, then why not make it happen now. Why wait for such a terrible end that results for our not seizing our opportunity when it was being handed to us. Could it be any worse than I had envisioned? I do not think so.

So as you are already aware, there was a decision made amongst us to silently back Judas, but with one condition that needed to be fulfilled. If Yeshua was to fall into Roman hands prior to the revolt taking seed, then we would immediately separate ourselves from his movement and deny any involvement. Better that we try again another day than all perish in a single purge. So word was sent to Judas of our decision along with information that Pilate's patrols were closing in fast and therefore Yeshua should leave Jerusalem at once. This he did, and the rest I will tell you of in another letter, for the daylight has already passed, and my eyes grow weary under the strain of the oil lamp.

Please tell me of events back home; I so long to know of what transpires. It seems like a distant memory to me now and I fear I will never see the beauty of my homeland again.

CHAPTER NINETEEN

"You're a hard man to follow Doc. I mean no offence, and I don't doubt what you have to say, because I've come to realize that you see and hear things in your head that the rest of us couldn't even imagine, but this insistence that Caiaphas had an ability to foresee the future is not something I am prepared to readily accept."

"Why not John? We've already talked how thoughts in a dream state could possibly meet or exceed the speed of light. So if they're not going back in time, then at the least they're moving forward in time. If our thoughts can escape our own time and space reference, then there's going to be an opportunity to peer into the future. Why shouldn't Caiaphas have been one of these people? Perhaps that it the true nature of prophecy. Not vision necessarily sent to us by God but an innate ability to peer through a window that we can create ourselves."

"I'm not saying he should or he shouldn't," Pearce replied. "But if it is true then I believe it should have been well documented by now. Don't you think so, Doc?"

"I think it is. I believe there are certain individuals that we are all familiar with and they are able to do it or should I say did it very well.

Pearce nodded his head as if he knew what I was going to say next. I guess after so much time together he could be precognisant too.

"What is the difference between a Da Vinci and an H.G. Wells," I questioned. "One we label as the greatest scientist that may have ever lived, the other we call a great writer of fiction. Or a Thomas Edison compared to a Jules Verne. Where is the uniqueness of either individual if both could see a world beyond their own? Whereas one could only describe it the other could actually make it happen. There are those that would laugh at Nostradamus, while other recognize that what he saw in his bowl of water fits perfectly with a world that appeared long after he was put to rest. So I have no doubt that Caiaphas could see well beyond the confines of his physical world."

"Are you saying that because you know it can be done, Doc, or are you just speculating? Because if it's all just his memories talking here, then it's possible you're just remembering something he himself wanted to believe. Do you follow me?"

I stroked the stubble on my chin almost in praise of John's comment. "Quite astute," I commented in response to his postulation. "Can a memory be a false memory causing later generations to believe in an error? I would think most definitely possible. Do I believe this is such a case? Most definitely not!"

"But how can you be certain," he interjected.

"Because I've seen time slip and move in my own reality, and with my own eyes, and therefore I know it's possible," I railed.

Pearce was sitting on the edge of the sofa cushion once again, leaning half way out of his clothes in order to get this story. I'd almost swear he was salivating.

"Well go on!" he begged.

I didn't' think I'd ever bring up this even again. I considered it buried a long time ago. I know my wife was glad that we never had to deal with it again because it certainly was a bone of contention when it happened. Now I was preparing to rip it open like the proverbial Pandora's Box and risk having to deal with it all over again.

"Well," Pearce repeated impatiently, his pen tapping restlessly against his notepad.

"What the heck," I muttered under my breath. "You obviously didn't do your homework well enough," I taunted him, "otherwise you would have known all about this already. There's a book. Not a very well read book, but a book that was published back in the late eighties. It's called Extraordinary Experiences; the Paranormal in Canada. It was written by a Toronto fellow, Robert Colombo, and if you go to page two hundred and sixty, there's a certain chapter; a certain chapter all about me."

Pearce gnawed unconsciously on the back end of his pen. "So you're saying you had a paranormal experience."

"No, I'm saying I had an experience with time progression slipping, but everyone else was saying I had a paranormal experience."

"I don't get it, what's the difference?"

I had to collect my thoughts for the moment. It had been a long time since I walked down this path of events. "The difference is that people search for ghosts and supernatural hobgoblins to explain what they can't explain. I saw it completely different. No supernatural, no calling from the graves. I was merely a spectator to one of time's screw ups."

With a wave of his pen serving as a magic wand, Pearce signalled for me to go on.

"Let me recount it for you. It was January 9, 1987 and it was an awfully slow evening and I decided to close the office early. It was already dark as it usually is in a Canadian winter. You get up in the dark and go to work and you come home in the dark and go to bed. Pretty bleak when you think about it. Anyway, I'm driving up Woodbine Ave., and there isn't a lot of traffic, but that's okay. It's two lanes both directions, so I'm making good time and figure I'll be home in less than half an hour. Then it happened."

"What!" Pearce lurched and almost shouted.

"It didn't even strike me as unusual when it happened. It was as if it was midday again. Everything was bright and what snow had been on the ground was suddenly gone. But then even stranger, Woodbine was no longer two lanes each way. It was back to being a single lane both directions and the buildings and offices that lined the road were no longer there. It was open fields, as if everything had disappeared. Up ahead I could see a car pointed in the other direction just sitting on the side of the road. Now I knew I had been driving at eighty kilometres an hour but it felt as if I was driving through gelatine. Everything was so sluggish, as if I was barely moving at all. There was movement from the passenger side of the other car and this tall woman stepped out and proceeded to open the back door. All I can remember is thinking when I saw her was how strange she looked. Tall, at least six feet but dressed all in black, a really long dress from high necked collar all the way down to her ankles. And her hair, it was platinum blonde in this bee hive style, as if it was straight out of the fifties."

"And then what," Pearce inquired almost as eagerly as when he's reviewing the story line of the book.

"She goes to the back door of the car and pulls out a child. I'd say about six years old, with a prince Valiant hair style, down to the shoulders. The child's crying; I can hear the crying. I can't tell whether it was a boy or girl. Only wearing a light cotton blue jacket, but then I have to remember, there's no snow, it's warmer now. I'm watching as she drags the child from the car. I'm thinking to myself that kid must have to go to the washroom, so they're making a pit stop. Simple explanation. But then she starts pulling the child out on to the road. Crossing to the other side of the road, over to a field. When she get to the middle of the road she sees me coming and stops. It seems to me like an eternity to pass by her and all the time she's staring at me, not with surprise but with this look of contempt almost. Hard to explain. The child is crying and wailing and by this point I don't know what to think. Next thing I realize, I'm almost alongside their car. It's a pale lime green. Actually the colour of guacamole. And I see the name on the side in chrome letters, or at least part of it. It says Bel, and right away Belmonte or Bel Air springs to mind. There's a man in the driver's seat. Balding head, large partially hooked nose, moustache. I can tell that he's of Mediterranean origin. Again, he's looking at me with this unemotional mask but I can see it in his eyes. He's surprised to see me. He's wondering what I'm doing there. I'm more of a mystery to him than he is to me. That's what his eyes are telling me.

I'm about a hundred meters past them when I convince myself that something isn't right. The child's in trouble. I know it. I have this overwhelming feeling that if I don't do something right there and then, they're going to seriously harm the kid. So I pull over to the side and stop. I look into my rear view mirror to see what they're doing. But they're not there. I swing around in my seat to look through the back window and there's nothing. No people, no car, and then blink, it's dark again and Woodbine is back to what it should be with cars going up and down the road, and there I am, parked on the side."

"And that was it? That's all?"

"No, of course not! It doesn't end up in a book if that's all there was to it. I was pretty shaken. I didn't know what just happened, since it was straight out of the Twilight Zone, and I knew I wasn't hallucinating. I made it home but I've lost a good hour of time that I couldn't explain That entire night I tossed and turned. My mind was racing a mile a minute and I could not get the faces of those people out of my head.

The next day I was still jittery and so I decided to tell a couple of friends in the shop next door about my experience. Bev and Avril listen intently but they didn't know what to say or do. I mean, what do you say to someone that just tells you a story straight out of from the Outer Limits?"

"Were they still friends with you after you told them," Pearce tried to joke about the situation but I could tell that he was taking it quite seriously.

"When I suggested to them that I thought I may have witnessed a murder that was about to happen, they didn't think I was nuts at all. We all were in agreement to watch the newspapers over the next few days to see if there were any reports of a kidnapping or murder of a little boy. I have to admit though, I was relieved when there was nothing reported. Then I thought, perhaps it was a hallucination. Maybe I had fallen asleep at the wheel. I couldn't really say any more. But the images weren't going away and I certainly wasn't getting a good night's sleep."

"So, did you then do something about it, or did you just continue to wait?" Pearce interjected.

I waved him to sit back and relax and just wait till I finished talking. "Physically it was beginning to have its toll on me. I must have looked a wreck because Bev said I had to do something and she and Avril came up with a plan. We had a common police acquaintance that worked at 41st Division, Bob Adams. They called Bob and told him that I had to see him about, as they labelled it, an incident. That was an awfully strange meeting. Bob sat in my office and I laid out the details of everything I had witnessed. He didn't flinch, but that was good, because he also didn't get up and walk out the door. He knew I wasn't spinning him a yarn and he decided to hear me out. By then I had come to a realisation that what I was describing wasn't in my own time frame. Something weird had happened and I knew that I was somehow watching an event that occurred back in the fifties. I don't know how I knew, I just knew. And Bob must have thought the same thing."

"And did the cops find corroborating evidence for your story?" That's what I like about Pearce, he jumps right to the essentials.

"Not at first. Bob did me the favour of going up to York Regional, since the crime would have taken place in that division if my report had been accurate. He asked at the desk if anyone knew of a young boy being killed up by Woodbine Avenue and the old highway seven back in the fifties. But the entire system had been changed over to computers in the last few years and a lot of the old files were simply discarded in the changeover. They had nothing on record. Bob was about to leave when one of the desk sergeants that overheard the conversation piped up. "There's something about an unsolved murder back then," he recalled. "Harvey Carps was the detective on that one. When he retired he still regretted that was the only unsolved murder in his files. Had his suspicions but could never prove anything."

I could see Pearce writing furiously while I spoke. He still had his tape recorder handy but I noticed John always preferred to write everything down in pencil. Don't know why exactly, and I've never talked much about it with him. But watching that pencil fly across the page was reassuring.

"What did they do next?" he questioned.

"That's when things got exciting. The crew up at York Regional took it upon themselves to make it their mission to find out more. Harvey may have been retired but he was still alive and was more than happy to tell Bob what he could. "There was this young girl," he told Bob. "Judy Carter was her name. About six years old when she disappeared from her Sherbourne Street home on January 9th, 1955. She was found face down beside a creek at the juncture of Woodbine and Old Highway 7 two days later. Except it wasn't a highway back then. Just the sixteenth line. No motive, no ransom request, nothing. Still had on her blue cotton jacket when they found her."

It got even more interesting when Harvey mentioned that his prime suspects were the housekeeper and her husband. Greek couple, but no one could find the proof to pin it on them. So the case went cold and finally it was dropped."

"How could they just drop it? I mean it's obvious that the housekeeper did it!" Pearce shouted, a scowl furling his brow.

"And that's when the interrogation calls started," I continued. "First it was just to find out if I had any more information. Then it was to find out if I could account for my whereabouts at that time. That was easy to answer. I wasn't born yet. Then they wanted to know if my father had ever told me the story, or if I had seen old newspaper clippings. I didn't know my father, still don't, and I certainly hadn't read old newspapers. It took a while to convince them, but eventually their questions stopped. But what surprised me most is they never bothered to reopen the investigation. No point they said, too late. Practically everyone involved was dead now, so they didn't see the point."

"But they can't just let it drop," Pearce got all excited. "You knew what they looked like!"

"John, if there's one thing I've learned, you can't hang someone based on a vision. Just not going to happen!"

"The story got out to the public though."

"Yeah, that it did. John Robert Colombo was writing a book on paranormal events. He received my story and gave it a lot of early book release publicity. Not too many stories from the paranormal can be corroborated from police files and all the discussions they had with me are there as public record. So he was making certain that he'd get maximum mileage out of it."

"And then the crazies came out."

"Yes, it was a three ring circus. The media mentioned my name. They even went as far as stating that I was a veterinarian in the Toronto area. I'd have people lined up in my office that wanted séances performed. It was absolutely ridiculous. No it was actually worse than that, it was a nightmare. I remember when people from the television show Sightings phoned from Los Angeles, wanting to discuss doing an episode based on my experience. Finally my wife and I had enough. We told them sure, but it was going to cost them. I would have full editorial rights, they'd fly us all down to L.A. for the shooting, and they'd pay for the story as well. They didn't want any part of that and shortly after that sanity was restored and everything became quiet and serene once more."

"Only one problem; this isn't about seeing the future, Doc, more like the past. Where's the connection?"

"Only when you look at it from my perspective, John," I corrected him. "You have to remember there were others involved. What they saw was the future. They saw me."

"How do you explain then that they went ahead with the murder? You think they would have abandoned their plans having seen you appear like that! Should have scared the hell out of them!"

"You know, I've thought about that for a long time. I

thought hard about how they were looking at me. And I think I may have come to an appreciation of what was happening. You see, what I saw felt like an eternity. Everything sluggish and moving like molasses. But I don't think they were experiencing it the same way that I was. I suspect I may have been moving at a blur to them. Fleeting seconds, at the most. That would explain that look of annoyance mixed with astonishment that I thought I recognized on their faces. Like a gnat buzzing around you, irritatingly but you can't do anything about it. You think you have a glimpse of it, but before you can even swat at it, the gnat is gone. They may have just been able to visualise myself and the vehicle, and then I was gone. Who knows what they thought afterwards? An apparition? A ghost perhaps? I can't really say what they thought. But what I can deduce is that for the briefest of moments, they witnessed the future."

"And from this you suspect Caiaphas could see the future?"

"From this I know that seeing the future is possible. This didn't have anything to do with spectres or ghosts like everyone would like to believe. This was physics gone berserk. A fracture or slippage in time. Which means they can co-exist and only the thinnest of walls keeps them apart. I got to see through one of those walls. Some have the ability to do it at will. Caiaphas was one of those. People want to use the term seer. That's fine. That's exactly what they do.

ROME: 39 AD

"And this I will tell you Elioneiai that the house of Lazarus was to be the downfall of Yeshua. When he left Jerusalem, he immediately returned to Bethany thinking that the reputation of the Exilarch's house and its prominence would somehow protect him from the Romans. And it was also during that visit to Bethany that the seeds were planted for Yeshua to resist the strategy laid out by Judas. It was Judas's intention that they maintain a very low profile throughout the Passover festival. There were to be no claims of leadership, no gatherings of large crowds, not a single world about Roman governance. But in Judas's plan he calculated that they would not stop the people from hailing Yeshua as the messiah.

They would not encourage it, but neither would they deny it. By the time Passover would end, the people's beliefs would be reinforced and all would hail Yeshua as their leader. Several days later Pilate would return to Caesarea with his guard and all that remained behind would be the legion stationed at the Antonia fortress.

As you are well aware by now, my son, messiahs aren't born they are proclaimed. Hysteria spreads rapidly through ignorant masses. And once they are affected then it is only a matter of time until the other classes begin to adopt the cause. A few tales of supernatural strength and wisdom are all that is necessary to unite a desperate people against tyranny. Think of the combination. With the Gideon legend behind him, the Davidic heir to support him, and Judas' religious tutoring to anoint him, not to mention his own personal charisma to propel him, Yeshua was formidable. Managed properly, there should have been no way that Judas should have failed in his plan. But fail he did.

When Yeshua found out that Judas had spoken to me without his permission, he accused his friend of plotting against him. Then he berated Judas for falling victim to my lies, saying that he had been duped by the sweet talk of a senile old priest. No matter how Judas tried to assure him that it was the priesthood that would offer safety and protection for a modicum of cooperation on his part, the more Yeshua became convinced it was a trap. Even when Judas tried to use logic, and explain that every time they entered the Temple, I had the opportunity to arrest him but I never did, was evidence of my sincerity. But Miriam and her siblings had worked their spell upon him, and more than ever Yeshua was convinced that I did not lay a hand upon him because I feared him. That I feared the anger of the people that would rise up as a torrent against my authority if I dared to do so.

What a fool he had become. He had come to believe that those that came to hear him would actually lay down their lives for him. Even his most loyal of adherents were not willing to do so. But he did not understand that nor did he recognize that the great majority were actually indifferent towards him. Judas knew it. He also knew that I was the only source of power and authority in the city that was not Roman. And even though Judas craved such power for himself, he was conscious that without my support they had nothing.

I know that you fear my talking this way, my son. Your concern in your letter to me is admirable but it matters not if the Romans learn of my involvement in what transpired those years ago. It is already clear that they have sentenced me to exile from my native land. They are content to let me live out the rest of my life in this foreign city where they can watch my every move. And I am at an age where it does not trouble me any longer. I realize that I am not long for this earth bound existence. My time is coming to an end and I welcome it openly. So with what little time I have left I want you to fully understand what took place and why I fear the consequences so much.

Fortunately we did not rely on Judas alone to be our ally and work together towards some harmony between us. Yeshua's brother James also recognized that survival was tied to an agreement of cooperation. It is why he is left a free hand to preach his teachings in the Temple courtyards even now. For that is an arrangement between him and I that has been long standing. James is an honest man. Dedicated to his brother's cause but smart enough to appreciate his security is best protected within Judaism and not without.

So much of what I relate now is exactly as James ben Joseph related it to me. For although he and his brother had grown apart, still they were tied by blood and no matter how much they disagreed on some of the issues, James was still his brother. And Yeshua's encounter with Judas bore heavily on his mind and for that reason he sought James' advice on whether or not he was correct in what he had said, passing on the words of their conversation in its entirety.

"Are you saying we should subjugate ourselves to him? I'm not his servant, and I don't bow to his commands," Yeshua scolded Judas furiously. "To adhere to his principles would negate all that I have preached and taught. I will never support a corrupt priesthood!"

"Neither shall I," Judas tried to console him. "I do not accept Caiaphas as my master but that does not mean we should be so hasty as to overlook his offer. A truly great leader is flexible, knowing when to shake an open hand and when to slap it away. Caiaphas is a stepping stone to much greater things. Surely you can see it."

"You only seek the priesthood for yourself!"

"And you seek a throne!" Judas retaliated. "Do not play

innocent with me for I have been with you too long."

"Then let us be honest with each other. You and your kinsman have devised a plan where I am the stepping stone. You'll try to seize the priesthood, and Caiaphas will attempt to rid this land of an occupying force. What matters if I die in the process as long as each of you achieves your goals? What kind of a fool do you take me for?"

"A dead one if you do not appreciate the opportunity that has been laid before us. What will you do when the Romans finally find you? How lenient do you think Pilate will be? You will be no more than rotting flesh hanging from their wooden cross. And then all that you have strived for will be lost."

"Without me you are nothing, a twig blowing in a stiff breeze, never coming to rest, never setting roots upon the earth."

"And without me you cannot receive what you desire most. Caiaphas cannot anoint you and proclaim you as deliverer. And as you well know, that anointing must be performed by the highest of priests. As Samuel anointed Saul and David, so it must be. Only I can do that for you. And you have my word that it will be done. Have I not advised you wisely all these years? Have you suffered in any way from my advice? Together we can achieve the ultimate goal, but if we are imprisoned, then all is for naught. We can only be free of Pilate's clutches by placing ourselves willingly into Caiaphas's hands."

"I need time to think,"

"What is there to think about?"

"My decision weighs heavier than you could ever imagine," Yeshua responded. "By accepting this offer I must evaluate whether I am betraying myself and all that I have stood for. The life you and Caiaphas are offering may in truth be a living death. This is one time that you cannot advise me. Only the Almighty God can tell me what I should do."

Even though I met with Judas the following day, he never passed on any of this conversation to me. I have my suspicions as to why. I believe he saw something in Yeshua that day, something that frightened him. I think he saw something more than a mere man. One whom did walk a path that other men could not imagine. Whereas James felt compelled to tell me because he wanted me to recognize the righteousness that coursed through his brother, I think somehow that righteousness sent a shudder of fear through Judas. Here was a man that could not compromise, could not sell out his convictions. A man infused with the Holy Spirit. A man closer to God than any priest could be. A man in possession of a force that Judas could never tap in to. And I believe he was afraid.

It was shortly after that everything began to unravel. Events grew strange and bizarre and hopelessly out of control. I don't know whether Miriam had overheard the conversation between Yeshua and Judas or whether Yeshua merely confided in her, but she took it upon herself to summon many of Bethany's leaders to attend the feast of homitz at her home.

While Yeshua pleased the assembly with his parables, Lazarus and Miriam carried an old sealed vase filled with perfume oil into the room where they all sat.

"This is the oil of anointing, handed down since the time of Zerubbabel," Lazarus informed the crowd. "When there shall come a king to sit on the throne of Israel once again, it is the time of its unsealing. Now is that time!" No sooner had he finished his words, Miriam opened the vase and poured its contents over Yeshua's head. The room was thrown into a state of panic and horror.

"You are a fool," one elder yelled at Lazarus. "That alabaster jar of Zerubbabel represented our single hope for a Davidic heir to sit once again upon the throne of Israel. If you are so willing to waste its precious oil, better that you sold it to feed the poor rather than anoint the head of one's whose birth ensures that he cannot make use of it."

"He's brought death to us all," another shouted. "The Romans will hear of this. They will accuse us all of being accomplices of this insurrection!"

"What have you done?" the elder continued. "The monarchy is a rite of birth, not a reward of merit. Many kings were unworthy of ruling but they were still kings. You have disgraced this house, your family, this land. Oh, that we had never set foot in this house to bear witness to such a travesty!"

"We are doomed," they cried out in anger and fear. "We are dead men. Pilate will have all our heads for this." The guests fled to the exits, desiring to get as far away as possible from the house of Lazarus. Yeshua tried to bar the main doors. "Wait!" he pleaded, holding up his hands to stop their panicked exodus. "Listen to me.

What Miriam has done for me is a beautiful thing. Didn't Jacob purchase Esau's birthright for a pot of soup? So too, has Lazarus given up his birthright for the pursuit of freedom. Have you all become cowards? Can't you even imagine what it would be like to rule your own country again? Miriam shall be remembered forever for what she has done. And to say that it would have been better to feed the poor with the proceeds from this oil. What a foolish comment to make. There will be poor always. You want to feed them? Feed them with the food of liberty. Let them drink from the sweet succour of victory. Their stomachs will become full and they hearts will resonate with the trumpeting songs of freedom."

"No, you are wrong," Judas shouted. "The elders are right. They will sing songs of mourning at your funeral. This was neither the time nor the place to establish your dominion. Our fates are now sealed!"

"If that be the case, then Miriam has merely anointed my body for burial."

"Lazarus and your beloved Miriam have seen to that."

"If that be so, then my survival is in your hands, son of Simon Boethus," Yeshua taunted him. "Think while you still have me. Take action while you still need me. Your life will also be forfeit once I am gone."

"You want a plan," Judas screamed. "Then here's my plan. We must go tonight. Perhaps our fleeing from this town will save the lives of all that were here in this home.

"And where shall we go?" asked Simon.

"To Jerusalem," Judas exclaimed to the horror of all that were there. "You have a wish to die. Then let us march into Jerusalem and challenge death to its face. Because after what you have done tonight there is no place to hide, no sanctuary that will take us in. We are all doomed men. I will go ahead and make arrangements. I will let you know my intentions before I leave. You will all join up with me later." Judas pulled Yeshua aside, taking him into a secluded corner of the room where he spoke at some length to his profaned master.

Bad news travels fast. Scandal travels even faster. The story of Yeshua's aborted coronation reached Pilate, who had taken to residing in the Antonia fortress during the Passover. The procurator was elated by the message. This was the evidence he required to finally bring down his retribution upon my head. Judas may have thought it was possible to reverse the damage that was done but not even his gifted tongue could alter the course that they had already set upon.

Judas came directly to me thinking that somehow I could sweep all that had transpired away. It was early morning and I could hear the piercing shrieks from my household servants. Not as if I didn't have enough trouble sleeping without Judas upsetting my house.

I shouted down from the landing high above his head,. "Evil tidings could have waited until later in the morning."

Judas' hands trembled uncontrollably as he paced the room. Here was Judas at his lowest; a scared animal pacing within a cage of his own making. Stripped totally of his normally exuberant self-confidence he was like a spider caught within his own web. He stared at the tiled floor as he paced nervously. "They're fools! All of them! Ignorant, stupid imbeciles! They don't even have a clue as to what they've done. We must work quickly. If I can convince the authorities that everything was just a symbolic ritual being acted out for the Passover, we might have a chance."

"You're losing touch with reality Judas. That which has been done cannot be undone."

"I knew it! I knew it! That house of Lazarus is nothing but a thorn in my side. Their ineptitude has thwarted every plan."

"What bothers you most Judas, this horrendous act that Miriam and Lazarus performed or the fact that what is done cannot be undone."

"You heard!"

"Everyone has heard. Something like that is not going to be kept a secret. Anyway, the fact is that Yeshua accepted their anointing. He didn't try to deny it. It is over. Any thoughts of freedom and liberty we may have shared are now over."

"No! It is not over yet! It's necessary that we shield Yeshua from the Romans. If we allow him to be taken and executed during the Passover it could stir a riot that we won't be able to control. The Romans would retaliate. Pilate would slice through us like ripe melons. We'd die in the thousands. So we must ensure that we can conceal him for at least the week."

"You are as much a fool as them, son of Boethus. How are

we to shield a wanted criminal without jeopardising our own lives? It may be best to let Pilate have him. The death of one man could save Israel."

Judas shook a fist in my direction. "There is another way. You could arrest him for crimes within your authority! Yes, it would work. If you take him into custody, then he's answerable to you, not to Pilate. You could place him under house arrest until all of this settles. Place him in custody for as long as it takes for the events of today to be forgotten."

"You're out of your mind. It couldn't succeed. The Sanhedrin has been dismissed for the Passover, so it's impossible. You know it can't be convened during the holy days. I cannot place him into our custody."

"Yes, but it still doesn't stop you from detaining him. You could hold him over until the Sanhedrin reconvenes and that will be weeks. You can protect him. Pilate knows our laws. He knows he can't touch him if he's held under your personal authority."

"But still you forget, it only will work if Yeshua agrees to cooperate."

"What choice does he have," Judas protested. "I've instructed him to go to my grandfather's house. I have an ass waiting to carry him through the streets. As written in the scriptures, he'll be borne by an ass' colt, and he'll be humbled for all to see, and he is marred by the cruelty of the nations. Don't you see? His appearance won't be regal at all. He won't look threatening and Pilate will have difficulty mobilising against him without good cause. Once I have Yeshua's agreement will you send your guards to take him into custody?"

"And what if he disagrees," I suggested.

"Then I'll bid you farewell, because if he disagrees then I'll be marked as a dead man either by the Romans or those close to him."

"As will we all if we are caught in this web we are trying to weave. Remember this. If he doesn't agree, don't come back here. Don't try to see me. Don't even tell anyone that we have been speaking together. Do you understand?"

"God help us all," Judas warned as he went out from my foyer and left my house.

It was a faulty plan at best, Elioneiai. Firstly, it was based on numerous assumptions and secondly it involved matters and men who I considered well beyond rational thought. Success was about as elusive as a forest growing in the Idumean wilderness. Yet, it was the absolute absurdity of the plan that lent it some credibility. Success or failure was completely out of my hands. Somehow I had become as much a pawn in this very elaborate scheme as everyone else. I don't know how, I can't even tell you why.

CHAPTER TWENTY

"Incredible. I never understood that entire thing with the anointing. It never made any sense to me. It just didn't have any rhyme or reason to it. Why would Mary be pouring oil over his head? And if it was holy oil, where was she going to get it from? They never tell you. No one ever gives you an answer. All they ever say was that it showed how much she cared for him and it made all the other apostles jealous. And then Jesus tells them off saying that she gave him what he needed but that didn't' make any sense."

Pearce was rambling but it wasn't as if he was incoherent. Merely putting the pieces together for the first time in a very long time.

"And now?"

"Now it's like this veil has been lifted and I can see it." Pearce was thrilled by his latest revelation. I can really see it."

"I'm glad for you John," I congratulated him. "Although I'll warn you, you have to be prepared for the possibility that you may never look at the origins of your religion the same way again. Are you actually prepared for that?"

"Doc, in case you haven't realized it, my world hasn't been the same since we first got together. At this point, I don't think it's going to shock me. My time knowing you has taken me well beyond shock!"

"Good on you John."

I'm beginning to give Pearce more credit than I have in the past. It's not easy to deal with what he's been going through. It's like finding out what's in Area 51. The revelation may satisfy your need to know but the repercussions could be devastating. He's actually handling this quite well. Might even be prepared to hear the rest of what I have to tell him. At least I'm going to find out.

"I assume you will be staying with us for dinner," my wife suggested as she stuck her head through the doorway. Pearce and I had been so preoccupied with our discussion that I hadn't even heard my wife come down the stairs. How long she had been listening to our conversation I had no clue but obviously she knew our conversation was still a long way from being over.

Jarred from his meanderings, Pearce responded cheerfully. "If it's not too much trouble, I don't want to be any bother."

"Well it's too late for that," she commented "We're having silverside tonight." And with that, she was off to the kitchen to start dinner.

"Silverside?"

"Corned beef," I answered.

"Oh," Pearce responded. "Looks like she's not mad at you any longer."

"Don't bet on it. She's being nice because you're here right now. But don't forget she's also mad because you're here right now! I'm certain I'll hear about it later. In fact I'll probably get jabbed throughout the meal. Just behave yourself and whatever you do, don't piss her off. "

"Me?" Pearce popped his eyes in feigned surprise. "How could I possibly be offensive?"

"Oh, I don't know, John. Perhaps you just have a knack. Like sneaking around a house and staring in through the kitchen window. Couldn't you have phoned first like a normal person? I could have even picked you up at the airport, which would have given me the opportunity to have explained to her that you were flying in. But hey, this is not getting us anywhere. I'm just rehashing old news as far as today's gone. Anyway, where were we...oh yes...talking about changing beliefs."

"That's where I think you wrong," Pearce rapidly waved his left index finger in my direction.

"What, about the mess I'm in or that you caused all this by not phoning?"

"No, no, about what you were talking about. About providing a different perspective of events in Jesus' life. I see it as reaffirmation. You know, you go through your entire life just taking for granted that things are the way they are simply because you don't have an explanation. And in fact you have a hard time believing it and it just sort of gnaws at you over the years. But you go on believing because that's what you're supposed to do. I guess you never had that problem because you have the answers already. But for the rest of us, this is like a breath of fresh air. It actually strengthens my beliefs because I can fill in the blanks. And it's this wonderful blissfulness that fills you inside."

"You're right, I can't see it. Too close to the fire perhaps. It's been the reality I've always known, but in saying so, it's probably why I put my test of faith up against anyone else's. I may be a scientist but that doesn't diminish my religious beliefs in any way. Just gives me a different perspective from most."

"Well, keep it up and my perspective may end up the same as yours."

"Heaven help us if that proves the case. I think the world just might have its hands full dealing with one of me," I warned before leaning back into my chair to think about how much more I could relate of Caiaphas's story before my wife called us for dinner.

ROME: 40 AD

Well my son, I guess it is official now.

My fate was left to Agrippa to decide and the bastard spawn of thieving Bedouin that dared to call themselves monarchs has sealed my fate. Apparently he has informed the Senate that my return to Judaea might demoralise the people who are currently celebrating Rome's most gracious and magnanimous restoration of the legitimate monarchy to the land. Returning someone of my stature that was closely associated with the suffering and domination of a regime to which they had borne such resentment, would only serve to confuse them and undermine the gratitude they now express towards Rome.

As a result the Senate has sent me word that I will remain a permanent guest of their city until the day I die. That may not be too long now, for I fear my health is failing. If that be the case, then I will be home sooner than you think.

In the meantime there is a letter that I have received from James, Yeshua's brother which has pleased me greatly. He has assured me that in spite of some of the teachings of certain apostles to the Gentiles, he will not be prepared to relinquish the demand that all members of their sect be circumcised. This is good news because it reaffirms his commitment to not shed the Jewish heritage of his church. You must do everything possible to provide James with support. The number of these Christians grows steadily and unless they are properly guided I fear that they will fractionate our religion. And this time it will be far worse than when the Samaritans broke away from our Temple in Jerusalem.

He will especially need your support when defending his position for rejecting Simon the Samaritan from the acknowledged group of disciples. You are aware that there are those that will try to do harm to James because of the dishonour he has brought to the one called Magus. There are those that say this Simon inherited the spirit of Yeshua upon his death and that his powers were even greater than those of his master. And remember, it was Yeshua that said, "He that follows shall be greater than me! All that he does shall be done in my name. He is your counsellor who'll bear witness to the power of the Almighty God." But James was right in casting that charlatan from his midst. He represented a danger far greater than he could even imagine.

There are those that said the Magus is kin to Yeshua through his mother's family. It matters not. Relationships are no guarantee of integrity and that is something I can attest Simon Magus had a total lack of. The feats he could perform were not done with any holy power. There was a black aura that pervaded each act but regardless of that, he had become well known, this man from Gitta. In the name of the Power, he performed his miracles but these were acts that God would definitely not sanction. James sent Philip to subdue the matter, and when he entered Samaria he declared in the name of their congregation that Simon Magus was not authorised to speak in their name. But Philip's declaration represented absolutely no threat to Simon as the people still flocked to see the Magus.

The matter soon escalated out of control. When Philip recognized that the people were not listening to him, he sent word to Simon Peter and John Zebedee to come quick and help him restore the path of their beliefs. But all the two did when they arrived was publicly banish the Magus from their sect, proclaiming that his power only served his procurement of personal glory.

But the Magus, he was smarter than most of the other apostles, gifted in magical arts and well-schooled, and he protested loudly to his excommunication, declaring that his power came from a much higher authority than either of these two glorified disciples. He immediately denounced Simon Peter for crimes against Yeshua, explaining to the assembled crowd how Yeshua died because of Simon Peter's denial of him. "If not for you Simon Peter, the Lord's servant would be here with us today. It was you who put personal safety and greed above all else. By what authority do you covet this prize of laying on hands which I possess, so that the Holy Spirit may enter? The true path can be found without you and your heinous band of apostles. All things come from the Power. That's the word of Yeshua and that's the word of myself. You aren't my master. You will never be my master. Only the Power, the Almighty deserves worship. You say that I should not have this power of laying on hands. But who are you to question that which God has given me?"

The assembly grew steadily more hostile towards John and Simon Peter. "You have no share in our work," Peter scolded. "Your heart is evil in the sight of God. You envy our authority and covet our practices. Repent and pray to be forgiven for your evil ways."

"I don't envy you," Simon Magus laughed. "In fact I pity you. You bought your authority with Yeshua's blood. Only through his death have you had the courage to claim authority that you never deserved. I don't need you to be blessed by God's gift. The Power has already blessed me with many gifts greater than yours. Remember what Yeshua said to you. 'Ha lachma anyah oichlu, ha eyin savil lishtu.' Are those words still familiar to you, Peter? They should be. Wasn't I there when he said them to you? The bread of affliction, the blood of suffering. That was the bread that was his body, the wine that was his blood. It was his body you afflicted, and his blood that you spilled. He accused you that night. Can you deny his words? If you hate me it is because I know your secret and for that reason you also fear me."

Philip, John and Peter had to flee from Samaria like whipped dogs. The fame and honour of the Magus grew even greater following that encounter. But what most don't realize was that James was correct in his assumption that Simon of Gitta only desired to serve his own cause. Excommunication was the only recourse with such a person, but this is because back in Judaea, Samaria and Galilee, you have no knowledge of what the Magus has been doing.

He is here now. Yes, here in Rome. And he is here with his own group of disciples that he has personally ordained. And the Magus speaks of one that is greater to come as well, just like Yeshua did. But in this case he knows of whom he refers. It is to Meander, his chief disciple, gifted in wisdom and certain powers that are way beyond any earthly explanation.

And the Magus is busily sending out his disciples to all the Gentile nations. And he has clearly condemned celibacy which is common amongst Yeshua's followers. By calling it unnatural and against God's teachings, he has issued a clear challenge to the Jerusalem church.

As a further emphasis, Simon has taken a wife named Helena. She's young, she's beautiful, and one thing more, she's a harlot. Like the prophet Hosea, he took to his marriage bed a prostitute. He is making a point that in his teachings, all can be forgiven, just as God forgives Israel for its sins. Dramatic, I admit, but also very effective. He is gaining quite a following here in Rome.

He's performing miracles here just like Yeshua did. Healing the sick, making the lame walk again. Although I am not allowed to travel outside of Rome, I have heard that entire villages and towns will empty in order to see him. They bring their infirmed, their aged, even their animals to receive his blessing. And the more he grows in popularity, the more he comes to believe in his own divinity.

I fear this man. I fear what he may do with this unnatural power of his. If his popularity continues to grow, there is no telling what he will do to those of us he considers his enemies. He performs some trick of flight. I know not how it's done, but it is clearly not a gift from God. That can only mean he has somehow channelled power from the darkness and that means he is a threat to all of us. He must be stopped and we must support all those that are willing to aid us in this cause.

You may be thinking that this is all merely the ramblings of an old man in exile that has lost touch with reality. You should know me better than that Elioneiai. I would not belabour this point unless I believed it to be far more significant than most could ever imagine. There is a storm brewing and it threatens to blow all of us into the sea of oblivion. We have utterly failed in our mission to enlighten the world to the worship of the one true God. Instead we have turned inwardly and not shared that which was given to us on Sinai with anyone else. And now that the rest of the world craves a sign from a living God, having lost faith in their own archaic beliefs of idolatry, where are we? Where are we, the children of Israel, God's anointed? Nowhere! But the various distortions, abominations and aberrant sects of our treasured beliefs, they in turn are everywhere to be found.

They are what the world is coming to believe is Judaism. They are the claimants to our most treasured beliefs and they will be our doom. For I have seen it in my dreams, my waking visions, and that which haunts my nightmares. I have seen our own downfall, our fall from glory from the face of the Lord. Others will take our beliefs, steal our heritage, live in our homes and it will all be because we let it happen. In truth, we have become our greatest enemies. Not the Romans, but ourselves. And we don't even realize it, which is how blind we have become to our own pending doom.

I have seen it here in Rome. It is like an insidious disease. It creeps slowly, consuming us from the insides. We have grown fat and lazy, desiring the life that those that rule us have provided. Already the young Jews here have abandoned their traditions, cutting their hair in the manner of these people, wearing their clothes, adopting their names. Do not let it happen in our own house. See to it that your brother Joshua does not stray from the path. He still has not written to me and I worry about him.

Guard the faith, my son.

CHAPTER TWENTY-ONE

"I'm curious. So what's your take on this?" Pearce asked while we sat patiently at the dinner table while we waited for the main course to be served following the salad.

"I'm not certain I understand your question," I responded. "If you're referring to the salad, I'm actually quite surprised." I quieted down to a barely audible whisper. "In the mood Marg was in, I thought we'd be lucky to get anything more than a corned beef sandwich and even that I thought we'd half to make ourselves."

"No, not that! I meant what Caiaphas had to say. You know, that you blew your chance to convert the world to Judaism/"

"Oh, that. I think it's all a matter of history now. I don't know if you recall as a child saying the little ditty that went, roses are red, violets are Jewish, if it wasn't for Jesus we'd all be Jewish."

"Yeah, I remember that. I hadn't heard that in such a long time. It was good for a laugh back then."

"The truth of the matter is, that if it was up to Jesus, we all would have been Jewish. The actual saying should have been if it wasn't for Paul, we'd all be Jewish. Left to Jesus, James and Peter, all Christianity would have been was another Jewish sect. But it would have been the biggest of the sects."

"But Caiaphas didn't see it that way."

"Caiaphas saw anything that wasn't Sadducee as not being Jewish. So even the Pharisees were an aberration as far as he was concerned."

"So, back to my question. What do you think?"

"I'm a Zadokite, John. And that means Karaite as far as my beliefs go. Anan ben David, my spiritual leader thirteen hundred years ago recognized that there wasn't any real difference between the major religions. That's way he told us all to read the book and if what we read seemed good to us then it was right. He was referring to the Old Testament, and he knew that no two people would read it and interpret it exactly the same. But it didn't matter as far as he was concerned. The intent would be the same no matter how you interpreted it.

But Caiaphas didn't understand that. All he could see was that for twelve hundred years we as a people failed in fulfilling our mission as dictated by God. 'Or Haoylum.' It's in so many of our prayers and yet it's meaningless."

"What's it mean?"

"Light unto the world. Can you believe that? God actually called us that and we've done our utmost to be anything but."

"I don't get it. Why didn't you go out and convert everyone if that was your mission? It doesn't make a lot of sense to resist a commandment of God when you guys were the only game in town at the time."

"That's where men can screw up even God's work. And in particular, one man, Isaiah. He's like the Tolkien of his time. Writes about the suffering servant, and that changes the entire complexion of the nation. It becomes an ageless literary masterpiece; sort of a chronicle of failure. In order to spread the religion, we have to suffer in the name of God. The entire world has to turn against us, scourge us, torture us, and then when they realize they can't break us, that's when they decide to join us because they finally see the light."

"I never looked at it in that way."

"Who would? It was the most insane concept that anyone could ever dream up. For the next two and a half millennia, as a people, we get beaten, enslaved, scattered to the four winds, despised, persecuted, locked behind ghetto walls, and finally almost totally exterminated. Now you tell me, how many people are going to say to themselves, wow, there's a people I'd like to be part of. They have something really going for themselves. I think I'll be one too."

"I guess not too many."

"I guess not! How about none? I'd be wanting to check to see if they have any active brainwaves if they truly wanted to join the Judaic club. We're not exactly the hottest show in town."

"But that's not the way it is. Not really?"

"Are you trying to tell me what being Jewish is all about John? You should have paid more attention to what was written in Blood Royale. Even there the plot line was delivering the same message. If there ever was an example of the suffering servant concept, that was it. So you see John, it's not a matter of whether or not I believe Caiaphas was right in his evaluation of the situation. He saw the future and in it we had been replaced as the people of the book. And for all intent and purpose that is exactly what happened. Whether we could have become the most prominent monotheistic religion of this age that I consider unlikely. We weren't willing to compromise God's commandments, and we certainly couldn't spread it by the sword, so minus those two options, we never would have achieved that position of prominence."

Pearce had just picked up on my double entendre hidden in my last comment and nodded silently. I guess he agreed with me, understanding how others succeeded by doing what we never dared. Or maybe it was Caiaphas that he was agreeing with. That's the problem with GLEEM. I consider it to be my take on the situation but there is that possibility that it was really his.

"I guess that's why mainstream Judaism is still very non-proselytising, accept for the Jews for Jesus bunch, that is." Pearce was trying to rationalise three thousand years of indifference as perceived by the outside world, and failing miserably in his attempt to find even one chink in this impenetrable armour that we surrounded ourselves within.

"Jews for Jesus? Complete misunderstanding of the entire nature of Jesus. If anything, he would have been the first to proclaim he represented the 'Jesus for Judaism movement.' What he wanted to establish was a softer, kinder, more accepting Jewish religion, within the rigorous dictates of the Torah and laws. Nothing separate, nothing beyond the scope of monotheism. That's where he failed. Not so much because of his efforts, but the lack of understanding from his own disciples, and certainly the efforts of Paul to shanghai the entire Christian community to a philosophy of his making."

Pearce looked penetratingly, directly into my eyes to make his next point. "You want to blame Paul for most of what happened, don't you?"

"It wouldn't be without good reason. Caiaphas didn't know him, other than as a tent maker that had a voracious appetite to hunt down Christians as if they were an insidious nest of vipers plotting to poison the world. And in that guise he not only despised him but feared him as well. All fanatics are something to be afraid of. And

Saul was about as fanatical as they could get.

Other ancestors of mine had to encounter and deal with him in his other persona. That of Paul. Just as fanatical, but even more dangerous than before. In this new guise he would tolerate no obstacle to impede him from his goal. Either outside of his circle or within. But we'll get into that another time, another story."

"You can't allude to a character flaw of that magnitude and then just switch to an entirely different topic."

"Sure I can."

"You mention something like that and the readership is going to demand an explanation," Pearce warned me.

"But Caiaphas didn't mention it. I did. All Caiaphas will talk about is the bounty hunter known as Saul. Fortunately for himself, he was dead by the time Paul manifested himself."

"And that's it? You're not going to say anything else?"

"You want to give the readership a clue? Then tell them this; Fuller's Club. And then they'll just have to wait until I talk about it in another story."

ROME: 40 AD

"I have never talked about this Elioneiai to anyone else. I have carried it inside of me all of these years but I remember it as if it all happened yesterday. It was that ill-fated night of the thirteenth of Nisan, in the twenty-second year of the Emperor Tiberius. Judas had arranged that they would all assemble in the house of his grandfather, he whom we referred to as the leper priest, cast out from our temple in which Herod had placed him above all of us. The Leper Priest, Simon Boethus, I spit upon his accursed name.

In the mansion of the Boethians, the meal had been prepared and laid out on the large marble table that filled the hall. Yeshua, his apostles and all of his favourites sat in reclining positions. Judas at that time did not know whether Yeshua had accepted his proposal or not. It's true that neither acceptance nor refusal would have made any difference by that time, but not even Judas was aware of that at the time. We never even conceived of the debacle that was to come. At the beginning of the seder meal, Yeshua removed his outer garment and tied a cloth about his waist.

I know what you're thinking Elioneiai. You're wondering, how the evening of the thirteenth day of Nisan could be the seder night, for everyone knows that it is the fourteenth. Rest assured I have not erred and neither have I lost my senses. What I will now speak of has obviously eluded all who try to explain the apparent contradiction. In our faith, Elioneiai, the Sabbath day is from sunset to sunset. This permits us to conduct our seder even on the Sabbath eve, because all preparations have been made long before dusk sets in. In this manner we aren't in violation of the Sabbath law that forbids the performance of any work. As for our misguided brethren, the Samaritans, they believe the Sabbath day is from the noon of the sixth day until noon of the seventh. As you can see, such a belief doesn't allow them any time to prepare the meal or conduct the ritual slaughter of the sheep which must occur between the third and sixth hours after noon has fallen. To accommodate for this problem, the Samaritans have a law that when the eve of the fourteenth of Nisan falls on the Sabbath day, then they must conduct their seder on the thirteenth, so as not to defile the Holy Sabbath.

I know that you would not be familiar with this law of the Samaritans. Few of us can be bothered to read their laws and study their books. I have made it a cause of mine to understand the half-breeds and their regulations so that we can refute their lies when necessary. Know your enemies, Elioneiai that is important.

That was why Yeshua conducted the seder a day earlier. In that year, the fourteenth of Nisan fell on the Sabbath. True to Samaritan custom, he obeyed its laws and performed the rituals on the thirteenth. I am not saying that Yeshua was a Samaritan. I've already alluded to the fact that his mother's family may have been of that persuasion, but in Yeshua's case, it was because he accepted the noon to noon restrictions of the Sabbath day. Now that I've explained this confusing matter, I will return to the original topic— what transpired after Yeshua tied the loincloth around his waist.

He poured water into a wash basin, then begged his disciples to come to him so that he could wash their feet. It was Simon Peter that stood up and came over to him first.

"If you are our master," Simon Peter asked, "why do you wish to wash my feet? Servants kneel and beggars kneel. Which is it that you are."

"Once more you don't understand what it is I'm about to do," Yeshua replied to him. "How long will it be until you understand?"

"You cannot wash my feet! You are my master. For you to do so, it would negate our relationship."

"If I don't' wash your feet," Yeshua began angrily, "then you will not be my disciple any longer. Can you understand that?"

"Then wash all of me if you wish to play servant," Simon Peter quipped in the dry humour for which Galileans are renown.

"I give not a bath but a lesson. Listen everyone! You call me teacher and master and it's right that you do so. I'm a teacher and I wash your feet like a servant. Learn this lesson well and follow its example. Even masters are servants to greater masters. Every messenger is subservient to the one whom has dispatched him. There are those that rule and those that are meant to be ruled. There's a time to give orders and a time to obey them. It has come time that we obey them for our own good. I've set an example for you to follow. In order that we preserve our mission we must allow others to dictate our immediate future. For that reason, I am allowing myself to be betrayed into the hands of my enemies."

"Who will betray you Lord?" Lazarus asked.

"Isn't that clear to you? This is the unleavened bread of our forefathers, who ran before the chariots of Pharaoh and had not time to let the bread rise. I dip it into the bitter herbs that are the sorrowful memories of our slavery and into the horozet sauce that is the mortar for the bricks of our bondage. Take this from me Judas and eat, for once more we must descend into the depths of despair, only to be redeemed at a later time. Hurry and do what you must Judas, for the time is growing late."

Judas left the table and ran into the night, bringing his message to me.

"I'll stop him Master," Simon Peter exclaimed, "before he can carry out this evil deed."

"Leave him!" Yeshua shouted. "Do you think he carries out his task willingly? Circumstances have made this necessary. It must be done. You can't go where I am going. Instead, you must remain free and spread my word while I am gone. Most of all, you must follow my last commandment to you — love one another. Love each other as you love yourselves. Cease your constant bickering. Judas must be given your love and forgiveness so all will know that you are my disciples and that you believe in me. Now sit and eat this last time with me. This unleavened bread is my body, this wine is the blood of my suffering. Don't consume me with petty jealousies, or all will be lost. Either my freedom will be sacrificed, or my life. I am prepared for either eventuality, but either case my true essence won't survive if you consume me with hatred."

That is what he meant when he spoke with Simon Peter. When you consider his words, you'll see how truly phenomenal was his insight into his disciples' thinking. He understood them better than they understood themselves.

"When they come for you Lord, I'll go wherever they take you."

"No! You shall not come when they take me. You'll follow later."

"Why can't I go with you immediately?" Simon Peter asked. "I'm ready to die for you."

"Are you truly ready to die for me?"

"Yes, Master!"

"My greatest trepidation is that you'll deny my existence. Three times you will be asked to acknowledge and testify on my behalf before dawn. Judas has arranged that I be taken into the custody of our own courts; I will be dependent on your testimony. I pray for you Simon Peter that your faith won't falter when I need it most"

"I'm ready to die for you Yeshua, I won't fail you."

The sons of Zebedee insisted they be chosen to testify for him, for they too doubted Simon Peter's sincerity. "No, it must be Simon," Yeshua insisted. "One is already chosen to speak for me, because there is no doubt about his heritage. Only he can fill the second void because his is recognisable as a Galilean and privileged to speak on my behalf. Too much time would be wasted identifying you as Galileans and we have no luxury of time. Simon has been with me from the beginning and is a reliable source of information about my deeds."

"What if your enemies haven't been sincere and decide to execute you without trial?" Simon Peter asked.

"I'm well aware of that possibility. Whosoever has a bag, let him bring it with him so we're prepared to flee into the wilderness. All shall carry a sword in case we must fight. We must be prepared."

Following the seder, Yeshua and his disciples went to the part of the estate known as Gat Simoni, the garden of Simon's wine press. Yeshua prayed for deliverance while his disciples stood guard, awaiting his captors. It was to be a long wait. Judas and I had much to discuss and coordinate if we were to be successful. Much wine was drunk at the seder and periodically one of the disciples lapsed into sleep, only to be roused by Yeshua and condemned for his lack of stamina.

It was impossible for me to have convened the Sanhedrin that night because our laws prohibit it, not to mention the Roman curfew that made a night time assembly impossible. It seemed Judas thought I'd have all the details taken care of by the time he arrived but that wasn't possible. In fact, I thought it was he that would inform me his plan was already arranged. He reprimanded me for slothfulness.

"Why haven't you put the legal structure into motion?"

"There can be no court held at this hour. Are you not Judas Iscariot? As scribe you know this thing cannot be done."

"And you are High Priest Caiaphas. You can make things happen for you are the law."

"Don't overstep your bounds and think that you can condemn me when it is your survival that hangs in the balance."

"Without a tribunal, how will our plan succeed? Our only recourse is to seek the protection of imprisonment and plead guilty to a lesser crime."

"I am well aware of this kinsman. There will be a trial. It just won't be tonight. For the time being, Yeshua will be arrested and imprisoned within the walls of my house. He'll remain there until the Passover ends and then we will weigh judgment to see if a trial before the Sanhedrin will be necessary. After the Passover, Pilate will retire to his palace in Caesarea and that will make Yeshua's release all the easier."

"It's too risky."

"Nothing is without risk. The key to any endeavour is minimising the risk."

"I don't know. Your plan still worries me Caiaphas. Acting alone doesn't empower you with the same authority as jurisdiction through the council. It's a vulnerable position and to be perfectly frank, not one which I had expected. It endangers not only Yeshua, but our entire mission."

"Don't fear for my ability to do what is required. Deliver Yeshua to me and with the proper testimony in evidence, I can shield him from Pilate."

"Are you certain?" Judas demanded to know.

"Yes! Once under my personal charge, Pilate wouldn't dare challenge me for fear that I'd lodge another complaint to the Legate for his constant usurping of my authority and interference with our internal legal structure. Already the Legate is looking for an excuse to send Pilate back to Rome."

"How can you be so certain? Pilate is a tyrant. He cares little for our legal system."

"On this you can be assured. I have information on this issue from some very important sources. One more serious complaint and Pilate will be standing before the Emperor Tiberius."

"But does Pilate know that?" Judas inquired.

"If I know it, then rest assured, he knows it."

My response was quite reassuring, but honestly Elioneiai, I didn't know if Pilate knew or not. He was a man that always underestimated his adversaries and never took threats against his person seriously. Pilate could be standing on the edge of a precipice holding a boulder weighing five stone and he wouldn't think his position as being precarious.

"My guards await you in the portico, Judas," I instructed him. "They will not draw any weapon unless they are provoked. See to it that they are not provoked. No harm is to come to anyone. Understood?"

Judas nodded in agreement.

"And does Yeshua understand that?"

"I am certain that he can control the other disciples. I do not give the rest much credit but one thing I do admire in them is their reverence for Yeshua."

"Then make certain nothing goes wrong, son of Boethus. Your family's resurrection of honour depends on it. Treat this entire episode with calm and civility and nothing should go awry. Make certain those Galileans that are with him understand that what Yeshua is about to do, he does so willingly. Any evidence of an armed confrontation taking place would immediately alert the

Romans. It would be under their jurisdiction at that point. And they will respond in true Roman fashion, of that I can assure you."

"I'll see to my responsibilities Caiaphas. Just make certain that your end is not wanting," Judas challenged me in return.

"Quick, go and perform your mission. The hour grows late."

Taking my honour guard in tow, Judas returned to his family estate. And the rest, as they say, my son, is history. Nothing went according to plan. Nothing was as it was meant to be. Those damned Galileans. A curse upon them. Ignorant savages that we should have disowned as part of our nation a long time ago.

As soon as Judas returned, the plan unravelled.

"Who is it you've come to see?" Yeshua asked when he saw them arrive in the garden.

"We seek the one known as Yehsua the Nazarene," my captain, Malachi replied to his question.

"I am he, let us be gone," Yeshua responded. And that should have been the end of it. But that damn fool Lazarus, who cannot bare not to meddle in affairs that are of no concern of his threw himself in front of Yeshua, barring Malachi from approaching.

"Move from our path Lazarus and let be done what is meant to be done," Judas demanded.

"You only seek me," Yeshua intoned, "is that not so, Judas."

Judas kissed Yeshua's cheek reassuring him of his intention. "If this prince of idiots does not cease his meddling ways, we'll be forced to take him into custody as well."

"Don't betray me with any kiss, Judas. The plan was for me alone to withdraw into your custody. Lazarus is to be left alone!"

And before Judas could even utter his consent, Simon Peter drew his sword and started to scream out, "It's a trick! It's a trick!" Without a moment to even think about what he was doing, the brutish, ignorant peasant launched himself towards my guards like a wild beast, knocking Malachi down. And with every intent to murder the captain of the Temple Guard, can you imagine that, after all that I had said and done, he was going to add political murder to his repertoire of crimes, Simon Peter swung his sword down with determined force. Fortunately, Malachi was able to roll quickly to his side, but not before his ear was cut through. I must give credit to my captain. Another man would have responded in rage and fury. With the complement of my guard behind him, he easily could have ordered the slaughter of them all in an act of revenge, but he did not, good soldier that he is.

With quiet resolve, he overlooked the blood that streamed from his wound and calmly gave Yeshua an order. "Have your men withdraw! If they pursue this folly, I will no other choice but to give the order for my men to defend themselves.'

"Put away your swords," Yeshua commanded. "If they had wished to come against us with weapons, they would have done so long before now. Wasn't I free to walk in the Temple without a sole to stop me?"

"I need Lazarus to come with us," Judas suggested. "He'll be able to explain how he erroneously interfered, and only when Simon mistakenly saw a prince of the royal blood threatened did he move to action. It will be accepted by all as an error of judgement, easily conceived by any one of us. Is that not correct, Malachi?"

"It could be misconstrued as such," my Captain agreed.

"Lazarus, where are you? Come out!" Judas shouted for the descendant of David. In the confusion of Simon Peter's attack, Lazarus had fled from the garden, leaving his white tunic behind, entangled in a thicket. If it wasn't so serious at the time, it would have been very funny. Could you not see it, Elioneiai, the heir to the throne running naked through the streets, terrified by his own ineptness, screaming that he is being pursued by the Temple guards? Except that if anyone looked, they wouldn't see a soldier anywhere within the vicinity. They would have considered him a raving lunatic.

In desperate resolution, what could Yeshua do but turn to Judas and say, "Do not fret for the others, I will manage without them. Only I am meant to drink from the cup of suffering."

No sooner had Yeshua been taken into custody, then all the other disciples fled as well, more concerned about their own safety than that of their masters. All that stood by him were Judas, who had set the entire affair into motion, and Simon Peter, whom Yeshua bade to swear on his behalf.

It was not long until they arrived at my courtyard, but Simon Peter refused to enter along with Judas, choosing instead to remain in the shadows of the stone gates. When I questioned Judas as to where the Galilean fisherman was, he advised me that he refused to enter. I had not anticipated his refusal to cooperate. Everything

thing hinged on Simon Peter's testimony. Without it, it would be impossible to declare Yeshua free of any political wrong doing. I begged Judas to go out and persuade the lout to come into my house, but Simon refused. It was then that I knew that our fates were sealed in failure. I recall turning to Yeshua, and whispering in a faltering voice, "We have failed."

CHAPTER TWENTY-TWO

"Works for me," my wife commented as she spread the food out on the table.

"Could you clarify that for me," Pearce responded to her unprecedented intrusion into our day long discussions.

"I don't often agree with my husband but this is one time when I think he's correct about events that were happening back then."

"You mean you agree with the memories being manifested from his ancestors, don't you?"

"Whatever," my wife shot back in her usual callous manner of rebutting anything that might have to do with GLEEM and the repercussions of the theory as it impacts on our lives.

"So, if I catch your drift, then you don't exactly agree with your husband's interpretation of how all these stories seem to be generated inside his head."

"I don't mean to alarm you here John, and I certainly can't object to the financial rewards that Allen's stories provide for this family, but let me make you understand, if I was married to Stephen King, it wouldn't meant that I believed we owned a car that was trying to run us down, or one of our dead pets kept visiting us from the grave."

"But his stories, they check out. Some of these events he talks about, no one else knew about and then a few years ago, they dug up evidence to support him. You can't say that was a coincidence."

"I can't tell you how my husband knows the things he does, I haven't really tried to figure it out. But he's a smart man and I'm certain he has his means in doing what he does. I just never bought into this mumbo jumbo theory that everyone wants to jump on board with. Sure, his family's real old, and I have never questioned that for a second, but that doesn't make him this great repository of ancient knowledge. Hell, half the time he can't remember a short grocery list when I send him to the store."

"Don't you just love her John," I interjected. "So supportive and reassuring. A real confidence builder," I joked.

"Hey, you're already in my bad books today buddy. Do you want to try and spread it over two days?" she threatened.

"But you have to agree that what he tells us in these books is sometimes spot on," Pearce tried to rein her in.

"So, he's a good guesser."

"Right, there's your scientific evidence, John. Guess-work! How ingenious," I rebutted. "Just like Ben Franklin's wife said to him after his discovery of electricity. "You old fool, I told you to hang the laundry out to dry, not fry it!""

John didn't know whether to laugh or not, trying to gauge his response by Marg's reaction. Only when she cracked a smile and then started to laugh did he feel safe to let out a good laugh as well. "So, are you saying that bit in Blood Royale regarding your two families coming together again after a millennia is not true?"

"No, I'm not saying that at all," my wife was quick to correct any wrong impression Peace might have entertained. "That is my family's heritage all right. We used to have the family estate back in Harkema, and that was in Harkemastadt, and our rule ended at the border which was called Harkema Opiende. And Henicke Harkema, whom we trace ourselves back to was the son of Antoine le Grand Bastard, whom was from the French royal family. So all that's very true. And Allen is who he says he is as far as ancestry goes. But the fact that we got together because of some inherited attraction that drew us together like magnets is what I don't accept."

"So, you weren't attracted to him the first time you saw him?"

"Well, yes. But that's not proof of anything."

"And your first meeting was entirely planned and conceived. Nothing to chance?"

"Not exactly."

I listened intently as Pearce manipulated the conversation to go directly where he intended. I guess he wasn't that bad an investigative reporter as I first thought. My wife is not exactly a push over and she would usually put up a good fight if she thought words were being put into her mouth. But the way Pearce was structuring the questions and answers, he was having her confirm everything he already believed.

"Not exactly it wasn't left to chance, or not exactly, nothing was planned?" he asked.

"Actually I just happened to be driving along the road, going back home and I spotted a new vet clinic, so I thought I'd drop in."

"And the reason you were interested in a vet clinic at that time?"

"This is beginning to sound awfully foolish, but I had just been to another vet clinic and it was time I felt that I should find another veterinarian to look after my dogs."

"So, this new clinic was close by the other clinic."

"No, not really."

"Then it was close by your house."

"No, that's not true either."

"So it must have been on the same road and therefore it was on a direct path home."

"It was a completely different street."

"And the reason you were driving on a road that wasn't the direct path between the clinic you went to and your house was…?"

"It seemed like a good idea at the time."

"That's it?"

"I don't know what else to say. It just happened. I ended up on Birchmount, saw there was a new clinic as I drove towards Steeles, and I dropped in."

"You don't think that's kind of weird."

"No, weird is trying to tie this all into GLEEM, as if in some way some mystical ties from the past drew us together. I know that's what you're trying to imply but that's not how it was. It was just a series of coincidences and that's the way it happened."

"Okay, if you say so," Pearce said in a voice that dripped with patronization.

My wife knew that she had been set up, fallen into his trap, and that there was no way on this earth that she could extricate herself. All that she could do was smile broadly and give Pearce credit for his performance. "Even if there was something to all of this, it doesn't mean our entire lives our governed by events of the past. That gives us a good excuse to blame everything on someone else and take no responsibility for our own actions."

"A good point," I supported.

"Shut-up," she turned on me. "I don't need your help on this.

Besides your still in my bad books," she smiled. "But I do believe it is time we eat before everything goes cold."

ROME: 41 AD

To Elioneia and Joshua. I hope this letter finds you both well. You must both remain steadfast in your beliefs. As my sons, you must let truth be your strength, and persistence be your advantage. Here in Rome, I encounter more and more of these Jews that profess to be of 'the Way'. Not only that, they have surrounded themselves with Gentiles that are even more vehement in the extortions of their new found beliefs. Normally, I have tolerated the sects of our religion quite well, but some like this new leader of theirs, called Barnabus, are a greater threat to us than all of the Roman legions combined. He has told all that listen to him that they should be wary of any of the teachings from the Jewish leaders, for he fears our persuasive arguments. He claims that it is better to listen to a heretic than to the preaching of a Jew, yet not only is he a Jew but a Levite as well.

I am reluctant to even suggest this, but whereas in the past our synagogues have been open to all the various sects to use as a podium from which to preach, I would now suggest that we ban these heretics from our holy places. Their tales of heroic struggle delude those women that fancy such things, and the young confuse reality with the mysticism they preach. I will no longer tolerate them to speak from our alter places. We must not permit our less observant members to fall easy prey to their ramblings. Condemn these professors of 'the Way' for they prefer to kneel before manmade objects instead of the Almighty God. They are like the heathen, unguided and untutored in the truth of heaven, seeking strength from their ignorance. Their followers fill the hordes that seek an omen from every thunderbolt and blame a demon for every unfortunate circumstance.

Waste neither time nor effort to try and stem their misleading teachings to the Gentiles. That lot is of no concern to us. When the time is ripe, even that ungodly mass will doubt the beliefs that are foisted upon them and will cast this 'Way' aside. As for the

Gentiles, time will be our greatest ally. But as to our own people, the more that come to think of themselves as Christian, the more I fear they will tumble from the true path. For them, the sands of time are running fast.

It was not always so. Initially, sorrow surrounded the events concerning the night that Yeshua was brought to me. The gaiety which those that claim to be his followers display results not from the salvation they proclaim as their reward but from the guilt they shared that day. Because if it was not for their weakness, Yeshua would still be alive.

"Fear not, Yeshua," I told him that night. "We wish you no harm. My father-in-law, Annas, and I will preside over this tribunal. As you can clearly see, this is not the Sanhedrin, and therefore any judgement is only of a civil matter. Calm your fears, for we have no authority to put a man to death. Witnesses have been summoned that will attest to events which have clearly brought you in defiance of halachah. If you should be found guilty, then you will be held in custody until such time that you repent."

"And who's to say priest that after you have me arrested you will not have me sent to a higher court."

"To do so would not serve any purpose for us. Incarcerating you within my prison will serve enough to protect you from Pilate, as he has no authority over any prisoner in my jail. Though Rome is everything you accuse it to be, an evil empire of warmongers, it has one saving grace — it is overly legalistic, tying its own hands with a mountain of rules and regulations. And one of those laws is the protection and preservation of the courts and laws of the country it occupies. Have you not wondered why the outer court of the Temple bares the sign placed there by the Emperor Augustus stating that no person of non-Jewish extraction can pass through the next gates? An example of our rules that they have made law. And should Pilate try to contravene those laws, he would be held accountable by the Senate of Rome."

"I want it known, Caiaphas," Yeshua insisted, "That although I appear before your makeshift tribunal, I have done no wrong. I don't deserve imprisonment, let alone death, for I am innocent. Didn't I speak openly and in public, with not attempt of concealment and certainly no intrigue? If I have done wrong, then why haven't I been arrested a long time ago?"

"Are you so dim-witted that you do not realize that this is not an issue of right or wrong? The context is immaterial. This is a matter of what is best for Jerusalem. Of what's best for your people. Your crime is that your presence here and now may result in a potentially dangerous disturbance that would grow into violent clashes against the Romans. I know that is not what you wish to happen. It is essential that we preserve the peace for the time being. Are you prepared to have the death of so many upon your head? All this can be avoided by simple answers to simple questions."

"Do not expect me to give false evidence which you can use to incriminate me," Yeshua warned.

"I said nothing about lying. All we seek is the truth. In fact, I have a solution that should satisfy all. With one simple answer we can dispense with the entire tribunal." I began to pace the floor in front of all that had been gathered within my house. "As you all know, it is not permitted for a civil tribunal to have jurisdiction over someone that isn't one of our own, nor over someone that is not in possession of their full faculties."

Everyone assembled nodded in agreement though I doubt any knew where I was heading with this train of thought.

"A declaration for either would mean that you are not able to be in violation of our laws. And should we free you, it would be under an amnesty that would be honoured by the Romans as well. What more could you desire? So, I ask you, Yeshua ben Joseph, is it true that you are either a Samaritan through your mother's family, or else that you suffer from episodes of insanity, manifesting themselves in the manner of visions?"

"A less than desirable exchange for my freedom priest. Either would serve to make me an outcast amongst my followers. A living death. What you ask is too great, and you of all people know that what I have heard and what I visualise, does not render me insane."

"Ah, but do you admit then to being a Samaritan?"

"Whether I am or whether I'm not does not in any way prejudice the fact that I speak for the Almighty God."

"Then tell me that you aren't a Samaritan and I'll believe you but know then that we must then bring you before this tribunal and pass judgement on you."

Yeshua made no reply. Now I know that Yeshua was a man

that would not lie. Left to interpreting his silence, I could only assume that he could not deny the statement and therefore chose to remain silent.

"You're not being wise," I said. "Failure to speak will only mean that I must rely on the testimony of others. Are you aware that even now one of your apostles has refused to testify? He whom you consider your friend and ally won't even enter into my house and speak on your behalf. I will give you time to reconsider before we proceed."

"What need have I of time Caiaphas? Time is of no consequence only an answer from you. Which serves you better — to declare me insane or to be a Samaritan? Since you already have your verdict, why not decide on the proper crime."

It was then that one of my guards slapped Yeshua across his face for speaking with such insolence.

"Refrain!" I shouted.

Yeshua glared at me, smarting from the blow. "If I've said something which isn't accurate, then tell everyone here. But if I speak the truth, what right have you to strike me? Would you have me turn my other cheek so that you may strike me again?"

"There will be no more violence in my house. I will not have this man struck again. All that come before me are free to speak. That is our law. That is our tradition. I will not have it violated. Let the witnesses come forward!"

Everyone shuffled into position. Being the night of preparation not everyone that I had called upon came to my assembly, preferring instead to be home with their families. Instead a group of Pharisees from the school came and requested entry. They said that they had spoken many times with Yeshua, but soon it was apparent that all too many of them knew nothing of which they spoke. A string of unfounded allegations, some irrelevant, and many preposterous. Fortunately our laws state that for every allegation there must be two unrelated witnesses to corroborate the facts before there is sufficient evidence to lay a charge. As you are aware, there has not been good blood between us and the Pharisees for two hundred years. And they had come to my house in order to put me on trial too.

"Take heed," the elderly Gamaliel cautioned me, "We may find our necks in a noose if we allow these students to make accusations so freely."

I nodded in agreement. "There will be no further questions regarding my involvement in this matter. As to why I haven't arrested Yeshua prior to this, it is because I found no wrong in him." The students became irate, and like mad dogs they hurled accusations of myself being in league with Yeshua. "The outer courts of the Temple are a place of free speech," I continued, "where all men are able to speak what is in their heart and on their minds as long as it does not cast disparage upon our sacred beliefs."

"Then why was he permitted to claim that he would destroy the Temple and rebuild one not made of men?" one of the Pharisees asked. "He has threatened to destroy our holiest sanctuary, the extinction of all that is sacred, an abomination to our ears."

"The Temple that I would build would not be of stone or mortar," Yeshua replied in his own defence. I sighed in relief that he finally decided to speak and hopefully put an end to his nonsense. "I will build a temple of hearts and minds."

"At the risk of being accused of being in collusion once more, I'd like to address our educated brethren from amongst the Pharisim. Yeshua speaks of inner spiritualism, forsaking all external trappings. Because you have no comprehension of any world but your own, you have made the mistake of accepting literally the same message that every prophet since Elijah has made. Continue to make these false accusations and I will have you dismissed from my premises."

"He claimed to be the son of God!" shouted another of the students.

"Am I to hear nothing but your blathering ignorance? This accusation isn't admissible either. We have no beliefs in sons of God. Since when have we become pagans? I should accuse you for even considering such a thing is possible within our beliefs. God is our father and we are all is children. Do you with to debate that with me? Nothing more is to be made of Yeshua's statement lest you deny that all of us are a firstborn son of God."

"Ask him Caiaphas!" the Pharisees demanded in unison. "The son that Yeshua speaks of is not as we know it. He blasphemes the law by saying that he is flesh and blood of God."

At that moment Nicodemus interjected himself into the conversation. "Such a question cannot be asked. All of you know who I am. I am Nicodemus, a senior of the council of elders, and I will explain to you the reason that such a question cannot be asked of this tribunal. If he should reply that his is a physical son of God, then he will have declared himself to be a pagan. And if he is a pagan, then he is not subject to Jewish law. And if he is a pagan and you have brought him into custody in defiance of Roman law forbidding us to exercise authority of non-Jews, then you have brought us all into breach of their law and we will all be brought to justice."

"That is not so," the students cried out. "Our laws clearly sate that any Jew that defames God is guilty of a capital crime. If he is a Jew as he claims, and he professes that God has fornicated with his mother, then his crime is blasphemy, and his must be stoned to death. That is the law Nicodemus which you must uphold!"

"I have heard him make such a claim," once of the Levites confirmed. "So did I," came another voice from somewhere across the room.

"Do any of you know how stupid you sound?"

"Be seated Nicodemus," I commanded reluctantly. "They are right, the law is the law."

"But Caiaphas…," Nicodemus tried to plead.

"It is the law. They have lodged a charge of blasphemy, no matter how outrageous their accusation appears to be. Unless Yeshua declares openly that he is not a Jew, as supreme religious cleric, descendant of Aaron, upholder of the laws of Moses, I must see that blasphemy has not occurred. Yeshua, do you claim to be that actual son of our Lord? You cannot be silent on this issue."

Yeshua turned to face his accusers. "You Pharisees have been an eternal thorn in my side. You claim to understand the law and are the voice of the people, but you are no different from the Sadducees. All you wish is to be a law unto yourselves. That is what you say I am but I have never made such a claim."

"Are there any here who can testify on behalf of Yeshua that he made no such claim?" I asked quickly.

"I can," Judas raised his voice in support. "Such a story has been spread, but that was by Simon Peter and Philip, even though Yeshua clearly expressed his displeasure with his disciples making such a contemptuous claim. He said so publicly at Gerasenes. Anyone who was there can prove I speak the truth."

"A second witness," I declared. "Is there not anyone that can bear witness and second Judas's story?"

To my surprise, it was a Pharisee, not one of the troublesome group that answered my call. "I was there," he said. "The accused recited the Shemah to the assembled crowd. I heard it with my own ears."

As all of know, the very heart of the Shemah is the confirmation of the singularity of God. For Yeshua to have recited it put an end to the foolishness once and for all. "What more needs to be said," I concluded. "Yeshua has been wrongfully accused. This charge is dismissed."

But this only antagonised the students further. For those that preach to the people that the God of Israel is a merciful Lord, it was clearly evident that there was no such mercy residing in their hearts. They sought a trap that I wouldn't be able to extricate myself from. Their grudge with Yeshua was secondary to the resentment they held for me. What happened next is only more proof that the worst miscarriages of the law only occur when there are too many laws. Perhaps we have become as bad as the Romans in that regards. We have laws that require representation of both Sadducees and Pharisees on every council, and similarly there is a statute that required the Pharisee students of law be present a hearing. This was the doing of Queen Salome Alexandra, who in her wisdom thought it would ensure that justice prevailed. I only wish she was alive now to see what the offspring of her decision has become almost two centuries later. I think she would regret what she had done. We now have a legal system that serves only to pit one religious faction against another, and it is justice which is held at ransom as a result.

Without a respite from having their last accusation rebutted successfully, the students were at it again. "Ask him if he claims to be the messiah," they demanded.

"And if he does, so what," I replied. "Many have laid claim to being the deliverer and just as many have failed in that ambition. What is one more to us?"

"Ask him!" they shouted.

"Are you the messiah?" I asked Yeshua.

"I am."

"That is not what we meant," a student screeched. "He has laid claim to being the royal messiah. Is he not the one that was anointed at Bethany? Has he not declared himself to be the one to lead us into the battle of Armageddon?"

Perhaps it was a premonition, or maybe it was just simple fear, but I knew that the noose was closing around us. The direction of their attack was obvious, and I knew that Yeshua was bound to stumble.

"This is not why we are here," I scolded them. "It is you Pharisim that believe literally in the war at the end of time. We Sadukim have no such belief in a resurrection and final battle. That is not what Zechariah nor Ezekiel were trying to say. How can I bring your personal beliefs into this tribunal?"

"As an appointee of the Legate, you must serve your master Caiaphas."

Here it was. Here was the club that they had kept concealed all this time and were now prepared to bludgeon us all with. For me to ignore their request would be immediately reported back to Pilate that I refused to investigate an exposed political threat. Any support for Yeshua would be seen as open dissension against Rome. I would have been removed from my position before the next day was out. I can assure you, as my present predicament has proven, Pilate would have taken great pleasure at that time in surrendering me in chains to the legate under a charge of treason. Damn the Pharisees. In order to have my head they were willing to sacrifice an innocent man.

"What say you to these new accusations Yeshua ben Joseph?" I had no choice but to lay the charge at his feet.

With an air of dignity, Yeshua straightened himself to his full towering height. "I am he who you call messiah. I am the son of Gideon. I have always proclaimed myself to be so — no more, no less."

"Are you the anointed of God, the chosen saviour of our people? The blazing sword that will crush our enemies beneath his heal?"

"Soon you will see that I am the Son of Man, sitting at the right hand of Power, whose legions are carried by the clouds in heaven."

"Sacrilege!" the Pharisees screamed. "He defiles your house with his threat of revolt. Send him to Pilate to deal with his sedition."

I tore my garments in response. "I mourn for all of you, for this is a sad day when a Jewish tribunal urges the shedding of innocent blood. If he uses the term Power, then he has a Samaritan tongue. If he be a Samaritan, then let him be. And if not, then declaring himself to be the anointed of God is no crime as far as I'm concerned. I am a Zadokite and therefore have no belief in a holy war against Rome. I do not find him guilty of any crime!"

"Take him to Pilate! It's your duty," they demanded. "He has preached revolt against Rome. He has confirmed that with his admission."

"You hypocrites! You hate Rome more than any others and you are willing to hand over someone who merely expresses what you all think. How can you believe that God will forgive you for what you are doing? A curse on your Pharisee heads!"

It was the wrong thing to say, I know it. But they disgusted me more than I thought anyone was capable of doing. Yes, I antagonised them further, but they are a fetid blot before God.

"We shall tell Pilate you are protecting a rebel," they fired back at me. "We will tell him that you have held this unlawful assembly at night?"

"I beseech thee! Do not make me pass a judgement like this. Upon your mortal souls, do not do such a thing. Will no one speak on Yeshua's behalf?"

Again Judas stood to speak. "The anointing at Bethany was not Yeshua's doing. You all know that is true. It was Lazarus ben Simon's doing. Bring him here and he will attest to it."

"Bring us Lazarus," they demanded, knowing full well that Lazarus had gone into hiding. It was only later that we found he had fled outside the city to hide at his family's country estate. "Produce Lazarus so he can confess," they taunted me.

"Lazarus has fled and is nowhere to be found," Judas replied. "Is that not proof enough to show his guilt?"

"Bring us proof to show us that Yeshua is innocent," they challenged Judas to action.

"Wait," Judas retaliated. "There is one outside who can bear witness to what I've said. Our testimony taken together should be sufficient to counter your charges. Is that not so, Caiaphas?"

"It will be sufficient." I sent out a servant girl to bring Simon Peter in from the courtyard. She was the most non-threatening person within my household that I could think of.

Within minutes she returned. "He refuses to come with me master. He denies knowing this man."

"Go again," I instructed her. "Make him fully aware of the urgency of this matter. He must realize that if he fails to comply, his master will surely die."

She went out again at my bequest, but once again returned empty handed after several minutes. "He says that he never knew this man."

He failed to live up to the name that Yeshua had given him. Cephas! Hah! He was no rock. He crumbled like dried mud. "Go out again," I ordered her.

"Wait," some of the Pharisees insisted. "We'll go out with her. If he fails to honour your request and denies you once more, then by the very laws that you uphold he has made any testimony he may offer in the future null and void," they grinned contemptuously.

"That is the law," I muttered. "Three denials shall be accepted as one truth. If he utters his denial of any knowledge of Yeshua then we must accept that as truth." I cursed them all as I rent my garments even further.

From the jubilant shouting I heard emanating from my portico, I knew exactly what had transpired. The rock was no more. Simon Peter had failed Yeshua when he needed him most.

"What is your verdict Caiaphas?" they laughed as they returned to the hall. "Is he not guilty of sedition? Did you not declare that this tribunal was a matter of civil law and therefore you are bound to uphold Rome's concerns in civil matters? Let us hear your decision!"

I buried my face in my hands. Never had I felt so alone in all my life. Abandoned by everyone that I had relied upon. Most of all, I knew that I had failed to fulfil my promise to Yeshua. "Take him to Pilate," I uttered. "God have mercy upon our souls."

CHAPTER TWENTY-THREE

"That's always been one of my favourite examples of how things get screwed up," Marg commented.

"I'm not certain I follow you," Pearce responded while stuffing the sliced corned beef between two slices of bread.

"For example, we are raised with these stories from the time they can lock us away in a room in the basement of the church and they expect us to accept it unquestioningly."

"Did I mention that my wife came from a very religious upbringing?" I interjected.

"Ignore him," my wife dismissed my comment, "you are instructed to believe events which are entirely illogical, such as the story of Peter outside Caiaphas's courtyard and accept that even though he never entered the house he in some way knew every single word that was uttered behind stone walls."

"There are some things we just have to accept on faith."

"Not blind faith, John. This is one case where I agree with my husband. There were too many unanswered questions. When Allen first told these event in the first print of the book, it suddenly all made a lot of sense. It was a typical man thing after all to do."

"Would you care to expand that observation," Pearce extended the invitation for Marg to clarify.

I looked down into my lap, eyes closed and shook my head. "Oh, here we go again," I muttered.

"Everything's about power. When it comes to men, that's all you are concerned about. Then, now, forever. Just go and destroy the world and mess up everyone's life just because you feel like it."

"Don't you think you've oversimplified things a bit," I asserted.

"No, no, let her continue Pearce urged. "This is quite interesting. It provides a perspective of what the reader is going to think when the book gets released."

"Let's face it," my wife continued. "Allen's family may

have called themselves priests but they were nothing more than an aristocracy that lived off the efforts of everyone else. They took their tithe whether or not some poor family had to go starving in order to produce their share. Don't get caught up in their sanctimonious holier than thou attitude, and everyone else, like the Pharisees were bad guys. Bottom line is that they were all bad guys. Every single one of them. And I should know. My family's history was no different. We ruled that state in Freisland with an iron fist. At least that's what we called it. The history books tell it a little differently. They wrote that when the Harkema's rode into town, everyone took cover. We raped, pillaged and slaughtered as we pleased. Why — because we could. That's what it was all about, power and the wresting of power away from those that have it. It was a game they all wanted to play. And it didn't matter whom got in the way. Their lives were inconsequential."

"Quite cynical."

"Of course, why shouldn't she be," I supported her. "She's right you know. You do have to remember John, when Caiaphas is telling his story, he views it from his own perspective. He's not going to see himself as one of the bad guys. Yes, the Pharisees were adversarial and just as corrupt as anyone else. They felt that they were better suited to interpret the laws and therefore saw the Kohenim, us priests, as an unnecessary evil. And from my family's perspective they were the hell –spawns trying to take an inheritance away that God had given to us directly. Yes, and it's true, in this battle between two opposing forces innocents suffered."

"That makes it even worse."

"Well at least it explains it," Marg inserted herself back into the conversation. "You thought the story in the Gospels was solely about finding a means to execute Jesus. He was nothing more than a bone to be picked over. You had a bunch of forces fighting each other in order to seize power, and he's the victim caught in the middle. Wrong place, wrong time. Nothing to do with the way it's described in the bible at all."

"That is a different perspective, I have to admit. But if I were to accept your point of view then it would pretty much eliminate the entire meaning behind Jesus' sacrifice to remove the sins of the world," Pearce commented.

"Do I get to say something here," I raised my hand.

"No!" they shouted at me in unison.

"Show me when the world became without sin." Marg tapped her hand against the table to make a point.

"Well, it's sort of figurative. He didn't literally remove all our sins. It's only meant to mean that he gave up his life because of our sins. Sort of a trade-off…"

My wife made no effort to comment letting Pearce stumble along in his explanation and he knew himself he was floundering.

"Help me here Doc."

"Hey, you told me to shut up. You get yourself out of your own mess," I advised with a huge smile beaming across my face

"Okay," he turned to my wife, "so it wasn't as if the world became a much better place after his personal sacrifice."

"How about it even got worse? How about it only led to more wars, more death, more suffering. The rich got richer and the poor suffered more than they ever did before."

"But they had hope."

"Sheesh, John, is that the best you can come up with." I was feeling a bit cocky as I watched his argument get picked apart by my wife. How many times I had been on the similar end of one of these discussions with Marg. I knew it wouldn't be long until she gave him the old one two.

"Perhaps if he had lived he would have been able to accomplish so much more," Marg suggested. "Caiaphas only saw him as means to an end. Those that opposed Caiaphas used him as a weapon against the priesthood. And when finally Pilate got his clutches on him, it was only one more cog in the wheel that would lead to the expulsion of the Jews from their homeland and the destruction of Israel."

"But from his death sprang Christianity."

"And everything else that went with it. It certainly wasn't the most enlightened period of mankind. The dark ages, the inquisition, the murder of heretics, and mass genocides."

"All right, this is getting a little too heavy," I commented. "The fact is that it happened. And Caiaphas was involved directly in making it happen. And right or wrong, it played out in a manner that we're all familiar. We know the what, the where, the when and the why. Sit back, have dessert, and let Caiaphas tell you the how."

ROME: 41 AD

Dear Elioneiai, I know that it must stress you to no end to hear what the followers of 'the Way' are saying in Damascus. I know, because it causes me no end of strife hearing it talked about in the streets of Rome. They speak to their followers as if they were in my council hall with us that fateful night, which as you know is a total fabrication. How can they make such a claim when even Simon Peter was too afraid to cross my doorstep? How dare them put words into my mouth and say that I personally prosecuted and convicted Yeshua. Such arrogance to even suggest that they know how our justice system works and making the presumption that one man has the authority to be both judge and jury. If those that listen to such nonsense would only take the time to study our laws then they would not lend any credence to these distorters of the truth.

They also spread the vile lie that I was removed from the office of the High Priest as a punishment for my involvement in Yeshua's death. Liars! They would like us to believe that Rome cared about one Jewish claimant to messiahship. Rome kills like a camel drinks — it is not satisfied until it has had its fill. The Christians have become so prejudiced against me here that they try to convince their fellow citizens that Pontius Pilate was forced to act as he did through coercion and treachery. As all of us knew in Judaea, he took pleasure in crucifixion and he certainly needed to excuse to execute a Jew. And when he finally laid his hands on Yeshua, I can only describe his mood as one of total elation.

So, let me write once more on the events of that night. As dawn approached, we, the great and noble self-righteous council members, the accursed Pharisees, and the assorted witnesses that were assembled, escorted Yeshua to the fortress where the procurator resided. Those that wished to humiliate Yeshua further insisted that he have his hands bound when presented to Pilate. And once we finally arrived, Pilate was summoned by his staff to receive the King of the Jews. Pilate was ecstatic to see all of us humbled before him.

"To what do I owe the pleasure of this visit?" he asked.

"I assure you, Governor, there is no pleasure to be had in this travesty of justice," I replied. "A hearing was held regarding this man known as Yeshua ben Joseph, a Nazarene. The judgement passed against him was one of preaching of the final ware of liberation."

"The final war of liberation Priest? Is that supposedly a synonym for insurrection?"

"He never openly preached revolt."

"That is open to discussion. And what of this hearing Priest? Have you forgotten there is a law against assembly at night? What were you really up to Caiaphas? Perhaps you were attempting to usurp my authority and take matters into your own hands?"

"This man isn't guilty of any crime!"

"That is from your viewpoint Priest. I am not a Jew. A crime against Rome means nothing to you but everything to me. Did you purposely try to overlook a crime against the Empire? It is obvious that your august assembly did not agree with you for why else have they brought him to me bound like a beast?"

"He's guilty!" shouted those pressing for a conviction.

"Of what crime?" Pilate asked mockingly.

"Treason!"

"Tell me more."

"He called himself king and spoke openly of war," some in the crowd replied.

"This is your man without guilt?" Pilate sneered. "Perhaps the Legate Vitellius would care to hear your explanation?"

"What you have our words Pilate. I have seen no actions. If each of us were to be held responsible for everything we have said at one time or another, then all of us would be guilty of a crime."

"Are you willing to confess to yours now Caiaphas? This man I have heard. This man I've seen what he did in the Temple. His words have incited disturbances. He is no stranger to me."

"What he has done does not warrant execution," I pleaded.

"Kill him?" Pilate feigned astonishment. "Who said anything of killing him? I merely want to talk with him." Pilate waved for his guards to bring Yeshua into his quarters. I tried to enter as well, along with members of the council but we were immediately blocked. "There's no need for you or your delegation to attend," Pilate scoffed at us. "I'm very capable of handling my own interrogation without your assistance. You are all dismissed.

Go back to your homes before I have you all arrested."

This brings up a very interesting point Elioneiai. These Christians spread the lie that we refused to enter the palace for fear of defiling ourselves. What possible defilement could they mean? It made no difference whether it was the Passover or not — we would never have partaken of Pilate's food or wine regardless. Since Vitellius had guaranteed our laws that Pilate could not bring his standards and ensigns into Jerusalem ever again after his previous fiasco, we had no worry that there'd be graven images within the palace. Even if that wasn't so, it would not have been an obstacle to us, since we had no intention to kneel down before any image. None should ever think that Nicodemus would willingly leave Yeshua's side, for he had sworn to protect him and only Pilate's order to leave could have separated them. What you may not know, Nicodemus was convinced that Yeshua was the true messiah. You know Nicodemus, my son, and you know he's not easily swayed once he sets his mind to something. Let these accuser ask Nicodemus if it is not so! Though he has fallen into disrepute with these new order of Christians because of his teachings, Nicodemus is one of the few that speaks with first-hand knowledge, and that is why they resent him so.

I can only speculate as to what transpired in Pilate's palace. Unlike these Christians, I make no false claim as to having eyes and ears where none were possible. Pilate would have been relishing every second that he felt he held Yeshua's life in his hands. He would have taunted him with that very fact, trying to make him squirm and eventually beg for his life.

But knowing Yeshua, he would not have said a word, which would have only served to infuriate Pilate further. Pilate would have tried to impress his hapless victim with the power he exercised but again Yeshua would have chosen not to acknowledge it. In fact, Yeshua would have lectured Pilate that any power he may have had was only the result of God wishing it so. And I can tell you exactly what Pilate would have said in response. "Am I a Jew," he would say, "that your God would reward me with power?" Then he would have said that he must be better liked that was Yeshua, for why else would he be rewarded by God. That exchange would have gone on for a while before Pilate would have realized that there was a much greater plot afoot.

Pilate must have asked Yeshua if he was aware of why he had been brought before him. To this question Yeshua would have indicated that it was never the intention for him to appear before anyone but me.

"But he has no law to put a man to death," Pilate would have mulled. "Then why would he have you tried only to bring you to me afterwards?" Knowing Pilate, it would not have taken him long to put together what had transpired. "Unless it was never intended for you to appear before me at all. Which could only mean that Caiaphas intended to secret you away beyond my reach." And that was how Pilate would have arrived at the charges he brought against me which ultimately resulted in my being here in Rome to defend myself. He would have been so delighted with the situation. Not only did my ineptitude deliver Yeshua to him but I provided him with a weapon to wield against me.

And the crimes for which Pilate sentenced Yeshua, these were recorded by his scribes and posted all about the city. For his crime of urging the people to pay no tax, he was to be flogged publicly. For having himself proclaimed as king at Bethany, he was to be crowned and raised up high on his throne to survey his kingdom. And for his treasonous acts against the empire, he was to be nailed to a cross until he died. That is Roman justice — that is Pilate!

First Yeshua was scourged with the tails of a scorpions whip. Then a crown of thorns was pressed into his forehead. And finally he was raised upon a cross of wood, just as Pilate had commanded. I never expected Pilate to carry out the execution on that very same day. I never thought him foolhardy enough to flaunt his spectacle while there were over a million and a half Jews gathered within the city for the Passover. Once again I underestimated Pilate's overwhelming desire to humiliate us at every opportunity.

By the time my messenger was received by the Legate Vitellius in Antioch, it was already too late. Too late for Yeshua, too late for any of us. Still, I'd like to think that it was my message which finally convinced Vitellius to order Pilate to go to Rome to face charges of corruption and misgovernment. I know I have told you in the past that it was the affair with the Samaritans that brought him down, but I believe that was only the final straw. Vitellius had already been primed to take action, Samaria merely convinced him to do it immediately. As long as I believe that, then I feel that a great loss still resulted in some good being done. Why Vitellius took so long to act I cannot say, but at least we can all feel vindicated against Pontius Pilate. He had made us suffer as a people for a very long time and now we as a people are able to do the same for him.

As for me, perhaps I deserve to have been accused of the charges laid by Pilate indicted me for collusion. In many ways I wanted Yeshua to succeed. Does that seem strange to you, my son? With all our powers and influence, we are not able to touch the hearts of the people we govern in the same manner as this carpenter from Galilee could do so effortlessly. He offered them something that clearly we are unable to provide. He gave them hope. He filled them with dreams. And if wanting to be free is a crime, then I am guilty as much as anyone. There are lessons here to be learned if we are to survive, if the priesthood is to endure. Too often we think only of serving God, but is it not also our duty to serve mankind. We are the bridge that spans two worlds. Through our intercession our people's prayers are herd and through our guidance the will of God is made manifest on Earth. This is what I have learned from this prophet from Galilee. I believe it is a lesson which can benefit us all.

CHAPTER TWENTY-FOUR

We had already shuffled back into my study, glass of Madeira Port in hand, with a box of after dinner mints that had been lingering around in the pantry for ages and now there was finally an excuse to break it open.

"Will your wife not be joining us," Pearce inquired.

"No, I don't think so. She's said her peace and she normally prefers not to get involved in too heavy a religious discussion. I think she heard enough of them in her house growing up that she prefers to steer as far away from theological debate whenever possible."

"Probably the smart thing to do," he qualified. "Especially when you realize that your books really do bring out the worst in some of the fanatics out there."

"Like I've always said, it's all about perspective. They probably feel that what I write is designed purely and purposely to antagonise them by challenging their belief systems. Remember they were raised to believe that if their right eye offended them, they should pluck it out. That's pretty strong religious dogma when you examine it. It's pretty damn well giving them permission to do their worst to anyone that offends them."

"Sound like you're giving them an excuse Doc."

"Just stating a fact. Have you ever thought about what this world would be like without religion?"

"People need something to believe in."

"True, but does it have to be in religion? Why can't it be science, or aliens, or even themselves?"

"Isn't that what atheists are all about," Peace postulated. "And they don't seem any happier than the rest of us. And if you think it could make this world a better place, then how come you aren't an atheist yourself, Doc. In fact, you're one of the strongest proponents of God that I know of. That doesn't make a heck of a lot of sense if you think we'd be better off without religion."

"That's not what I said John. I merely asked if you've ever

given it some thought. Because you see, I have, and the more I thought about it, the more I rationalised that we need our religious beliefs."

"Are you trying to suggest then that Caiaphas was wrong?"

"Let me try to explain this as simply as I can. I've looked at our science, our technology, and even our arts and the conclusion I came to was that they're soulless. Sure, we can play with DNA and probably in about twenty years we'll have created a new life form, not to mention we'll have started playing around with manipulating our own genetic structure and who knows what that will result in. And our video games will take us further into cyberspace than we'll probably ever want to venture, because I'm certain we'll be hooked up by chip implants in the not too distant future. As an extreme technophile and a scientist, I should be delighted, but the deeper I look into the heart of our creation the more difficult it becomes to find anything there. It's empty. Black. As I said, soulless. And that's how I came to realize there is a very big difference between a world that we create and one that's divinely inspired. In God's creation there's a purpose, a sense of fulfilment. It's that inspirational essence, that touch of heaven which raises us above all that has come before. And that's why we need religion."

"Surely there must be something more than just a gut feeling that makes your faith so strong. As Mrs. Pearce says, you're holding back."

"There is, but that's between myself and the Lord. I doubt very much I'll take the time to put it in a book. I'll only tell you that there are some things in this world that can't be explained by science."

"Gee Doc, I never thought I'd hear you sat that."

"I'm not going to be someone that you'll easily label, John. Science is merely a way of finding answers. A tool, a resource. It must never be seen as the solution to every question. "

"Let me get this straight. You're the proponent of this theory that even our unexplained memories have a scientific foundation. That we're the sum total of our DNA passed downward through countless generations. That even those mysteries that we label as love at first sight, have an enzyme basis to them. And now you're telling me that science isn't 'the be all to end all' answer."

"You want to know why I'm such a strong believer John."

"Yes I want to know," he demanded.

"I'll tell you why. For three hundred million years reptiles ruled this earth. They dominated it. And they had the predators and the prey just like we mammals do. But at no time, did some weak little dinosaur pick up a club and take out a T-Rex with a few good swings. Yet the rat like creature that ran between their toes, did manage in sixty million years to evolve into a bent over, chimpanzee like creature, that not only did take out a sabre tooth, but found ways to do it faster and easier and more effectively with each passing generation. Even better, in just over two million years this little guy ended up developing into us. You see John, science can't explain that. Evolution can't explain that. There is only one explanation. There was an interfering hand in the process. An unseen catalyst that made something out of nothing. Order out of chaos. And there is only one force that could be behind such an overwhelming turn of events. That's God. And it really doesn't matter how you want to picture him or her or it. Because that's only a frame of reference. I look at the world as my frame of reference, and that's God."

"You ever think about taking up a job at the pulpit Doc?"

It was one of Pearce's better lines. Almost as dangerous as putting the fox in charge of the hen house, I would think. It's not easy talking about one's own belief systems. Sure, I can talk about what a Caiaphas believed, or a Bustenai, or a Natronai. But those were their beliefs and I can distance myself from what my ancestors believed. But John was trying to tap into my own personal beliefs and this was myself I was talking about. Strange as it seemed, having myself as the topic of discussion made me feel that same way when John first came to my house after discovering my identity. It was as if I was reliving the event all over again. The exposure, the loss of anonymity, the failure to protect my own privacy. And I didn't like it at all.

"Never gave it a thought," I responded. "Because like I said, there are some things that are better left between myself and the Lord. And I'll leave it at that because we have much more important things to discuss."

ROME: 41 AD

My sons, I am sending you this scroll as much for its entertainment value as its importance to our future. It is quite popular here in Rome. They call it the Gospel of the Infancy and it is being circulated amongst the Greek community that has adopted this Christianity. As you read through it, you will see that it speaks of a boy who accidentally ran into Yeshua and was struck down dead as a result. What is the purpose of such a bizarre story, I cannot fathom. For this community to not only write but to adhere to such a fabrication makes no sense at all. I actually find myself defending Yeshua against such inaccuracies. There is even another story in this gospel of a young man that was transformed into a donkey. By riding on his back, Yeshua turned him back into a man. Perhaps there is some symbolism that this story masks that I just don't quite understand. Surely they cannot believe such things are possible.

There is another story that has been circulating amongst these followers of Yeshua and I can recognize the source of their material but it is truly a distortion of the facts. They tell this lie in order to incriminate all of our people. By bringing our beliefs and heritage to the pagans, those that preach 'the Way' have cast a pall over us. They have used this story of Bar Abbas to embarrass and accuse us falsely. The heathens still fail to understand the intricacies of our language. Within their capacity to reason they have no knowledge of what Jesus Bar Abbas truly signified.

Firstly, I have tried to point out to those that advocate this meaningless tale, that in spite of what may be the Roman's better qualities, the freeing of a prisoner at the time of the Passover was not one of them. It spits on the grave of all who died by the blood on Roman hands. I have thought of three possible ways in which such a distortion of the truth could have occurred.

One would have been the freeing of those prisoners that we held in the high priest's jail for crimes of a minor religious infraction. Having those in our custody partaking in the seder within their own homes was of far greater import than the punishment of an individual for a minor civil infringement. This to me would be the most logical explanation to explain this pardon that they speak of.

But then, their story of a Bar Abbas says that one prisoner Is set free in place of another that must die. This is reminiscent of the sacrifice of the scapegoat on the Day of Atonement. While one animal is sacrificed on the altar, the other is set free to run through the streets with a red ribbon around its neck. Every citizen casts their sins upon the fleeing animal until it carries them far beyond the city gates. That is the second possible explanation.

When their followers talk about the sacrifice of the lamb so that Bar Abbas could be set free, then I can also think of our practice of choosing two lambs for the Passover ceremony. One lamb is sacrificed for our service in the Temple much in the same way that the goat is selected for the Day of Atonement and its blood is splattered on the horns of the altar to remind us of the blood we painted above our doorposts when the Angel of Death came through Goshen in the time of Moses. Following the Temple services the second lamb would be carried in a ceremony back to its mother's care, much in the same way that we were led from Egypt and returned to the care and protection of the Almighty. Whichever explanation serves as the basis for their concocted fallacy it is more important that we address them with the truth.

After Pilate ended his interrogation of Yeshua, he came out on to the portico of the palace to address all of us that he kept waiting outside. "So, Caiaphas," he addressed me, "will you have me crucify your king?"

He was hoping to trap me with that question, knowing that if I did not denounce Yeshua's claim to kingship that I would be guilty of treason. "What could you possibly mean, Excellency? You know very well that we have no king but Caesar."

"Isn't this you king?" Beckoning his palace guards with a wave of his hand, he had Yeshua brought out from the shadows. It was a horrible sight. He had been whipped so badly that he could scarcely stand upright. Over his shoulders they had placed a purple robe, the colour of Imperial Rome. A crown of twisted thorns adorned his head, its barbs clearly piercing his brow. This was a prime example of Pilate's cruelty. Roman justice as only they could perceive it.

"Look everyone! I bring you your king," Pilate shouted to us. "Tell me why I should condemn this man. I find no fault with him."

There was no reply.

"I can't hear you Priest. Tell me, is there a reason that I should condemn him?"

I still made no attempt to answer his taunts.

Pilate grew angrier with my silence. "Can I presume that you still don't see the crime he's guilty of? I bring him before you dressed as the king he claims to be and you all stand there silently."

Then all of a sudden, Nicodemus threw himself to the ground and rent his clothing. Tossing the dust from the ground upon his head he pleaded with the governor. "I beseech thee Excellency, I beg thee, release this man."

"Finally Nicodemus, you show me some respect. What a pitiful site you and your companions make. Now, let me see all of you beg upon your knees."

"He is guilty of no crime," Nicodemus lamented. "I beg you to let him go. He is an innocent man."

"How can you say such a thing Nicodemus? He claims to be a king. Can you not see his crown?" Pilate laughed hauntingly. "I hear that he's even had himself anointed. What do you say to that? Do you truly believe that his is your messiah that you have prayed for, the son of your ancient King David, the one who will shed my Roman blood and liberate your miserable lives? Come on and tell me Nicodemus, who is this man."

"Don't do it," I shouted towards Nicodemus but I was too late.

"He's the son of the Most High God, a teacher of the Lord, a true child of the Almighty in both purity and righteousness. He our Master, Jesus the son of the father, Jesus Bar Abbas."

Now that I think of it my sons, that is where this Bar Abbas name probably came from. How could I have not seen it before? When Nicodemus used Yeshua's title in the Latin tongue he must have originated this entire narrative. Jesus son of the Father, Jesus Bar Abbas. Of course, what an old fool I have become not to have seen the obvious. Here was Nicodemus pleading to have Jesus Bar Abbas freed and in the end Pilate had Yeshua executed. How could these Greeks not comprehend that they were one and the same?

"Shall I find your king guilty," Pilate questioned Nicodemus.

"You have no authority over him Excellency. He is only answerable to God."

"Oh foolish old man. Do not let your delusions rob you any

more of your senses. Behold him! See how he bleeds. He is no son of your uncouth desert god. He's just an ordinary man. With his own lips he told me that he's a king. He even dared to attempt to impress me with some fable of being raised up from among men to walk among the mighty. What do you say to that, all of you that have brought this man that walks among the mighty in bonds to me? Will you have me crucify your king?"

The Pharisees that were still amongst us repeated their charges against Yeshua. "We have no king but Caesar!"

"What shall be his punishment?"

"Crucify him!"

"What do you say to that Caiaphas?" Pilate turned to me.

"Such things are not for me to decide Pilate. I have no power to put a man to death. This decision is yours and yours alone."

"Let me rephrase this for you then Priest. Knowing that treason is a capital crime under Roman law, what do you then think the verdict should be?"

That cunning weasel had trapped me. I had no recourse but to say exactly what he wanted to hear. If I was to suggest anything less than death, then I would be condemning myself to a similar fate. And by agreeing, it was no different than as if I had gotten to my knees and succumbed to Pilate's authority. That was what he really wanted. All this was merely a charade to make me crawl before him He didn't care about Yeshua — he was nothing more than a tool designed to humiliate me.

"If one is found guilty of treason," I answered, "then there is no other choice but to execute him. That is the law. That is Caesar's will."

"Did you all hear it," Pilate exclaimed. "Sentence has been proclaimed!" The procurator exalted in his victory. "Take him to be crucified. Nicodemus, no need to fret. Your son of god will soon be joining his father."

Pilate was gloating. It was a day that was emblazoned upon my memory. A day that the world cannot forget.

CHAPTER TWENTY-FIVE

Pearce was yawning, barely trying to conceal his state of mental exhaustion as he slouched back on the couch, his head weaving back and forth as he tried to maintain a façade of being alert.

"Is it finally wearing you down John," I surmised.

"Actually, I think it might be the port getting to me."

"Well we can call it an evening if you wish. There's still so much more to talk about and it's no use if you're going to be snoring away on the couch."

"I'd really love to call it quits for the night but I didn't give myself the luxury of that much time before heading back to the office."

"You didn't John…"

"Yeah, I'm afraid I did."

"Hope you don't mind my saying so, but that's pretty dumb. Twenty-one hours to fly out here and the same to get back and you're not giving your body a rest in between. You'll be absolutely useless when you get back to Toronto. So when did you book the flight back?"

"Tomorrow at six p.m."

"John, I'd say that Caiaphas is only about half way through the telling of his story. We're going to have to pull another all-nighter. You're going to be a basket case by the time you get on the plane."

"Them the breaks."

"Well, we better get on with it then. No use engaging in idle chit-chat then."

"Except that I have to ask a few questions like any good reporter," Pearce corrected me. "I need more detail on this Nicodemus fellow. I know he was a big shot in the early Church, but I'm not entirely certain where he came from. Without the background information it's difficult to see how he can have a foot in both camps."

"He's actually one of the more interesting fellows. Firstly, he has wealth, a rich merchant operating in Jerusalem."

"How rich?"

"Rich enough to donate the outer doors to the inner court of the Temple. These were a set of massive brass doors. Worth a fortune at the time and quite ornate. Beautifully tooled and engraved so that everyone that ever saw them spoke about their exceptional beauty when they returned home from their pilgrimage. And because of his great wealth, he had a seat on the Sanhedrin."

"You've mentioned the Sanhedrin a few times already but it would be good to describe it to the readers more fully."

"Okay, the Sanhedrin was the end result of a very old custom established by Moses. When Moses needed to legislate he appointed seventy elders to do the work. It was this body that ran the courts and legal system, although in some cases Moses did make decisions on his own. For the sake of the people, they were better off appearing before the Sanhedrin because Moses liked to hand out the death penalty quite often. And the customary judicial house became known to us as the Beth Din, the house of judgement. As time passed, the structure of the Sanhedrin became more formalised, with a balance of legislators and the wealthy class in approximately equal proportions. By the time of Jesus there were two levels of legislators. The priesthood, and this new group from the Pharisees known as rabbis. They were interpreters of the law focusing from the collective viewpoint of the common people, whereas, the priesthood interpreted the law from a completely religious standpoint based on the cult and rituals. And the wealthy class, well they were what they always were. A privileged group that had to ensure that they protected their own interests whenever a new law came in to being or an old one was being revised. Not much different from the House of Commons and the House of Lords in the British parliamentary system in the manner by which they represented the various classes. The big difference being that not only did the Sanhedrin make the laws, they also enforced them. An all in one legal entity."

"So Nicodemus would be part of that wealthy group?"

"Exactly. He was there because of his tremendous wealth. That's not to say that he didn't have quite a bit to offer in the manner of erudite and educated discourse but that wasn't the reason he sat on the council.   At the time of Jesus, he was the president of the council.   Comparable to what we would call the Speaker of the House in our parliamentary system."

"And his relationship with Pilate?"

"Pilate loved the wealthy class.   Rome loved the wealthy class.   They would do everything within their power to keep them entertained and supportive because if you were able to ally yourself with the rich and powerful in a subjugated nation they would most likely remain subjugated.   Problem was that Judaea was unlike anywhere else in the Roman Empire.   As a Roman you couldn't get very close to those you considered your Jewish peers.   They wouldn't eat with you, partake in the circuses or theatre with you, participate at the gymnasium, and give you their daughter or anything like that.   So it became a constant battle between the aristocracy and Pilate's ego."

"So it was Pilate's goal to humiliate Nicodemus."

"All the time, any way he could.   The same held true for Caiaphas.   So, if you knew that these two men were desperate to keep Jesus alive, then the best way to exact your revenge on them and also to humiliate them was to execute Jesus.   And when you humiliate the two leading men in Jerusalem you're also slapping an entire population across the face."

"This is all beginning to make a lot of sense now," Pearce determined.

"I always told you it would.   So, are you going to manage to stay awake in order for us to finish or not?"

"Let's get that coffee rolling again, hook me up intravenously, I'm ready, I should do just fine."

"Well if I'm not mistaken, Marg's bringing in a plunger full of coffee now." I sniffed the sweet aroma of a fine Columbian brew coming down the hallway. "Let me just see now where Caiaphas left off." I closed my eyes and cocked my head to one side as I searched for that one singular voice amongst all the other voices.

ROME: 41 AD

I am so delighted that your last letter to me Elionciai was personally delivered to me by my grandson.   He has grown in to such a fine young man. I barely recognized him. And when I called him Yonni, he was quick to remind me that he is grown up now and prefers to be called Jonathias. He does you proud, you have tutored him well. I hope that before I pass away in this God forsaken land he will bring glory to our family again by wearing the vestments of the High Priest. He is such a balm to my sore and tired eyes.

He also was quick to remind me that I've been negligent in sending a wedding gift to his sister. Martha has returned to Jerusalem with her new husband Jeshua ben Gamaliel and Yonni said I have been very remiss not to have congratulated her on this momentous occasion. He's right, I should know better. Jeshua has always been like a third son to me. I will search for the finest gift in Rome to send them. Personally delivered by Yonni, of course.

And why I'm at it, what about my other two grandsons. Your brother hasn't bothered to write to me often, but that's no excuse for his sons. After all, Jonathan Cayapha is my namesake. You would think he'd write a letter to his grandfather. His brother Menahem I can excuse. He's still young, but Cayapha has no excuse. Tell your brother Joshua I have said so.

I hear that the Sanhedrin is considering sending a mission to Rome to try to arrange the release of all our political prisoners here, including myself. Although I would love to return home as would the other's held as prisoners here, I fear it is not the right time for such an endeavour. We are not exactly popular here, and I doubt anyway that Agrippa will permit it. Why would he want those that could contest his reign back in Jerusalem? I hear that it has finally been made official that he can bear the title of King of Judaea and produce coinage with that title stamped upon it. That being the case, he is better off leaving us to rot in this far off city where we can cause him no trouble. And as I mentioned our popularity in the Empire dwindles with every passing day. With this Saul of Tarsus persecuting the Nazarenes and the other followers of 'the Way', they have retaliated by accusing all of us as a people of having the sin of murder upon our hands. That we have killed not only Yeshua but the other prophets as well. They say that we are an evil race, hostile to all mankind, and that the wrath of God has fallen upon our necks as a heavy yoke. And even though most of the Gentiles here in Rome have absolutely no conception of what is being said, they are quick to support the wave of discontent that has arisen against the

Jewish Quarter in the city. Most have never even been to the Quarter and wouldn't recognize it even if they passed it. Just a squalor of a suburb harbouring craftsman and artisans of all trades, with their braided hair and their long beards. They turn up their noses at the stench of the fish markets and are close to hysterical if the dye from the vats even come close to sprinkling upon their fine togas but they pay no notice to the arms of the dyers that will never be able to wash away the stains of their labour. But what those whom do visit notice is the wealth in the quarter displayed through the windows of each home, and the possessions gained from hard toil and an equally hard life. And this they covet it and in order to hopefully take possession of these items one day they are more than happy to spread these lies that falsely expound our hostility towards all mankind.

The stories concerning Lazarus are of no help to our reputation either. You know that he ran from the garden when Yeshua was arrested, only to turn up much later, feigning ignorance of his part that was intended to save Yeshua that night. The other apostles wished to make him pay for his cowardice. Those Galileans are a rough edge to mankind and cowards they do not tolerate. It is said that Simon Peter consulted with the other disciples to see what they should do about Lazarus. Apparently they prayed for Yeshua to give them guidance on this issue and although I cannot verify the story, apparently they say a voice did come to them that said, "If I wish for him to live until I return, then that is not your concern if you believe in me." What am I supposed to make of this? I do not know. But Lazarus took it as a reprieve that provided him with the time to leave the hotbed of Judaea for safer regions in Anatolia. He was smart enough to know that he'd not receive a second pardon from his former colleagues. Where the other apostles encounter danger and hostility from every direction, Lazarus has been able to claim his cowardice had the full approval of Yeshua. This wouldn't surprise anyone that knew him. He was weak-willed as a boy and he was even worse as an adult. But he should not be careless in thinking that Ephesus is a safe refuge. Nowhere is safe if your enemies wish to do you harm.

Don't be concerned about the material Lazarus writes with marked frequency. These epistles form John are already being condemned by James' followers. As for these Greek Christians, as I mentioned previously, they'll believe anything, but this is a phase that these people go through on a regular basis. In a few years they'll have a more popular philosophy to flock after. So if Lazarus talks about himself and the other disciples conversing with the spirit of Yeshua, then so be it. His explanation is quite clever. He claims that the reason no one else can confirm it other than the disciples is that Yeshua never appears to them in the same physical body. His appearance changes each time. So of course no one else can recognize him. The disciples know it's him only by identifying the inner spirit within the person. How could anyone accuse them of lying if that should be the case?

As for when he will appear to the rest, tell them not to be too optimistic. Remember, I heard it all after his crucifixion. He was to return two days after his entombment, then it was two weeks, and last time it was two years. But it never happened. I hear them now talking about two decades. I have better advice for them. Tell everyone two centuries and then they don't have to be caught in their own lies.

Lazarus is probably the worst for spreading these rumours, but I have heard that his propensity to write these ridiculous statements has even earned him the disdain of their clerical leader that they have in Ephesus. Apparently this Diotraphes has countered by stating that he does not recognize Lazarus or John as he prefers to call himself nor any of the people that Lazarus has appointed as disciples.

As to the accusation that somehow we priests were responsible for the death of Yeshua, I blame no one else than myself. I will take that blame. After all, I am guilty of having helped conceive that ill-fated plan. Just recognize that my guilt is one of failure, not of murder. Let those that falsely accuse me have their words be scattered in the wind like chaff that blows across the earth but fails to ever take root. If anything I have said is not true, then ask James, Yeshua's brother. James will not lie. As a Nazarene, he has sworn to God to never shave his head, nor drink wine, nor profane the truth. He will not lie when questioned and all that know James recognize this fact to be true.

Ask James about the final days of his brother. Ask him about the burial and the role I played in that. What I did was to say to all that I failed him and for that I wear my guilt. And what I did has only made the Senate of Rome certain that I was in some way involved with Yeshua and plotting the overthrow of the Roman occupation.. When I am dead and finally laid to rest, I ask Elioneiai that you engrave the following on my ossuary box: Here lies Joseph Caiaphas, the Lion of the house of Matthias, son of Zadok, High Priest of Israel. So that all that pass my tomb will know the truth. For already they tell the story of how Yeshua was brought down from the cross by Joseph of Arimathea and laid within his tomb. Is it not obvious that this Joseph from a house called Lion of Mathea is none other than myself?

As best as I can recall that day, Nicodemus came to me following the crucifixion, suggesting that there was still time to save Yeshua. The hour of the Passover seder was quickly approaching and as is our custom, no corpse can remain unburied past sunset on festival Sabbath. Not even Pilate was foolish enough to violate our customs with so many Jews gathered within the city. I agreed to go with Nicodemus and request that all the victims still on the crosses be brought down for burial before the sunset.

Pilate was expecting us. "I suppose you've come for the bodies of the criminals Caiaphas?"

"It's my duty to remind you that you must deliver the dead to me for burial prior to the onset of the seder."

"Am I a Jew that I care about your customs?"

"No," I shook my head, "but neither are you a fool. You know it is just as important for you to release the corpses as it is to me."

"Why do you vex me so High Priest? I need no reminder from you. I'll send one of the captains of my guard to accompany you. He'll break the legs on all those we hung today to make certain they asphyxiate quickly before I release them. Is that not fair enough?"

"No," Nicodemus cried in an outburst before composing himself. "There's no need to break their legs," he explained. "I have heard that they are all dead."

"Do you also take me for a fool Nicodemus?"

"They're dead, I assure you. All we ask now is that you deliver up to us their bodies."

"Dead so quickly — I don't think so. Send for Rubrius. I want to hear from him directly. He's standing watch around the hill, so he'll know. We'll let my tribune determine what shall be done. Until then, stand there and amuse me as there will be no bodies brought down until I have a full report."

One of the procurator's servants raced outside the palace to retrieve the tribune. It wasn't long until he returned with the soldier, but to Nicodemus and myself, it felt as if we were standing there in silence for a lifetime. I shouldn't have been surprised. After all, Pontius Pilate was the commander of the Praetorians before he was elevated to the status of a governor. The praetorians are synonymous for evil. They worship death; they feed on it and no matter how much Pilate scrubbed his flesh, the blood stains would always be there.

"What news Rubrius of those you crucified today?"

"They are crucified, Pilate, I fail to understand why you are questioning me thus." Rubrius was obviously concerned that someone had levelled a charge of dereliction of duty against him.

"I mean are they all dead," Pilate clarified.

The tribune looked at the procurator as if this was a trick question of some kind. "Of course not," he finally answered. "Most don't die that quickly on the crosses." Rubrius took a lengthy pause and then qualified his answer. "But some do, like that one today."

"Which one?"

"That one they call King of the Jews."

"Don't you think that a little strange," Pilate inquired.

"I didn't give it much thought. He cried out for a drink. We put the sponge of wine-vinegar to his mouth to revive him but it didn't help. Usually we can do that several times and keep them alive for quite a long time. You don't want them dying quickly."

"Go on! What else happened?"

"Just after he took the drink he said something very peculiar."

"Well man," Pilate insisted, "tell me!"

"He said that 'it is finished.' "

"What's finished."

"I didn't know," Rubrius responded.

"Anything else?" Pilate asked impatiently.

"'My God, My God, why has thou forsaken me' and then he died. All of a sudden he just slumped and died."

"And you're certain of this?"

"Yes. My Aramaic is quite good."

"No! Not what he said. Are you certain he is dead?"

"He didn't move. I couldn't see him breathing any longer."

Pilate turned from his tribune to face us. "Well gentlemen, it looks like this king of yours is ready for you to take down. The others you'll have to wait for. It shouldn't be too long after we break their legs. Rubrius, help Nicodemus take down that body."

I had become suddenly very aware that Nicodemus had not told me everything he had done that day. Even his words that he used were peculiar when I re-examined them. When Nicodemus first asked Pilate for Yeshua's body, he used the Greek word soma, which is a reference used for a living body. But when Pilate told Rubrius to help take down the body for Nicodemus, he used the world ptoma, a distinct reference to a corpse. I didn't see the significance of it at the time. Mistaken use of a word by Nicodemus, nothing more. But how does one with a total command of the Greek language make such a mistake. Pilate, not being fluent in Greek would not have picked up the subtle difference in words but I most certainly did.

I passed no comment as I walked with Nicodemus and the tribune to Golgotha. Once we were there, I looked upon Yeshua hanging high above us and for all intents and purposes, he looked very dead. I too could not detect a breath upon his lips. Thinking this was still some trap by Pilate, Rubruius had the body re-examined before he gave the order to bring it down. But once again he was reassured that Yeshua had expired giving him the confidence that he had passed whatever test Pilate may have been contemplating.

It was when they were removing the nails from Yeshua's wrists that the soldiers were startled into action. Perhaps it was just a twitch of a nerve, or maybe even the iron nail scraping against bone and tendon, but everyone saw it. The clenching of the fingers on the right hand. Without a moment's delay one of the guards thrust his lance deep into Yeshua's side and then withdrew it.

Nicodemus became hysterical. "What have you done?", he screamed. "It is not permitted to defile the dead! You have desecrated the laws of this land and those of Rome as well. Tribune, I demand that you discipline this man immediately."

"Sir, I defiled nothing," the guard explained to his

commander. "I saw him move. See! See how he bleeds."

Almost as if relieved, the tribune nodded his approval. If this was a test by Pilate, then surely he had done everything to demonstrate the proper response. "He'll die for certain now. Finish bringing him down and hand him over to Nicodemus"

By this time Nicodemus had made the transition from hysteria to absolute shock. Once more I sensed there was an undercurrent of some plan that had definitely gone awry by this time. Taking the body, Nicodemus began the preparation for burial back at his estate. And when the linens had been packed with spices and the second cloth was wrapped around the head, the small procession carried Yeshua to my own tomb within my garden and laid it to rest. I had offered my own tomb only as a temporary solution for the Passover, until such time that I could contact Yeshua's family and have them make their own final arrangements.

Nicodemus never said a word about what may have been his intentions. I had my suspicions though. It was obvious to me that the wine-vinegar had been tainted with something far more potent. An opiate perhaps. Had it worked, Yeshua would have survived his crucifixion and the greatest miracle ever would have been foisted upon the people.

Several days later, still in the middle of the Passover my tomb was empty. No arrangements had been made to explain it, but I was not surprised. His followers must have carried him away in the cover of the night. How could they leave their messiah to rot in my tomb after all? Such things are for lesser men, ordinary men, mortal men. Such were the events surrounding Yeshua's death. There were no miracles. There was no fault to be cast upon me. There was no sin other than my failure to save him.

Once again I caution you that I think the time grows near to prepare my tomb. I think I will be returning to Jerusalem very soon. The pains I suffer are being exacerbated by the cold dampness of a Roman winter. I fear I will not make it until the spring. I love you my son. Tell your brother I love him too.

CHAPTER TWENTY-SIX

"So why use his own tomb," John pressed his pencil to paper awaiting an answer.

"Wouldn't you do the same for family?" I asked in return.

"You've mentioned that before, but I still don't see how they were connected. Other than being from priestly families."

"That connection started about 230 B.C. with a common ancestor named Alcimus. I mentioned him earlier as an interesting fellow in his own right. You had several sons vying to be High Priest at that time and in order to do so they had to win the favour of the Seleukid Kings of Syria. That in itself was pretty difficult since these kings liked switching around the vestments of the High Priest more than even the Romans did. One of the sons was Alcimus or Joakim as he was known amongst the Jews in the province of Judaea where God's name was most commonly known as Yahweh. But he worked out a deal with the Seleukids to unify the Samaritans back into mainstream Judaism. To everyone in the northern provinces he was known as Eliakim, where God's name was Eloh or El for short. And the Seleukids Greekified it to Alcimus. So now you have a little idea about this fellow. He's shrewd, he's power hungry, and he's constantly fighting for his political life.

Now Alcimus has two sons, Mathias and Sadok. Five generations down from Mathias, Joseph Caiaphas is born. But Sadok is the more interesting son. Because he has his own son, Achim, whom in turn has Elius, who is father of Eliud, the father of Eleazar, the father of Matthan, the father of Jacob, the father of Joseph. And Joseph as the story goes, married Mary and they had several children, one whom we know as Jesus of Nazareth. There is the connection. They were cousins, distant cousins. Very distant."

"But family is family."

"Exactly! You have to appreciate that it was a different world back then. Just take a look even now. Two thousand years since Caiaphas and those in my family still recognize ourselves as Kohenim. We know our tribal affiliation is Levite but in truth none of this is really of any significance in today's world. But we can't let go of our ties, our past, our family. Back then it would have been even stronger. As far as Caiaphas was concerned, Jesus was family. Therefore he was entitled to lie in the tomb until such time that his own family would have transferred him. As they say, 'blood is thicker than water.' "

"I guess under those circumstances it makes some sense," Pearce acknowledged.

"When you put the pieces of the puzzle together it really does make a very complete picture. There's no mystery men, no anonymous benefactors, no conspiracy theories. Just a bunch of men playing politics with the lives of those less fortunate, just as my wife described it."

"But still…"

I knew exactly what he wanted to say. "But still you want to believe that God had a hand in all of this. I'm not saying that divine intervention didn't play a role. After all the fact is that the tomb was empty and one of the world's great religions was built from these events. That tells you that there was something special about Jesus that set him apart from every other spiritual leader. It shouldn't though have to be a case of all or nothing. Believing in what Jesus stood for shouldn't depend on having to accept all the hocus pocus as part of the package. It's ludicrous to think that his teachings couldn't stand on their own merit."

"I'm not denying that Doc. We've been down this avenue before and I'm willing to be open to what you're saying. But you have a lot to learn about people. We need the hocus pocus. We don't like to think everything is ordinary and common place. It's the out of the ordinary that excites us and gives us hope. Because if we can't believe that our dreams might actually be possible, then you've taken away one of the primary reasons for living. We want to be deluded." Pearce presented his case to me as if he was in a court of law. "You don't see it do you?"

"You know I'm that odd hybrid of scientist and religious proponent. In order that the two don't consume me in a pitched battle for dominance I have to rationalise a compromise. And if I can do that using memories from antiquity, then so much the better. You're right that I don't see the need for mysticism. I just don't believe there is a need for it. The truth makes a much better story as far as I'm concerned!"

ROME: 41 AD

My son, I just had a very entertaining night with Jonathias. He is like a salve for my old age. When he is around I don't have time to worry about my infirmity. We have so much to talk about. That doesn't leave me any time to immerse myself in self-pity.

He's very knowledgeable about events occurring in Judaea. I sometimes wonder whether he is looking for a political career greater than what can be found through Temple service. He's been asking about our kinsman Judas. While he was in the market square today he came across a preacher from 'the Way' that was telling his version of Judas' death. He questioned as to why the truth has apparently become a secret of what really happened to Judas the Iscar, son of Joazar the Boethian, son of Simon.

I know that it's well recognized that I had no great fondness for Judas, but his memory does not deserve the false accusations that are being spread by these Christians in Rome. What I find even worse, is that as I understand it, these falsehoods have actually originated from Judaea. True, no one has any love for the Boethians but still to besmirch the memory of Judas like this is a travesty. Jonathias had his first taste of how these lies have become nothing but a series of accusations that paint us as a people in a very bad light.

To recount the events as they really happened will have little effect in dispersing the fallacy they have fabricated. But the reality was that few amongst the followers of Yeshua would bother to listen to Judas after that night. In fact most were openly hostile to him. Simon Peter was the most vehement, but that was to be expected. He railed against Judas, accusing him as the betrayer of Yeshua. Who could believe Judas' version of that night? No one else had witnessed Simon Peter's act of cowardice. Denial was one of Simon's greatest assets. He continued to even deny the denial. What chance did Judas have? The betrayal was seen by all, but the denial by none.

Initially, there was no attempt made to silence Judas since Yeshua had told them that night in the garden that the betrayal was both necessary and to be expected. How could Judas be punished for something that he was expected to do. Simon Peter must have feared that given enough time, Judas might have started in succeeding in persuading people to believe his version of that night. It's not known whether Simon Peter slew Judas or had someone else do it. One day Judas' body was simply found lying in the field of Akeldama, his belly slit from top to bottom. Most of the apostles have denied any complicity. Others counter that wasn't Judas as the real Judas hung himself instead.

But there are those of us that know better. For one, his family had to prepare his body to be placed in the tomb. They certainly knew in what condition his body was returned. Saul of Tarsus is another that knows the truth. He has levelled a charge of murder against Yeshua's original disciples. He hunts them down under this premise. He's like a lion on a bone. He won't let it go until he's proven that they were all involved in killing Judas. Eventually the truth will come out as this Saul is very tenacious. I do not agree with his methods of persecution but I would not suggest to you that you try to stop him before he resolves this issue. Judas deserves this much. Fire can only be fought with fire.

Please don't think for a moment that I am condoning Saul's methods. Fanaticism from any perspective is just as dangerous. But in this particular event he works to expose the truth and therefore I can pardon his methods. I recognize full well that this Saul is a danger to all of us and in time he will have his own judgement passed against him. But now is not that time.

Enough, it is time for the good news that you'll probably be wanting to hear. I will be sending Jonathias back to you on the next tide. I cannot tell you how much his presence here has meant to me. As I mentioned he has been like a tonic to me but I know that I cannot keep him here indefinitely. He has been my strong right arm this past month. Not to mention my eyes and my ears. If there's any advice I can share with you, it is not to grow old Elioneiai. I can tell you now that you will not take pleasure in it. You expect to find wisdom in age but instead all you do is become decrepit. It's not fair but that's the way God has ordained it to be. Who are we to question the ways of God?

They say one must grow old gracefully but that is a contradiction of the highest magnitude. We are only reminded of how frail and weak we become with age. As we come in to this world so do we leave but enough about my complaining. There is still so much that I must write to you about. The world is changing and we must do more if we are to stem the rising tide before it washes us out to sea.

First we must make the Pharisees accept that we are all one people. If they continue to make divisions between themselves and those that don't believe in the same beliefs that they do, they will only fracture our society beyond repair. They claim that they wish to return us to the pure beliefs of our ancestors but they completely misconstrue the truth to suit their own misguided purpose. I have heard that they are trying to have James removed from the Temple courts but you must ensure that this does not happen. As long as James and his followers are permitted to teach openly as one of us then he will always be one of us. Do not let them force James and his followers from the court. To do so would drive a wedge completely between us and his church. They will be lost forever to us.

Damascus must reign in these followers of 'the Way.' The synagogues must keep the leaders of this faction from the pulpit. This sect has transgressed well beyond the teachings of James and his church. They no longer respond to his leadership and the proof of their guilt is contained in letters that they have sent to their disciples here in Rome. You must be vigilant in your expulsion of this pestilence. Treat them as lepers and keep them as far away as is possible from your flock. Remember that the youth of the congregations are the most susceptible. They are always searching for answers to questions that have none. These tales of fancy and fantasy from these heretics will entice them by making promises that do not exist. I fear that if we do not strike now against them they will grow like weeds in our gardens, poisoning our flowers and robbing us of our fruit.

Yeshua would never had tolerated his existence upon this earth being mitigated into a justification for turning people away from the laws of Moses. Remember it was his claim to his followers that he did not come to change the laws of Moses but to reaffirm them. Does this sound like a man that was trying to undermine the beliefs and traditions of his people? And if it was not his intention then surely we cannot let those that claim otherwise to do so under the protection of our laws of sanctuary that have come down through the ages. For these laws are only intended for those that are true believers in the Torah and it is clear that those that are the followers of 'the Way' are no longer believers in the word of God. Therefore, they are not to be extended the same privileges as if they were still a segment of our own people.

Though I urge you to be vigilant at no time is it to be done violently. There is no crime that these misguided fools have committed other than believe that there exists a dichotomy of rules and laws, one set for them and the other for the rest of the world. Have pity on them for they cannot see the errors of their ways. Man must serve God, not God serving mankind. If our laws seemed stringent, our rules harsh, then it is for a reason, so that every man comes to understand that the path of the Lord's is not laced with frankincense and myrrh.

Why not eliminate this problem once and for all you are probably thinking? We only have to leave the likes of Saul and his men to do that for us. But I have a bad premonition in doing so. I fear that we will only be making martyrs of them and that in doing so they will haunt us throughout our existence. I cannot take this chance that such a vision should prove true. We must bide our time and trust in the Lord. As long as we let all know the errors of their teachings then where can they possibly find adherents from amongst us?

Let your brother know what is to be done. He must ensure that the leaders in Jerusalem support your strategy in Damascus. I want it written that both Elioneiai Ha Cayef and Joshua Damneus are in agreement with the implementation of this policy. Otherwise we will not be able to ensure that the Diaspora follow suit. Their participation is essential since there are more of us living outside of the regions of Israel and Syria than in them and I would think that the disciples of the Church have recognized this is where they will find our weakest links in the chain. Only your combined authorities can exert an influence over the communities and synagogues in distant lands. This could prove to be the greatest challenge of your lives as I would not wish to even imagine the consequences of failure.

CHAPTER TWENTY-SEVEN

"Seems a lot more complicated than I've given it credit before," Pearce suggested.

"That has always been the biggest hurdle for anyone trying to study or examine the Judaea of Jesus. In order to do so correctly, they have to see it through Jewish eyes but most certainly not the Judaism of today and definitely not the Hasidic Judaism of the Hasmoneans. There was essentially a different Judaism back then. Tolerant, yet pedantic. Uniform but the result of a cultural mix. Consciously preserving its core foundation of basic monotheism but recognising that they were an island awash amongst a hostile sea of polytheism. And every time those waves washed across the island, it would leave behind puddles of water that would be absorbed by the vegetation. So it grew on a steady diet of heathen dogma."

"And in English Doc?"

'Forget everything you thought you knew and picture a world in which the coexistence of Judaism and Christianity was nothing more than two sides of the same coin. Problem was that you could never visualise both sides simultaneously just like the coin. Mutual exclusivity which meant that in order to survive, Christianity had to undergo expulsion."

"Justification for persecution is not easy to accept." Another attempt by Pearce to rationalise the history he knew with the world as he believed it to be.

"No, the world we know today is the result of Caiaphas' excommunication of the early Church congregations."

"You're saying Caiaphas did the right thing?"

"What's right, what's wrong? If everything that happened in the last two thousand years was meant to be, then Caiaphas did the right thing."

"What would have been the alternative?" Pearce challenged.

"That's where it gets interesting. Had he not forced them out of the congregation then in most likelihood there would have either been a dilution of Christian teaching so that it became no more than another sect of Judaism, or else Judaism itself would have been transformed so that there was a hybrid religion that was a little bit of both but having a definite resemblance to Jewish secularism."

"And what about that option of hunting them down and terminating the problem as he described it?"

"What you would have had if that was the case would have been an early example of ethnic cleansing. Never happened since we know that Christianity went on to grow and spread quite well after its inception. What we also know is that the first real attempt to eradicate the early Christians came from the Romans starting about twenty years after Jesus' death. Why? — Because they were becoming too prolific. And they were too prolific because they were pretty much left alone."

"That's not the way they describe it,"

"I would have thought John that you gave up believing everything you read a long time ago."

"You mean after we met."

"Especially after we met!" I corrected him.

"You want me to accept so much, Doc. Do you ever think that sometimes it's just too much?"

"Too much?"

"Yeah, too much. You want to change the world and that's too much for any one man to achieve."

I began to laugh. Pearce was becoming quiet amusing even if it was unwittingly.

"What's so funny?"

"I was just thinking that line must have been used a very long time ago. It wasn't true then. One man did change the world."

"Maybe so, but just because it happened once don't go expecting to see it happen again. Because it won't."

"There's a lot of evidence to the contrary," I managed to say in between my laughter. "History's all about men changing the world. We just don't look hard enough to see it when it is happening. That's why we call it history. Because we only see it much later, well after the fact."

"I should have known better to start this discussion with you," Pearce muttered.

"That's never been your forte, John. Knowing better would have been never trying to find me in the first place. Now that you've let the genie out of the bottle, it isn't going to go back in. And you want to know the irony of it all. Let's just say that everything I've told you becomes verified, as I expect it to be — still a few bone boxes to be uncovered, not to mention a few scrolls that will come out of hiding. Then it won't be a case of anyone else but you having changed the world."

Pearce thought about it momentarily then conceded that I had a point there. After all, had he left me to my own life without his interference, none of this would ever have become known.

"Not really much different from the situation Caiaphas faced," I suggested. "Whether he acted or remained passive would one way or the other ultimately change history."

"And so you've come around full circle," he observed. "It's going to take me some time to consider an alternate perspective of Caiaphas."

"That's all we can ask," I assured him. "That's what it's all about. Making people think about what may have really happened back then. It's not good enough for me just to say it was so. Because you got to remember that the only one seeing the pictures rerunning over and over again in his head, is me. If we do a good job translating my images into words, then maybe, just maybe those that read my story will have an appreciation for what I see. But having an appreciation doesn't mean they necessarily accept it. That comes much later. That occurs when they recognize there's only one way things happen. Could be more than a half dozen explanations but the actual event has a singularity of focus."

"I can agree with that, Doc. Used to report traffic accidents for one of the papers I worked for in the past. There were times I couldn't believe how there could be so many variations on a single accident by so-called credible witnesses. I used to think that they couldn't possibly have been reporting the same accident, their stories were so different."

"Makes you wonder if we even have the capacity to see things the same as anyone else," I postulated.

"Or maybe it's like the Matrix," Pearce proposed.

"Let's not get ridiculous John," I cautioned. "That's a movie. Science fiction. Don't cross wires here. It's hard enough to establish the truth without going off on a tangent into never-never land."

"I just meant…"

"I'll keep emphasising the fact that Caiaphas was not the bogey man he's been described to be over the last two millennia. He was a father, husband, grandfather not unlike anyone else. He was born to affluence, power and heritage.   Privileged? Yes. Unsympathetic? No. If anything, he cared about too many things. He saw the survival of his entire nation sitting squarely upon his shoulders and that meant he had to walk a tightrope between life and death knowing that the souls of all those people were his to care for."

I must have been getting tired because I was starting to sermonise.   That was something I found myself doing frequently when I wanted to bring a long overdrawn discussion to an end. I found myself actually beginning to do it now and took a quick glance at my watch. The day was almost gone. Felt like it had flown by. I started to apologise to John. He didn't need me coming down on him so strong. How was he to know anything different from what he had been taught as a little boy? The entire world was grey but when it came to telling the story of the Passion and the Crucifixion, suddenly the world was in Technicolor. Clear as a bell. Caiaphas did it, the Jews all took part in it, and now let's get out there and beat them to a pulp because sixty-five generations ago, one of their political leaders is accused of a crime we don't particularly like. Deicide!. Of course that's a little incongruent because you can't really kill a god since to be a god you have to be immortal. But what the heck, we'll punish them anyway.

"Hey Doc, you with me?" I must have just started slipping into a sleep because there was Pearce shaking my shoulder in order to get my attention. "You seemed to have disappeared on me there," he suggested. "See anything unusual?"

"Actually wasn't visualising Caiaphas' thoughts at all."   I tapped my forehead with the first knuckle of my right hand in an effort to shake the cobwebs from my brain. "Getting harder to keep focused. Maybe we should continue this in the morning?"

"Perhaps we can just finish off telling those last few days," Pearce suggested. "Then I'll have a complete chunk of the story I can work on tonight if I can't sleep."

"I'll do my best but without that intravenous drip of caffeine I can't guarantee I'm going to make it."

"Hey, how about you just have Caiaphas fill in the blanks as to what happened after Jesus was put in the tomb. That had to be important to Caiaphas at the time. A body goes missing, it's got to be a concern."

ROME: 42 AD

The fatigue now grows increasingly weary my son. I know you have heard it from my lips for quite some time that I am in the last of my days but at this juncture I believe my span is measured in weeks rather than months. I have no regrets. I am an old man and the Lord has been kind to me most of my days. What has transpired has done so because of weakness. My own failure to stand up against the tyranny of one Roman. One self-serving, pompous, sadistic man that for ten years governed us by grinding our spirit beneath his heel. And that will become my legacy. Not for what I've done but for what I failed to do. Such fickleness this fate of ours. To live, to die, but rarely leave a mark to our passing.

I seek nothing more than is my right. I ask for nothing that is not my due. And if in wake there is but one life to which I have made a difference, then all was not for naught. I will teach you a song Elioneiai. It has been passed down through our family since Aaron first wore the ephod. They say that his sister Miriam taught it to him much in the same way that she taught all the Children of Israel to sing at the time of the parting of the Red Sea. Since childhood I have heard it resound within my head, and somehow I know that my father heard it, as did his father, and his before him. As if the song is alive in our memories and passes magically from one generation to the next. Perhaps you have also heard it.

My heart is raised in joyous song,
My eyes see the glory in all its manifestation,
But my lips are silent like the still of the night,
Fearful of man and his condemnation.

Voices no longer shout from the wilderness in these days,
Proclaiming the greatness of Your being,
Can You not see, these are wicked days and evil times,
When the lone voice can be silenced forever.

Who am I Lord, to know Your message,
This worthless vessel of organic clay,
Tainted by the vanities and pleasures of our age,
Chained by fears and doubts of worthiness.

Look and see the backslider that I am,
Why then do you persist in Your pursuit,
Can You not witness the failing of my lips,
The faltering of both my desire and will?

You have sent Your signs and wonders,
Reaffirming Your faith but I know not why,
How can You believe in one who does not believe in himself,
Do not taunt me with Your everlasting promises.

Where are the golden bells that ring with each step I take,
Or the blessing of Your name, lying flat against my forehead,
There is no incense burner hanging from my hand as I pass amongst
them,
What has been is gone, and what is gone is no longer known.

But who am I to tell You what I can and cannot be,
All things are possible within the unfolding of Your power,
If You so desire to resurrect the past, it is within Your awesome
glory,
Though I have not the right to question, You still tolerate my
iniquity.

You, who are so willing to overlook my failings,
Placing Your trust in one that thinks himself unworthy,
Nurturing my spirit which is weak and faltering,
Who am I to doubt Your undeniable will?

Instill in me the confidence to uphold Your divine mission,
Raise the standards so I may carry them proudly before my enemies,
Carry before me the shield that turns aside the anger of the many,
And I will trumpet Your song to the ends of the earth.

I will not ask You to make for me the smooth path,
Nor do I seek the burden of a lightened yoke
The weight upon my shoulders will not cast me down,
For I know that I am in the service of a fair master.

When I have been disobedient, You have shown patience,
At times of my unruliness, You have been tender,
My waywardness has not brought an evil word from Your mouth,
And always You have welcomed me into Your heart.

Ask and I will give, speak and I will listen,
Give me strength and wisdom and my burden will be lightened,
I know that which You desire of me must be done, I will obey,
Yours is the Glory forever and ever, I will not fail You.

It has a certain ancient beauty, would you not say so, Elioneiai? It rings so clear of how we once used to live our lives. When we were free, when our kings ruled and God marched in the lead of our armies as a pillar of fire. It is our song. The song of the Kahana. Sung by our family through the centuries and now it heralds my coming home to the Lord. As long as we live there will be someone to sing it. I trust you will ensure that your brother will also take its words to heart. Perhaps you know them already, just as they were imprinted upon my soul the day that I was born, so may they have been gifted to you.

There have always been songs amongst our people. Whether sung for victory or times of defeat, they have raised our spirits and brought us hope. What were they singing that day when Yeshua was nailed to a Roman cross? They had lost hope, filled their hearts with despair, resigning themselves to the loss of their master. Theirs is a song of lament extending through time. For no matter how long it has been since the passing of Yeshua, they still sing of his passing and glorify his name. I bear them no angst. Their loss was in part my loss but never would I have dreamed that they would delude themselves into a false sense of reality in order to preserve failed hopes. My good friend Nicodemus has become the worst of their lot. Rather than prepare for the coming day of our retribution he lives in the memories of the past

The Romans posted guards over my tomb in order to secure

the area against thieves in the night. Because my tomb was only serving as a temporary resting place until his family came forward to take his body, the sealing stone had neither been sealed nor even completely rolled across the entrance. Our occupiers are a strange lot, fearing the unknown more than the truth of reality. Pilate was especially convinced that Yeshua's body would be taken and in so doing his followers would raise it as an icon to worship. I too thought it may be stolen even though to do so would be a desecration of our laws for the dead must be properly buried within three days, so that their bones will be ready in a year's time to be relocated into the ossuary. That is our custom but these were unusual circumstances. Their cause outweighed the preservation of our customs. I was not surprised when it was reported to me that the body had been taken just as the procurator had predicted.

Who did it I cannot say. What was even more suspicious was that both the body linen and the head cloth were left behind. Why remove the burial cloths at all? Why indeed. What if there was no one to be buried. And then I thought over again our conversation with Pilate. And Nicodemus' choice of words. Nicodemus will not lie, which for a politician is an amazing feat. So his failure to refer to a corpse may have been intentional. The more I thought about it, the clearer it became. When Pilate questioned how Yeshua could have been dead already after only a few hours on the cross, there was no sudden expression of grief from Nicodemus. Not a single tear. How could one that loved Yeshua so much not even shed a tear upon hearing that his Master was dead?

In fact the only time I saw any sign of emotion from my old friend was when the Tribune pierced the side of Yeshua's body with his lance. Not anger as I would have suspected, but fear. What could he have been afraid of? I wrestled with that question for a long time.

Not too long though because several days after the crucifixion, there were reports of Yeshua appearing to some of his closest disciples. The appearances were brief and for the most part they ended almost as quickly as they began. Then he was no more. Never seen again as if he had never been. To this day Nicodemus will not say a word about what truly transpired.

It is only conjecture on my part but I believe it to be well founded and as about as close to the truth as anyone will get. This is what I believe. Several hours following Yeshua being hung upon the cross, the guards posted at Golgotha were distracted. I've even heard it said that they were playing dice, so it would not have taken much to add something to the draught of wine vinegar that they keep in the barrels by the site. You see, Elioneiai, that is how I presumed it was done. They would be the ones to provide the drink so no one would suspect a thing, least of all the guards themselves. After all, they'd be the ones administering it. The frequency which it's given is quite predicable, since the Romans use it as a stimulant to maximize the entertainment value. It was pointed out to me by Marcus Bibulus that there is no lesson to be taught the populace by an unconscious victim on the cross. But one screaming and wailing conveys the most important of lessons. 'That this is where you will end up if you defy Rome and it will not be pleasant.'

Place shephen into the vat of vinegar and it will produce a deep sleep not unlike death. And with that sleep of death, Nicodemus would race to the procurator's palace pleading for the body to be brought down for the Sabbath. Only a physician would be able to determine the shephen induced sleep from actual death, since the body responds to very little. Neither pain, nor touch, nor even sound can stir one from the effects of the seeds.

Although I have never directly asked for the truth, there is little doubt in my mind that there was a carefully conceived plan spearheaded by Nicodemus that went awry. But it would not be in their best interests to admit to such a plan and therefore the full truth will likely die along with their last breaths. Had they trusted me enough, perhaps together we could have made it work. Now we will never know!

CHAPTER TWENTY-EIGHT

Pearce wrote furiously as he put the final touches to the letter just completed by Caiaphas. "And then he dies, I guess. Is that how it goes?" he asked.

"I wouldn't know," I commented.

"But you'd be able to see his last thoughts and memories, wouldn't you?"

"No."

"But what about GLEEM."

"I may be the embodiment of genetically recorded memories, but they're not from Caiaphas. At least not these ones."

"But you're telling me what Caiaphas was writing at the time. How can they be his memories and not be at the same time?"

"Think about it John. If the memories I carry within me are part of my inherited DNA, then I certainly didn't inherit them from Caiaphas at the end of his life. Elioneiai and Joshua Damneus were already grown men. Their days of inheriting anything from their father were long gone by then."

"So how then?'

"Jonathias," I answered.

"His grandson?"

"Yes. Do you recall what it was like to lose a family member when you were young, John? A grandparent, perhaps even a great grandparent."

"I was about twelve when my grandfather died."

"It's hard when you're young. You're never prepared for it no matter how much the adults try to explain it to you. And the images never fade away. All the events surrounding their passing remain firmly imprinted upon your memory and you carry them with you all the remaining days of your life. And their faces, of those you loved and had to say goodbye to are as vivid now as they were when they were alive. That's exactly what Jonathias experienced when he came to Rome to be with his grandfather Caiaphas. And when he had children of his own, everything he saw, everything he felt was passed on to his progeny. That is the true nature of GLEEM. Transference of data that has a highly emotional contextual value as demonstrated by its ability to cause a physiological response."

"So you're saying that everything I felt when my grandfather died was passed on to my children."

"That's correct. The only catch being that there would have to be a trigger to release it. And your children won't know what that is until it actually occurs."

"So, they may never experience it."

"Most people never do. And that's probably better in the long run for their own sake."

"I still think it would be an asset to be able to look at current reality and have an appreciation as to how it came to be. Mankind has always been searching for answers but we find them so rarely." There was the sound of disappointment in his voice.

"We've been through this before John, trust me, it's not that great a gift for a whole lot of reasons. Oh, it's nice to know your origins. But you don't have to experience what I have to live with in order to know your roots. Yes, I am born from the line of high priests, but so are many others and they don't have these persistent visions. And it's not like I'm any more deserving than anyone else. I am religious, but not as religious as those that people point towards. My slate is neither clean, nor am I guiltless of sinning. I have tried to live a good life, but there are those that have lived much better lives. For that reason, I ask just one very simple question, "Why me?" And the answer comes back each time that unlike the others there's been this constant recombining of the same genetic material occurring amongst my ancestors. The result is that I don't have need of a trigger to release ancestral memories. They release themselves. The only justification I can make out of my curse other than the fact that the recollection of memories is more pronounced through inbreeding, tends towards a religious explanation."

"I didn't think you'd attribute your situation to a religious epiphany," Pearce goaded me.

"You know John how I said I wouldn't talk about my personal relationship with the Lord, well I'm going to break that promise but just this one time. Make of it what you will but I did get an answer to my question of 'why me.' The answer provided was actually quite simple. It went like this, 'If I was to cast a rock against the door and knock it in, then they would say, 'Who has thrown this rock and broken in our door? Perhaps it has rolled down a hill and on its own and came through our door.' But if I was to cast a pebble against their door and knock it in, then they would all say, 'Surely this must be the hand of God for how else could a pebble break in our door!' That's the answer I can give you."

"What kind of answer is that?"

"The obvious kind. As Lazarus once said, 'think simply and you will understand'."

"I still don't get it. I've never been very good at riddles."

"Read Zechariah!" I instructed. "You want to have a better understanding Pearce, then read something that's been around for a long time. In Zechariah, you will find all the answers to all the riddles. You will understand not only yourself but all that has happened to me as well. Not only the why, but also what was so special about my family and what it is that I'm expected to do. And once you have an understanding, when I speak to you next, we will finally have a bridge between us built and we'll speak a common language. It won't be such a mystery to you any longer. And who knows, maybe I'll restore your faith in the process. And just perhaps when it's all over, I'll find peace within myself. And I'll go back to where I belong!"

"Oh, like that makes even more sense to me…"

"I guess I'm going to have to explain it further to you, aren't I? The Zechariah for Dummies version," I laughed but Pearce didn't find it that funny. "I'll let you in on something few people recognize. Most of the prophets were from the priesthood. From the highest order and intermarried into the royal family repeatedly. This should sound familiar to you since it's my story as well. Besides the memories passed on, we also communicate through time by composing books. So when I was reading Zechariah, I knew that in a way the prophet was speaking directly to me. That he was telling me what was going to happen in my life. And from my perspective Zechariah was not the least of the prophets but in reality the most important of the prophets. That his was the only text and all the others were merely commentaries. Each time I read the book, I see more and more of my life through his eyes. It was a personal revelation of major proportions but virtually impossible to explain to anyone else. Do you follow?"

"We have been working pretty hard tonight. Maybe we should call it a night and start again in the morning."

Obviously all this was far beyond Pearce's comprehension and it was apparent he was avoiding even trying to think about it.

"Don't patronize me, Pearce. I'm not any crazier than you are. On second thought, let me rephrase that. I'm not crazy. Nothing should surprise you any longer. With all you've learned about me you know that there is more to this world than you'll ever have time to learn."

"There are more things in Heaven and Earth, Horatio…" Pearce mused.

"Maybe Shakespeare knew something most others don't realize."

"I'm not dissing you, Doc. It's just that you shove an awful lot of information in front of my face and I know that so far it's had a good track record in proving itself to be true but I also have to view it from the angle of the reader as well. And there's certain areas that you cross easily from belief to disbelief. Trust me on this. I know the business. And voices from heaven is one of those areas you just don't want to go."

"Then we're okay because this has nothing to do with heavenly voices. All it has to do with is an old family member passing a code through his written pages and then GLEEM taking over because the code breaker is genetically wired into the family's future generations. Remember John how I explained how a trigger can release a stored memory. Although most of us wouldn't have a clue what those triggers might be, there's always a possibility that someone would have that knowledge. Zechariah appears to be one of those people. He knew exactly what to say in order to elicit the right response from his descendants. And the most amazing part is that it all occurs rather benignly. One day I just turned to Zechariah in the bible and began reading for the umpteenth time and as I began to read a particular paragraph it was as if I hit a brick wall as these words began transforming within my consciousness. I had zoned out completely to my immediate environment and then I found myself saying silently over and over again, 'that's not how you are meant to read Zechariah. You read it exactly as you have been named.' Probably lost you there again, didn't I? This didn't make any sense at all to me at first either. Firstly, I couldn't figure out why I was even saying this, and secondly it was all pretty cryptic."

Pearce smiled with an almost euphoric expression lighting up his face. For a moment I thought he was going to shout out, 'Eureka.'

"Actually Doc, I know exactly where you're coming from. I'm not lost at all. You are named Aryeh-zuk but if I was to reverse the syllables, you could have been name Zukaryeh. That's pretty close to your Zechariah., I'd say."

I was amazed. No, I take that back, I was absolutely flabbergasted. I personally struggled breaking this clue regarding the two names for at least five minutes back then before it dawned on me what the meaning of the repeating words in my head were trying to convey. Now, here was Pearce giving me the answer spontaneously before I even had the words out of my mouth. "Full credit John. You're dead on. But even so, it's not until you tie it in to a common phrase of the prophets that you realize the significance. That's the expression of that which is first shall come last and that which is last shall come first!"

"Did you apply the name reversal thing to the prophetic writings afterwards?"

"I certainly did. Having received that instruction I began reading chapters nine to fourteen first, followed by one to eight. The book suddenly takes on an entirely new meaning when you read it that way. No longer was it a historical update of the then current high priest Jeshua, followed by a few chapters of unassociated apocalyptic events. Now, it was entirely about the apocalypse, followed by an explanation of the new order and covenant. And what's really amusing that for two millennia every theologian has read the book in the usual way, and completely accepted the fact that as it's written it appears extremely disjointed with no flow at all."

"And now?" Pearce chimed in.

"When you read it in this particular fashion it takes on a whole new significance. It holds all the answers to our future."

"Really? You saw all that in the Book of Zechariah?" Pearce sounded more astonished than disbelieving.

"What it becomes is one seamless, homogeneous story about the time to come. The occult meaning of the twin crown, unsightly priest, and poor lambs, became crystal clear to me. My fear was that once I understood, I became afraid that I couldn't live up to the expectations."

"Well, aren't you going to tell me," Pearce pleaded.

"Like I said, John, it was a message being passed down through the descendants. That's where it belongs."

"But if you can see something that could change the course of the world…"

"Then I'd do exactly what I've done so far; nothing. Because as I've learned from Caiaphas, trying to change too much of the future can have devastating effects. I'll settle for just having an impact."

ROME: 42 AD

I write to you Elioneiai to let you know that your son will not be returning to you quite as soon as I had previously indicated. I need him more than ever now. As you are aware, the Emperor has brought bad tidings to our land and seeks to break our will. He has summoned me to appear in his court in two days' time to have me answer for our people's defiance to raise a statue to Caligula in the outer court of our Temple. Such a base and treacherous plot to do what no other emperor had ever considered. But I have renewed vigour in my soul, and my heel steps lightly upon the ground. I go to do battle once again. I shall not undertake my task frivolously. I have seen in my dreams what the result of my failure would be and I shall not let it happen. If I must rail against the Emperor, like a solitary tree standing against the might and fury of a raging storm, then that I will do most willingly.

Surely it must be a sign that we are at the end of days for never have I seen the world spin so quickly. With the rise of Agrippa to prominence, it sent a wave of fear down the spine of Herod Antipas. If Agrippa was to earn the complete confidence of Caligula then it would spell the end of Herod's reign for surely Caligula would hand all of Galilee to his friend. Of this Herod was most correct for anyone that knew Agrippa knew that to rule over us has always been his intention. How then could Antipas even think that he could demand of Caligula that he be made King over Galilee instead of tetrarch? Perhaps knowing that all was lost gave him the false courage to demand what he knew would never come about. As a result of his audacity, both Herod and his wife Herodias have been exiled to Gaul. What role they'll play there I do not know.

And now all of ancient Israel has been laid at the feet of Agrippa. From the heights of the Golan to the Gulf of Aqaba. From the land of the Nabateans to the desert border of the Egyptians. All is his to rule. The prince has returned now to Rome from Alexandria where Caligula will formally present these lands to be his possession and declare him ruler of all. I do not know what such power will do to such a man. It leaves him one step from being supreme in our world and our history with omnipotent kings has always been a rocky one.

It will be my intention to meet with Agrippa as soon as he arrives in the city. I have sent word of my summons to an audience with the Emperor. I know that Agrippa, Romanized or not, will not condone what Caligula intends to do in the Temple. And there lies my advantage. For above all men, Caligula loves Agrippa and he will pay him heed. There is my opportunity to save our people and our religion. With the persuasion and presence of Agrippa by my side I intend to thaw the heart of the Emperor and change him from this course of blasphemous action.

Jonathias will be by my side where he will learn first-hand what it means to be of the line of High Priests of God's chosen people. We bend no knee before any man, not even one that now calls himself a god. Do not fear for his safety, for the Lord will protect us. Of that I am certain. It has been a long time since I've felt the fire in my soul and now that it rages once again, it will be like a might inferno, tearing down the horrors that are set against us. The Righteous Lion of Kamithea will roar again and its roar will deafen and shake the very foundations of this wicked city. And the Holy Spirit will be infused into my grandson and he will see with eyes that are the gift that has been given to us by God and passed down from generation to generation.

God has charged me not to allow an idol be set within the Holy House. Even if it is to be my dying breath I ensure that such a travesty shall not take place. But I do not fear, for as I said the presence of God is within me and his voice rings within my ears. He has sworn to me Elioneiai that no matter what evil befalls our people he will watch over us and nurture us. Though we may not even pretend to understand the working of the Lord's strange ways, we must at least believe in his promises. He has declared that the rod and the sceptre shall not fall from between our feet for all eternity. Though we may suffer great losses, and be cast amongst the nations so that they may do evil things to us, He will never desert us.

I fear not these insane visions of this lunatic emperor. He will press his good fortune too far and will be made to suffer for it. No man no matter how noble of birth, nor how powerful can escape the judgment of the Lord. The great shall be humbled and their bones will be crushed beneath the heels of the common man. Caligula's fate will be no different. He has challenged the Almighty God and he has been found to be wanting, an insignificant speck of dust that stings the eye momentarily when the wind blows but it soon washed away by the tears that it creates.

For all our existence we have been tested. It will be no different in the distant future. This appears to be the fate of those that bear the imprint of God. Our trials and tribulations are predetermined and God measures us by the strength of character which we raise against adversity. Do not think that in some way we can change this destiny. Merely learning the manner in which we can survive will be reward enough. Every other nation has withered and passed away through time never to return. But we have survived the heavy hand of them all and while they have become nothing more than memories that quickly fade and cannot be recalled, we are still here. Recognize this for the miracle it truly is. And see to it that we do not forget the importance of its lesson. We are entrusted with the survival of our people and in order to do so we must know that at the proper time, just as much can be won with an open hand as with a closed fist.

Yeshua was not unaware of this. He foretold of the suffering that we would incur. He knew that the yoke of Rome would be a heavy one to bear. And the other-worlders would mar us with their whips; scar our bodies until we are scorned by all that look upon us. We will suffer in God's name. But this fate will be our strength. The more they oppress us, the stronger we will rise from the flames. And we will be a light unto the world in all the days of darkness. This message Yeshua carried from God. Of that I have no doubt.

CHAPTER TWENTY-NINE

"I thought he was dying. Just how long did Caiaphas keep on going?" Pearce was becoming somewhat impatient. Understandable since the hour was late and he was rapidly growing as tired as I was.

"You want to know the full story, don't you? He just didn't disappear from history after Jesus died. In fact, his involvement in history continued to be just as important from the Jewish perspective afterwards as what is the very singular view of the Christian perspective."

"I didn't realize…."

"Of course you didn't. That's why I'm telling you this. You have to understand something John. When we first started this book you had nothing but scorn and contempt for my ancestor."

"No...No, that's not true,' he interjected.

"Come on now, John. Don't try to deny it. You're no different from the other ninety-nine percent of the Christian world that exists. You were nursed on this stuff from the day you were born. Caiaphas did this, Caiaphas did that. It was on your face the moment you spotted his name on the genealogy chart. You can deny it all you want, but I know what I saw."

"But that's not fair," Pearce tried to excuse his behaviour. "I will admit, I was a little shocked when I first saw his name there. Only because it's hard to think of him as a real person. And that he would have descendants."

"That's the problem. He was a real person with real wants and needs just like everyone else. Except he wasn't like everyone else. He was entrusted with the wellbeing and care of an entire nation. When he made decisions, he had to do in on the basis of ensuring that his people benefited from the outcome. The awesome responsibility he bore on his shoulders was frightening when measured against anything comparable that we could think of in today's society. You'd have to place it on the level of a Harry

Truman ordering the bombs dropped on Hiroshima and Nagasaki. The unleashing of a horror that is immeasurable on the scale of what we consider humanity in order that a greater evil was prevented from occurring."

"I admit that I never contemplated that comparison before."

"Really, why not?"

"I don't know," Pearce defended his failure to look beyond superficial evidence, "just never thought about it. Didn't know enough!"

"I'll tell you why. Because like everyone else, Caiaphas was a black figure synonymous with evil. He didn't have another face. He wasn't allowed to have one. But as you'll come to realize, as I tell you about the rest of his life, he had many more dimensions to his character than you could ever imagine. Yes, I have the advantage of seeing his life in its entirety, but that's no excuse for the world never to have looked deeper than just scratching the surface. I can only hope that by the time you're finished writing all this down you'll at least understand why I can say I'm proud to have him as an ancestor."

"I'm already changing my views by what I've seen so far," Pearce defended himself. "I'm realizing that he was operating within a whole bunch of conditions that I never had considered before. I'm not making excuses for him, or anything like that, but you've made me appreciate, Doc, that he wasn't living in a vacuum either."

"There's so much more you have to learn about that time, John. I'll do my best to educate our audience but they'll have to do the rest. As Caiaphas had said, everything was in a political turmoil. Caligula was one crazy mother of an emperor if you excuse me for saying so. He started off well, but something snapped and before anyone could react, he was nominated his horse as a senator, then as coregent, and everything you heard about him sexually probably doesn't record half the things he did. Then you have the entire old order of Herodian tetrarchs tossed out on their ears and a quarter Hasmonean, three-quarters Herodian king put in their place. But as far as the Jewish world was concerned, that one quarter made him one hundred percent Hasmonean in their eyes and that's all they cared about. Then you have Caligula threatening to erect a statue of himself in the inner court of the Temple which is about as sacrilegious as you can get in Judaism. The whole thing smacks of Jesus' comments of derision against the Temple, which had to make some think that he had powers of precognition. To the Christians and the followers of 'the Way', they saw it as the clearing of the road to make their big push. With Judaism faltering, they were ideally placed to fill the lacunae that would be left behind."

"You'd think there would have been supporting documentation for what you're suggesting, Doc. All these events and yet no one ever took the time to really write about it as a historian. It may surprise you, but I have read Josephus, and he really doesn't' record much about it."

"So you figure if he didn't write about it, then it didn't happen. The fact that he only gave Jesus a single paragraph didn't do him justice either, but we know as a single individual, he ended up changing the world. How could Josephus have missed that?"

"I dunno."

"I mentioned to you once before John, history belongs to the victors. They get to write it the way they want everyone to see it. They also have the power to obliterate everything that runs contrary to their version of the world."

"You're suggesting that Josephus' book was tampered with?"

"Anything is possible. But you're wrong about documents not surviving. One very important document has survived. It's called the Zadokite document. I happen to have a copy in the house. Not the original, just a recent copy. It's in Hebrew and for that reason most scholars haven't bothered to do much with it, considering it just an interesting artifact from a group of priests without a Temple cult to work within any longer."

"What does it have to do with the history of this particular time?" Pearce asked.

"Everything! In case you don't know the story, it was found in the ancient archive of the genizah of the main synagogue in Cairo. And it has laid there for a very long time, being copied once the older copy began to disintegrate with age, so that there was always a version preserved."

"That's nice, but I still don't see the connection."

"See, that's where you have to start asking questions. Why take such care to preserve it. What was its legacy that it had to be maintained for almost two thousand years? For all intents and purposes, it's an irrelevant document having absolutely nothing to do with Rabbinical Judaism. In fact, it was what you could probably call the opposite faction."

"You mean the priests?"

"No I don't. With a name like the Zadokite document that is exactly whom you'd expect it to be from, but it's not!"

"Then who?"

I rose from my seat and walked over to the bookshelves where I began to fumble through the stack of books until I found the one I was looking for. Having found my prize, I returned to my chair and immediately began to flip through the pages of the book, almost unconsciously. I made certain that Pearce saw it for himself. That he realized that it really did exist

"When I translated it for myself I came to the conclusion that it was definitely not a Zadokite document, and being from the long line of priests, I'd definitely know, and it wasn't from the Essenes either, as others have claimed."

"Oh, for crying out loud Doc are you going to tell me or aren't you?" Pearce cried out in frustration.

"It was written by those that called themselves 'the Many' and they claimed to follow 'the Way.' These weren't a priestly faction, nor the 'Sons of Light' as the Essenes referred to themselves. These people considered themselves to be children of righteousness following the teaching of the 'Righteous Teacher', whom we know to be an Essene personage, but also following the 'Unique Teacher'. There is no Essene correlation to someone called the 'Unique Teacher'. This particular person had been recently involved in their lives, only to have been taken away from them suddenly. This 'Unique Teacher' was none other than Jesus and 'the Many' were the initial members of his following within the Jerusalem Church. As far as they were concerned, they had inherited the new covenant between man and God. And what they write about is how they were finding themselves being overwhelmed by their contemporaries that had hijacked their teachings and were now distorting them beyond recognition."

"Therefore, you're saying this is a Christian document."

"Indeed. One of the very first."

"Well then, that doesn't make much sense, does it? Why would it be stored in a synagogue for all those years? That's the last place anyone would go looking for it!"

"Exactly what they would have thought. You just proved their point, John."

His mouth opened releasing the all intelligent, "unghhh?"

"Early Church history John; there's the Jewish sect, doing exactly what was laid down for them by Jesus and followed through by his brother James and cousin Cleophas. Then there's the breakaway segment, that's floating between two worlds and trying not to make any decisions either way. That's Peter's group. Another group has formed around John Lazarus. More abstract in its thinking, not concerned with the real world. Very ephemeral and cultic, trying to plant both feet firmly in never-never land. And finally there's Saul's or now known as Paul's group. This man plays for keeps, takes no hostages, and when he sets his mind to something, he's a force to be reckoned with. You have to remember that as a bounty hunter he didn't let anything stand in his way, do you really think he was that different when he decided to take the helm of Christianity?"

"You still didn't answer why it was hidden away in an Egyptian synagogue."

"I thought I did."

"No, you definitely did not."

"Well then, you didn't understand my previous answer. I'll give you the subtitled version." I regretted saying that. It wasn't John's fault that he didn't pick up on my innuendo. "I'm sorry John. I'm tired. I shouldn't have said that. Guess I lose a bit of my patience as I get tired. You might even say I get cranky."

"No harm done, eh?"

"No harm done. The Jerusalem Church, the original church was failing. It was too much like any of the other Jewish sects to be considered anything different. They used the synagogues to preach, they broke bread with their fellow Jewish congregations, and the only thing that separated them was their belief that the messiah had already come. And that's what most theologians fail to realize. It's not a crime to believe in the coming of a messiah in Judaism, or in the fact that he came. Messiahs come and go. That's a basic tenant of Judaism. Yes, there are the big two that I mentioned earlier, and they are the ultimate, end of days messiahs, but in the meantime it was fine for saviours to appear regularly if need be. Messianic belief is core to Jewish fundamentalism. So why would there be a problem if one part of the congregation wanted to believe that a messiah had come and gone in their lifetime. So the bonds in the early days of the Church were still quite strong with mainstream Judaism. With the death of James, all that changed. Cleophas wasn't charismatic. A claim to leadership simply because he was a cousin to Jesus wasn't enough to hold his group together. Those that preached alternate realities to the original church teachings were becoming stronger, especially since they began converting the gentile populations. Essentially they were diluting the early teachings through the introduction of pagan beliefs in order to decrease the adverse hardships that adopting the religion represented to the new converts."

"You are mentioning hardships that had to be relaxed but you're not spelling it out for the reader, Doc."

"Offhand I can think of a couple that really presented a problem to the Gentiles. Circumcision was one that really gave them a lot of difficulty. If there was going to be pain involved, they didn't want any part of it. Paul was the first to sell out in that area. He wanted adherents and if eliminating a stipulation handed down by God directly to Moses was what it was going to take, he was willing to do so. After all, what did it matter if God said to do it! Dietary laws were next. A choice between your eternal soul or a good pork roast, and the pig won. Once again it was Paul that made that happen. Amazing isn't it?"

"What's that?"

"How easy it was to throw away twelve hundred years of tradition, heritage, and doctrine."

"So why do you think it was that easy to do," Pearce inquired.

"Because Judaism was already in a flux. Over the previous two centuries it had absorbed Galilee, Peraea and Idumaea. Sure, it converted the people there to Judaism, but it wasn't the fire and brimstone Judaism of Moses' days. This was a modernized, tolerant, almost 21st century religion for today. And because it wasn't as stringent as we're led to believe, it was prone to be exploited. And that's what strong individuals like Paul did."

"First of all, I don't know where Peraea is, so I don't have a clue where you're talking about. And secondly, if they're as lenient as you're saying, then it doesn't make a lot of sense that they'd even put someone on trial for blasphemy, let alone allow him to be crucified."

"Now you've got it!" I congratulated him.

"Got what?"

"Your first break through. I told you, John, everything you thought you knew, you had to forget. You're half way there. You remember how Caiaphas told you that Jesus followed a Samaritan custom of holding the first night of the Passover a day earlier."

"Yeah."

"Well, he didn't tell you the whole story. In the Mishnah, the codified laws of Judaism, Pes. 4:5 to be exact, the rabbis of the time mention that all of the Galileans started the celebration on the previous evening. There were variations within the religious practices everywhere, which is like extending an open invitation to extremists to make an attempt for radical change."

"So where's the problem?"

"The problem is that whereas mainstream Judaism was fairly tolerant up to a point, the offshoot extremists weren't tolerant at all. And the Christian radical groups certainly weren't accepting of a group like the Jerusalem Church which wouldn't have any part of their expansion into Gentile lands without proper conversion. And if they couldn't get approval from Jerusalem, then these radicals decided they would do just as well without Jerusalem. That got ugly after a while, because when the daughter detests the mother, it only spirals downwards until one party is eliminated. In this case, it was the Jerusalem Church that was being eradicated. They ran for their lives, most of them ending up in Egypt, and the only support group they had was the still very tolerant Jewish sects of the time, which welcomed them to worship within their synagogues and when they finally became extinct as an early Christian sect, they laid their ancient documents to rest in the Genizah of the synagogue. And that's why it was found there."

Pearce scratched his head which I have come to realize is an unconscious signal that he gives when the kernel of an idea is finally boring down into the centre of his brain. "This is all very difficult for me to absorb. On one hand you're telling me, or I should say Caiaphas is telling me or his son that they have to make a clear separation from the Christians, because he's feeling threatened by them, and you're saying that isn't the case, that Judaism is very tolerant and accepting of the this new sect. In fact it's all warm and fuzzy and there's even a willingness to share their houses of worship and who knows what else."

"You're forgetting about Caiaphas' perceptive abilities. He's seeing a future relationship that isn't very warm and fuzzy as you call it. Let's face it John, Christianity over the last two thousand years hasn't exactly been the biggest supporter of Judaism, has it? Between attempts of genocide, ghettoizing, branding, burning, torturing and converting, I'd say Caiaphas had it figured out pretty damn right! Wouldn't you? But he didn't fully realize this until the audience with Caligula. Things got awfully ugly then. That's when Caiaphas switched from being very accommodating to self-preservation mode for his people. He was forced to swallow his pride and realized just how small a speck Judaea was in the eye of a Roman Emperor.

ROME: 42 AD

I cannot believe that we have fallen so far and fast into the pits of Gehenna. Elioneiai, the battle of my life is about to be engaged. Never have we been tried as a people as we were today. So great is our tribulation that the heavens cried tears enough to fill the ocean. We are to be sorely tested, but I have prayed continuously since I returned to my apartment in the hope that God will intercede on our behalf.

It was fortunate that Agrippa stood with me before Caligula. The emperor is completely depraved of his senses. Whatever he has become afflicted with has left him bereft of any intelligence. Rome is in the hands of a madman and there seems little to stand in front of him as he heads down a path of recklessness. But the Jewish Prince has a settling effect on Caligula's madness. Agrippa has a unique ability to still even the hottest rage that the emperor railed against us. Had it not been for Agrippa, I do not know if I would be back in my apartment now or in a dungeon deep beneath the palace walls.

Caligula has demanded that we as a people begin to pay homage to him, not as our emperor but as a god. At first I thought he could not be serious. No one has ever made such an outlandish claim in this manner. The Romans had always had a custom of deifying their dead glorious leaders, but never had one had the audacity to demand such honour while still very much alive. For this, God will curse him beyond measure and his life will be forfeit before I set foot in the grave. Of this I am certain. No one can mock God and escape his retribution.

When both Agrippa and I tried to explain to Caligula that his demand could never be met, he grew furious and began to cast objects about the room. The clang and clatter of metal as it crashed against the walls was all about us. At any moment I thought he would pick up a spear or a dagger and thrust it at us, erasing our lives in such a thoughtless and ignoble manner.

Not even Agrippa could soothe him with talk at that juncture. Caligula's eyes were wide with insanity, the spit spraying from his mouth as he screamed relentlessly. And then he made his most nefarious comments for which I hurl a thousand curses upon his head. When I thought there was little more he could do to offend our senses by demanding us to pay homage to his assumed godhood, he found a way to make even that demand blanche by comparison. In his scorn for us, he demanded that we erect a statue not in the outer court as first proposed but now well within the inner court, our holy sanctuary. Not any statue, but one of Caligula as Jupiter. And this statue is to be twenty cubits tall. May Asmodeus seal the tongue of this wicked and vain little man so that it cleaves to the roof of his mouth preventing him from ever uttering another word, so painful are the ones that he did issue this day. Had I a weapon in my hand that moment I would have cut his heart from his chest and ended this evil once and for all.

I thought I could reason with the madman. I tried to explain that our religious laws would forbid such an erection but to no avail. No sooner had I mentioned that both Augustus and Tiberius had guaranteed that we would not be subjected to placing statues of the Roman pantheon of gods within our holy places in respect for our antiquity of traditions, Caligula challenged the sanctity of our beliefs by insisting that our own Jewish teachers in Rome had been the first to state that the deification of a man was not incongruous with Judaism. I asked him to identify who would say such a thing and he immediately answered that both Aquila and Priscilla had said it was so. Here is where the Christian heresies have come back to haunt us.

Aquila and Priscilla are no more than Jewish Christians that have grown rich upon their preying on the ignorant of Roman society. True, Aquila was once a respected Jewish scholar but now he is nothing more than a pariah sucking the life blood from the Roman aristocracy at the same time he empties their coffers. He has created an entire set of beliefs based on the resurrection of Yeshua with but a smattering of the parables that Yeshua preached amongst the people. This falsehood of life after death has obviously reached the ears of the Emperor and he has chosen to believe in it literally. And based upon this misguided philosophy he has extrapolated this resurrected messiah dogma into a justification of placing himself into the centre of our universe. By claiming Yeshua to be the precedent, he's now opened a door which we are unable to close without a terrible loss, I'm afraid.

Blessedly, it took the quick thinking of Agrippa to provide the opportunity for us to find a temporary resolution to this situation. Without placing ourselves in jeopardy he made a proposal which has bought us the most precious commodity, time. Our prince did not recoil in horror, nor did he show any evidence of revulsion while listening to Caligula's suggestion. Instead he fed the Emperor with exactly what his dementia required. He provided the reassurance that it could be done, but only if it was left to those best suited to see that it be created with the proper honours and decorum that would be required for such an augmentous event. This suggestion immediately enthralled and enchanted Caligula and his manner grew suddenly calm and less bellicose. He urged Agrippa to continue, to which our prince leaped to the opportunity to demonstrate his mastery over the most powerful demagogue in Rome. If Caligula was nothing more than a musical instrument then Agrippa would have been its lyrical master. By the time Agrippa had finished his soliloquy, the Emperor had agreed to give all of Galilee and Trachonitis as a tetrarchy to the prince. And as for me, he has ordered me to return to Jerusalem in order to oversee the construction and installation of his statue. Surely this is the hand of God. How else can I explain this miracle of being able to see my home again when all seemed lost and that I would die so far away from those I love and cherish?

So prepare a welcome for me, my son. I will be returning to Jerusalem and not as some feeble old man but I feel as if I'm in the prime of my life. This task that Caligula has placed upon my shoulders will be a burden that I must make certain that I carry for many years. As long as I'm alive, I can make certain that this statue will never be completed. And Agrippa can ensure that the Emperor's vanity will never let him be satisfied to think his statue is at a state of readiness to be erected. And I feel that the Lord has invigorated me in order that I keep His Temple cleansed of these pagan idols. If I should falter in health, then I entrust you to make certain that this statue never sees the light of day.

I only wish that my Anna was still here to welcome me on my return home. I miss your mother so much. There isn't a moment of the day that I'm not thinking of her. She knew exactly what to say and how to behave in every situation. Her advice would have been most welcome when I had to appear before Caligula. Although the situation has worked well in that he has made me his caretaker for this loathsome scheme of his, I somehow feel your mother would have been able to guide me in saying the right words to have dissuaded him completely from his insane plan. There are times I wish I could believe like the Pharisees in an afterlife and resurrection. If I was to share their beliefs then I would have the cherished hope of being with Anna once again when I depart this world. But I know this is not the case and the Lord welcomes us all back to the Shekinah as nothing more than the spirit in which he formed us. Alas, this is the fate of man and no matter how we may wish it not to be so, it makes no difference. Dust to dust, ashes to ashes, nothing more, nothing less. This being the case, I promise you I will not depart this world until I have completed this task, which the Lord has entrusted me with.

Be prepared for our return, Elioneiai. Your son is looking forward to returning and being with his family. He longs to return to the place of his birth. He realizes we do not belong in this strange foreign land. Next time we speak it will be in Jerusalem.

CHAPTER THIRTY

"The Way was obviously making some headway but in the wrong direction," Pearce speculated.

"That's the odd thing. When you look at the Zadokite Document and you examine it as an outline for the early Christian Church, it has a clear and definite strategic plan. The document is essentially all about preparing for "the Way". And this 'Way' wasn't about walls or intolerance. Nor was it about exclusivity and possession. It was about as middle of the road as you could possibly get. Not about turning right nor left, but walking that central pathway. Enduring derision and scorn, because the early leaders recognized that they lived in a world that would not tolerate the middle ground. All this was explained in the Zadokite Document, and was their summation of the entire teachings of the one they referred to as the Unique Teacher."

"And this Unique Teacher you claim was Jesus."

"Couldn't have been anyone else. You know what, I'm not feeling that tired any more. Instead of letting Caiaphas tell his story for the rest of the night, I think I'm going to take some time and tell you a bit of mine. How's that sound?"

"I guess fine." Pearce started to vibrate his writing hand in eagerness for a change in pace.

"Well, good then. Because Caiaphas isn't the only one with something to say. You know Pearce, when you first barged into my life I've wrestled with the idea of how was I going to talk about all that we covered over the years without sounding like one more lunatic with a theory. And more importantly, how was I going to convince everyone that I wasn't merely spinning a good yarn, that what I was saying was for all intents and purposes true. Or as true as anyone could possibly get to providing historical truth. On the surface, that's a major issue because no matter what I say, there's all those centuries of dogma that will try to bury me under an avalanche of distortions and lies now accepted as historical truths. Again, the big question becomes, 'How am I going to make a world believe in a doctrine that is contrary to what they have been raised upon since the day they were born?' The first thing anyone would likely say is that I'm delusional."

"So how do you deal with it?" Pearce asked genuinely concerned that I was thinking about throwing in the towel after I had taken him this far along the path of the story.

"It was actually surprisingly easy to deal with," I responded. "For the moment I stepped outside of my framework and asked myself a simple question. I said, 'What is more important to you? God or the word of God?' To further qualify the challenge I rephrased it as follows, 'If I had the power to choose which would disappear from my existence God or His Word, which would I want to remain behind and continue to exist?'"

"Wow, that's putting the tough question to yourself, Doc. And you were able to make a choice?"

"Oh yes! It was an awkward question, but I reasoned that if I had to choose, then the Word of God should be left behind.

"Why," Pearce asked somewhat surprised by my answer.

"I instinctively knew that if I had the Word of God then I would always have God there as well. By keeping the commandments and laws and the ethical standards, God's presence would be manifest regardless. Do you follow my reasoning? Just having God isn't enough. It doesn't mean you live your life any better. But if you actually live the Word as prescribed by God then you achieve heaven on earth. It doesn't matter if God is physically around any longer or not. You've attained what is ultimately the purpose of God's existence and in turn, our existence."

"That's pretty heavy," Pearce sighed.

"It is far better for God to live in our hearts than to reside in heaven. To a Christian, they have to say to themselves, 'What is more important? The Word or the man?' As soon as they choose the Word then they will be united again with Jesus' original doctrine. And the Jews have to say to themselves, 'Did God not make them as a light unto the world?' And when they acknowledge that was His purpose, then they have to ask themselves why they have chosen to hide that light under a basket. That's when they recognize they are no different from the Christians asking themselves their own question. One people, one set of beliefs, but unfortunately, two thousand years of confusion in between that resulted from those wishing to use God as a tool or a weapon and forgetting, or choosing to forget that it was not about God but the Word."

"And then what?" Pearce prodded.

"From the house of Ephraim and from the House of Judah there will be a gathering. To quote Zechariah, 'You shall be a shepherd of a poor flock.' Now you know the message my ancestor wanted to pass on to me. You're helping me put into motion a plan that was set for me a long time ago. You should feel like a part of making history."

"So that was the instructions he passed down to you."

"That was part of it. A very key part. That's why I figured the first time you came by my house it was no accident. Like everything else in life, you had a role to fulfil. You just didn't know it and I'm certain you had no idea what you were getting involved with when you tracked me down."

"Don't mistake me for too much the fool, Doc. I probably had far more knowledge of what I was getting in to than you give me credit for. After all, I didn't spend all that time tracking you down with the hope that there wasn't going to be a story in it." Pearce winked knowingly as he tapped the side of his temple.

"Yes, I have to agree with you there. You wouldn't have gone to that extent if you didn't think there was something unusual. Or at least if your wife didn't think that. After all, it was her that put you on the scent."

"Credit where credit's due. But the fact is it was no accident."

"Okay, it was no accident. Granted. But the fact is that things happen for a purpose. There is an unseen hand that guides our actions. It doesn't' really matter what you call it. Fate, kismet, divine guidance, it's just there. And the fact is that without your showing up that fateful day, I would have had no vehicle by which I could have fulfilled the obligations placed upon me by Zechariah. When is coincidence not a coincidence? When it's meant to happen."

"Perhaps. I'm not overly convinced. Although we have quite a large readership waiting in anticipation for this next book."

"Not to mention a bunch of government agents that ran amok in your offices. They're not going to be overly happy with any inspired mission designed to change the established order."

"True, but if there's one thing you've taught me Doc, is that the world's about change. If everything that was supposed to be true has been changed by those with their own missions, then it would suggest that something like this Zadokite Document could just as equally set a course in a different direction. Might even be the correct direction."

"Change is well documented in the Zadokite Document. It may be an ancient scroll, but it too has suffered misinterpretation since its rediscovery in the 1890's. The authors knew even then that there'd always be people that choose to believe in the lie because they cannot accept the truth. Truth, as we learn from the Hebrew word 'emet' is the same in the beginning, as it is in the middle, and as it will be in the end. Hence the use of the first, middle and last letters of the Hebrew alphabet. The message in all that is that we never had the authority to choose what we wanted to believe and alter it to meet our needs. The truth is supposed to be unalterable. But as both you and I know, that's not the case.

This document, this obscure document, was relegated to the trash heap, the Genizah, of the Ben Ezra Synagogue in Cairo. When found by Schechter in 1896, even he failed to realize the significance of the document. Assuming that it must be essentially Jewish in context because after all, it was found in the Genizah, Shechter translated in a completely Jewish character and tone. Or perhaps he didn't fail to realize its significance. Maybe he did understand it perfectly well and chose not to reveal the truth. The motives of individuals are as varied as there are people.

Here's a book, copied all the way into the twelfth century, when suddenly the Jewish community in Egypt loses the reasons for its preservation. Only with the knowledge that it bore the name of the Lord, and that it held religious significance at one time, even though they no longer knew why, they placed it into the Genizah, which would serve as its tomb.

Schechter's intent to maintain a Jewish character to this document, only led to subsequent interpretations by Yadin and Burrows based on the initial incorrect assumption. This only served to entrench an elite Essene flavour to it, even though it is very different from any other Essene doctrines. It was Yadin that gave it the name of Zadokite Document. Burrows called it the Damascus Document. What does that tell you? It says they didn't know nor understood it.

Firstly the author uses a term for the community in which he refers to it as the 'Hagu'. As a term, it helps explain and demonstrate why this community was actually the early Jerusalem Church and in fact constituted James' circumcision party. They were Jews that followed the teachings of Jesus the Nazorean as taught to them by James the Just and then by Simeon ben Cleophas. The time of its writing is either the occupation of the Temple by the Zealots and rebels during the Jewish-Roman War, or just after the Temple's destruction. In all likelihood, the Jerusalem Church recentered itself in Egypt after the fall of Jerusalem. This movement to Cairo and Alexandria would account for the essential difference between mainstream Christianity and the Coptic Church.

I can demonstrate all this from those early writings. Similarly to my unique understanding of Zechariah, so too did the words and phrases of the Zadokite Document literally open up before me. An entire ancient world was literally revealed to me. No other Jewish or Christian document will refer to its congregation as 'the Way', as many times or in the differentiating manner that this manuscript does. Modern religious books and epistles will talk about following 'the Way', but the Zadokite Document or Hagu talks about being 'the Way'. They were 'the Way' and as far as their relationship with God was concerned there was no other 'Way'.

The author of this document is fighting several battles on a multitude of fronts; Pharisee, Helenism, and those that thought they had joined 'The Way' but who were now following the alternative teachings which had surfaced in Damascus. The community of the document were followers of the true path, the original 'Way', according to the teachings of Jesus, and they were appalled by the corruption of his teachings. The author discusses how these teachings had been twisted by another individual, who had created a perverse teaching that was more readily accepted by the Gentile world. Do you think that if this was really an early Jewish document that they would be talking about the corruption of their teachings by those that distorted them in Damascus? Not at all."

"Okay, so it's an early Christian document. But what's so important about it. Jewish, Christian, does it really make a difference?"

"That's my whole point. As a Christian document it makes

a world of difference. As in this world could have ultimately been changed completely from the way we know it, had this document seen the light of day and been accepted as the primary Church doctrine as it was intended to be."

"We had a Church doctrine. You know well enough about the Nicene creed and all that stuff."

"Oh, I know about it very well. Problem is, they chose the wrong doctrine. How appropriate do you think a doctrine written by Constantine the Great and the Bishop of Rome is going to be. As if they had anything in common with the Church in Jerusalem or Jesus, himself. Constantine wanted the Christians to join his army and fight against Maximus, and the Bishop of Rome wanted power over the masses. This creed was nothing more than a business agreement."

"And this Zadokite Document was any different," Pearce interjected in a desperate attempt to salvage a last vestige of Church history before I trashed it completely.

"For all intents and purposes, let's stop calling it the Zadokite Document and refer to it as the 'Hagu'.   Whereas the author of the 'Hagu' saw himself failing in his battle, losing to the tide of falsehood and disbelievers, I see it completely different. I see him as a herald of the coming age in our time. I do not see him as failing; merely starting the process which has now come full circle and that you and I are going to bring to fruition through these books."

"I thought your mission was to tell your family history. That's the one our paper signed on to."

"John, as you'll discover, it's all family history. And if one listens carefully, they will hear the song of the new dawn."

"A little over the top, eh Doc. Song of the New Dawn?"

"I take it very seriously, John. Strange how these words can explain some of the things we do subconsciously. I'll digress a little bit."

"Oh, as if that would be something new for you?"

"Tsk, tsk. Don't be nasty," I taunted. "If it wasn't for my digressions, you'd only have half the sales your recorded.   Before my son was born, we were having difficulty arriving at a name for the new baby if it was a boy. My mother suggested James. As Ashkenazi Jews, we always have used names from our dead ancestors. James was not one of them. It was not common for Jews to use the names of the apostles and usually it was deliberately avoided because of the persecutions those names represented. But when it was suggested, I knew that it was appropriate because his second name was to be Aaron. Therefore his Hebrew name would be Yom Aharun in Hebrew, meaning the Day of Aaron. Without knowing why, this seemed significant at the time.

And when my daughter was born, she was named Charlotte Eve. And her Hebrew name is Shechar-Shear-Lot or Song of the Coming Dawn."

"So you named your children after significant events in the articles you read. Lots of people do that. You and Frank Zappa have something in common."

"Except that the children were named long before I even read my first copy of the Hagu. Coincidence, I don't think so. Deliberate, if that was the case, but not of my doing. And then you'd have to seriously look at the events of my life and realize nine years ago I wouldn't have had been aware of half the things I recognize now. I believe we are influenced by many things without having the faintest realization that it's being done. Certainly GLEEM plays a significant role but it' not the only thing. Some may call it fate, others coincidence, I choose to believe in that little thing we call divine inspiration. In today's world we are so determined to believe in our own abilities of self-determination that we tend to overlook the obvious or are even more determined to deny it."

"I think it may just be a case of our world having a lot more tools at our disposal to explain what used to be considered the unexplainable."

"Correct me if I'm wrong, John, but you're a religious man."

"You already know that I am Doc."

"If you're a religious man then why do you find it so hard to accept something as simple as believing in divine intervention? You would think that as a person with a strong foundation in religion you'd see it no differently than taking a breath. An undeniable reality. Yet giving God his dues seems to be incongruous with today's theocracy. Don't you think that's a little strange? People believing in God but not willing to let him play a role in their everyday lives?"

"You make it sound practically criminal Doc. It's not like that at all. I think we can still be believers without having to have personal conversations with God. Most I would think go through their lives without having the Almighty take a direct hand in it."

"So why bother/"

"Why bother what?"

"Why bother having any religious affiliation if you don't expect to have an encounter with the Lord?"

"You're confusing me now. Lots of people are very religious and they don't need to hear voices, or see visions in order to do good things and feel close to God. It's all about believing, even if you only do it on faith without ever getting a direct intervention from heaven. The reward is not intended for this life, it's for the afterlife."

"No! I don't agree. And neither did the people of the 'Hagu'. That's the difference between us and the people back then. We are willing to live in a vacuum but back then they expected to have regular encounters with God. The Righteous Teacher, who first led the sect of Essenes and ultimately made possible the coming of the Unique Teacher, is described in the Zadokite Document as being well aware of how the hand of God influenced every aspect of his life. What is quite astounding is that whereas others would have looked upon him as shunned, outcast, and exiled from the position of High Priest, he simply considered himself divinely inspired, given a new task and purpose. I'll fill you in on another little twist in history that goes against the grain of historians. For the sake of argument, let's just say that the Righteous Teacher happened to be my early ancestor, Joakim. We already talked about him as you may recall. Common ancestor of Jesus and Joseph Caiaphas. If it is Joakim, Alcimus in the Greek, who was the Righteous Teacher as I believe, then he was the last of the Zadokite priests prior to the displacement by Lysimachus and soon to follow afterwards, the Hasmoneans. The Hasmoneans or Maccabees as they are now commonly called were not of the ordained Zadokite families considered for the high priesthood. Therefore, their assumption of this position was not permitted. In fact it would have been considered an affront to God and the entire Jewish world. But as I mentioned, history has a way of whitewashing certain facts. Following the Hasmonean occupation, history was to record Simon as being the Just and Joakim as being a tool of the Greeks and therefore a defilement to the position. But it was the Maccabees that ended up having a quid pro quo relationship with the Seleukid Greeks.

Whether history sees Joakim as a good high priest, or not, was never the issue. He was by God's selection, the rightful High Priest and therefore the proper choice. The only choice. Even if the claim was true, that he was a puppet of Antiochus, put in power by the whims of a foreign king, it is still immaterial. By blood and promise, he was still entitled to serve as High Priest. By forcing him into exile and eventually hunting him down, those followers of Lysimachus and Menelaus set in motion the series of events that led to the destruction of the Temple and the desolation of Judaea by the Romans. Because if they could depose the rightful High Priest, then the Hasmoneans could take over the role for a hundred and thirty years without feeling guilty.

From the Psalms written by the Righteous Teacher, we can develop an appreciation for the torment he suffered, being so far removed from the Temple. We feel his anguish and recognize the he was condemned unjustly. Had he been left to his own devices, his pursuit of peace rather than war with the Greeks would have changed the entire history of the land and the destruction of the Temple may have never occurred."

"I need a little more than gut feeling Doc. Anything that would suggest you're correct in assuming that it's Joakim as your man."

"A few things. At the beginning of the Zadokite Document there is a provision of a time frame for the Righteous Teacher. It says that three hundred and ninety years after the conquest by Nebuchadnezzar, God remembered the covenant with our forefathers. That would be 196 BC. He caused a root to grow forth from Israel and Aaron, being a redemption led by the high priesthood. But it would take another twenty years before he raised for the true followers, the Teacher of Righteousness. This would be about 176 BC which fits roughly with the time period of Joakim."

"That sounds pretty plausible. But help me here Doc. It seems pretty obvious even with my limited capacity for history. Yet no one has put the pieces of the puzzle together and from what you're telling me, they'd have to be blind, deaf and dumb not to have done so."

"It's not that uncommon for people to choose to be all three."

"For what purpose?"

"Perhaps they considered the truth dangerous. If the truth was to be known, it might have undermined their intentions, their goals, whatever. There are those that would be very concerned about the truth."

"Who's intentions?"

"Now that's an interesting question. Are you sure you're ready for the answer?"

"C'mon now Doc. I've been through thick and thin with you so far. You can't think about pulling out on me now!"

"I'll tell you what. I'll provide you with the details and you can then answer your own question. It should become pretty obvious. Deal?"

"Okay, deal."

"In the document, it is written that there comes a man of scoffing, a phenomenal preacher, who causes the adherents to fall away from 'the Way'. He does this by removing the distinguishing mark which was passed down by their ancestors. He appeals to those seeking the smooth way and the fair neck, thereby justifying the wicked and condemning the just. Others in turn will break the ordinance which only serves to cause dissention amongst the followers and a rivalry which threatens the movement. The true followers had 'living waters' but those that follow this man of scoffing have nothing but 'lying waters.' The author predicts that the wrath of God is set against this false congregation, which has become a large multitude and has developed many false scriptures. Their works, referring to their books and epistles are unclean before God. . The author proclaims that they will be condemned by God because they abhor the ordinance and the Lord will wipe them out completely. They will never be the inheritors of the covenant as God did not choose them from the old, because those that have had the covenant were there before these new proclaimers were even established."

"From the references and phrases he uses, it almost sounds like he's talking about the Church but then he's also making it sound like there's two Churches. Am I on the right track?"

"You're very warm. It's clear that the author was not speaking of another Jewish group. That's evident from the reference about removing the distinguishing mark. The reference is to a group comprising people that weren't even of a known nation at the time the covenant was made with Israel. To highlight this further there is this line that reads, 'That He knew their works or history and He detested the generations or stock from which they arose.' You couldn't get much clearer that this wasn't another Jewish group being written about.

Now some pretty heavy hitters amongst the biblical archeological groups translate this section as being nothing more than the Essenes criticizing the works of the Maccabean rulers. But contrary to their opinion, it doesn't fit. There were very little scriptural works regarding the religious changes of this period and in fact, the majority of works not only proclaim but celebrate the re-establishment of the ordinances and requirements, not the contrary as this one does. Helenism was not being promoted and therefore it is clear that the author is writing about a different time period.

This inherited or distinguishing mark or ordinance he writes about is without a doubt, ritual circumcision. The scoffing preacher makes it his purpose to eliminate this requirement for membership and in so doing, he attracts those that want an easy path and have no desire to learn the true teachings. The smooth things are mere delusions, a breaking of the laws of Moses, with no basis in Torah or Judaic law. The true believers according to the author still take the hard path, because they are the only real God-approved followers."

"If that's the case Doc, then you'd be intimating that this scoffing preacher was no one else but Paul because he's the one that did away with the requirement for circumcision."

"You're on to it now, John. That's exactly whom I'm saying that the author of the 'Hagu' is referring to. He makes an appeal for all true believers in 'the Way' to listen to his words carefully and not to become lost like those following the false preacher. Clearly a reference to the proselytizing and conversion of the Gentile races and equally as impossible to confuse with Israel and therefore this particular document has absolutely nothing to do whatsoever with the Maccabeans.

In sentence twelve of the document, it is written that God sends His anointed ones, which you notice reads in the plural as messiahs, possessed of His holy spirit and His truth. God's messiahs will preserve portions of the flock and their names will be exactly identified. They will spread their seed across the world and spawn congregations worldwide. Sounds pretty familiar, doesn't it. Clearly not a reference to the extremely reclusive Essene community. But it is very interesting that the author refers to the duality of messiahs. Obviously it was quite common to have been anticipating the two messiahs as I explained earlier, rather than waiting for only one."

"I can see what you're trying to say Doc, but I don't see why this couldn't be another sect of Judaism that was in to proselytizing to the rest of the nations."

"I thought that would have been obvious," I responded. "Firstly, we know there were three sects to Judaism, what you are proposing is a fourth and all the historical records don't indicate there being a fourth. And secondly there is a statement cleverly incorporated into line eighteen of the document that reads 'because it is ours'. This comment was in reference to the promise of God to his chosen people. This particular group, much like the Essenes felt that they had inherited that promise, but they weren't the Essenes."

"How can you be so certain? Maybe it was the Essenes but written by one of their more radical members?"

"Always a possibility to consider but one that's totally blown away by line eighteen of page three. There's a recounting of some ancient history demonstrating God's constant redemption of his people. It is a testimony to how He will always forgive the people of his covenant. This line eighteen reads as a condemnation of Judaism for failing to take the message to the world as they had been instructed, 'to be a light unto the world'. We had been commanded to proselytize and consciously disregarded that instruction. Nevertheless, in line nineteen, God overlooks our transgression and failure to do as we were commanded and still built for us a sure house, destined for eternal life."

"But how does that prove anything?"

"Because the Essenes did not condone proselytizing. They were not accepting of conversion of the Gentiles. There's lot more in the document that dissuades anyone from thinking that it was written by the Essene community."

"Well, don't stop now."

"I wasn't intending to, I was just taking a moment to catch my breath. Page four gets very interesting as it indicates that there will come at the end of days, a Zadokite whose genealogy is known from the Diaspora. This Zadokite will know the times of the last days. During these final times it says that each man will be judged by his own merit. Being a Jew will not be the only criteria. In fact the author talks about those that came after the righteous one and the wicked one, who accepted the teachings of the forefathers and were like the original covenant but were not."

"Am I supposed to decipher what you just said?"

"You have to think outside the box on this one. The author is stating that in the final days there will be a union between Jew and non-Jew. And it will be brought about by a Zadokite, a descendant of priests that's from the community outside of Judaea. You have to remember that as far as the Jerusalem Church was concerned, Jesus was coming back, the resurrection of all the righteous was a definite, and that ultimately the Gentiles would join and adopt Judaism which by their definition was Christianity. The author goes as far as stating in lines ten and eleven on page four, that this new group will not be united with the house of Judah until the last days. And the reason that this new group was not one with Judah at this particular time was summed up in line twelve where the author says 'The wall is built, the ordinance is far removed', referring to the other group placing an obstacle in their path by disregarding the commandments and not enforcing the laws of Moses on those that joined them and thereby erecting a wall between the Jewish community and these new recruits. One event naturally precipitated the other. By abandoning the circumcision ordinance, the requirement to be Jewish first in order to become Christian as was the case in joining the Jerusalem Church, only served to promote the schism that developed between the parent and daughter. The separation of the sects became inevitable."

"That's clearer, I'll have to admit that, and I can get the gist of the author's angst but I still don't think it's as cut and dry as you make it out to be."

"Oh, ye of little faith," I quipped. "I guess I'm going to have to hit you with everything I've got. Ultimately you're going to have to read the document for yourself. It's a shame you're not fluent in the Hebrew language, then you'd be able to translate if for yourself as well and not have to rely on the Standard English translation. But until you do get the chance to read it, I'll fill you in on the psyche of the author. He's very disturbed that the wall was created. He attributes it to three causes. The new order had become immoral, desired power and affluence, and was being led by an unholy clergy, as described in lines seventeen and eighteen on page four. He analyses it and comes to the conclusion that the way everything had unfolded was not a natural progression. Instead it was the result of one man. This wicked preacher, whom in his pursuit of power led the people astray and his name reads as TSOW. The name isn't very cryptic, bearing a close relationship to the same person that John accuses in Revelations. This wicked preacher that caused the rift and distorted the teachings was Saul, who went by his Roman citizenship name of Paul. Once again, a word with a double meaning or purpose is used. Close enough to suggest Saul but also having a translation of excrement."

"Shit? His name meant shit?"

"No, no. It's a play on homonyms. The word TSOW is not the same as Saul, though they have a similarity in the way they'd be pronounced in the Aramaic. For now, let's just say that the reference was double edged."

"I didn't realize that the writers of the time could be so clever. You'd almost think they had a sense of humour."

"I would think they showed a wit far beyond any of our authors of today."

"If it's Saul that he's got so much hatred for, then you've got to provide me with more reasons than you've offered me so far Doc."

"Why's that? Just because Paul's been made a saint doesn't mean that he was one. At least not to the author of the 'Hagu'. If anything, as far as the 'Hagu' were concerned, he was the devil incarnate. Page five of the document deals in more detail with the schism that this TSOW or Saul created in his wake. The followers of Saul are accused of saying that the laws of Moses have been repealed and they speak falsely against the Torah, all of which was true of Paul's adherents. The author compares them to being vermin. It is interesting that in line fifteen on that page that the author mentions that some of the followers of 'the Way' are forced into following Saul's teachings. I don't know of anywhere else that such an accusation is made against Saul's followers. It is almost suggestive of the cults we have today where once you join they won't permit you to leave. I can't speak for what he might be referring to exactly. I don't have that memory stored away anywhere in my mind. I can safely assume that none of my ancestors felt the urge to join. So whether this force that he refers to is through intimidation or actual physical punishment he's not stipulating. It is explained in line twenty of this page that the desolation of the land is a result of the removing of the boundary and because of this, Israel was led astray."

"This boundary if I guess right is referring to the division between Jew and Gentile? Am I right?"

"You're getting good at this John. The circumcision was the most important boundary between the Jews and the Gentile world. By removing it, the Damascene sect brought about the final days. That was how they referred to Saul's following, as the Damascenes."

"And as to the final days that he refers to, would that happen to be the destruction of Jerusalem?" Pearce was taking great pleasure in putting the pieces of the puzzle together.

"That and much more. Not only did he see the Damascenes causing the destruction of Jerusalem, but more importantly the end to James' Church, Judaea, the Zadokite cult, the world as he knew it, etcetera, etcetera. Not to mention the scattering of the Jews to the four corners of the earth."

"He saw all that, did he?"

"Perhaps not all that but most of it. There's a lot that this author of the 'Hagu' saw."

"Any idea who it may have been?" Pearce asked eagerly.

"I've asked myself that question quite a lot. Obviously had to be someone quite intuitive. Almost a seer. Well educated, knowledgeable about the Temple practices. A leader, highly respected. And a true follower of Jesus and his teachings. The original teaching as Jesus first presented it, which meant he had to be familiar with Jesus himself."

"And what does that all suggest to you?"

"If I was a betting man…"

"Oh come on now, who do you think it was?"

"Well, if I was a betting man, I'd put my money on it being James. The insights are too great for it to have been just anyone. In the document he describes the true 'Way'. The well of living waters is described as being the well of the Law. The Staff is the searcher of the Law and is a reference to the staffs mentioned by Zechariah.

The twin staffs being Faith and Union. The staff is also symbolic of being the tool of God's shepherd."

How do I know that a singular staff refers to the twin staffs? That's where GLEEM comes in. Certain memories are triggered as soon as I read specific references and this is one such case. When I read lines nine and ten on page six, where it makes reference to the Nobles of the People for they are the ones that have come to dig the well with their staffs which the one Staff instituted. One staff has obviously transmuted into several. And in the end of days, there will come another Teacher of Righteousness, which is the key message of this passage. He is to be the shepherd which tends the poor flock of Zechariah. Now you may look at these lines and not view the entire panorama that pops into my mind but at least now that I've pointed them out you will see that there is far more meaning from these few simple lines. Everything is a conundrum unto itself. Every answer only begs another question. Now you can at least have an inkling of what I see."

Pearce weighed out the riddle which I had just tabled with an invisible balance that teetered between his hands. "I think you do have the answers, you're just not sharing them all with me. Granted, you see things with a greater clarity than the rest of us do but to take a page from my wife's book Doc, you're holding back. I've got this gut feeling that you're not telling me everything you know about this document. Now don't get me wrong. I'm not saying you are doing it intentionally but I'm only getting the Readers Digest version. "

"Don't give me that much credit John. There are answers and then there are answers! We still have a lot to write about and I'm thinking a series of about ten books should do it. Then, just maybe, you'll have all the answers. So don't be so impatient my friend."

"Aha! So there is a lot more that you've held back."

"If I had the answers it certainly wouldn't be spread over that many books. I'd sum it up in a few lines. Problem is that I don't have them and therefore I can only talk around the subject without zeroing directly on the target. Do you ever experience that feeling John, where you know something's right in front of you but you just can't grab it. You beat around the bush but you can't nail it. That's where I'm at. I have my suspicions, can weigh out probabilities but I just can't find that one piece of the jigsaw that would finish it off."

"I can relate to that. I've been there before. Frustrating as hell!"

"I have no doubt that Paul is the culprit in this document. He founded the Damascene order. He was its spiritual leader. And his followers are the ones the author of this document refers to when he says, 'They are like those that have come into the sanctuary to kindle the Lord's altar in vain. The Lord will shut his door against them. If they are to be accepted then they must return to the letter of the Law.'

I mean, just take a look at the language on page six at line fifteen.

I flipped to the right page and flashed Pearce a quick look as much good as that would do him considering it was printed in Hebrew.

The laws are set down for those that are followers of the 'True Way.' That's a reference to those that adhere to the teachings of Jesus as taught through his select apostles, James and John. They have established a new set of Ten Commandments. Right there it's telling you that these are not just another Jewish sect. By setting up their own commandments to follow they have drawn a line in the sand that separated them from all the other groups. There's no way you can ignore these commandments. They pretty well say it all." I thumbed through the page until I found what I was looking for.

"What do you got there?" Pearce leaned forward and craned his neck trying to see what I was pointing at.

"Thou shall keep away from the Children of the Pit. First commandment."

"They being….?"

"That should be obvious by now. The Gentiles and the Damascene Church, what else. Thou shall refrain from the wealth of wickedness gained by appropriating the wealth of the congregation, which is intended for the poor, the widows and the orphans. Second commandment." I didn't give Pearce a chance to ask his next question. I knew what it was going to be so there wasn't much point in waiting.

"Clearly a charge against certain Church leaders of misusing funds. They weren't too keen about funds being used by the leaders for travel and living fairly comfortably while those that the tithe was intended for continue to starve. The third commandment. Thou shall put a distinction between the unclean and the clean, the holy and the common." I held up my hand to stop Pearce before had a chance to ask his next question.

"The dietary laws were not to be abandoned. The circumcision was not to be abandoned. The laws of Moses were to be preserved. Just as Jesus had said that he did not come to change the laws of Moses but to confirm them. A clear challenge to Peter's and Paul's teachings that the dietary and ritual laws were no longer in force.

The next commandment was quite interesting. To keep the Sabbath day according to its rules and appointed days. Fasting was to be done according to the Damascene rules. Obviously, the other brotherhood had discovered a better explanation and marking of the fast days.

Fifth commandment that all shall set aside holy offerings according to the rules. And the tithe was to be maintained as the Temple was still the centre of religious life. Can't get much clearer that this is the Jerusalem Church. The Temple was still very important to the 'Hagu'. The Essenes on the other hand wanted nothing more to do with the Temple. Very important point when identifying the author of this document."

"And the other five commandments?" Pearce was able to sneak in his question while I was taking a breath.

"These should sound very familiar to you. Love each man his brother, like himself. This was the sixth commandment. What I find unusual about it is that the Golden rule was obviously cherished but was not the primary rule. It's sixth, not first. Funny how it became pretty much the only commandment of the Christian Church today.

The seventh was to strengthen the hand of the poor, the needy and the stranger. The eighth to seek the wellbeing each man of his brother. It was not good enough to only love your brother, but you had to also act. You did whatever possible to help your brother in the community. You were not bear rancor against your brother. Three commandments concerned with brotherhood. So even though they weren't in the first five they were extremely important."

"And that leaves two more."

"Do not sin against his kin of flesh. This ninth one is a little more mysterious at first look. I see it as having two distinct interpretations. One is not to sin against other members of the community as in the sense of community as family. Which could mean that sinning against anyone outside the community was perfectly acceptable. The other meaning could be construed as a reinforcement of the incest laws from Leviticus. Only because kin and flesh are used simultaneously which would suggest flesh is to be taken literally, not as a synonym for kin. Which leads to the tenth which says, thou shall refrain from immorality."

"Well that's pretty broad. That could mean almost anything."

"Immorality is broad. If they were going to list everything there would have been a hundred commandments. They only wanted ten. They were very optimistic. As you can see on this page, they felt that adherence to the commandments would bring about a lasting peace in the world for a thousand generations."

"And you see something of significance hidden in there."

"Very astute. You are getting good at this John. It would be easy for one to draw a connection between a thousand generations and the millennium concept in Christianity. But what is more significant is when you look at this in the context of line nine on page seven. Very unusual phrase used. It actually refers to God's actual presence on earth in the final days. This is not a passing literary phrase as the earlier translators deemed it. Therefore not giving it the recognition it deserves. This phrase implies the physical presence of the Lord amongst his people, fighting directly against the wicked. It's Armageddon but with a Christian twist in that God actually comes down to Earth at the end of time. That's not anywhere else in the Jewish religion. It is the closest link you will ever find between Judaism and Christianity because it has a foot in both worlds."

I got out of my chair and walked towards the doorway.

"Where are you off to?" Pearce asked nervously at the thought that I was drawing our conversation to an end.

"I'm off to bed. If you're smart, you'll do the same thing as well. Come, I'll show you where you can sleep for the night. Tomorrow's another day and I'm definitely too tired to continue any longer. Pack it up John and call it a night."

Reluctantly Pearce laid down his pen and closed his note book.

CHAPTER THIRTY-ONE

"Morning John. Good sleep?"

Pearce tenaciously hung on to the duvet resisting the wakeup call. When he started pulling the cover over his head I knew that it was time to take drastic action.

"I hope the pull-out was comfortable."

Still no response other than a grumble. It was eight in the morning already and by now the children were desperately awaiting the return of their living room so they could watch the television.

"Not to disturb your beauty sleep, God knows you could use it, but we still have a lot of ground to cover before you get on a plane and fly out of here." He continued to ignore me until I began to wave the cup of copy just above his head.

Reluctantly Pearce propped himself up on his elbows and then began a ritual scratching exercise that seemed to go on endlessly. And then in a moment of awareness he started sniffing the air with anticipation. "Is that a coffee I smell?"

"Yes it is! Here's the first cup and there's a fresh pot brewing as we speak," I informed him. "But I warn you John, around here pots of coffee don't last long. Between my wife and myself we go through quite a few pots during the day and if you're not quick enough to finish this one and then grab your own refill, you're going to miss out. Comprenez?"

Throwing off the covers, Pearce was lying there in an old pair of pyjamas I found in one of my drawers. Which means they had to be very old, since I haven't worn pyjamas since I was a teenager. You could tell they were quite dated simply by some of the sports team logos they had printed on the material. Can't remember the last time the Minnesota North Stars have been a team but I know it wasn't recently. There was a slight titter of a giggle coming from behind the doorpost.

"Is that you Charlotte? If it is, you better come out and say hello to our guest. It's not nice to hide behind the wall and laugh at him no matter how ridiculous he may look in daddy's old pyjamas."

"Oh, thanks a lot Doc. Why don't you just embarrass me completely?"

"I thought I did. Did you want me to try harder then?"

My daughter came into the room and greeted Pearce with a 'hello' followed quickly by a, 'can I turn on the TV.' No sooner had I given an approval and she pressed the button on the remote, my son James magically appeared out of nowhere and was sitting in front of the screen.

"Why don't you get dressed in the bathroom John and I'll meet you in the kitchen. We can continue our conversation over breakfast. There's still a lot of ground to cover if you're to catch a flight out of here."

Once John had managed to pull himself together he joined me in the kitchen over a plate of scrambled eggs and toast. He was still quite dishevelled but for John that was a pretty normal state of affairs. Marg joined us at the table fully prepared to add her two cents whenever possible into our conversation. As much as she insisted that she never believed in any of the hocus pocus I professed, she was still eager to listen to it. She insisted that she only did it out of a courtesy, but on occasion I'd overhear her passing on some of the information she learned from her own conversations with me and I would break out in a broad smile knowing that as much as she denied it, she couldn't ignore it completely.

"I had a lot of things to think about last night," Pearce rolled into the conversation. "And I'm still not one hundred percent certain about this Zadokite Document. I know what you told me makes a lot of sense but I guess my question is why are you the only one that sees it. So many people have had the opportunity to read and translate it and none of them came to the conclusions that you have. And not to question your expertise Doc, but these are trained theologians and linguists and not to mention, historians. How is it that they never saw it?"

"It's a fair question John. It brings to mind the story of the jewels in the dung heap. You can hide them in the centre of the heap and all anyone will ever see is the pile of shit and nothing more. It's not until one person actually sifts through it all with their fingers that they can find the jewels. And those that missed the opportunity will comment that they always knew that they were there, but they weren't going to lower themselves to do it."

"Yeah but that doesn't apply completely to this situation. These after all are experts in the field. They do sift through it and they don't see it? So that doesn't make sense to me!"

"Okay, then let me go one better. Homer writes about Troy and everyone reads the Iliad and calls it a myth. These are historians, archaeologists, museum curators, the best the world had to offer. Von Schliemann says that the Iliad is an actual road map to the lost city of troy and he was going to not only find it but uncover its hidden treasures. These world-respected experts label him a madman, a buffoon, and dismiss his claims completely. And after he uncovers it they still manage to condemn him for his extravagance, his failure to adhere to proper archaeological cataloguing systems, you name it. So what's that tell you about experts John?"

"I dunno."

"It tells you they're experts because they have their colleagues pat them on their backs and call themselves experts and they live within their mutual admiration society, afraid to move outside the boundaries lest they lose the support and admiration of their colleagues. So they not only close ranks, but close their eyes as well."

"So, you're saying you're like Von Schliemann, able to see what the others can't."

"In retrospect, I can understand how it is that certain forces wished for me to examine the Zadokite Document as a keystone to my calling."

"Oh brother," Marg interjected. "I don't know if I can listen to this any longer. A calling yet!"

"That's just another way to look at GLEEM, John. People talk about their calling. This little voice that tells them what to do and where to go. GLEEM is exactly that. A genetic imprint that tells you what to do and where to go simply because it's been transferred into your grey matter from time immemorial. There's no real difference when you examine it. And if predecessors experienced the same knowledge, then they knew that I or someone from the family line would be able to translate it from the original, be familiar enough with Jewish law and custom and have a passion for ancient history to put it all into perspective. But most of all, they knew I would be able to spot the incongruities immediately and draw the right conclusions."

"So which one of your ancestors passed on the insight do you think?" Pearce was back into the thick of things, scribbling madly as I spoke, his tape recorder whirring wildly in the background.

"I can't tell you how I know, but I know that these particular insights and memories are from Jeshua ben Gamaliel, whom had watched the destruction of the Temple by the Romans. His world had been laid to ruin by a mighty and powerful empire. In so doing, before he was beheaded, he disguised a prophecy which he passed down through the generations by directly telling his son to memorize it. It went like this:

'Know this, son of Aaron, son of Zadok, I have set this time upon the lips of my prophets long ago, but your world will not listen. So heed the words of your ancestor, as he watched Jerusalem be laid to waste. For then I planted the seed within the womb of your birthing, and for fifty generations I have nursed it. Did I not say to him that your world has become like a new forest of trees planted in the valley. And the trees grew until the valley was pregnant with their shoots and impassable, surrounded by a wall of majestic mountains.

And I made the vine grow above the forest and below the ground I made the waters flow so that a fountain sprung from the earth to nourish all the trees of the forest. But the flow of water became like a torrent and the fountain sent out great waves that eroded the soil and felled the trees. And when the forest had been destroyed, the waves crashed against the mountains until they were levelled to nothing more than grains of sand. The entire valley was laid to waste, covered by the waters, except for the presence of one lone cedar. The vine then spread out from the fountain and approached the cedar, and a mouth sprouted from the vine and it spoke. 'Are you not that cedar remaining from the forest of wickedness? And was it not you that turned the forest away from being righteous? You kept taking what was not yours, without compassion, until your conquests took you to the distant reaches. Those that approached you were caught in your wicked net. You spread your canopy above all the others, preventing the sun to reach their leaves. But now you are undone. You shall become dust along with the forest that has been washed away, And you will try to rise again from the soil, but your seed will be devastated even more than this time. And the dust of your wood will be burnt until it is ash and you will never come again.'

"Sounds pretty biblical."

"It was. Contained in a gospel referred to as the Gospel of Barnabus. Had absolutely nothing to do with Barnabus as you can tell but was something that Jeshua ben Gamialiel had jotted down during one of his prophetic visions. And he did so because he knew when the time would come. He knew it then just as I know it now. Not unlike a message in a bottle. He set it upon a sea of time and it floated home to me."

"Okay, it's a message but what does it mean," both Margaret and John questioned simultaneously.

"Rome was that forest that filled the valley of Israel with its trees and surrounded the city with its mighty fortifications that stood like mountain walls. And there came this vine which spread its fruit across the skies above the forest and the fountain which sprung from the living waters. Doubly fruitful were the vine and fountain as was the meaning of Ephraim. I bet you didn't know that. Every Hebrew name has a translation and that was Ephraim's. The vine was the teacher and the fountain was the congregation. And the waters grew until they toppled the trees of the forest. But the congregation was uncontrollable and soon they became more destructive than the evil empire which they swept away. They flooded the valley so it did not grow as it once did."

"This is sounding very prophetic to me Doc. I'm going to need a scorecard if you intend for me to follow all of this."

Hold your horses, John. Let me finish the prophecy and then I'll lay it out in a more orderly fashion for you. Okay?"

"Okay."

"But proving resistant was the powerful cedar which grew out of from the waters of the Empire which had concealed it. This cedar inherited the Middle East, and was more treacherous than all the wicked trees that had preceded it. The cedar distorted the truth and forced its words through conquest and torture until it spread out its canopy in order to fill the world. It reigned in power over several cycles, until the zenith of its power was reached in the final cycle where it attempts to seed the valley, but then it is destroyed forever in a fiery holocaust. The Cedar of Lebanon will be gone forever, and only then shall peace reign. The teachings of the vine will then prevail, and the hand of the Lord will rest easy upon the earth. Do you understand it now?"

"No."

"I thought it would be perfectly clear to you by now. How about you Marg?"

My wife shook her head.

"It is pretty obvious what the prophecy means. I don't understand why you don't see it. But then again, no one has properly interpreted it for two thousand years, so I guess I shouldn't be too surprised.

The valley is Judah and Israel, just as was the valley of the Rose of Sharon. The mountains were the Diaspora. The conquest of Rome destroyed the valley and took control of the mountains. The remnant of Judah and Israel could still be found in the Diaspora but barely existed in the homeland. Rome filled the valley until it was unrecognizable and the Jews suffered under the hand of Rome. But then Christianity sprung into being and though the message of the vine should have been like the underground spring, guiding and nourishing the forest, it grew out of control until it had in many ways become more evil than the Roman forest.

As powerful as the uncontrolled waters had become, there arose a greater power that rose above the waters and could not be felled. The cedar is Islam, peaking and subsiding over the centuries until just before the end of time, not even the waters can knock it down. The cedar attempts to seed the valley with nothing but its own seedlings and that brings about the time of the End of Days.

The vine revives and the original message of the vine is restored to its original form. This is 'The Way' of which I've been trying to explain to you in regards to the Zadokite Document. A war is fought between the vine and the cedar, on a scale of devastation never witness before. Only after massive suffering does 'the Way', become triumphant. Order is restored and the world is at peace.

Pretty simple, n'est-ce pas? At least I think it is. Do you see it now?"

"So you're suggesting that we're at this End of Days period?" Pearce appeared to shudder just thinking about it.

"Hey, prophecy is alive and well. Do you think that all that was recorded in the bible was nothing more than the ranting and raving of lunatics?"

Pearce was about to say something.

"Be careful how you answer that question. It' the ruination of a lot of people. Because if you deny it, you've effectively stated that you feel that parts of the bible are legitimate and the rest is garbage."

"I wasn't going to say that. I was only going to suggest that we may not fully understand the true meanings behind the prophecies."

"Sure we do John. If the bible says in a prophecy that God says the Jews are his chosen people and they will be forever in order to keep his promise to Moses and David, and He goes on to say that I will bless those that bless them, and curse those that curse them, what do you think it means? It's a prophecy, a guarantee, and it's pretty obvious. So if certain religious leaders stand on a pedestal and claim that God has abandoned the Jewish people and the inheritance has been taken away, you know for a fact now that they're full of crap. God never said that. The prophets never said it and what will happen is a lot of people are going to suffer for believing in these preachers that want to ignore prophecy and make erroneous statements."

"But what about the statement that prophecies were only appropriate for the times in which they were made. Doesn't that suggest that things can change and they don't have to be guaranteed forever?"

"Hello… What is a prophecy if it's not prophetic? I really have a hard time with people not understanding this. It wasn't my intention to move into my religious mode because I like to think of myself as a scientist but there are times when I don't seem to have much of a choice. A prophecy for the end of time is for the End…. Of…..Time! Where's it going to change or play itself out? There are no wild cards here. Like Einstein said, 'God doesn't play dice.' Things proceed in the manner they're meant to proceed. There's a plan. And neither you, nor anyone that wants to hide behind the clergy and speak differently is going to change it. That is why I have a good laugh at those that say they're religious but choose not believe in the prophecies. It's like being a little bit pregnant. You either are or you aren't."

"This prophecy then is saying that there's going to be a war between Islamic nations and the West. And that it all ends with a fiery holocaust which engulfs the Muslim world and ultimately destroys it."

"Bingo! You got it! So, almost six hundred years before Mohammed even started his campaign, my ancestor envisioned not only Christianity dominating the Western world, but a corrupted version of the original teachings at that, only to have the Holy Land surrounded by a more evil empire than the Romans, which ultimately threatens the Western world, but in which a combined Judeo-Christian civilization arises in order to defeat this threat to their existence. And in doing so, the restoration of the original teachings of the way results in a reunification of Ephraim and Judah. In other words a single Judeo-Christianity that everyone can believe in. And the world in the most part is finally at peace.

Now there's something for you to think about for a while."

CAESAREA: 43 AD

It is so good to have my feet back upon our soil. I weep with tears of happiness that I have returned safely. Without Jonathias, I do not know if I could have managed the voyage back home. He watched over me the entire journey like a lioness protecting her cubs. And with good cause. A finer group of ruffians and cutthroats you wouldn't be able to find on board a single vessel. It was as if Rome had emptied her prisons and was exiling all of the inmates to our country.

I have already sent word to the Legate of Syria, regarding the Emperor's intention to set up a statue of himself in the inner court of the Temple. I have warned him that this could result in the insurrection he is trying so hard to prevent from occurring within our borders. He is a wise man. I have faith that he will join us in making every effort in preventing such an occurrence. Agrippa has assured me that he will prevail upon Caligula to rescind his order but he must do so in a manner that does not put himself into jeopardy. Caligula is quick to execute those that he finds disagreeable, even those that are his friends.

I had thought that you and your brother would have been here to greet me at the port of Caesarea. I know your duties in Antioch keep you extremely preoccupied and that your presence here was unlikely, but I still have not had word from Joshua. Whatever his anger is that he bears towards me, it is time that he rises above it. What is he searching for? A father that is always there to guide him every step he takes in life. That I have not been and should not be expected to do. I did not have two sons to care for; I had a nation to watch over. I'm sorry if he feels abandoned by my decisions but now is not the time for him to immerse himself in self-pity. Our people need us more now than ever before and we must stand united against our common enemy. I don't know what to say to him any longer. Hopefully you will be my mouthpiece and tell him that his angst towards me, although justified in his own mind, is not going to be resolved at this time. We must prioritize our problems and deal with our situation accordingly. Now is the time we work together. He can nurture his hatred for me afterwards.

And since my return I have already had a visitor that I did not expect to grace me with his presence. It has taken extraordinary circumstances for him to overlook our differences and humble himself to ask for my help. Jacob, known as James son of Joseph, brother of Yeshua has made known his fears to me. He is a man of visions and in one of these premonitions he has seen Ephraim becoming ruler over Judah, and those that failed to accept this were given over to the sword. We knows that all Hebrew names have a second meaning and Ephraim implies doubly fruitful or the second fruit. James is certain that this second fruit is the followers of his church, a development of the Judeo-Christian heritage which now exists. But he has envisioned a darker reality, a breakaway group from 'the Way' that eventually supersedes Judaism and in fact is responsible for terrible persecutions of the Jews well into the future.

He has seen a star that comes out of Judah in the final days. The star is a searcher of the Law and he will come to Damascus and there as the sceptre of Israel he will strike against the children of Seth. Damascus he is certain represents the evil power, where the Kiyyun and Tabernacle has been taken. What he was trying very hard not to reveal to me is that his authority is being challenged and seized by the church in Damascus. Now Kiyyun can be translated in several ways. As Saturn, and as images referring to pictures found on medallions. The tabernacle, or essentially the true house of the Lord has been taken over by a group centred in Damascus that had adopted practices that are contrary to the true "Way". For him to even suggest to me that this group considers itself to be the caretakers of the Tabernacle can only indicate that the power shift may have already occurred.

But James told me much of this breakaway group's customs. This Damascene order has integrated the Feast of Saturnalis into their religious beliefs and has begun the use of images, medallions, and assorted icons, contrary to ban on graven images, which has James extremely concerned.   By creating a hybrid of our beliefs with those of the Gentile world, this church has made itself attractive to a wide variety of adherents.   James has proven himself most inefficient in the task his brother left for him. Even he is aware that the flock had become ill kept. The shepherd and those that serve him have failed to perform their duties. This is quite true. The flock that Yeshua raised has been ill kept by the shepherds he left in charge following his being struck down. They have become large and fat over the years but they have been led by shepherds that have taken them astray.

Ignoring James' natural resentment for this group that refuses to acknowledge his authority, I see them as being nothing more than rebels masked by a covenant of repentance, good-will, tolerance, but in fact they are clearly the exact opposite in every characteristic. Faithless, immoral and wicked, pursuing wealth and doing evil things against their fellow man. They will never be able to heal the rift because the primary goal is self-gain. James has no chance of ever bringing them back into the fold. Their wine is the venom of serpents and the cruel heads of asps.

They have chosen to be part of the nations of other races and therefore they have placed the kings of these foreign nations in roles of leadership before God.   James attempted to instruct me that the apostles were men of perfect holiness, a select group, but were still loath to carry out the commands of the righteous. He admitted that they had failed to achieve and do all that they were expected to do.

This he has suggested has led to the opportunity for the one I knew as Saul to go from bounty hunter to advocate of 'the Way.' Elioneiai, how is it that you failed to tell me of this sudden change in purpose by our Tarsian nemesis. James has described him as, 'one whose lot has not fallen in the midst of those taught of God.' Saul was not chosen by Yeshua and those that are knowledgeable in 'the Way', men of intellect will reprove him, until the day that he shall again stand in the conclave to be judged. James is certain that those that have been led astray by the Damascene Order will one day return to 'the Way.' Of this I cannot say that I share his belief. Until then, they shall have no share in the house of the Law. We must reject them completely.

It is evident that the Damascene Order is already subjugating the influence of the Jerusalem Church, which they accuse of being completely composed of Judaizers. Apparently this is a charge that Saul, now called Paul has brought against them. One I don't believe James fully understands because this breakaway order will only be content with the eventual defeat of all those adhering to the instructions and teachings of the Jerusalem Church. If being a Judaizer is suddenly to be condemned then it is not an issue of replacement as James chooses to believe, but one of total eradication. Mark my words Elioneiai, if this Damascene Order is allowed to rise to flourish it will not only herald our own decline but actually precipitate it.

James has become irrelevant. He no longer exerts control over these renegade churches. I do not know how much longer we can help him retain what little authority he still possesses. If these New Christians are going to introduce practices that are in direct conflict with the laws of Moses then it may be best that we disassociate ourselves from James' Church immediately. That is not to say that we no longer permit his followers to use the courts of the Temple because it is best we do so that we do not alienate those that still adhere to our laws but be alert that we do not lower our guard and find that their heretic followers bring non-Jews into the inner courts. This would be pollution and a violation of our sacred house.

Be wary for I fear that we are on the verge of a precipice. Armageddon may very well be upon us and the fulfillment of the prophecies at hand. Stay strong, my son, for when I am not here then our people will be depending on you to be their source of strength in troubled times.

CHAPTER THIRTY-TWO

"Sometimes I get the feeling Doc that you think I have a PhD or something in antiquities. Let me make it perfectly clear, I don't!"

"Is there a part you're referring to specifically?"

"You know that medallion thingy you talked about. And all that other stuff."

"You mean the Kiyyun."

"Yes."

"The Kiyyun that Caiaphas talked about, not me."

"Okay, the Kiyyun that Caiaphas talked about."

"Funny, the original translators failed to understand that these images and Kiyyun were not a sign of approval but were actually a condemnation, just as Caiaphas mentioned."

"So there is something actually written about this," Pearce jumped on my statement.

"Oh yes. Very well described in the Zadokite Document. But where it's mentioned in this document is also supported by the quote from Zechariah in which the shepherd is struck down and the man that is with him. The flock is scattered. The Lord turns his hand upon the shepherds. The poor of the flock are the ones that give heed to the Lord and are therefore saved. And it is the Star from Jacob which is carrying out the punishment in Zechariah. In the final days, they will be scattered, implying destroyed, and the poor of the flock, those that are true believers in 'the Way' will be redeemed."

"But being the book of Zechariah, doesn't this make the other document more Jewish than Christian."

"You really are determined to try and separate this document from the early Church, aren't you? I see I'm going to have to give you even more examples why that isn't the case. Page eight of the Zadokite document states that all that's described in Zechariah will happen on the day that God visits Earth. The visit is seen and described as an actual physical visitation. I find that amazing. You should see it that way as well. In line three of this page; it is again clear that this is not an Essene document but a document of the

Jerusalem Church." I went out of the kitchen and quickly returned with my copy of the Zadokite Document, placing it in the centre of the table and flipping to the correct page where I pointed out the statement. "It states that the Princes of Judah have become like those that removed the landmark. If this was an Essene document, then it would automatically imply that the non-Essene Jews had removed the landmark, because the Essenes considered mainstream Judaism to be riddled with sin. The landmark is that feature which separated us from the Gentiles. In other words, the circumcision. To say that the leaders of the Jews had become like that group which the author earlier claims are the wicked children of the pit that had removed the landmark, makes a clear distinction between the two. Jew and the Uncircumcised Party, which the author does not consider the latter to be Jewish in any context. And now he has grown concerned that the so-named Jewish Princes, ie. the Jewish leaders of the sect are now willing to condone the entry of non-circumcised members to their sect.

Now let's look at line four of this page where the Lord explains why he will take out his wrath against the Damascene Order. All of this is laid at the feet of one man by the author. He states, 'All this they did not consider, who built the wall and daubed it with plaster, because one walking in wind and raising storms and preaching to men with lies, preached to them, so against all of the congregation, the wrath of God is kindled.' The separation of those that perverted 'the Way' was caused by a single preacher who travelled over the known world as indicated by this phrase 'walked in wind' and was a powerful commanding orator as suggested by the phrase 'raising storms'. But his teachings were nothing but distortions and lies, he goes on to say. This man whom we saw was earlier called TSOW by deeds alone is shown, to be no other than Saul of Tarsus. So, because of him, the truth was lost and now the end of days must come to pass according to James and Caiaphas.

Line eighteen here reinforces the resentment against the Damascene Order as the author states, 'God hates and abhors the builders of the wall and His wrath is kindled against them and against all those that walk after them.' You can't get much clearer than this. James in not very happy with what has occurred in this breakaway church."

"I can't argue with any of what you're telling me Doc. Like I said, I don't have a PhD, so I have to believe everything you're telling me but I don't see how all the scholars that have examined this document haven't seen these passages in the past."

"They have, without a doubt they've seen them, translated them, and for whatever reason came up with theories that are completely implausible in some cases. For example, Burrows wished to call this the Damascus Document thinking that the Essenes referred to Qumran as Damascus so the Romans would not find their village. This is a ridiculous concept since roads existed which led to their outpost and it was already well known. This was not a hidden society, just a monastic one. He also failed to recognize that the writings weren't actually praising the people of Damascus but condemning them. Why in the world would the Essenes condemn their own community? Now you tell me how a scholar like Burrows could overlook a paragraph like that beginning with line twenty-one of this page, extending all the way onto page twenty of manuscript B, which reads, "All the men that have entered the new covenant in the land of Damascus have acted faithlessly again, forsaking the well of living water, and shall not be reckoned with the gathering of the people. And their writings shall not be any longer from this day when the Unique Teacher was gathered up, until a Messiah arises from Aaron and from Israel.' I don't know about you but it is clear to me that this means that those that entered the New Covenant in Damascus where Paul started his order and base, were no longer to be considered partaking in the 'living waters' and their writings were no longer reflecting the true teachings of the Unique Teacher following his death and they would never return to the true path until the priestly messiah comes at the end of days. Can you see that?"

Both Pearce and Marg nodded their heads as if they were children sitting in class.

"Why would a reputable scholar overlook all of this? I still don't get it."

"I don't get it either." They were both stunned into silence by my response. "Come on! I can't be expected to have all the answers. This is one of those times. It really doesn't make sense to overlook something so obvious. Yet, Burrows has done it and so has everyone else."

"I know you to well Doc," Pearce said suspiciously "You do have a theory about this. I can tell. You got that look."

"If I did, it would go something like this…" I hypothesized. "There are several statements being made that would run contrary to what we consider mainstream Christianity today. Firstly, the Damascene Order was not considered a proper follower of 'the Way'. Secondly the letters and epistles as well as certain scriptures being produced by this group were considered heretical and not part of 'the Way.' But most importantly, this break away occurred shortly after the death of the Unique Teacher. Now remember, this Unique Teacher is an entirely different individual from the Righteous Teacher of the Essenes. Whereas the Righteous Teacher was referred to as hruwm, the Unique Teacher was most often referred to as hrwyui. I know you don't have a PhD John, but trust me, this difference in spelling is very significant. The fact that the death of the Unique Teacher is referred to as a day of gathering, similar to Elijah's, it suggests a unique death or disappearance. Put it all together John and it's obvious to me, and it should be to the rest of you,   that the Unique Teacher is Jeshua or Jesus and his uniqueness was the result of his teachings being very different from the Essenes, Pharisees, and the Sadduccees.

But notice that the original Jerusalem Church members were expecting his death to be followed by the appearance of the Messiah from Aaron and Israel. Not a return of Jesus! No second coming! Imagine, a document written by James and his followers that is so completely different from the Christian beliefs of today! Who changed it? Who made up the lies? What's true and what's not? I can guess why an accurate translation may have been buried. Can't you?"

"Conspiracy theory, conspiracy theory," Pearce began shouting.

"Hey, you know what they say about paranoids thinking there's always some Machiavellian plot being hatched behind everything."

"No, what?"

"They're probably right! That's what they say."

"I will admit that it does look like there's something suspicious taking place here," Pearce admitted. "I don't know if I want to agree with the concept of a plot to protect modern Christianity. There may be some simple and plausible reason we just haven't thought of yet. What I do know is that you've got the makings here Doc for a major publication. I've got that gut feeling again just like I had with Blood Royale. Anyone reading this is going to know that it's very different from your first release of the Caiaphas Letters. What you've added so far makes any comparison of the two editions like night and day. I can't even describe how excited I am."

"You mean you're no longer upset that I've turned all your personal beliefs upside down?"

"I didn't say that. I'm actually pissed off that you've done that, but it still doesn't stop me from being excited."

"Then this little titbit should make you even more excited. There's a time frame provided in Manuscript B in line fourteen of page twenty." I pointed out the specific paragraph I was referring to. "It reads that the time that the Unique Teacher was gathered in until the time that the destruction of the community took place as a result of war which followed the 'preacher of lies and man of falsehood', was forty years. Then Israel had become homeless, without a king or judge to lead them. I'm surmising that the author of this little epitaph was one of James' closest associates, since if I'm correct about the reference, James would have been dead by a few years at this time. Because he says that it is forty years, he's indicating that it has already taken place within his own time. Now get this. This is good. Inexplicably, Burrows translates it as 'was forty years' trying to make it a prior historical event more fitting of the Essenes and the Righteous Teacher. The fact is that it does clearly state 'it is' as the correct translation making it present tense.

As Jesus likely died in 33-34 AD, then 40 years would coincide nicely with the end of the Roman-Jewish war. Thirty-seven years until the fall of Jerusalem and forty to the fall of Masada. The chronology fits, and the Jerusalem Church was expelled from the city along with the Pharasaic schools at the end of the war. Without the Temple, the Sudduccean movement was doomed and there would not be another Jewish government to rule over Judaea, Samaria and Galilee until 1948. So how's that for being a fitting reconciliation of events to what is described?"

"How certain are you?" Pearce questioned.

"Very."

"Okay, I'll buy it."

"I do too," Marg interjected. "But what could they hope by

covering up the manuscript like they've done?"

"As cover-ups go, it was fairly effective. Most accepted what they had to say as gospel." I laughed at my little pun but no one else seemed to be sharing the joke with me. "Take it as gospel...didn't anyone get it?" Still no response. "Anyway, there aren't that many people that are aware of the document, let alone go about translating it from the Hebrew. Intentional? Oversight? Who's to know? Fact is the document exists and it is probably the most significant finding of the last century and hardly anyone knows about it."

"Until they read your book," Pearce was quick to emphasize.

"Let's hope so. You've got a church that doesn't want it to be uncovered because it would condemn some of its current practices. And a rabbinical society that wouldn't want to admit that the two religions were so close at one time that they could share documents and heritage. Can you imagine the consequences if both parties recognizing that the degrees of separation at the inception of the Church were so minor that there really wasn't a distinction between them? It would be tantamount to admitting that at some point in the past the teachings of both were not that dissimilar and as such any conflicts existing today were not the result of God's word but man's. All the righteous sanctimonious reasons to preserve ancient prejudices become irrelevant."

"That's good!" Pearce declared.

"Not from everyone's perspective. There' a lot of people that have benefited over the last two millennia by emphasizing the differences. There'd be a lot of unhappy people thinking that they and their ancestors may have been duped over that same time period."

"And hence the government boys trying to get hold of you at our offices."

"Not all information is good information John. Even the truth can be undesirable. If we look at an extreme example, can you imagine the devastation that a revelation of this nature could wreak? Business havoc, major corporations disintegrating because their major shareholders are religious affiliates, political upheaval, even more terrorism by religious fanatics. All because there could be a shift in population dynamics structured by a new set of beliefs. Best to keep it under wraps and avoid any ramifications."

"You don't seriously mean that."

"Why should I know what is best for the world? I don't think any of my ancestors were overly concerned about the repercussions of the messages they delivered. They never questioned their actions. Neither did they ever question their beliefs. That is until Jakob Goldenthal came along. And I guess I'm more in tune with his memories than the others. Because I question almost everything and anything. Didn't you ever wonder why it took your detective work to track me down before I ever decided to reveal the concept of GLEEM in any of my books?"

"Tough decision."

"Extremely. By telling you all, I knew I'd be unleashing a genie that I could never force back into the bottle. So all those years I kept it all under wraps until you came along. After that, I really didn't have a choice any longer. You would have eventually exposed the story, so by giving it to you directly I'm able to ensure that it stays accurate. Doesn't make it any easier though. I know that with every word I give you, I could be altering the future by clarifying the past. And with every chapter I don't give you, I'm preserving and perpetuating a falsehood that we all have lived by for a long time now. Yeah, you're right, a real tough decision!"

CAESAREA: 43 AD

Elioneiai, I don't know if you're as confused as I am regarding this Christian sect, but it seems to be dividing rapidly into so many segments that it no longer has a single voice. And most serious of all the Gentile adherents have become disruptive. They still claim to respect the authority of the Jerusalem Church, but they have made a clear distinction between themselves as Christians, the Nazarenes up north and the followers of 'the Way'.

I can assure you that Saul will already be taking advantage of this segmentation. He is preaching of defiance of the circumcision law. This man won't desist until he creates his own theocracy. Many of his statements are appended with the comment, 'by the consent of James, brother of Yeshua, Bishop of Jerusalem.' James doesn't even know that Saul is making these claims in his name. The situation is totally out of control.

Everything is becoming so complicated. Even the Pharisees

are wielding a disproportionate amount of power lately. Given enough time, they'll find ways to subject the sun's brilliance to their laws of purification. I don't understand this world any longer. I returned from Rome to find everything turned upside down. Although I have honoured my promise to the Emperor to stay out of Jerusalem affairs and hence my residing in Caesarea, I am still of everything that goes on in my beloved city. I thought I had witnessed everything until I saw Pharisees wearing gloves so that the air wouldn't soil their clean hands. The world has gone mad. The Pharisee adherence to ludicrous extremes has made fulfilment of Judaism a hardship rather than a pleasure. With every step they take they make a prayer for they have ventured upon a new path. This behaviour is absurd. God has never asked us to burden ourselves in this manner. Increasingly, they're gaining popularity among the people in spite of this, especially among the women. Given the right circumstances, I think they would even try to do away with the priesthood. After all, the Pharisees despise us. Already they are dictating how they would like to see the services in the Temple conducted. They are hypocrites, wearing their Judaism like a fine cloak, just for the sake of others to see and be impressed. Their audacity is so great that they claim that the tephillin on their heads and on their left arms are holier than the ephod that the high priest wears. They have used it to mock the ordinance of the ephod and coronet that God has provided only to the house of Aaron.

How have we let this happen? Whoever humbles himself before God shall be rewarded, for the humble are more righteous than all the sages that have proceeded them. Unlike are Pharisee counterparts, we have no belief in an afterlife nor a resurrection during which we can correct the errors we make in life. We must make the most of the life we have.

A Jew who doesn't attend the synagogue regularly is no less a Jew than any of the Pharisee who spend the better part of their lives within the holy sanctuaries. When a Jew is crushed beneath the heel of Roman oppression, is his suffering any less than that of a Pharisee? Is the blood of a Pharisee when shed any redder than that of any other Jew? God did not give us the Pharisim to tell us otherwise.

I don't know which is worse; these Pharisees or the Christians. Both are determined to send me to my grave. Their determination to alter the Holy Scriptures is unquenchable. And yet neither is to be considered a true enemy of God, merely misguided in their interpretations. There have always been those like the Pharisim that force themselves to adhere more stringently than others, and like the Christians that follow a set of ordinances that relax the regulations. Everything is relative. It is not our role to condemn our brothers for their variations to the practices of Judaism, what is important is to ensure that we do not permit them to do so. Most important is to cease our silence against those that wish to change the face of Judaism all together. That will be our greatest challenge as guardians of the true faith.

Whether it be the Nazarenes, Christians, or followers of 'the way', we must keep them from splintering us into a multitude of factions. Any introduction of pagan beliefs from the Gentile world will ultimately lead to the decline of our civilization, the abandonment of the covenant with Abraham and Moses, and will be abhorrent in the eyes of God. This must be undertaken with a fervent zeal if we are to survive. All that I know regarding the origins of these groups and the falsehoods they spread, I will relate to you. It is your duty to ensure that these words are to be continued through the successive generations of our family. They must be remembered, and all must know that they are the truth. We must speak in the synagogues, the meeting places, the forums both here and in foreign lands. Every ear that crosses our path must hear our message. Fire can only be fought with fire. We must not falter. We must be shepherds protecting and tending our flocks, not only in Judaea, Samaria Idumea, Galilee and Peraea, but throughout the world, wherever there is a Diaspora community.

We are the standard bearers for the army of the Lord, and with His word we will slay our enemy's falsehoods. We must remain strong and our courage adamant. God established our race at the beginning of time and has declared us to be eternal in order to spread his message amongst all the people. The paths of the Jew are truth and therefore the path shall be continuous without end. While civilizations have faded into the distant memories, we have survived them all. Our seed shall be carried like the milkweed on the wind to the four corners of the world. All the people will come to learn that the burden of the Torah is a glorious one. It is the everlasting word of God and all those that seek the fountain of knowledge that comes from the sacred scriptures shall share in its blessings.

The Nazarenes will not find it easy to change even a single word of the truth. We'll use their own distortions and misinterpretations as a noose around their necks to silence them forever. They'll choke on their own incredulous myths until all their breath is gone. Those who call themselves Nazarenes will be like a ship floundering upon the sea. And when they discover that they are lost, they will curse their captains for taking them upon such a perilous voyage.

We must be like a wall my son, preventing heathen fallacies from penetrating the minds of our people. Heathen teachings are like weeds. They must be plucked constantly from fertile soil or else they will strangle the fruits of the garden until nothing remains. We must remain vigilant, for like the weeds, when one is pulled, others will grow in its place. We must never forsake the garden and say that there are too many weeds.

Waiting for James to deal with the segmentation that is taking place within his church will be of little help to us. The Jerusalem Church is losing its influence over the churches in Asia and Mesopotamia. Even now, letters purported to have been written by Saul are circulating freely. His philosophy is gaining more adherents rapidly. He challenges the Nazarene doctrine by encouraging its followers to drink wine to prevent illness. He challenges those in the Jerusalem Church to abandon their adherence to the dietary laws. And in general he claims that any Gentile can become a Christian without converting to Judaism first.

What Saul is trying to create is a church that is no longer part of our reality; a foreign cult that only resembles us superficially. Any common beliefs between us will soon be coincidental rather than intentional. In these Churches outside of Israel they are dominated by people that have no knowledge of the one and only God. Yeshua the Jew has become superseded by Jesus the incarnation of whatever God they wish to worship at the moment. To this pagan horde, the Torah and our laws have absolutely no significance. How can anyone debate the oneness and uniqueness of the Almighty with a people that previously worshipped a pantheon of gods? In their own simplistic way, they say, 'If one God was good, then two is better.'

We must strive hard to contain this plague unlike James,

whom has resigned himself to the consideration that it is all well beyond his control. Our major concern must be the preservation of our sacred beliefs and not allowing them to be distorted by those having no entitlement to them. They have said, 'Let us take what we like from Judaism, Zoroastrianism, and Hellenism and make a world that pleases us.' This hybrid that Saul wishes to create and call his new Christianity is intended to supersede the spirit of Israel. Let us challenge him by raising the spirits of our people and stoke them with the fires of our Holy God. Let us raise the spirit of those that have lost hope and make them understand that the Lord has not forsaken those who bear His sign.

This I entrust to you Elioneiai. I pray that your brother Joshua will be there by your side to aid you in this most difficult task. I know that it is his wife Maxima that has driven this wedge between us. I hope he can forgive me for the angst that he knows I have borne against his marriage. I have come to realize that it was not for me to dictate whom he should marry and whom he should not. Times have changed. These are modern times. The selection of Anna as my wife when I was but a young boy by my father Kamithos and her father, See, was the practice of a bygone age. They had chosen wisely for me, because not only was your mother loving, caring and beautiful, she had always been my best friend. But now those of you of this generation seek more in a marriage. Perhaps it is time to change my old fashioned ways if I am to bring your brother back to me. How could his wife not object to me if I had let it known that I objected to her? I do not want to pass on to the Shekinah with the knowledge that he still remains angry with me. Please tell him that I am sorry, and beg him to stand with you on this task.

CHAPTER THIRTY-THREE

We returned to the salon following breakfast to go over the remaining chapters of the book. I calculated with a little luck and by restricting Pearce to a minimum number of interruptions, we should be finished this last section by the time lunch rolled around. Of course, keeping any type of control over Pearce was more easily said than done. I could tell that he was already putting together a series of questions regarding the Zadokite Document.

"So Doc, I've had a lot of time to think about what we talked about last night. And I was thinking, if this document really was a Christian document, then it would probably give an indication of how the resurrection really took place. At least that's what I'd think would be in there."

"That's a fair statement." I commented. "There is an answer to it as well. At line nineteen of page twelve there's a summation of the laws but the translation provided by Shechter and the other experts fails to acknowledge that these laws served to bring the congregation closer to the Unique Teacher who still acted as an intercedent even after his death. The actual reading should be, 'And these are the laws of the sanctified one to become a walker amidst all of the living to judge you, and you whom are judged to be this, will walk with the seed of Israel and will not be cursed.' So where's the error you're probably asking. The experts interpreted the sanctified one to be the Essene member that was ministering to the uneducated masses. If they were to become enlightened by these ministrations, they will become one of the true followers within Israel and will attain salvation. Now when you first read this you probably tend to agree with that interpretation, since initially, it does appear reasonable and logical from an Essene perspective. But what you have to remember is that unlike Essene documents, this manuscript has introduced a new character, the 'Unique Teacher.' Therefore the impression that it is actually conveying is that the Unique Teacher is now walking amongst the congregation even after his death. This occurs because we read the line of him being an intercedent and then the reference to the sanctified one being the walker. If you notice, there is no plurality here. The reference is not to sanctified ones, which would be the case if it was referring to all the Essene preachers that were moving throughout the region seeking converts. My mind, on the other hand, automatically assumes that the references are singular for the simple reason that they are not referring to two individuals, and the Unique Teacher and the Sanctified One are one and the same. We don't have enough information to make the conclusion whether the walking amongst the living is literal or figurative. So if others wish to interpret it as Jesus actually returning from the dead, then so be it."

I could tell Pearce was satisfied by my reply. He was merrily jotting down notes around the outer periphery of his main body of writing. He looked up momentarily, pausing his scribbling, to challenge my Unique Teacher-Jesus connection.

"I don't believe there are too many candidates that can fill the description," I counselled him. If you look at line twenty-eight on this page, the author instructs us to listen to the voice of the Teacher. Interestingly, he does not stipulate whether he refers to the Righteous Teacher or the Unique Teacher but taking into consideration that in line thirty-two he calls those that listen, men of the unique one, then it is obvious that he is referring to the Unique Teacher. The fact that he is suggesting that so many years later you could still listen to the voice, even though the Unique Teacher has been killed, suggests that all of this particular Teacher's sayings had been gathered into some form of book. In that way, the voice could still be heard. Also, the Teacher of Righteousness is mentioned secondarily to the Unique Teacher and is responsible for creating ordinances, whereas the latter passed righteous judgments as explained in lines thirty and thirty-one. Therefore, we have a spiritual leader whose words of wisdom had been written down, and he actually passed judgments on people based on a set of ordinances or values that pre-existed., and he had been killed but his words thrived even after his death. Once again, it's obvious that whoever was going to leave such a legacy would have something written about his life. This person wasn't going to be kept secret. His name would have been on everyone's lips. We only have one person that fits this description. So it has to be Jesus."

"Learned a long time ago that there's no such animal as 'has to!'"

"That's nice John, but in this case it's a matter of it has to! If there were a lot of others matching this description then the reference of 'Unique' would have hardly been appropriate."

"So what about these ordinances you mentioned, Doc. You said something about the Righteous Teacher writing them."

"Now you have to remember John, that the Righteous Teacher was an Essene fixture. He was responsible for the leadership and direction of that group. So he came up with a list of ordinances or rules to keep them focused. It would appear that many of these are also common to the early Christian Church, which only serves to raise the question of how intertwined these two organizations may have been in the beginning.

On page nine there is the start of the section entitled the Laws of Proper Behaviour of the Community. Oddly, the first ordinance of this group deals with the issue of homosexuality. The translation by Shechter does not come out and directly say this. In so doing he fails to provide the student with a truthful accounting of the phrase which reads 'All men which are uniting man from man'. It would appear that the deleth of uniting was replaced by a rosh as the statement was found to be offensive. One who commits homosexuality is no longer to be considered to be a living man and is to be put to death by use of the Gentile court system. By using the Gentile courts, the congregation is not guilty of committing murder of one of its own which God would frown upon. An interesting use of the legal system.

There's really nothing much to the other ordinances until we reach number seven which prohibits sinning against the Torah. Again, it's emphasized by this ordinance of how close the Jerusalem Church was initially to mainstream Judaism.

Then there's the tenth ordinance which outlines the membership of the Elder Court or Tribunal. There are to be a minimum of four priests, and six of Israel that have been instructed in the teachings of the covenant and the 'Hagu'. All members must be between twenty-five and sixty years old. This is where we first have mention of the 'Hagu' court. Since we know from tradition that these elder courts are to be made up of seventy judges, then the ordinance is only requiring about a seventh of these to be well versed in the original covenant or to simplify it further, to be Jewish. The rest can be converts, those that have followed the requirements to become Jewish first before entering into the Church.

I like the next one. The eleventh clearly states that men over sixty have diminished capacity and therefore cannot remain as judges. This is one of the few references to age where it's not viewed as the onset of wisdom but as the advance of senility. This is a very un-Jewish concept if I might say so.

Ordinances fourteen to thirty-nine all deal with the proper details for the keeping of the Sabbath. Remember, to the early Jerusalem Church, the Sabbath was Saturday, and the preservation of the Sabbath was based strongly on Old Testament law just like their Judaic cousins.

Where we encounter a bone of contention is ordinance thirty-seven which cautions against having Sabbath in a place where there is contact with Gentiles. This would directly oppose Saul's instruction to his followers to encourage services within the congregation made up of both Jews and Gentiles. You have to remember this was a major source of conflict between the rival Christian groups and amongst the apostles. The Jerusalem Church was always clear about it. You became a Jew first, then a Christian. What food could be eaten still followed the kosher dietary laws. Therefore any area where Gentiles prepared their food was considered 'traif'."

"There had to be some major difference too, didn't there," Pearce suggested more than asked. "After all, Christianity did break a way ultimately which meant there had to be irreconcilable differences somewhere!"

"Your right, John, but again I ask you view it with the mind of someone living two thousand years ago. What you might consider as not highly significant in today's day and age, would have been catastrophic in their minds back then. Take a look at Ordinance Thirty-nine which gives us a glimpse of the elimination of the animal sacrifices in the early Christian church. We've talked all about the personal offerings in the Temple ages ago when I mentioned the incident where Jesus caused a bit of a riot in the outer court. In this ordinance, for all intents and purposes, the personal offerings have been eliminated. Only the single sacrifice for the Sabbath is continued and this would have likely ended up being the congregational meal. It is well understood by this time that Jesus' sacrifice eliminated the need to continue the practices of the personal offering. This was one of the main breakaway points of early Christianity and here it is mentioned as one of the ordinances of the community. But those offerings on God's behalf are still to be continued as seen in Ordinance Forty. But the alter sacrifices mentioned in this particular ordinance refers primarily to the grain and non-animal sacrifices with the emphasis on prayer being the greatest offering. As it says, 'but the prayer of the righteous is like an offering of delight.' Clearly a change of thinking from the traditional Jewish animal offering has taken place. As I said, in our minds this may not seem to major but at that time this would have been a major deviation. Trust me, this is huge!

And if ever there was an incongruity that demonstrated that this group no longer was traveling on the same path as its parent, it would be Ordinance Fifty-four, the last law of the community. It reads, "And every utensil, nail, or peg in the wall which are with the dead in the house will become as one unclean like a working tool." By Jewish law, organic materials in contact with the dead are defiled but sometimes inanimate objects with which they had contact at time of death could become unclean but this was always a bone of contention and discussed *ad nauseum* amongst the Rabbis. The tools of the dead person's trade were often considered imbued with the essence of the person and therefore could become defiled. In this manner, cooking and eating utensils, always in contact with that person were by some considered defilable. But metal objects rarely in contact, being non-organic, were almost always considered impossible to become defiled. Nails in the walls or floors, never. You'd have to burn down their house if that was the case since their entire abode would be considered unclean.

So, why the concern about nails? Why the reference to nails or pegs or any other object inserted for hanging purposes in the wall? Why make the issue of defiled nails the last law of the community? Nails hammered into an upright board being considered as one with the dead person is unique to this particular community. It's quite perplexing when you first examine it. But if we think about the possible significance of nails in relationship to the dead long enough, you eventually come up with the answer. It is not so much a law of defilement as it is a custom of sanctifying a sacred memory. I view it almost as a re-enactment by which those entering into the home of the dead person are automatically drawn to relive the crucifixion, recall their origins, and sanctify the memory of their fallen brother or sister in the Church.   The nail becomes not an object of simple hammered metal but transmutes into a religious experience, reminding the mourners of Jesus' death upon the cross. Thus it is not to be seen as the last ordinance but as the beginning of a new life since the crucifixion was merely the prelude to the resurrection. Later it became more common to hang a crucifix on the wall as the sacred artefact but that took centuries to develop into a custom."

"I thought that might be the case when you mentioned the nails."

"Sometimes the obvious is nothing more than what it appears to be," I saluted him. "There are an awful lot of people out there that make a living from trying to make things difficult. And most don't see the forest for the trees. Hopefully we'll be able to correct a bit of that."

ANTIOCH: 43 AD

I grieve for you Jonathias for the greatness of our loss. I mourn the passing of the one whom embodied the soul and spirit of Judaea. It pains me to know that the time you spent with your grandfather was so short before he has passed on. May his spirit bring glory and illumination to the Shekinah. I weep for your sister Martha that she may no longer bask in the radiance of his smile and share the laughter of his delight. I cry tears of pain and sorrow for myself and my brother, Joshua, that we may no longer benefit from the letters of his intelligence and the teachings of his wisdom. Oh wail and shriek you creatures of this world, for this day the earth has become bereft of a great jewel. Joseph Caiaphas is dead but his memory will never depart from this world. You are still a young lad, barely in your teens but now is the time to pick up the mantle left behind by your grandfather.

My father was a great man with a single-minded purpose which he asked that we, his children, guard and preserve. Having known him for all the days of my life I can attest that he lived his life entirely in the pursuit of truth and any humility which he displayed came from the light of inner truth of his being. There never was a need on his part for bellicose arrogance, because he always knew that the truth could speak for itself. Its voice can never be stilled.

Indeed, Joseph Caiaphas was blessed above all others because the Almighty gave him knowledge and insight well beyond other men. I can only pray that the Lord grants me even a fraction of the blessing he bestowed upon my father. And I will reiterate that any man who could consume the degree of knowledge that my father encompassed, without proclaiming his own greatness as a result, is in my opinion the epitome of humility. If there be one word by which I can label your grandfather it would be righteous. It's a word that the Pharisees easily banter about but do not understand. Caiaphas was a true Zadokite. If you should find that the Pharisees are gladdened by his death, it is only because they know their greatest adversary is no longer amongst the living to frustrate their every subterfuge to confuse the laws and traditions of our people. Today, we the descendants Aaron, of the priesthood of Israel have lost a little bit of our radiance when the spark of Caiaphas ceased to exist. And the Pharisee know that a shadow hovers above us this day and that the glory of heaven has been dimmed.

But as your grandfather would point out, from every tragedy there comes a miracle, no matter how minor. Your uncle, Damneus and I have agreed that the memory of our father must be preserved and the sanctity of his name glorified above all others. After so many years of being apart, we have come together at this time. We must not let the work he has done as the High Priest of all our peoples for nineteen years be tarnished. It is sad that it took the death of Caiaphas to bring my brother and I back together. I know it was my father' wish that it would be so. I only wish that he had seen this reunion with his own eyes.

But above all Jonathias we must take on the heavy burdens that oppressed Caiaphas in his final days. He had great insights into both the past and future and he knew that as a people we were facing the greatest battle of our existence. To fight the enemy that lies within our midst will surely prove harder than the enemy without. Rome will never defeat us, but the failure of our people to resist the temptations of the pagan world will surely be our downfall.

I recall in one of his final letters to me that your grandfather asked that I ensure that his memory won't be altered like that of Judas the Iscar, son of Joazar the Boethian, the son of Simon.

Notably, Caiaphas had an unusual relationship with this Judas, which I personally found difficult to appreciate, since all men dislike the Boethians, but he was able to define that this Judas had a significant role that has been now completely expunged by those that call themselves Christian. We must ensure that the same does not occur to his memory.

Our father had been ill for some time but he did not let his infirmity deflect him from his responsibilities. God has graced him by letting him slip away while he slept. At last his troubled mind and discomforted body will find peace. The knowledge that he has imparted to us will live forever. His words to us are an eternal gift. We will make preparations to lay him to rest in the tomb of our forefathers. We will do him great honour when we carry him to our tomb. But afterwards we must set about continuing the work that he began.

Damneus and I agree that this situation with the Christians is growing intolerable. The church which Saul is creating is no longer to be considered a Jewish sect. It is to be considered a foreign cult which only resembles us superficially. Any common beliefs between us are only a faint whisper of what once was. This Christianity of Saul's is no longer the deviant sect that Caiaphas believed it to be. Our goal is very different from his as we can no longer be concerned with preventing its development as it is now a reality that has gone far beyond that pursuit. It now behoves us to prevent ourselves from being engulfed by this hybrid of our world and that of the pagans.

Saul entices those Jews that are weak in their faith by proclaiming his religion is the fulfilment of the Jewish prophecies. Therefore we must meet every challenge with debate until we can make it obvious to all whom examine the basis upon which both religions that they aren't merely interpretations of one idea but instead two entirely different concepts. Our origins stemmed from the peak of Mount Sinai, from a fiery cloud and a stormy blast. Theirs comes from the mouth of Saul, a man that sought first to eradicate them and now seeks to lead them. We were the few that fought enslavement and pursued the freedom that is the right of all mankind, while they, as their numbers increase, will become the enslavers and taskmasters.

What we must provide to our people is a reaffirmation of our ideals, and though that may ultimately lead us into confrontation and conflict with the Romans, at least is will serve notice to the world that Jews will not forsake the freedoms granted by God without a fight. And all shall know that liberty is only achieved when you possess something worth fighting for.

So let us not view our mission as a reintegration of those belonging to the Jerusalem Church and the Nazarenes for they will likely return to the fold once they separate any association they have with the Damascene Church of Saul's as they recognize it to be nothing more than a mockery of their beliefs. We must instead pursue a course of casting the Damascenes out of our prayer houses, our sanctuaries and our synagogues. We must declare them banned from our services and ceremonies. A separation is to be drawn between us and them and no longer are we to call them brother. All the world must know and see their order for what they truly are. Something foreign and blasphemous to our way of life. Separate and apart, without hope of ever joining the folds of Judaism, for whereas the other sects still adhere to our laws and customs, this one has chosen to replace them and that we cannot abide.

Once more, we're a nation awash amongst a sea of heathen gods, only now there is one that ridicules our cherished beliefs through its desire to emulate our relationship with God. It is a deception. All that they do is a lie. Is this not proven by Saul's letter to his followers in Corinth in which he states, 'All things are lawful for me.' He mocks the legal systems by which men govern themselves. And how can men find righteousness in this man from Tarsus when he writes, "To the Jews, I come a Jew in order to win Jews. Those under the law, I came as one under the law, though not being under the law myself, so I may win those under the law. To those outside the law, I become as one outside the law, that I might win them too.' This is a man that does not know honour or integrity. Any who would choose to follow him would have neither concept of truth nor righteousness and therefore there exists nothing to reason with.

When anarchy becomes law, and distortion becomes the accepted moral, then you know that these are not people imbued with the same spirit as us. They no longer listen or heed the words of Yeshua, their Christ. Did not Yeshua say that he came not to change the laws of Moses but to confirm them?

Unlike the civilizations we survived in the past, Assyria, Babylon, Greece, empires that lived and died by the sword, this new enemy is one that come from within. Its weapon is the word and the greater the lie the more that come to join its ranks. It conquers feeble minds and feeble souls. Stopping this deception will be our greatest challenge. This, your grandfather understood all too well. Those from among us that are weak of heart will fall to their conquering sword. Once again we are being challenged by the offspring of Dathan and Korah.. And once more we pray that the Lord opens the bowels of the earth to swallow them from our midst.

In Caiaphas' name, we must unite our people behind the banner of the Lord and fight His holy battles. Before us He shall march as a pillar of fire and a cloud of smoke. We will reconfirm our covenant which the Almighty made with our forefathers. Our enemies shall be scattered before us. And those that bless us shall be blessed themselves.

He has set us as a nation apart, an island standing alone in a raging sea. Like a beacon, we must hail passing ships on those waters and guide them to the safety of our shores. Those who seek tranquillity and love of God shall make it to dry land. Those who ignore our shining light will ride the squall for all eternity. And we must ensure that none of our children attempt to sail out upon those waters. Those that forsake the security of the safe harbour offered to them shall surely perish beneath the waves. The Lord will have no pity on them, for they've turned from the light and have chosen the dark. His heart will become cold to their prayers and He'll cast them into the depth from which they will never return.

Caiaphas died so that his work may live. His life will not be in vain. We will accept the mantle of his mission to safeguard our people from the threat that he did personally bear witness to. In our hearts and in our minds he will live as a part of us, forever.

Your Loving father Elioneiai

CHAPTER THIRTY-FOUR

"He died?"

"No one lives forever, John."

"It's just that I didn't expect that when we started on this book that he was going to die in it." Pearce's tone was somewhat scornful.

"Hey, you don't even like the guy," I reminded him. "Don't you remember? You basically accused me of whitewashing his reputation when I first started telling his story."

"That was then," Pearce cast aside my comment. "Now that I have a better appreciation for what he was doing, I'm a little disappointed that it's over now."

"Oh, I wouldn't say that it's over. Caiaphas' memory has lived long after his body was put in that tomb. He's very much alive. But more importantly, he's key to everything that James wrote and preached subsequently."

"Isn't this supposed to be about Caiaphas? I don't think we want to confuse the issue by introducing other personalities into the framework."

"Now, I don't want to lead you astray, John, because it was our intent to write about Caiaphas and let him tell the story of what transpired all those years ago. But we changed that venue quite a while ago."

Pearce rolled his eyes in disbelief at my suggestion. "I got it all recorded and written down Doc. Hours and hours of the stuff and I don't know which conversations you were participating in but the ones that I was listening to seemed to be about Caiaphas."

"But now if you were to look closely at you notes you'd see that we have been spending a heck of a lot of time discussing a document that most likely had been put into circulation by James. But it's important for you to recognize that although it might appear that I've gone off topic, these two people played a major role on influencing the society of their times merely through their interplay and interactions with each other. In fact there was a definite synergy as a result of their relationship. What developed or blossomed from either of them was bigger and greater than what would have been produced had they not had this relationship. So I think it's important that we continue to examine the Zadokite Document because what it contains had a major impact on Caiaphas and ultimately determined his reactions. Most of what we know of Caiaphas is the product of his reactions to events and circumstances. So you see, to comprehend Joseph Caiaphas you must fully understand the people and times he was reacting to."

"So we're not stopping here because he's now dead."

"No way! We're just beginning. What comes now ultimately changes the course of history. You have three people that try to pick up the gauntlet and they unfortunately couldn't achieve the task that Caiaphas set for them. Between Elioneiai ha Cayef, Joshua Damneus, and Jeshua ben Gamaliel, the three not only fail to avert the rise of the Pauline Christianity, they also were in some ways responsible for the Great War against Rome that ended the Jewish nation. I'd say we still have a lot to talk about!"

"But not everything today. I still have a flight to catch."

"A little more on the Zadokite Document and that should provide you with the finishing touches of Caiaphas' life."

"Sound good."

"If we take a look at page fourteen," I flip to the appropriate page, "it deals with the fact that the community overseer must be between thirty and fifty years of age and that he must be fluent in all the languages of the families within his congregation. I find it very interesting that this early Christian community is far worldlier than the Jewish communities it shares the Temple grounds with. It views itself as being decentralized, involving people from foreign lands, and spreading across the continents and granting each community equality as seen by the demand that its leader essentially be fluent in all the languages of its brethren."

"And this is unique?" Pearce questioned.

"Very! It's pretty much in direct opposition to the Jewish position at that time. As a Jewish community, communication of a religious nature was performed in Hebrew. Therefore it was essential that any pilgrims to Jerusalem had at least a basic understanding of the language. This wasn't too difficult since Aramaic was fairly universal at the time and it was closely related to

Hebrew. But the overriding difference is this outward perspective of the Church versus the inward centralized view of Judaism. How they were able to achieve a hundred and eighty degree shift in attitude so quickly is remarkable. Incredible! It's as if it came out of nowhere."

"It came from Jesus," Pearce instructed me almost immediately.

"That may very well be the case because it certainly wasn't the Jewish perspective. Even this restriction on the age of the community leader is quite surprising. Amongst us Jews, age was always associated with wisdom. After all, Moses was already eighty when he was leading us through the desert. This attitude of senility restricting the age at which those amongst the Church could lead contradicts the predominant Jewish view of the time. It would appear that leadership was only to be given to those that were approximately the same age as Jesus was when he was preaching, give or take a few years."

"And what else is in the document?"

"The remaining pages of the document deal with the individual's commitment to the community, the undertaking of oaths, and a generalized explanation of the morality expected. In most cases it is undistinguishable from other Judaic congregations in this respect. Its only significance is the emphasis, that the early Jerusalem Church did not see itself as a distinct entity, separated from its Judaic heritage."

"But how can that be? You already said they did away with the centralization Even their choice of leaders was different from the rest of the Jews. And what about everything else you've told me so far about this early church. How could they not see themselves as being distinct?"

"That's probably James' influence manifesting itself. He taught that the only way by which Judaism could find the correct path or "the Way" was by building a bridge between the old and the new. The Judaism that had become introverted and protective and the "New Covenant," which saw Judaism spreading across the face of the Earth. Therefore there was no distinction other than being either old or new covenant. No matter which, it was the Judaic heritage which bound them together."

The message of the Jerusalem Church expounded the

teachings of both the Righteous Teacher and the Unique Teacher, both of whom postulated ways to unite the Jewish and Gentile worlds. A Judaism for everyone so to speak, that provided the strength to transport its followers through the epoch of wickedness that would exist between the coming of messiahs. Christianity, not as it is now, but as it was meant to be; the type that Jesus preached, then James. Do you see it now John. Jesus didn't come to provide the Gentiles with a new religion. He came for the Jews. To propel the Jews into an evangelistic phase of their development that would consolidate the world into the New Judaic Covenant. He was a Jewish prophet for a new age. But what happened afterward was all one big mistake as far as the Jerusalem Church was concerned. The wires got crossed, circumstances changed, the spiritual centre for Judaism got destroyed and what resulted was a schism rather than unification.

And now, as we look back on all that I have shown you, you must realize that Jesus' calling by the Lord was one of far more extreme difficulty than you have ever been taught. He was a Jew with a message that at the time neither the right nor the left appreciated nor liked. Bottom line was that the only 'Way' God wanted to see created was the path which James taught. More than anyone else, he knew his brother, his message and his purpose."

"Christianity was for the Jews, not for the Gentiles, that's what you're trying to say here, isn't it? Well that's a humdinger of a revelation."

"Everything I've been telling you so far has been pointing to a major revelation. A reinterpretation of known events and known facts. None of this came out of a vacuum. These were all real people with their own motivating factors. Religions have tried to sterilize the subject so much that they've dehumanized it. It's time we put the people back into religion. Don't you think so, John?"

"Sterile is something I can agree with Doc. There are times I question why I do what I do. Seems that it's become more of a paint by numbers event rather than something you put your own personal input in to. Doing a lot of things simply because we're told what to do even though half the time you can't relate to it."

"You're absolutely right," I congratulated him. "Tradition has its place but if you can't relate it to your everyday real world then what's the point. I don't know about you, but I want a personal

God. I want a God that deals with me one on one. That's religion. The rest are just mindless cults that people go through the motions but don't seem to practice what they preach. I have gone through a lot of soul searching myself and have forged that personal relationship which I believe was the doctrine 'the Way' was trying to achieve.

GLEEM has been a help there. During all that time that I was compelled to find my soul, my roots, my heritage, my essence of being, I also discovered my ancestors. Yes, I am the descendent of a long line of the high priesthood. A Zadokite, traceable back to Jeshua ben Gamaliel, who married Martha, the granddaughter of Joseph ben Kamithea, called Caiaphas. Yada, yada, yada, and so forth, and so on, etcetera. That's all fine and dandy but the real importance was being able to glimpse into their souls. See how they wrestled with the same questions. Find out how they forged their own relationships with God. Because that's exactly what they did. They had more than just routine and hollow ritual. Something far more. They had faith based on a personal relationship that was bi-directional.

Some of my ancestors that followed Caiaphas were able to achieve that, others couldn't. Some didn't bother to try. Many went on to play a leading role in Rabbinic Judaism, the exact opposite of finding that one on one relationship with God. This was confirmed by the memories of my ancestor, Jacob Kahana Goldenthal. Not only did he refuse to become the Rabbi of Brody, like his father and grandfather, but he reacted in a completely unorthodox manner. Pun intended! He started to study philosophy and history. Actually it wasn't that simple. As long as I'm telling you this bit of the story I might as well give it to you straight. The community of Brody raised the money to send him to rabbinical school in Leipzig, Germany. Jacob went to Leipzig all right, but he used his money to enrol himself into the regular university there. There's a copy of the warrant for his arrest over in the Central Jewish Archives in Jerusalem. You just didn't do things like that back then, especially when you're the son of the Rabbi!"

"We're definitely going to have to do that story on Jacob Goldenthal soon," Pearce practically pleaded. "Like you said Doc, the bit they leaked out about him and the Empress of Austria isn't right, so why not make that our next effort."

"I'll give it some thought John. There's just so much to tell before then. Anyway, to make a long story short, Jacob had discovered that as a family, we were also descended from a long line of Karaites far in his past, and that helped explain why Rabbinic Judaism did not hold any of the answers he was searching for. Just so you have a clue what I'm talking about, the name Karaite means "to be called." It was a Jewish sect started by the Exilarch Anan ben David and it represented a return to older traditions, those more typical of the Sadducees. Following principles laid down by the Zadokite priests. It was a natural following for him because like myself, he had a very good understanding of GLEEM even though he may not have had the same scientific background to analyse it with."

"But the little bit I know about his time in Austria may suggest that he went off the deep end Doc."

"Not at all. The more he read, the more he challenged everything he had been taught. The voices in his head told him there was something more. He just became determined to find out what it was. Most of us would probably behave the same way when you take off the blinkers."

"You're certain you're just not making excuses for him," he teased.

"The more your question your values, the more you'll discover they're probably someone else's that you adopted. Perhaps your parents, your peers, and in my family's case, values that have been passed down since the dawn of time. Jacob found that those values in some cases were diametrically opposed to what his father and grandfather expounded. Questioning is praiseworthy, blind faith I personally consider contemptible."

"Well, then there must be an awful lot you find contemptible about today's world because blind faith is something we have by the bucket load."

"You are so right. We can't even think for ourselves today. We need someone to interpret about everything before we accept it. And it's funny. Almost two thousand years ago, Lazarus saw this same thing and he was at a loss to stop it too!"

"What are you referring to, Doc?"

"One of the most significant indicators of this failure to think for ourselves is something that John or Lazarus expounded in

Revelation. As he cautioned, 'those that are meant to understand will understand by thinking simply. It is the number of man. Then and there he was telling you, no hidden meanings, no fantastic extrapolations. Just think simply. He even gave you a key, a numerical key to it all. John provided a single number that would unlock the entire book. But did anyone take his advice and approach it very simply in order to understand. No! The Catholic Church built an entire set of myths and prophecies to terrify all their adherents in order to keep them in check based on that book."

"You're saying you understand it."

"I'm saying Jeshua ben Gamaliel understood it. Elioneiai ha Cayef understood it. Joshua Damneus understood it. Even though John didn't publish it in its final form until close to 90 A.D., it still circulated in an oral form long before that. They heard it, they understood it. So did many others. I share their memories, so I guess that means that I understand it as well."

"Oh, come on, Doc. Don't just sit there all tight lipped. Tell me, what's it mean? You gotta say something about it."

I closed my eyes and laid back in my chair. My breathing became deep and prolonged. "You know what John, rather than me tell you about it, why don't I have Jeshua ben Gamaliel fill in the blanks for you. He was very involved as well in undertaking the mission that Caiaphas had left to them all following his death. I think he can say it best of all."

JERUSALEM: 56 AD

To my brother in spirit, Elioneiai,

Your daughter is well. The birth of our son was not without difficulty but she has provided you with a strapping and healthy grandson. We have decided to name him Joseph after your father. I hope that you are pleased with our choice of name. May he grow up and honour the name he bears and in so doing bring honour to the entire family.

I have taken the opportunity to read the letter you sent me regarding the epistle that Lazarus has sent to me, thinking I will have influence on the Jerusalem Council. The key is not as difficult as some may think. As John he may consider himself out of harm's way in Ephesus but I'm certain he is still apprehensive about the far reaching arm of Roman authority. As such, I cannot blame him for trying to conceal his message in a cryptic fashion. John has provided this number merely to conceal the hidden message of his discourses from the Romans and the other dioceses of the Christian Church Now that you know where to look for the key, I do not expect that you will have much trouble resolving his comments in the future.

As a Jew, Lazarus could have sent us these warnings in either Hebrew or Aramaic. He acknowledges that he chose Hebrew so that it would be best for us to comprehend. Not to mention, what better way to hide it from prying eyes. Had it been intercepted, how many in Ephesus could be counted as being that fluent in Hebrew to have made any sense from it.

John provides the first key which is about this time; our present. In Hebrew the number is not just six hundred and sixty six using letters to represent numbers, but if we let the letters be exactly that, just letters, then they spell out a word, Tarsu, or the Tarsus of the Roman world. Clearly the man from Tarsus is his greatest threat. He who proclaims himself to be a Jew from Tarsus, his followers to be considered Jews no matter what their heritage, inheritors of the promise that God made to the Jews, this John points to as the enemy. John says it clearly, but the meaning is lost by those that read this word but refuse to accept what is so clearly obvious. John bears witness to the destruct effects of this apostle who claims he is no less than those superlative apostles whom had actually known Yeshua. John has recognized that the followers of the teachings of the Jerusalem Church are threatened.

But there is also a duality to this unique number selected by John. The second key that he has cleverly concealed is the Roman world which we live in; a clear revelation of the beast of our own and future time. Remember that in Roman numerals, this number would be DCLXVI, which is the most unique number in all of the Roman counting system. It is the only number which uses all of the Roman numerals, only once and in their proper descending order. The uniqueness of this number is a clear indication that he wished us to recognize Rome as the beast of our eventual destruction.

Whereas Saul of Tarsus destroys us from within, it will be Rome that possesses the power to destroy us from without. Should these two forces ever come to be united they will overpower us and we will succumb to their relentless attacks. Now I do not say that Lazarus is possessed of the ability to prophesize but I do strongly recommend that we take seriously what he has said in this letter, Elioneiai. I know that Caiaphas, if he was still alive to be with us, would agree that John has identified the threat accurately.

I think it is important that we make certain that John's words are circulated freely amongst the people. When they come to see that which he has concealed within its words then we will at least have a chance to resist these evil forces of decimation. This warning must be taken seriously. I am not gifted as your father was, but I fear that John may not have even done justice to the severity of the threat that these two forces represent. In my soul I feel as if I have looked into the face of my own death. There are evil tidings that are coming our way.

If ever there was a time to think about revolting against our oppressors now would be that time. We must act before both of our enemies become too powerful for us to overthrow. Already I have begun discussions with uncle Damneus in regards to how we should first approach the threat. He suggested that we must first find a way to bring back our council leaders that have been held as prisoners in Rome. To do so, he says will win over the hearts of the people and invigorate them with a spirit that Rome can be overcome. There is still a chance if we act now that this may be possible. They have been in Rome for so long that I suspect many will be succumbing to old age. Discussions of how to finance such a mission I will leave to Damneus as he says he has his ways. This may take a few years but I am hopeful that it can be done. Once accomplished, we will look at the next steps and that is where I will need your guiding hand father.

I beg you father, take this letter of John's seriously. You have asked me to interpret its meaning for you and now that I have provided you with the key, I pray that we will unlock the passiveness that we have expressed so far against those that have subjugated us and we bring the hand of God against them with a mighty force.

May God be with us in this troubled times

Jeshua ben Gamaliel.

CHAPTER THIRTY-FIVE

Pearce just sat there, staring at me in disbelief, while he cleared his throat repeatedly but never bothered to say a word.

"I don't know what you're doing John, but cut it out, it's annoying," I threatened him.

"What?" he asked innocently, oblivious to the sounds he was making. "What are you talking about?"

"You've got a question. I can tell when you have a question and this is that time. So why don't you just ask it instead of making sounds like you're gargling razor blades?"

"Getting a little testy this morning, aren't we."

"Obviously, you're working very hard at avoiding asking whatever it is you're struggling with."

"When did psychoanalysis become one of your degrees, Doc? I don't remember seeing that one up on your wall."

"Now, who's the one that's getting testy? But if it's any consolation to you, I probably know already what the difficulty is."

"Why are you insisting on there being a problem? I don't have a problem," Pearce insisted. "I don't know why you keep saying that I have a problem."

"Then ask your question," I challenged him.

"Okay, you want me to ask, so then, here's my question. Why should I accept that this guy, Jeshua ben Gamaliel, is able to solve almost instantaneously what no one else has been able to do in two millennia? And these were some of the best theological minds that ever existed over that time span. Don't you think that's a mystery that needs explaining?"

"The only mystery is how something so simple could be overlooked by these experts. Right from the onset, John is telling you that you don't have to have a code breaker machine to solve this one. He wouldn't have said that if he knew that he had made it so cryptic that it could never be resolved.

But Jeshua ben Gamaliel had an obvious advantage since he co-existed in the same world in which John was residing. Speaking the same language, having an understanding of the same idioms makes a major difference. That is a feature that became lost over time to those living outside of that particular environment. You follow what I'm saying?"

"Still too simple. It couldn't have been that simple!"

"Why not just accept what John was telling you. Why do people always insist on making things more difficult than they need to be?"

"Because Revelation was all about prophecy. Where's the prophecy if all it was, was a nothing more than current day events wrapped up in a bit of gloss?"

"See, that's where you're making your big mistake, John. Revelation is very much a prophecy. It's current events and it's prophecy. But Jeshua ben Gamaliel wouldn't have known that the third key was a prophecy of the future. In his mind, he wouldn't be thinking that, even though he is an ancestor of mine. I'm afraid Jeshua didn't have that particular gift.

You see, John made use of a number system that he was not even aware of, as it didn't really come into being until much later. Therefore by definition it is a genuine prophecy. Of course I'm referring to the Arabic system using 666. So Jeshua would have been oblivious to the third key and John may have had a gut feeling that there was something more to his Revelation but unable to put his finger on exactly what it was. Sure, he was living in a part of the world where Arabic language was being spoken, but it was not a major tongue and in all likelihood, it would have been ignored. So the fact that the Arabic numerals fit into a prophecy of the future may have been occult to John at the time."

"You still haven't told me what the prophecy was," Pearce blurted.

"I'm getting to it. Since all he would have been familiar with was an alphanumeric system, the Arabic system of pure numbers was unique. It's our world which was able to identify with this new system. And it's through our hindsight that we can pinpoint to the Muslim world as a future beast. The question becomes what was he pointing to and because we know the history, we can answer that it was a particular date. Six hundred and sixty-six years after the birth of Jesus, born in about 6 BC, the Empire of Islam established itself. For two decades it had been tearing itself apart through rival claims to the Caliphate. And in 660-661 AD, Ali was assassinated and

Islam was finally ruled by a single unified Caliphate. Had this not happened, it was on a path of self-destruction. It would have completely disappeared due to the greed and power-lust of those that ruled it. By eliminating the intense rivalry from within, it transformed itself into the next beast."

"I didn't see that coming. Funny how you can read the same thing over and over again but it isn't until you hear it from someone else can you even conceive of alternatives."

"But simple now that you've had it pointed out to you."

"It is," Pearce reaffirmed my comment. "So that's it."

"No, there's actually a fourth key, which is also a prophecy of the future. And guess what, it points to our time. And it's not a number but a symbol this time."

"How can six hundred and sixty-six not be a number?"

"When it's a symbol! And it's a symbol we've seen thousands of times in our everyday lives. We don't even visualize it any longer because we've seen it so many times. Picture the belly of the sixes overlapped, the stems pointing to 12 o'clock, 4 o'clock, and 8 o'clock.

Take a good look and start fleshing out the numbers by giving them some depth. You will recognize the beast and it is the most terrifying of all, as it does harness the power to obliterate civilization as we know it. See it, recognize it, and you will know it intimately."

"It looks like the radiation symbol," Pearce speculated as he finished putting the finishing touches to his drawing.

"Or the biohazard symbol. Either one works."

"Coincidence?"

"John, when are you going to come to realize that there is very little that occurs by coincidence? Lazarus had Davidic blood coursing through his veins. That family made for some awfully good prophets. Now ask the next question John!"

"What's that?" he responded.

"Why four? That's what you should ask me next.

"Why four then?"

"With four keys to the number of the beast it means that there would be four separate beasts. And John tells us that it is four. He talks of the four beasts that serve the angels. They are not in any way representing the evils of the number of the beast but they do serve to tell us the number of times or keys that we as mankind have and will experience.

To reinforce this number four, John tells us there will be four horsemen. The first horse is white, under the guise of purity. It represents a false holiness, armed with a golden bow, or a false covenant based on wealth, and it crowns itself in false pride and power. This is John's interpretation of the rival power that challenged the Jerusalem Church for rule over Christianity. He could foresee that death and suffering that would be wrought in its wake under the guise of purity and righteousness."

"Saul?"

"Yes, Saul. The second horse is red like the cloaks and the plumed helms of the Roman officers. Red like blood, shed by the world's mightiest military machine. This horsemen is only concerned with warfare and conquest. Living by the great sword, enemy to true peace. How clearly we see Rome as this beast."

Pearce gasped as he followed closely how the pieces of the puzzle were coming together.

"The third horse is black, based in darkness. Black like the cloaks of the mullahs and the fanatics that misinterpret its purpose. This horseman does not attempt to prosper through the purity or holiness of John's teachings of the Jerusalem Church. In fact it will prove to be the exact opposite, like a black wind that will try to spread darkness upon the earth. And in its hand it carries the balance. Not only the balance of power, but it will be able to determine the fates of world economies. It will rise to ultimate power because the world will not stop it from gaining control of vital resources. In fact, it will pay its price, support it without questioning, until it is too late. And then we become embroiled in endless wars designed to stem the current rise of Islamic fundamentalism, impede and slow its progress as it attempts to take control of more and more countries towards its goal of ultimate domination.

And lastly, John sees the pale horse. It is without description. It is simply death. What it represents is simply beyond John's imagination. He cannot even fathom the destruction that this fourth beast can manifest. But we can. We have the knowledge to appreciate exactly what power that fourth horseman has. We know what radiation and toxic waste can do to this world. Prophecy? Oh yeah, very much a prophecy! And again, it all ties in to the number four but that will be your homework. If I tell you that the number four is significant in Islam, then you'll have to find out why and then you'll understand how it is the third horseman than causes the forth to be revealed."

"This is going to sound strange," Pearce cautioned me, "but I suddenly have this feeling inside my gut, like it's all churning or something because I can see it all. I know you'll think I've probably started hallucinating on you but I can really see it. I can't tell you how many times I've read through Revelation and I never saw any of it .before. Not like this. Not like now!"

"It's a strange feeling isn't it? Almost as if there's a chill running up and down your spine at the same time you're feeling ecstatic, like your opening the big present on Christmas Day."

"Exactly! That's just like it is!"

"And there's an awareness, a sense of pure knowledge that you can't describe, but similar to standing at the edge of the universe and admiring the view."

Pearce clapped his hands together resoundingly. "You've hit the nail on the head. That's exactly how it feels. You must have read my mind. I was just thinking that."

"The edge of the universe bit?"

"I couldn't imagine what that would look like. I meant the sudden awareness; that mystical feeling of bliss." Pearce corrected me.

"Not that mystical," I assured him. "It's a feeling I get quite often. I knew it was unlikely to have been any different for you. Now that you're being let in on some of the biggest secrets of our time you're thought patterns are quite predictable. So, I'll ask you this because I think you may have become enlightened, so to speak, do you have an appreciation for was happening in Caiaphas' timeframe?"

Pearce nodded his head in confirmation.

"Do you have an appreciation then for Caiaphas?"

He was reluctant to answer that question. It was something he had been taught since his youth to not even consider. Caiaphas is was and would always be the ultimate bad guy. That the time and circumstances could have dictated the decisions that were made and no matter how much you want to believe they could have been different, there never was another choice. Pearce withdrew into the seat, he didn't even bother to jot down on his paper an attempted reply.

"Makes you think, doesn't it?" I challenged. "How can you condemn anyone if we're all victims of fate? Caiaphas, Judas, Paul, Peter, even Jesus all had roles and a predetermined destiny. Their lives were intended to be intertwined. Their roles predetermined by circumstances that they themselves never fully comprehended."

"You're suggesting again that Caiaphas was a victim," Pearce responded incredulously.

"I'm saying they were all victims. Victims of their own beliefs, their prophecies, their myths, their expectations. Because the ancient scriptures predicted a series of events must take place, they in fact did take place. It's a case of fulfilment occurring through necessity."

"And what of John's prophecies then?"

"Same thing. They had to happen. Even if let's say the explanation that I have just provided to you was well known, do you think it would have changed anything. Do you think Paul would have been condemned by the very Church he had established. Or that Rome would have disappeared prior to making Christianity its official religion. Or that Mohammed may have never been born. Or mankind, if we had known the interpretation of the last horseman would never develop nuclear or biological weapons? Do you really believe anything would have changed?"

"That's a tough one," Pearce made one of his classical understatements that I had come to expect from him and appreciate.

"You know it all would have played out exactly as it did. Even if you had the power to stop it, you wouldn't have done so. The universal truth is that both fate and destiny find ways of fulfilling themselves no matter how much one may try to avoid it."

"That's sounding pretty…"

"Fatalistic? That's my point exactly."

"But what about all that talking yesterday about the way time flows and how any interference could alter the course of events?"

"I think if you look back on your notes you'll see that I said going backwards wouldn't be allowed. The universe has its built-in protective mechanisms exactly for this purpose."

"That's a shame Doc. I'd like to still maintain my beliefs

that we can change life's directions by our own choices."

"I'm not saying you can't. Everything is on a proportionate scale. On a personal level you have free will to make or break it within your own life. But on the greater scale, that one level that really counts, I have come to believe that we're just here for the ride."

"How can you as a scientist say that?"

"How can you after all you've heard, deny it?"

"There are times I can't make you out Doc. We've talked about an awful lot of stuff over the last thirty-six hours, a lot of science and a lot of religion but I never took you for a fatalist."

"I'd like to think that God taught me how to be a realist."

"Realist, eh?"

"Yea, just like Caiaphas."

ANTIOCH: 64 AD

Alas Damneus, I no longer know what we should do now that our father is not here to guide us. Everything is slipping away like the sands beneath the waves. Every moment slips through our fingers until we are left holding nothing but the emptiness that resembles the hollow within my heart. What are we to do? Tell me brother, because I cannot find the answers on my own.

I fear that we will lose everything should we try to wage war against an Empire that knows no equal. And the battle rages against those that try to distort our teachings but every blow we strike against them they counter with the lies that spew from the serpent's tongue like honey from the hive. This Jew from Tarsus has made a mockery of our teachings, saying that for too long we have basked in decadence and no longer do we deserve the blessings of the Almighty. Caiaphas had warned us to beware the teaching s of this man and yet we have done little to limit his influence. No effort must be spared to bring him to heel before he causes further damage with his hatred and lechery.

This is not the way God intended the world to be. He did not set us upon our path only to see us scattered from the trail by a runaway stallion that has bolted and now tries to crush us beneath the flailing of its hooves. Then again, the fact that the horse had broken its reins is no fault of anyone but ourselves. Did we not know that he had only intentions bent on destruction? Was this not obviously the metal of the man from the moment he encountered Caiaphas? A man that chose willingly to hunt other men into extinction. Why should we have even considered that the leopard had changed its spots? The only difference being now that he has raised his sights even higher. He has chosen to try and force our world, our way of life, our traditions over the precipice and in so doing, destroy over thirty generations that lived their lives solely by the grace of God. It cannot be allowed to happen. We will not allow this to happen. We must gird ourselves for battle against the forces of Gog and Magog that assemble about us. Armageddon is at hand. Brother, there is no other explanation than the end of days is at hand.

Brother, I now know what must be done. The Lord has delivered to me our answer. This shall become our war cry. Let them muster their forces against us. We are not afraid. I am the Cayef, you are the Damnea. Let them fear us for together we shall raise the standard of the Lord and march an army against them that shall make the world tremble. The hand of God is upon us and he will not leave us to fall beneath the onslaught that has set itself against us. We shall endure while all else fades into the mist of half-forgotten memories. The Lord's covenant is an everlasting promise.

For God has spoken of these times and warned us of this sinner that was to come amongst us and set us against each other, brother against brother, and son against father. And the Lord warned us that he would try to twist the words and laws of our people and delude us into following a smooth path. None of this should be new to us. All this was written in the third book of the law, the Book of Priests, as was given to Moses from the mouth of God.

And the Lord said, "If you shall no longer hearken unto Me, and no longer follow My commandments, and reject My statutes and your soul rejects My ordinances, so that you will not follow all My commandments and choose to break My covenant for another, then I will curse you and appoint terror over you so you can no longer see the truth and your soul will languish. All the seed that you plant will be reaped by your enemies and all shall come against you to rule over you and hate you. And you shall constantly fleeing through all the days of your life even though there be none pursuing you. And I will break the pride of your power. And your heaven and earth shall become your technology of working iron and brass and your strength shall be nothing more than your own vanity. And you're children will be lost to you. Taken by your enemies and turned away from you and refusing to honour you.

And though ten women may bake your bread in a single oven, when they serve it to you, you will not be satisfied. Your hunger will never be satiated. I will destroy your high places and cut down your sun-pillars. And My soul shall abhor you. You who have become the uncircumcised of the heart, I shall humble thee for you have chosen to be contrary to Me. Only when you have been humbled, and recognize the iniquity of their ways, will I remember My covenant with Jacob, and My covenant with Isaac, and My covenant with Abraham."

In His wisdom, the Lord has seen all which is transpiring and He has spoken to us long ago of what will come and informed us of all that we must do. Nothing is not known to Him, not even the future can remain hidden, and we have been charged to see that His flock does not stray too far from the shepherd. And though it may seem by all appearances that this Saul of Tarsus may be successful in his intentions to set up a nation of Gentiles that worship a false covenant in direct opposition to us, in the end of days his following will perish beneath the just hand of the Lord.

Of this I am certain. The documents that I received from Lazarus in Ephesus, I delivered to my son-in-law, in order for him to render his interpretation for the content was of a prophetic nature. Joshua has confirmed my own interpretation of this most recent revelation that the war is coming. The worst will happen but it will only set off a chain of conquest that will ultimately see our people reunited in order to wage the final battle.

When all is done, Rome shall be no more and those that follow this Christianity that Saul professes will become mute and divided. There was but one voice that resonated with the law as it came down from Sinai. Moses stood before the Almighty and talked to him as one would speak with their elder. And God has taken no other from amongst mankind to walk in His footsteps since the days of our Lawgiver. Many have come and gone that have laid claim to be a prophet of God. Many will be the false prophets that are yet to come. But like all that choose to deceive, their tongues shall cleave to the roof of their mouths and their lips will be sealed like the tomb of Machpela.

When all have come and gone, we shall still be here. He will not forsake us. Our people will still live according to the true Way, the only Word. There are no others. There is but one God and He does not revoke His promises.

EPILOGUE

There was nothing left to say. My memories of this particular ancestor had run dry. Every last thought that Caiaphas had planted into my subconscious had been expressed. I think Pearce was relieved to know that our exchange had drawn to a close. Our conversation had taken quite the turn with its constant duelling over moral issues. The constant exchange of the high ground caused its fair load of bruising. He was now left to question all that he had held true for so long, and I had gained the relief of releasing myself from the burden of memories that weighed me down like an anchor on my soul. All in all, a fair exchange.

We had already made our way to the front door and were doing the usual perfunctory farewells. Marg had joined us in the foyer wishing to say her goodbyes to our guest, the man that had startled her so badly the previous day. By now all had been forgiven and she was telling Peace how delighted she was to have had the opportunity to finally meet him. I think she was still playing the part of being a good hostess and I'd get the lowdown of her true sentiments later.

Slowly he doffed that well-worn overcoat of his, putting one foot forward onto the threshold. "So what do you say that next time we do this story about your ancestor and the Empress of Austria?"

"Perhaps. All depends on the mood you catch me in," I responded not willing to commit to any topic of future endeavour.

"So you're saying we could very well be doing a different story then." Pearce's demeanour expressed disappointment. He had wanted that story from the moment he showed up at the house.

"That's a distinct possibility. But don't worry; we have a lifetime of memories to analyse. We'll get to it eventually."

"The story on the Empress will attract a heavy female readership so if you're going to spring something different then it's got to be good. I need the stuff that sells books."

"I'm surprised at you John. I didn't think you'd be having

anxiety pangs at this stage of our relationship."

Pearce smiled at me knowingly as if to say he wouldn't push the issue any further. He'd have to trust me on this.

"As you already know Pearce, there's far more to me than you've encountered so far."

"Considering you're background Doc, I'm not too surprised. With all those genes swirling around inside of you, the truth is, you really aren't you at all."

"I'm not certain I agree with that particular description. I was simply implying that there's more to me than meets the eye. But we'll explore exactly what that is over the next series of manuscripts."

"And what exactly will I discover?"

"Most likely what everyone else discovers."

"Well that's not telling me too much Doc!"

"You're about to climb into a taxi and head to the airport John. I don't think we have time for another marathon discourse."

"How about a titbit? A little teaser that we can drop on the readers just to wet their appetites for what's coming next."

"I'll leave you with a parable that will give you something to think about. Just so you have some background history I have this anomaly which occurs every time I contemplate taking a trip to Israel. It's actually one of the triggers that stimulates certain visual and cerebral memory responses. In the old days they would have called me 'korai'; one who's been called. History has been littered with those that would be considered korai. So, every time I have this particular stimulus of visiting Israel I endure a calling."

"But who's calling you?"

"That's part of the parable John that you're going to have to figure out for yourself. But let me continue. My father-in-law talks to me about us all taking a trip to Jerusalem where he has accommodation in a house on Mount Zion. I tentatively agree but explain to him that for reason too hard to explain, I've sort of avoided taking a trip to the Middle East."

"Because of this korai thing."

"Yes, because of it. It's one thing to be called, quite another to respond. Well, anyway, I go to sleep that night and I have this dream. I'm a boy in Israel, but not the Israel of today. From the clothes I'm wearing, I'd say it was probably quite a long time ago.

I'm hot and tired. I've been playing with the other boys but they've disappeared suddenly. I'm walking by an orchard containing pomegranates and figs and some other kind of fruit that for the life of me I can't recall, other than remembering that they were high in juice content and looked a bit like an apple. I'm thinking, I can grab some fruit to quench my thirst when this thought pops into my head. More than a thought, I'm being instructed. It's a powerful voice and it begins by laying down the law. I can only partake of the fruit that has fallen to the ground. But that fruit which is within the shadow of the branches belongs to the farmer and I am not to touch it. And that which has fallen and subsequently become split and bruised is to be left where they lie as that fruit is only fit for the beasts of the field and the worms of the ground. But the fruit that has fallen and is undamaged but which lies outside the shelter of the tree is mine to partake in and do with as I please."

"So what's it all mean?"

"Yes, what's it all mean," Marg interjected. "Why didn't you tell me before of this dream of yours?"

"Because it was appropriate to think about it now," I said somewhat disapprovingly. As if most husbands discuss everything that pops into their heads immediately with their wives. We'd all be in serious trouble if that was the case.

"But what does it mean," Pearce insisted on knowing.

"I can't tell you!"

"Can't tell me or won't tell me?"

"It's a parable John. It's meant for you to interpret. There is very little purpose to a parable if I tell you what it means. That's why one tells parables. Next time we get together you can tell me if you've figured it out. And if not, perhaps I'll give you a further clue then but I'm not willing to give it away now.

"That's not really fair!" Pearce whined.

"Since when does fair have anything to do with this? I don't recall saying anything about being fair."

"But you'll tell me later, right?" my wife questioned me.

"Am I going to solve this?" John was desperate to know.

"I think so. Considering you're a big part of it. I have this suspicion that it will dawn on you. Probably sooner than later."

"And are the readers of the book going to figure it out too?"

"Some will, some won't. That's the way parables work. But

in the end, I believe it all works out."

"And how's that, Doc? Just what is your take on all this? If anything, I'd say that you're the real enigma!"

"Every man must come to his own conclusions. Without sounding too patronizing, I am just a guide."

"Oh, come now Doc. Without dismissing the fact that you do have a particular insight into events of the past and you may also have an awareness of certain religious aspects that were particular to your family of priests, that doesn't make you a prophet, you know."

"Pearce, as I have always insisted, it's all a matter of perspective. To the Christians, in the past they would have considered me to have been an Ebionite. As Jews, my family were Karaite, but in my heart of hearts I am nothing more than I've always claimed to be, one hundred percent Zadokite. So, why's that so hard to accept?"

"And they'll understand that? I don't think the word is in the vocabulary of most people. You know Doc, you have to admit you that you're a bit peculiar."

"And the same goes for you John," I smirked.

"I guess that's why we make such a good pair!"

"Could be Mr. Pearce, could be."

"Well, this is it. Taxi's here, so I'm on my way." Pearce extended his hand and I shook it heartedly.

"Let me send you on your way with that tried and true ancient quote, 'that in time, all men shall know.'"

"And when's that supposed to be?"

"Only God knows John, only God knows!"

A Zadokite Prayer

⌘

Hear,
Oh, Israel,
Yahweh is God
And our God is One,
And I am His servant,
He is my eternal master.
Lord, hear the prayer of thanksgiving from Your humble
servant, true son of Abraham, Isaac and Jacob, our
forefathers: Priestly son of Aaron and the son
of Zadok, his descendant by their blood
And through Your heavenly graces,
Protect me each day as You have watched
And guarded over my ancestors since we left Egypt.
Guide me on the path before me of true righteousness.
Let me walk in Your footsteps, and be good in Your Eyes.
Strengthen my forearms,
Keep my heart from
Fear and weakness
Let me sing out
Your praises
Amen

⌘

www.ingramcontent.com/pod-product-compliance
Lightning Source LLC
LaVergne TN
LVHW051621080426
835511LV00016B/2104